D1066383

Plant Manager's Handbook

Plant Manager's Handbook

Charles H. Becker

Prentice-Hall, Inc.   Englewood Cliffs, N.J.

Prentice-Hall International, Inc., *London*
Prentice-Hall of Australia, Pty. Ltd., *Sydney*
Prentice-Hall of Canada, Ltd., *Toronto*
Prentice-Hall of India Private Ltd., *New Delhi*
Prentice-Hall of Japan, Inc., *Tokyo*

© 1974 by
CHARLES H. BECKER

Fourth Printing . . . . . October, 1978

Library of Congress Cataloging in Publication Data

Becker, Charles H
   Plant manager's handbook.

   Includes bibliographical references.
   1. Production management.   I.   Title.
TS155.B39   658.2   74-4451
ISBN 0-13-680694-5

Printed in the United States of America

To
Anne Bruce Becker, my wife
and
James, Lesley, and Edward, our family

About the Author

Charles H. Becker writes from nine years experience as plant and facilities manager at Polymer Industries, Inc., Stamford, Connecticut, with a variety of responsibilities in production, engineering, maintenance, quality control, and collective bargaining activities. His background in industrial production management totals 23 years, and includes assignments as shift foreman, department supervisor, and assistant plant manager.

Mr. Becker has also lectured and chaired seminars at the American Management Association in New York, primarily in the areas of training first-line supervisors. He has also served as senior program director for American Management Association.

The author holds bachelor's and master's degrees in chemical engineering, and is a registered professional engineer in Pennsylvania.

What This Handbook Will Do for You

This book gives you the specific information you need to reach top performance in the four major areas of plant responsibility: leadership, profit, operations, and facilities. You can use its ideas in any size operating facility, whether manufacturing or service, profit or non-profit. It will become an indispensable desktop reference for plant managers along with production superintendents, operations executives, supervisors, facilities managers and plant engineers—all those who have a stake in the operation of a plant or service facility. What will it do for you? Why do you need this book? Here are the answers:

- This book tells what is expected of you in the SIX MAJOR AREAS of a plant manager's responsibility. Chapter 1.
- It defines the PROCESS OF MANAGEMENT, describes the MANAGEMENT CYCLE, and gives a detailed example of its application in the plant. Chapter 1.
- The book supplies the guidance you need for MOTIVATION of your plant team toward a superior job. Chapter 1.
- It provides step by step instruction in developing the most EFFICIENT ORGANIZATION STRUCTURE for your plant. Chapter 2.
- This book tells how to put together a PLANT OPERATIONS MANUAL, and what to do if you don't have sufficient time or manpower to do it all at once. Chapter 2.
- It gives three different systems of CLASSIFYING HOURLY OPERATORS in your plant, with detailed examples. Chapter 2.
- The book tells you what to do to avoid UNIONIZATION of your plant, and gives the STEPS TO TAKE when the union appears. Chapter 3.
- This book helps you tackle the persistent problem of ABSENTEEISM, and tells what you should expect of your employees. Chapter 3.
- This book tells you how to assemble the most effective COLLECTIVE BARGAINING TEAM and get it moving toward successful contract negotiations. Chapter 4.
- It tells how to PREPARE FOR A STRIKE and the ACTIONS TO TAKE when it occurs. Chapter 4.
- The book shows you how to recruit, train, and motivate the FIRST-LINE SUPERVISOR. Chapter 5.
- It tells when OVERTIME SHOULD and SHOULD NOT be used, with examples of the economics involved. Chapter 6.
- It shows you how to make the most effective decisions in establishing SHIFT OPERATIONS and HOLIDAY SCHEDULES. Chapter 6.
- This book tells you how to set up a profit-generating PREVENTIVE MAINTENANCE program with a common-sense approach. Chapter 7.

7

- It tells how to constantly improve MAINTENANCE EFFECTIVENESS by measuring PERFORMANCE. Chapter 7.
- The book gives FIVE AREAS in which to look for opportunities to improve PRODUCT QUALITY. Chapter 8.
- It tells you how to start reducing the accident rate in your plant by giving the four essential steps you must take to set up a PLANT SAFETY PROGRAM. Chapter 9.
- It spells out your obligations and possible penalties under the OCCUPATIONAL SAFETY AND HEALTH ACT. Chapter 9.
- This book lists the eight cost-saving fundamentals you must consider in setting up the most efficient MATERIALS MOVEMENT SYSTEM. Chapter 10.
- It leads you step by step through the establishment of a COST REPORTING PROCEDURE tailored to your plant's unique needs. Chapter 11.
- The book shows you how to TAKE CONTROL OF OPERATING COSTS and _keep them under control._ Chapter 12.
- It shows you how to set up a permanent, self-motivating COST REDUCTION PROGRAM. Chapter 12.
- It sets out five fertile areas in which to look for NEW COST REDUCTION IDEAS. Chapter 12.
- This book will guide you through the critical phases of any PLANT CON-STRUCTION or CAPITAL EQUIPMENT PROJECT, from original concept to post-completion audit. Chapter 13.
- It will help you avoid costly construction errors by improving your skills at BLUEPRINT REVIEW. See checklist, Chapter 13.
- This book enables you to make important contributions to the DESIGN OF A NEW PLANT, and offers valuable hints for REFURBISHING AN OLD PLANT. Chapter 14.
- It helps you to boost profits by getting the best buys in EQUIPMENT SELECTION. Use the ten easily applied criteria of Chapter 15.
- The book shows you how to CONSERVE ENERGY and cut power costs by adjusting the power factor of your electrical distribution system. Chapter 16.
- It gives you seven basic operating rules and seven inspection points to prolong the life of your STEAM BOILERS. Chapter 17.
- This book shows the six design criteria you must consider before specifying a PROCESS VESSEL. Chapter 18.
- It will give you money saving tips on DRYER DESIGN. Consult the list of selection factors on Page 247, Chapter 18 before buying expensive equipment, and the operating hints on Page 248 before using it.
- The first six pages of Chapter 19 will help you select the HEATING SYSTEM for your plant with the greatest fuel efficiency.
- This book will show you how to set design goals and select the right equipment for your AIR CONDITIONING needs. Chapter 19.
- It will give you instant reference to METRIC CONVERSION units in nine categories. Chapter 20.

HOW THIS BOOK IS ORGANIZED

PLANT MANAGER'S HANDBOOK is built up into four parts, each containing two to eight chapters. Written entirely by a practicing plant manager, it moves rapidly on each topic from the basics to practical ideas for day-to-day application.

PART I deals with the organizational and human relations aspects of the plant manager's job:

The responsibilities of the plant manager within the manufacturing department and his relationships with other corporate departments are described in Chapter 1, along with an explanation of the management cycle. Chapter 2 offers a detailed analysis of organization structure at the plant level. The plant manager's problems in industrial relations in union and non-union plants are dealt with in Chapter 3, and a complete guide for collective bargaining is provided in Chapter 4. The crucial problem of development of the first-line supervisor is covered fully in Chapter 5.

PART II is the plant manager's ready reference for how-to-do-it techniques in every day plant operations:

Chapter 6 provides practical ideas for solving operating problems common to all plants—production scheduling and reporting, use of overtime, start-ups and shutdowns, and many more. Chapter 7 gives concrete examples of ways in which the maintenance department can be developed for maximum performance, while Chapter 8 does the same thing for the quality control department, adding the background information you will need for an understanding of statistical quality control. Chapter 9 sets forth detailed procedures for establishing and continuing a cost-cutting safety and housekeeping program. Chapter 10 completes the operations section by establishing the fundamental requirements for efficient materials movement and showing how they can be applied with modern equipment.

PART III provides real help in the never-ending battle with costs:

Chapter 11 shows you to measure economic performance by building cost and budget systems up from their most basic elements, with specific examples of expense budgets, capital budgets, and depreciation methods. Chapter 12 tells how to achieve and maintain control of operating costs, as well as how to set up a *continuing* cost reduction program.

PART IV is the engineering-technical section of the book.

Chapters 13, 14, and 15 comprise a comprehensive guide for handling plant expansion, equipment, and design projects. Chapters 16 through 19 offer a wealth of practical information for managing and improving the electrical, mechanical, process, and heating-ventilating-air conditioning facilities of your plant. Chapter 20 provides a set of the most-used tables of technical data, including the handy metric conversion group.

HOW TO USE THIS BOOK

- KEEP IT HANDY, in or on your desk for immediate reference, even during phone calls. Having it at your fingertips will save innumerable trips to the bookcase or library and wading through irrelevant information in a variety of other books.

- STUDY THE TABLE OF CONTENTS. By becoming familiar with the chapter and section headings you will be a step ahead the next time you need information in a hurry.

- BROWSE THROUGH THE ILLUSTRATIONS. Each is a thought-provoking example of an idea awaiting application in your plant. The suggested forms and checklists can be used as is, or revised by you for specific applications.

- PRIOR TO ATTENDING A BUSINESS MEETING use the book to brush up on the subject matter involved. You will be better prepared to ask questions and assure yourself that *all* of the relevant factors have been considered in the decision-making process.

- DISTRIBUTE COPIES to your key subordinates. They will understand your directives better and be able to carry out your wishes more effectively if they have access to the same information you do.

- USE THE INDEX and Table of Contents for cross-reference. For instance, if you are interested in reducing plant costs, you will find cost-cutting ideas not only in the chapter on Cost Control and Cost Reduction, but also in the chapters on Plant Operations, Quality Control, Safety and Housekeeping, Materials Movement, and Choosing Electrical Equipment for Cost Effectiveness.

Charles H. Becker

ACKNOWLEDGEMENTS

A word of acknowledgement is due to my friends, associates, and organizations whose ideas and achievements have shaped my ideas of good plant management; I think especially of those at the Koppers Company, Inc., The Plastic Products and Resins Division of Monsanto Company (formerly Shawinigan Resins Corporation), and Polymer Industries, Inc. A special word of thanks is owed to the late Richardson Thurston of Polymer Industries who encouraged the study of management as a science; to William Meier of Crawford & Russell, Inc. and Perry Welch of the Hartford Electric Light Company, who contributed technical advice on certain aspects of Chapter 16; and to the following manufacturers and publishers who provided and permitted use of their materials:

Akron Gear and Engineering, Inc.
Allis-Chalmers Manufacturing Company
American Air Filter Company, Inc.
American Conference of Governmental Industrial Hygienists
American Iron and Steel Institute
Cleaver-Brooks Division of Aqua-Chem, Inc.
Conveyor Equipment Manufacturers Association
Dodge Manufacturing Division, Reliance Electric Company
FMC Corporation, Link-Belt Material Handling System Division
Gulf Oil Corporation
Harper & Row, Publishers, Inc.
John Wiley & Sons, Inc.
Mixing Equipment Company, Inc.
Modern Materials Handling
Modine Manufacturing Company
National Fire Protection Association
Proctor & Schwartz, Inc.
The American Society of Mechanical Engineers
The Falk Corporation
The Patterson-Kelley Co., Inc.

C.H.B.

Table of Contents

Decisions in Advance. Hard Questions. Lost Time. *Preparation for Bargaining.* Start the Day After. Negotiating File. Team Meetings. Essential Steps in Preparation. *Where to Obtain Information.* Data Required. Sources Within the Company. Sources Outside the Company. *Legal Aid. The International Representative and the Shop Committee. Notification of Contract Expiration.* Physical Arrangements. Take Charge. Businesslike Tone. Team Discipline. Late Hours. Keeping Records of Bargaining Sessions. Stenographic Reporter. Tape Recordings. Take Notes. *Union Demands. Company Demands.* Counterproposals. Own Demands. *Bargaining Manual. Contract Language.* Compare Contracts. Get a Book. Legal Help. *Role of the First-Line Supervisor.* Company Demands. Calm Shop. Upward Communication. *Strike Preparation.* Sales. Operation Decision. *When a Strike Occurs.* Communications. Protection. Operations. Aftermath.

Recruiting. Recognition of Status. Motivation. Compensation. Training. Information to Pass On. Job Descriptions. Conducting Performance Appraisal. College Graduates as Foremen. *Conclusion.*

PART 2: Plant Operations

Scheduling the Plant. Changes in Schedule. Use of Overtime. Plant Start-Ups and Shutdowns. Emergency Procedures. Holiday Operations. Shift Operations and Schedules. Production Reporting. Utilization of Manpower. Outside Personnel Working in Plant. *Conclusion.*

Organization of the Maintenance Department. Maintenance Scheduling. Major Work Order System. Preventive Maintenance. Shop Facilities. Time Records and Charging Out Costs. Maintenance Supplies. Outside Contractors. Measuring Maintenance Performance. *Conclusion.*

Where to Start on Quality. How to Organize the Quality Control Department. How to Develop Test Procedures. Statistical Techniques: The Normal Distribution. Statistical Techniques: The Quality Control Chart. Statistical Techniques: Assorted Useful Methods. Quality Control and the Cost Function. *Conclusion.*

Safety. Responsibility for Safety. What Accidents Cost. Establishing the Plant Safety Program. Issue Safety Procedures. Investigate Accidents. Safety Statistics. Sources of Safety Information. Fire Prevention. Occupational Safety and Health Act (OSHA). *Successful Housekeeping Practices.* Tie-in with Safety. Further Reasons for Good Housekeeping. Implementing the Housekeeping Program. *Conclusion.*

Fundamentals of Materials Movement. Movement of Materials in Bulk. Liquids. Solids. *Containers for Material Storage and Movement. How to Move Containers and Bulky Items. External Traffic.* Integrate with Internal Handling Systems. Go for Bulk. Specialized Shipments. Hazardous Materials. *Conclusion.*

Heating. Choose Between Centralized and Decentralized Systems. Select a Fuel and the Medium. Pick the Best Heater. Include All Gains and Losses in the Design. *Ventilating.* Reasons for Ventilation. Types of Ventilation. Techniques of Ventilation. *Air Conditioning.* Why Air Conditioning? How Air Conditioning Works. Choose the Right Equipment. How to Set Design Goals. *Conclusion.*

Decimal Equivalents of Fractions. Metric Conversion. Temperature Conversion. General Conversion Factors. Circumferences and Areas of Circles. Sheet Metal Gauges. Wire and Wire Rod Gauges. NEMA Electric Motor Dimensions. Steel Pipe Dimensions. Weights of Materials and Angle of Repose. Corrosion Resistance of Metals. Tank Volumes. Properties of Saturated Steam.

Plant Manager's Handbook

PART 1

The Plant Organization

Chapter 1

The Full Scope
of the Plant Manager's Job

The plant manager functions at that point in the corporate structure where the company's plans turn into action. The success or failure of those plans depends on the energy and ability with which he applies the corporate resources of people, money, raw materials, and equipment to the task of producing the company's products and services.

The demands upon the plant manager in his application of these resources grow heavier as the complexity and pace of our economy increase. New products move from the laboratory and design stage to full-scale production faster than before. Corporate management, caught in the profit squeeze, requires closer compliance with the budget, and expects cost reductions to be achieved on a pre-planned basis. New plant processes require more steps, more complicated equipment, and tighter quality controls. The community expects the plant to reduce noise, air and water pollution to lower levels with each passing year, aiming ultimately at the vanishing point.

The purpose of this chapter is to help the working plant manager put his sometimes bewildering array of duties and assignments into a comprehensive whole, to understand the relationships between them, and to specify the management tools he will need to cope with them. In it, we will examine the basic responsibilities of every plant manager's job, some of the additional assignments he is likely to have, and his relationships with other departments of the company. The fundamentals of management science will be presented, along with valuable ideas for leadership development and self-improvement.

RESPONSIBILITIES OF THE MANUFACTURING DEPARTMENT

The job of the manufacturing department is usually given in the simplified statement, "To make a quality product on time at lowest possible cost." Sometimes the phrase, "safely, and with good employee relationships," is added. There is nothing wrong with this old definition, except that it does not go far enough in describing the larger role present-day corporations expect the manufacturing group to play.

Let's look at "production." Of course the manufacturing department must produce the company's products in required quantities on time to meet customer demands. But, more than that, it is expected to communicate knowledge developed by its operations which may lead to new products or substantially improved old ones. It helps guard the company against obsolescence by responding quickly to meet changes in markets, technology, and intensity of competition.

Consider "cost." Manufacturing at lowest possible cost is a taken-for-granted objective. But the corporation looks for broader cost activities by its manufacturing department. It expects manufacturing to make profitable application of capital funds; it looks for wise use of money in the purchase of equipment which is labor-saving, maintenance-free, reliable, and offering maximum flexibility for future operations. The company must rely on the manufacturing people to protect its investment by proper maintenance and physical protection of plant property. And it expects the manufacturing group to help gain a competitive edge by continuously reducing costs.

The maintenance of good employee relationships is no longer considered a fringe activity by any serious manufacturing manager. But the company may expect more than just a low incidence of grievances and strikes in its plants; it may require the active development of good relationships with the entire communities in which they are located, including neighbors, civic authorities, the business and professional community, minority groups, and those concerned with the environment, as well as its employees.

RESPONSIBILITIES OF THE PLANT MANAGER

While the plant manager occupies an important place in the broader development and operation of the company, he must continue to meet his basic responsibility for the operation of the plant. The "plant" may range from a small unit with ten or twelve workers to a mammoth complex with thousands of employees. No matter what the size, the plant manager is expected to produce results in six basic areas. They are production, quality, cost, safety, housekeeping, and employee relationships.

Production

This is the job of manufacturing the required quantity of finished goods in time to meet customer demands. It is the most fundamental demand upon the plant manager, and the one with the most obstacles to success. Late raw materials, absenteeism, strikes, bad weather, power outages, equipment breakdowns—all conspire to prevent his reaching the goal. It is the function which calls for the manager's greatest powers of leadership, to foresee and overcome the obstacles to meeting production deadlines, and to motivate his people to get the work out in spite of the difficulties. He accomplishes this by setting the example of refusing to yield to obstacles, and exhibiting a tough-minded approach in fighting for the way to get the job out on time no matter what the difficulties. He really has no choice—failure in this area of responsibility drives away valued customers.

A second responsibility is to determine accurately the production capacity of the plant, so that the corporation can make profitable decisions regarding sales and marketing strategy. When you must develop an estimate of production capacity, include the time the equipment must be out of service for repairs, cleaning, and preventive maintenance. Report the additional capacity available if the number of shifts are increased.

Quality

Most manufactured products are subjected to quality tests before they are declared ready for shipment. Material which does not meet specifications has to be scrapped, sold at a fraction of the price for prime material, or returned to the process for reworking—costly alternatives to making the product right in the first place.

Occasionally the quality goal is very simple—as when a machined shaft is made of a specified grade of steel to a length and diameter of so many inches plus or minus definite tolerances. Any shaft meeting these standards is shippable and will satisfy the customer. More often, however, the quality problem is much more complicated. The quality tests may not cover all of the possible product properties of interest to the customer (who, for reasons of his own, may not be willing to tell how he uses it). And the quality tests may not be capable of uncovering every possible error made in the manufacture of the product. Customers buying these products must depend on the manufacturer to make the product in exactly the same way every time it is produced.

Faced with this situation, the plant manager must establish an attitude in his organization which reaches far beyond the passing of quality tests; he has to establish a program of *product integrity,* which means that the entire organization is committed to making the product according to standard process instructions every time it is made, without shortcuts or individual deviations. Instilling this respect for total quality places heavy demands upon the leadership abilities of the plant manager, but it is a responsibility he cannot ignore in an economy where customers steadily grow more demanding in quality performance, more sophisticated in evaluating supplier's quality, and more willing to hold the supplier legally liable for the cost of difficulties caused by defective raw materials.

In the quest for quality, do not lose sight of profit responsibilities. If the plant is manufacturing a product with an allowable moisture content of 1.00 percent, it is a costly error to turn out a product at 0.25 percent moisture when the process could be operated within allowable tolerances at an average 0.75 percent moisture—it amounts to giving away a half-pound of product for every one hundred pounds sold.

Plant experience may reveal that a product can be made with higher quality than that required without additional cost. Pass this information to the marketing department, for whom it might represent a competitive edge.

Cost

The requirement that he produce a product at standard cost is the most obvious element of the plant manager's cost responsibilities. When the plant cannot produce at the cost which has been previously agreed upon by sales, manufacturing, and engineering, the company may find its profits dangerously reduced, or eliminated altogether.

A second responsibility is to prepare annual operating budgets for all plant functions such as production, maintenance and shipping—controlling expenses within the limits of those budgets throughout the year. Since he cannot personally approve each single expenditure, the plant manager faces the leadership task of creating a cost and value consciousness throughout his organization, and a system of workable controls.

Corporate managements are no longer willing to accept the once-a-year crash program for cost reduction, but expect plant managers to set up result-producing, continuing programs. The cost reductions predicted from a carefully planned and executed program are included in the company's profit projections.

The plant manager participates in the corporate capital expenditure program by the very nature of his job. He makes recommendations for new plants and equipment to expand production, reduce cost, and improve quality. And he carries a continuing responsibility to protect the investment in existing facilities with sound maintenance practices.

Safety

Any human being worthy of the name will do whatever he can to prevent injury to another in the work environment, and plant managers are no exception. But humanitarian feelings do not go far enough, and the plant manager must realize that he cannot meet his production schedules or cost commitments in a plant where accidents are frequent. In most companies he reports his safety performance in terms of the frequency and severity of accidents to the plant employees.

The keys to an improved safety program are these:

    1. A continuing program of safety education conducted primarily by the line supervisors.

    2. Inclusion of a safety section at the beginning of every standard operating procedure.

    3. Designing new equipment with the safety of the people who must operate and maintain it in mind.

    4. No-nonsense enforcement of safety regulations.

Housekeeping

Safety is impossible in a plant which allows spilled materials and debris to accumulate. Product quality is threatened by dirty surroundings. Morale and efficiency of the work force are lowered if the plant is not clean. Plant managers who once thought of housekeeping as a sporadic "cleanup" function—performed only when there isn't much else to do—are coming to understand that it has to be an ongoing activity for which they assume full responsibility. Corporate managements are also taking this view, and in some cases are conducting elaborate interplant housekeeping inspections.

The perceptive plant manager realizes that his plant is often visited by members of higher management who may know little or nothing about the technical operations. But they do know a clean plant when they see one, and base judgments about the ability of the plant manager on the physical conditions they observe. When these men later confront important decisions about where the company's capital is going to be invested, their recollections cannot help but influence the decisions.

Employee Relationships

Throughout his career the plant manager is exposed to all sorts of materials dealing with employee relations. Books, articles, seminars, company meetings and memoranda—all tell him how to conduct employee relationships, but rarely tell him what results are expected from his efforts. Here are four result areas (three of them measurable) in which to judge the plant manager's performance:

    1. Plant operations are not interrupted by events arising from poor employee relationships.

    2. The prevailing atmosphere in the plant is not one of laxness, but of a sense of purpose. Admittedly this is a subjective evaluation, but one very real to men experienced in plant operations.

    3. When company-employee relationships are put to the test by complaint or grievance procedures, the plant manager will be found to have taken sound positions. The plant manager should not be rated on the number of grievances filed—after all, that is up to the union—but on the number he loses in arbitration.

    4. Absenteeism, lateness, and accident frequency are all at low levels.

It is not the job of the plant manager to keep everybody happy; that's an impossible task anyway. It is the job of the plant manager to put his employee relationships on a businesslike basis, with the overall goals of the corporation in mind.

The Total Job

Plant managers sometimes make the mistake of attempting to do a good job in one or two of these result areas, while neglecting the others. Management men who are in a position to observe numerous plants agree on one point: Those plants which consistently meet their production, quality, and cost targets turn out to be the plants where safety, housekeeping, and employee relationships are also in good order. Avoid slogans like "Safety first, quality second, production third." They oversimplify and obscure the real fact of life in an industrial plant: A good job has to be done on *all* of these responsibilities.

HANDLING SPECIAL ASSIGNMENTS

Corporations vary so widely in size, organizational structure, and management style that no single list of responsibilities will fit every plant manager's job. One or more of the following functions is likely to appear on the individual list of responsibilities.

Engineering

The plant manager who does not bear responsibility for some kind of engineering function is a rarity. In a small plant or a small company, he and one or two subordinates may constitute the entire engineering capability; when this is the case he relies on outside engineering firms to handle the detailed engineering, and draw up the blueprints and specifications for major projects.

In a large corporation the services of a central engineering department with hundreds of employees may be available. Even so, the local plant may still have its own engineering staff to take care of smaller projects not suitable for assignment to a large department. Engineering responsibilities of the plant manager fall in one or more of these categories:

1. Plant Engineering and Maintenance. The plant manager is always expected to take the responsibility for keeping the buildings, grounds, and equipment in good condition. An uninterrupted flow of utilities must be maintained, and a preventive maintenance program instituted to prevent surprise outage of production equipment.

2. Process Engineering. The plant manager may have reporting to him a process engineer (or engineering section) whose function is to troubleshoot bottlenecks and problem areas in the manufacturing process. The effectiveness of this activity is judged on the basis of quantitative results—increased production output, statistical measures of quality improvement, and cost reductions which can be translated into lower budgets.

3. Project Engineering. Once the decision has been made to expand the plant, add new equipment, or replace old equipment, an engineering project begins. It should have clearly defined goals in terms of the equipment to be installed, the cost of completing the project, and the date at which it is to be turned over to the operating work force. Good performance is required in all three phases of a project; the company's position in a new market, or its profit performance for the year, can depend on the successful completion of its important capital projects.

Purchasing

Corporations assign the purchasing function in a variety of ways. In some small organizations, the plant manager *is* the purchasing agent. In other, larger companies, the purchasing agent reports to him. In still others, the purchasing function does not report to the plant manager, but is part of a materials management group reporting to a different management echelon.

If the plant manager is in charge of the purchasing function, he is expected to:

1. Assure the company of a continuing supply of raw materials and supplies of acceptable quality.

2. Arrange for delivery of materials in time to meet the requirements of the manufacturing process.

3. Reduce the cost of buying, moving, and storing raw materials.

If he is not accountable for the purchasing function, the plant manager's responsibilities shift to the area of communication—keeping the purchasing department fully informed of late deliveries or substandard quality. Close cooperation with the purchasing department is required in the scheduling of plant trials for the evaluation of materials submitted by new suppliers offering lower prices.

Traffic

When this responsibility is his, the plant manager is expected to provide for movement of the company's incoming and outgoing shipments on time and at the lowest available cost. Like purchasing, the traffic function offers strong possibilities for cost reduction, ranging from the simple selection of cheaper routings all the way up to company ownership of its own means of transportation. Traffic activities include scheduling shipments, selecting routes, choosing the mode of transportation, reviewing bills and charges, and the pursuit of damage claims.

Community Relationships

Seldom is this aspect clearly spelled out in the plant manager's job description, and the way it is handled is set forth in less formal communications from top management. At the minimum the company wants its plants to enjoy good relations with the communities in which they operate, and expects the plant manager to maintain those relations with the long-range interests of the company in mind. The plant manager's job can involve him in these facets of community relations:

1. Liaison with municipal authorities—fire, police, public works, planning and zoning, water resources, and pollution control departments.

2. Participation in trade, civic, and professional organizations.

3. Handling complaints from neighboring residents and businesses concerning noise, traffic, air and water pollution.

4. Socio-political activities. Some companies encourage their managerial employees to engage in political work in the party of their choice. Others are deeply involved in joint business-government-community programs to train and employ the handicapped or the disadvantaged.

5. Cooperation with charity drives—usually the United Fund or similar give-once-for-all type.

RELATIONSHIPS WITH OTHER DEPARTMENTS

The company cannot survive unless its divisions and departments form a smooth-working team. The company's customers don't care whether the manufacturing department gets along well with engineering, or R & D with accounting—they want quality merchandise delivered on time and will make no allowances for internal bickering. Within the company, however, the interests and objectives of the various departments differ so much that sometimes conflict seems inevitable. This section is designed to help the plant manager put into proper perspective his relations with other departments, and to sort out the important factors affecting them.

When handling situations of actual or potential conflict, keep two points in mind: the plant manager who agrees to every special request made of his organization will find that he has saddled it with so many inefficient procedures that operating costs are increasing without corresponding return. On the other hand, if he blindly refuses to consider the requests of other departments the entire company may suffer in such important areas as customer relations, new product development, and the effective completion of major engineering projects.

Sales

There is one overriding aspect of the relationship between sales and manufacturing which may seem—and sometimes is—unfair to the manufacturing department: If sales has committed the company to deliver a product at a specified time to a customer, there is no choice but for everyone in the company, including manufacturing, to strive to meet the requirement. Again, the customer views the company as one unit, and is not interested in its internal communications.

This is not to say that the sales department has no responsibility for maintaining contact with its accounts, avoiding "rush" deliveries and manufacturing surprises. The sales department which makes promises to customers without first checking the manufacturing position is living dangerously indeed. Similarly, manufacturing must keep sales advised of actual or potential interruptions of production, and problems affecting quality.

Accounting

The points of contact between the accounting and manufacturing departments lie in the areas of cost reporting and cost control. Manufacturing expects the accounting department to develop cost reporting systems which allow manufacturing managers to make the optimum financial decisions in day-to-day operations. It also expects accounting to issue cost reports promptly—a monthly report issued three weeks after the month has ended is useless as a tool for controlling costs.

The accounting department expects to find a climate of cost consciousness in the manufacturing operation, and a willingness to cooperate in cost control projects. To render prompt reports, it must have speedy submission of the production department records on which they are based—production totals, off-grade reports, receiving and shipping documents, and inventory totals.

Engineering

The engineering department's largest projects usually deal with the installation or modification of production facilities, and the relationship between the two departments is a close and continuing one.

The degree of independence which engineering has in designing plant equipment and layout differs from company to company, but at the minimum manufacturing looks for engineering to:

1. Design equipment and installations with operating problems in mind—ease of maintenance, safety, convenient access to operating controls, and housekeeping, as well as production rate and quality.

2. Make use of the experience acquired by the manufacturing department with present plant and equipment.

3. Submit its preliminary plans and specifications to the manufacturing department for review and comment.

The engineering department should expect manufacturing to:

1. Supply complete and accurate data on the performance of existing equip-

ment, including special studies when the regular process records do not contain the information needed.

2. Review plans and specifications promptly.

3. Keep in mind engineering's responsibility for the cost of the project.

4. Participate in the post-completion audit to determine whether the project is generating the profit it was designed for.

Financial justification of engineering projects can fall to either department. When corporate practice calls for the engineering department to prepare the economic justification, it will need the help of manufacturing in projecting labor and operating costs. When the manufacturing department justifies the project, it needs accurate cost and completion date estimates from engineering.

Research & Development

Some plant managers hardly ever see a research man, especially in those companies where the engineering department bridges the gap between development and full-scale production. In companies and industries where products must move from the research stage to manufacturing very quickly, the association can be very close.

When R & D approaches manufacturing, it usually wishes to make arrangements for experimental production of a new development on plant equipment. Manufacturing should expect R & D to come in with a carefully thought-out proposal, and to present a detailed operating procedure for the experiment in advance of the work. It will also want to see evidence that sufficient laboratory and pilot work has been done to justify a full-scale attempt on plant equipment and time.

Manufacturing's requests to R & D are usually for assistance in solving technical plant problems. R & D will look for clearly stated objectives and sound reasons (preferably financial) for devoting its time to the problem. It will also expect that manufacturing has applied all of its own resources to the problem before approaching R & D.

The two departments can help each other by keeping a two-way communication going:

1. Manufacturing should keep R & D supplied with up-to-date copies of all operating procedures. It should inform R & D of changes in manufacturing capabilities, and pass along any technical information discovered in the plant which might not turn up in laboratory or pilot plant investigations.

2. R & D should keep the manufacturing department informed on the progress of new development projects, especially those which may require new machinery or new personnel skills.

THE SCIENCE OF MANAGEMENT: THE MANAGEMENT CYCLE

As he approaches this imposing list of assignments, the plant manager may not be entirely clear on exactly what the management function is. He already knows that "management is getting things done through other people," or he would never have risen to the post of plant manager. What he may not realize is that management is a clearly defined set of activities, and that the techniques used in its practice can be defined, described, and learned. The purpose of this section is to put the elements of management into clear focus, and to help the plant manager achieve an overall balance in their use.

Management: Pinpointing the Term

It would be hard to find another word used so much but so loosely defined in the minds of those who use it as "management." Many think of management as "the people who run a business." The dictionaries aren't much help either—they talk about "direction," "control," and "executive skill," without stating precisely what it is that managers do.

Perhaps the best definition available is the one promulgated by Lawrence Appley, past-President of the American Management Association: "Management is the guiding of human and physical resources into dynamic organization units, which achieve their objectives to the satisfaction of those served, and with a high degree of morale and sense of attainment on the part of those performing the service."

The Management Cycle

Most managers have been exposed to bits and pieces of the management cycle throughout their careers. They have heard of "budgetary controls." They have submitted "organization charts." They have attended "planning seminars." And they have been through periodic campaigns emphasizing some part of the management cycle—"management by objectives," "management by exception," "management by *total* objectives," and so on. There is nothing wrong with any of these concepts in themselves, but they are misleading to the extent that they fail to capture the full scope of the management function.

The practice of management consists of three essential activities—*planning, organizing,* and *controlling.* No human activity requiring management can be successful without them; they are always present, to a greater or lesser degree, in every organized enterprise carried on by groups of people. Together they constitute the *management cycle,* a term which implies, quite accurately, that the work done in any of the three functions is never complete in itself, but must be adjusted on a continuing basis to accomodate changes in each of the other two. Let's examine the elements of the management cycle more closely, and illustrate their application to a specific plant problem.

1) Planning is the first step taken by a manager as he approaches a task assigned to him, and he develops his plan by pursuing two highly disciplined activities. The first is to develop an exact statement of the objective which is to be reached, including not only *what* is to be accomplished, but *when* it is to be completed.

The second step in planning is to determine exactly what activities must be carried out to reach the objective. These activities must be defined clearly at this stage in terms of their cost, manpower demands in numbers and skills, requirements for tools and materials, and the order in which they will be executed.

2) Organizing is the management process by which groups of people are assigned to the activities stated in the plan. As he structures the organization, the manager assembles the appropriate number of people with the required skills, and establishes lines of authority and responsibility between himself and the working groups. He coordinates their activities to avoid conflict and duplication of effort. And he sees to it that no one reports to more than one superior, and no supervisor has more people reporting to him than he can reasonably handle.

3) Controlling completes the management cycle. In this step, the manager evaluates the progress of the organization toward its goal. He establishes methods of measuring and evaluating the difference between the goal and the accomplishment at appropriate times. He sets up checkpoints which warn him that the effort is going off target before the situation gets too serious. When the warnings are received, he takes corrective action in time to bring the effort back on target.

Now we come to an understanding of why planning, organizing, and controlling are called the *management cyle.* When he evaluates the signals he receives in the control phase, the manager may decide that the proper corrective action is to change the organization, or even go back to the planning stage and add or detract activities. In some cases the objective itself may have to be changed. When that happens, organization and control must be reviewed again, and the cycle may be repeated many times before success is achieved.

Consider the application of these principles by a plant manager to a specific case. This manager has decided, after a series of near-miss accidents, that he wishes to establish a safety glasses program in his plant.

He starts with the planning phase, and his first step is to define the objective as clearly as he can: "After March 31, 197—, safety glasses will be worn by all employees and guests of the company in production, maintenance, and shipping areas of the plant."

His next planning move is to decide what activities must be carried out to reach the objective, and he writes down the following list:

A. Conduct an Educational Program
    1. Assemble facts about effectiveness of safety glasses, including eye injury case histories and statistics for the nation, the industry, and this plant.
    2. Conduct safety meetings with each plant work group, stating the reasons for requiring safety glasses, and presenting the information assembled in 1.
    3. Support the campaign with a series of articles in the company newspaper.
B. Provide Safety Glasses for All Personnel
    1. Plano glasses for personnel who do not wear glasses regularly.
    2. Prescription glasses for those who do. Each employee to submit his own prescription.
C. Establish Plant Regulations
    1. Draft a plant safety rule requiring safety glasses, and publish.
    2. Make it a condition of employment that safety glasses be worn.
    3. Establish disciplinary procedures for failure to comply.
    4. Post signs in appropriate areas.

The planning phase completed, the plant manager moves next to the organizing step. In this case the plant manager won't even look at his organization chart. He knows that he can find on it groups of people who can operate the steam boilers, perform processing operations, and ship finished goods. But nowhere on the chart will he find a group of people set up to work on a safety glasses program. He will have to organize a group to carry out the program.

His first step in organizing is to decide what abilities are needed. Reviewing the activity list reveals the need for the ability to 1) research the information required for the educational program, and develop it into a presentable form for worker meetings; 2) communicate the information to the employees and enforce rules developed by the program; and 3) measure and fit each employee with a suitable set of frames and lenses.

The second step is to hire or assign people with these abilities. This plant manager feels that his personnel director has the skills required for (1) above. The production superintendent meets the requirements for (2). But there is no one in the organization who can accomplish (3). This skill will have to be acquired outside the company by engaging the services of an optometrist.

The third step in organizing is to establish lines of authority and responsibility. Our plant manager feels that many of the decisions to be made by the group need not involve him directly, so he delegates his authority by putting the personnel director in charge. The production superintendent is made accountable to the personnel director for matters relating to this project.

The fourth step is to establish the relationships between the elements of the organization. In this case, the plant manager decides that the personnel director will assume responsibility for hiring the optometrist, and conducting the research and publicity work. The production superintendent is made responsible for the meetings with plant personnel, for drafting the safety regulation, and posting of signs. By assigning the activities carefully, the plant manager avoids conflicts between the two men over who is to do what.

Now that the organization is complete and ready to start work, the plant manager turns his attention to the controls he will use to satisfy himself that the program is proceeding according to plan.

He arranges monthly meetings with the personnel director to receive a verbal report on the program's progress. He notes on his calendar the dates when the accident statistics and publicity material are due, and asks to see them. He requires written reports from the production superintendent on the plant meetings, and asks for them when the meetings are due. Several days after the March 31 deadline he walks through the plant to see if safety glasses really are being worn. At each control point, he takes corrective action if the goals of the program are not being met.

Our manager may have to go through the cycle several times before he can call the program completed. He may get halfway through the preparatory stage only to find that a state law prohibits him from making the wearing of glasses mandatory. This does not mean the end of the program but it does mean that he will have to go back to the planning stage and review his objectives and procedures. One hundred percent compliance may now be an impossible goal, and must be reduced to some lower figure. Certainly the new plant regulation will have to be eliminated. Obviously the method of control will have to be revised in light of the new situation.

IMPLEMENTING MOTIVATION AND LEADERSHIP TECHNIQUES

The management cycle does not set itself in motion. The basic driving force which gets things done is the leadership provided by the organization's leader; in the industrial plant that man is the plant manager.

Volumes of information and advice concerning motivation and leadership have been written, and it is almost certain that any reader of this book has been exposed to some of this material. It is a good idea to become familiar with this literature, and to select from it those techniques which seem to best fit your personality and situation. Here are five approaches to leadership which will be useful to any plant manager:

Take the Initiative

There are really two parts to the plant manager's job. In the first part he responds to forces outside his control: customer orders, union grievances, assignments from his superior, equipment breakdowns, and many more. This work is necessary and important, but its successful completion will earn the plant manager only a reputation for competence.

The second part of the plant manager's job consists of the work which he assigns to himself. It consists of the improvements he makes and the programs he carries out which are *not* required by outside forces. It is based on his assessment of the opportunities open to his organization, and the objectives which he sets to take advantage of them. It can be in the area of cost, safety, technical improvement, or in many other areas. Whatever the area, the work which he does on his own initiative is the work which sets him apart from the competent caretaker, and establishes him in the eyes of his subordinates and his superiors as a leader.

Set the Example

The plant manager can rely on one key principle: the example he sets in energy applied to the job, in determination to reach objectives, and the wisdom and ability with which he carries out the management cycle will not be exceeded by his organization. He is fortunate if it is matched. Therefore, if he expects high standards of performance from his subordinates, he must set even higher standards for himself. His example determines the tone of the work climate in the plant.

Fulfill the Needs

One concept of motivation is that people are prompted to action by an ascending order of physical and psychological needs. The lowest needs on the scale are those of physical survival—food, clothing, shelter. Higher on the scale are recognition, security, belonging, and self-fulfillment.

When the nation's economy is healthy, the lower needs are taken for granted. A plant employee can acquire food, clothing, and shelter by working almost anywhere, and sometimes by not working at all. Therefore, his willingness to stay and to work hard at a particular plant depends upon the degree to which his needs for recognition, for belonging, for feeling that he is involved in something worthwhile are filled.

Sometimes the needs of the employee and those of the company are in conflict, and the plant manager must realize that not all psychological needs can be provided by employment. His task in motivation is to identify those areas where the needs of each coincide (as in safety) and use this fact to the greatest advantage of both; and having identified the areas of conflict (as in absenteeism), to face them squarely so that employees know where they stand.

Delegate the Work

The plant manager who entrusts as little as possible to subordinates, but tries to handle all the problems and projects himself, is missing an important element of leadership. If employees are to feel that they are growing and developing in their jobs, they need to take on more challenging assignments; as these are successfully completed their self-confidence and sense of participation increase. The manager who develops such subordinates not only has a stronger team working with him, but opens up valuable blocks of time in which to pursue the initiative on his own job.

Be Yourself

Management styles are often described as "autocratic vs. democratic," or "production-oriented vs. people-oriented," or in other this-versus-that expressions. Studies of the personalities of many managers indicate that there is no one type of personality or set of personality traits attributable to the successful manager. The important points in developing your leadership style are: 1) study your own personality and adopt those leadership techniques which suit you best, 2) modify those personality traits which will bring you into conflict with the objectives of your job or with company policy, and 3) don't try to imitate someone else or his style of management. You'll be unconvincing and appear insincere if you attempt it.

CONSERVING MANAGERIAL TIME

Every manager is confronted with the problem of dividing his time among the many demands for his attention. Aware of the critical need for time in which to pursue self-assigned tasks, he uses these techniques to make more time available:

Delegation

Delegation is not only a sound principle of leadership, it is an essential device for gaining time. It is a simple axiom of cost efficiency that every job should be performed at the lowest possible level in the organization. The manager must constantly review the tasks he performs to see if they cannot be assigned to subordinates. If he can recover thirty minutes per day, he will free 125 hours per year for "initiative" work.

Get Rid of Crises

Every plant has emergencies which legitimately demand the attention of the plant manager. But when the same crisis occurs again and again, an opportunity exists to reduce the erosion of his time by establishing routine procedures to prevent (or take care of) the emergency. The production equipment which breaks down every seven or eight months, creating an "emergency," can be taken out of service on a planned schedule for repairs twice a year.

Study the Use of Time

The plant manager who is willing to keep—or have someone else keep—a record of how he spends his time for a month is in for some surprises. He will find that his time is not really being spent where he thought it was, and that much of it is consumed in activities which further his objectives not at all.

The techniques of personal time management are not complicated, but they do require self-discipline.

1. Plan your time. Obtain an "executive planner" or similar booklet from the stationery store, and use it to block out the time you want to spend on each activity. Even if the unexpected interferes with the schedule, you will at least know what you deviated from, and can adjust to the change with the minimum loss of time.

2. Minimize the pleasantries. Subordinates, associates, even your boss—all seem to have unlimited time for social talk. You do not want to offend these people, but there is a lot you can do within that limitation to keep these conversations short, allowing you to get back to the work that counts.

3. Control your availability. Not every salesman who shows up in the reception room should be admitted to your office by merely asking for the privilege. If it appears that you might be interested in his product or service, talk to him on the inter-office phone before inviting him in. You can then quickly terminate the contact if it is not worthwhile.

You want your subordinates to bring certain matters to your attention. Without further guidance, they will bring a great deal more than you are interested in. Steadfast refusal by you to handle matters which should be taken care of elsewhere is your only defense against this waste of time.

4. Match the time period to the job. If you can depend on having two solid hours alone next Tuesday morning between 10:00 AM and Noon, that's the time to tackle a two-hour job (perhaps review the blueprints for the new building addition). Don't waste that good block of time by handling four half-hour jobs which could be fitted into smaller time slots available throughout the week.

SELF-IMPROVEMENT: HOW TO KEEP ABREAST OF THE JOB

If the plant manager has a written job description for his position, it will undoubtedly contain a section on self-improvement, calling upon the manager to increase his knowledge and ability in his field. This requirement is hardly necessary; any manager attempting to operate today with only the knowledge and skills he had ten years ago is headed for failure. Time and the economy do not stand still; the man or company who does not move ahead inevitably falls behind.

There are three areas in which the plant manager needs to keep abreast of the times. One is the technical field of the plant operation—metal fabricating, plastics molding, electronic assembly, chemical processing, or whatever. Another is the field of management science—the continuing development of management as a body of knowledge in itself, and the development of new techniques for applying it. The third area is that of social and economic trends—developments in labor law, union organization, pollution control, employment trends, and civil rights legislation, for examples, have potential impact on the plant operation. The plant manager must be fully aware of all of these trends in order to adjust successfully to them.

The plant manager can choose from a number of ways to keep up with his technical field. Most colleges offer evening courses in a wide range of technical subjects. Seminars lasting from one day to two weeks are offered periodically on technical subjects. A large number of technical and engineering societies publish magazines which report new developments in their fields. And there is an interesting trend toward the mailing of free magazines to people working in a particular field; in one recent year a plant manager in the New York area received all of the following publications without cost, and mostly unsolicited: *Plant Engineering, Data Processing Magazine, Packaging Digest, Science & Technology, Industrial Water Engineering, Business Management, Modern Manufacturing, Material Handling Engineering,* and *Distribution Manager.*

Similar resources are available in the field of management science, with many colleges offering evening courses and short daytime seminars. The American Management Association conducts workshops, orientation seminars, and management courses up to a week in length in a number of large cities. Private management consulting firms also conduct seminars in many areas. The Society for the Advancement of Management organizes local chapters of people interested in keeping up with the management field; they meet periodically to discuss management topics in the same manner as the technical societies.

Keeping up with social and economic trends is largely a matter of reading. Newspapers and general circulation magazines are a good source. Some technical publications do a good job of keeping their readers advised on these matters as well as technical developments. A wide variety of commercially published bulletins and newsletters are also available for the price of a subscription.

Chapter 2

Making the Organization Match the Work

Ask any plant manager what his most important resource is, and you will most likely get the reply, "people." With some pride, he may go on to explain how he has carefully recruited the best people available in the labor market and thoroughly trained them to do their jobs.

But these efforts are not enough. People, competent and well-trained though they may be, do not work in isolation; they must work with each other in a system which obtains the best results from their combined efforts, and minimizes the detracting elements of conflict, confusion, and frustration. Devising that system is the job of *organization,* and it is among the most important tasks a manager performs. If it is done well, he is far along the road to a smooth-running, efficient operation. If it is done poorly, a never-ending series of problems interfering with plant performance will be the result.

This chapter will show you how to tackle the job of structuring the plant organization, what the choices are in organizing the hourly work force, and how to handle some special organization problems.

HOW TO ACHIEVE A SMOOTH AND EFFICIENT ORGANIZATION

Keep the Goals in Mind

Among the first questions the plant manager will ask are "What am I trying to accomplish with organization structure?" and "How will I know when I have a good structure for my plant?" The broad answer is clear: The organization structure must make its full contribution to the plant goals of quantity, quality, and cost. The specific answer is contained in this list of objectives for the plant organization. It must:

1. Accomplish the work. Not only must it provide sufficient numbers of people with the ability to carry out the production tasks, but it must also furnish support personnel to move materials, judge quality, repair equipment, and supervise the operation.

2. Minimize cost. Organization structure can contribute mightily to reducing costs. It should avoid wasting labor just as a good production process avoids wasting material. Every task performed should be assigned to the lowest wage or salary level at which it can be performed competently. And while it is providing

sufficient numbers of people to do the work, it must not provide excessive numbers.

3. Maintain flexibility. Every industrial plant experiences peaks and valleys of production output. Changes will occur in equipment, processes, and kinds of products manufactured. Key people may be absent for periods of time ranging from a few days to months, or may suddenly leave the organization altogether. The organization structure must provide it with the maximum ability to meet these changing situations without losing its ability to continue production, and without incurring excessive cost.

4. Provide clear-cut lines of authority and responsibility. Unless each individual and group within the organization understands what his job is and where his authority begins and ends, its performance will be damaged by confusion and internal friction.

5. Offer maximum opportunity for advancement. People will leave when they see no chance to achieve higher positions and earnings. The organization structure can be built to encourage employees to broaden their skills, and to reward those who do; in return it gains employee loyalty and greater flexibility.

6. Harmonize with the physical layout of the plant. An existing arrangement of buildings and heavy machinery dictates to a large extent the shape of the organization which will run it; to ignore the boundaries of departments and sections so determined is to create administrative problems for the foremen and supervisors who must later lead them.

When a new plant is to be built, the physical layout should be adjusted to meet the requirements of good organization structure; at this stage changes can be made at little or no cost which will save many thousands of dollars in operating costs over the life of the plant.

Follow These Steps

Structure your organization from the ground up; start with the most basic tasks that must be performed and work your way up through the people who will perform them to the managerial and administrative system which will run the plant. The section headings which follow comprise this list of steps to be followed in order:

1. List the tasks.
2. Decide what workers are needed.
3. Establish sections and departments.
4. Develop the supervisory and managerial structure.
5. Assign responsibilities.
6. Coordinate activities.

List the Tasks

The use of the word "tasks," rather than "jobs," is quite deliberate. Decisions about job content and the types of workers needed should be delayed until a complete listing of the elemental tasks which must be performed is made. By following this procedure, you can build up job content from the basic work elements and keep open as long as possible the opportunity to make the most efficient combinations for your plant.

As an example of the listing of tasks, consider the Shipping Department in a plant which receives solid raw materials and supplies in cartons and 100-lb. bags, and liquids in 55-gallon barrels and tank trucks. It ships out solid and liquid products in 50-lb. bags, 55-gallon barrels, and 5-gallon pails. A list of the work tasks performed by this department, and set down in no particular order, would look like this:

Unload boxes, bags, and barrels from incoming trucks.

Transfer finished goods from production area to warehouse.

Sweep floors.

Transfer raw materials from shipping dock to warehouse.

Collect broken pallets.

Transfer outgoing materials from warehouse to shipping dock.

Take daily inventory of bulk storage tank levels.

Take completed receiving reports to accounting department.

Compare incoming bills of lading against purchase orders.

Move broken pallets to Maintenance Department for repair.

Attach labels to each piece of outgoing shipments.

Draw small quantities of products to fill sample orders.

Unload bulk liquid receipts into storage tanks.

Repackage outgoing shipments to meet customer requests.

Complete customer order form and return to office after shipment.

Unload incoming supplies.

Sign receipts for incoming shipments.

Remove trash to pickup bins.

Type labels for shipments.

Package samples in appropriate containers for parcel post.

Take weekly supply inventory.

Prepare bills of lading for outgoing shipments.

Call trucking companies to arrange shipment pickups.

Fill 55-gallon barrels from bulk storage tanks.

Decide What Workers Are Needed

The many separate work tasks can now be combined in different ways to make up jobs. What you are trying to achieve in this step are the most efficient combinations for your plant—those which will give you the greatest output at the lowest operating cost. No handbook can tell you what the best combinations are; that must be decided on the basis of your particular conditions and circumstances. Let's see how three plant managers might make up different job contents using the same list of tasks developed in the previous section:

Plant Manager No. 1, running a medium-sized shipping operation with a strict requirement to keep costs low, chooses to combine the tasks into jobs this way:

Shipping Clerk

Complete customer order form and return to office after shipment.

Compare incoming bills of lading against purchase orders.

Attach labels to each piece of outgoing shipments.

Sign receipts for incoming shipments.

Type labels for shipments.

Package samples in appropriate containers for parcel post.

Prepare bills of lading for outgoing shipments.

Call trucking companies to arrange shipment pickups.

Materials Handler

Unload boxes, bags, and barrels from incoming trucks.

Transfer finished goods from production area to warehouse.

Transfer raw materials from shipping

Unload incoming supplies.

Unload bulk liquid receipts into storage tanks.

Take daily inventory of bulk storage tank levels.

dock to warehouse.

Transfer outgoing materials from warehouse to shipping dock.

Draw small quantities of products to fill sample orders.

Fill 55-gallon barrels from bulk storage tanks.

Utility Man

Sweep floors.

Collect broken pallets.

Take completed receiving reports to Accounting Department.

Move broken pallets to Maintenance Department for repair.

Repackage outgoing shipments to meet customer requests.

Remove trash to pickup bins.

Take weekly supply inventory.

To keep his costs low, this plant manager has examined the task list for the simpler operations, and combined them into the job of Utility Man. He can pay a lower rate for this job, and hire relatively unskilled people for it. By keeping the number of levels down to three he avoids the upward pressure on the Shipping Clerk's wage rate which might result from having to include wage differentials for too many levels.

Plant Manager No. 2 runs a larger shipping operation which has been growing by leaps and bounds, and now threatens to outstrip its physical facilities. Not pressed quite so hard on costs, his problem is to get the day's work done in a limited amount of space. He divides his task list into jobs somewhat differently:

Shipping Clerk

Complete customer order form and return to office after shipment.

Compare incoming bills of lading against purchase orders.

Sign receipts for incoming shipments.

Type labels for shipments.

Prepare bills of lading for outgoing shipments.

Call trucking companies to arrange shipment pickups.

Dock Man

Unload boxes, bags, and barrels from incoming trucks.

Repackage outgoing shipments to meet customer requests.

Attach labels to each piece of outgoing shipments.

Unload incoming supplies.

Remove trash to pickup bins.

Warehouseman

Transfer finished goods from production area to warehouse.

Sweep floors.

Transfer raw materials from shipping dock to warehouse.

Collect broken pallets.

Transfer outgoing materials from warehouse to shipping dock.

Move broken pallets to Maintenance Department for repair.

Storage Tank Operator

Unload bulk liquid receipts into storage tanks.

Fill 55-gallon barrels from bulk storage tanks.

Take daily inventory of bulk storage tank levels.

Sample Man

Draw small quantities of products to fill sample orders.

Package samples in appropriate containers for parcel post.

Take weekly supply inventory.   Take completed receiving reports to
                                                 Accounting Department.

This is a somewhat more expensive system than used by Plant Manager No. 1, because it has more job levels, and a greater degree of specialization in each job category. The Utility Man is gone, and his chores have been distributed among the more skilled and higher paying positions of this organizational system.

But Plant Manager No. 2 has accomplished his objective of covering each major activity with a specific job, so that the activity can be accomplished quickly without holding up the rest of the operation. For instance, he established the position of Dock Man, so that there would always be workers at the shipping dock to load and unload trucks quickly, avoiding a pileup of materials there. He did the same with the position of Storage Tank Operator, so that a man would always be available whose primary duty is to unload bulk liquids, avoiding delays at the bulk liquid station. Obviously, a high level of activity is required to provide economic justification for establishing such specialized positions.

Plant Manager No. 3 approached the problem very differently. He ran a small (less than ten men) operation, subject to wide variations in work load distribution—heavy on truck loading one day, tank farm work the next, and sample preparation on the third. He was further concerned about the effects of too much specialization. If the Shipping Clerk were absent or quit unexpectedly, or if the same happened with other crucial skills such as tank farm operation or sample preparation, he might be in serious trouble. For these reasons, he wanted maximum flexiblility in his organizational structure.

To get flexibility, he used a system in which every man in the department is trained to do every job. Instead of using job classifications as in the previous examples, he divided the list of tasks into five work areas or "fields:"

Shipping Desk   Tank Farm
Loading Dock   Sample Preparation
Warehouse

(The individual tasks are not listed here for the sake of brevity, but would follow closely the division used by Plant Manager No. 2 in the previous example.)

As each man is hired, he is gradually trained in each of the fields. As he continues his training, he passes through a series of grade levels, each commanding a higher wage rate. The schedule of advancement might look like this:

	Time Required in Previous Level	*Qualifications for Advancement*
Beginner	—	—
Warehouseman D	2 months	Automatic
Warehouseman C	4 months	Automatic
Warehouseman B	12 months	Performance Review and Examination
Warehouseman A	18 months	Performance Review and Examination

The time intervals and the nature of the performance reviews and examinations are tailored to meet the needs of individual plants and departments. A fuller discussion of the Operator Grade system appears on pages 49-50.

Plant Manager No. 3 is using a somewhat more expensive system, because if every man he hires is capable of advancing to Warehouseman A, he will be paying every man in the department the top rate. In return, he can count on every man who shows up for work being able to perform any task, and he avoids squabbles about seniority in promotions or the assignment of overtime between classifications. Under the conditions prevailing in his plant, this manager felt that the cost of operation would be lower in the long run with the flexibility provided by this system.

By reserving decisions about job content until they had made a list of the basic tasks to be performed, these three managers gave themselves the maximum opportunity to find the best job arrangements for their plants.

Establish Sections and Departments

The next step is to set up the sections and departments of the plant organization. Some groupings are immediately apparent—after all, doesn't every plant have a maintenance department and a shipping department and aren't their functions obvious? But careful consideration of the following issues will help you achieve optimum cost efficiency; they can apply to the reorganization of old plants as well as the structuring of new plants:

1) Choose between process and product orientation. The manager of a plant (somewhat simplified for this example) producing refrigerator cabinets, wastebaskets, and metal storage bins might decide to organize *by process.* If he does, he will establish these departments: Stock Preparation, Cutting, Metal Forming, Painting, and Trim. Each department will carry out its process on all the products made—whether cabinets, baskets, or bins. Or he can decide to organize *by product,* setting up a Cabinet Department, Waste Basket Department, and Storage Bin Department, and each department would perform all of the steps required to make its product.

How to make this choice? By finding the system which requires the least number of people. Under the heading *process orientation* write down the names of the departments required; opposite each department put down the total number of people required to run it. Do the same for *product orientation.* (The usefulness of this procedure can become quickly apparent; in our metal products plant example the manager found that under product orientation he would need a cutting machine in each department and one operator, for a total of three machines and operators. In process orientation he discovered that two machines and operators could handle the total plant needs.) Choose the system which requires less people, but verify your decision by looking for offsetting cost factors: Would the chosen system require such highly skilled people that the total labor cost will be higher? Does it require additional support functions such as quality control or materials movement which wipe out the labor savings? If so, a thorough cost analysis may be the only way to settle the question.

2) Centralization vs. decentralization. This question applies most often to the support functions. Should a central department be set up to handle all material movements throughout the plant? It would have advantages: maximum use of equipment, better training of lift truck drivers, better control of safety and maintenance practices. Or would it be better to give each department its own material handling equipment and personnel? This method has advantages, too: smoother operation within the production department, no material pileups while waiting for help to arrive, no time wasted in sending verbal or written communications to get material moved. Partial decentralization might be useful; would it be more efficient to have the production departments perform their own in-process quality controls, leaving the final checks to the Inspection Department? Would it be better to assign a pair of mechanics to a production department which can fully utilize their services, rather than have them report to the Maintenance Department every morning, only to be sent out to the same production area?

There is no "book" answer to these questions. The point is that they should be considered when departments are being set up or reorganized.

3) Conform to physical layout. Large buildings and major units of process equipment

create natural outlines for sections and departments, and it is wise to follow these outlines. To ignore them—perhaps by having a foreman cover the activities in one building and half of another—is to create supervisory and managerial problems which will seriously interfere with plant efficiency. Sometimes equipment is so specialized as to require its own organization and a high degree of centralization; an example is a battery of distillation columns in a chemical plant. The unit may serve different departments of the plant, but is assembled in one part of the plant with its own operating group because of its unique size and mode of operation.

Develop the Supervisory and Managerial Structure

Some describe free enterprise as simply "competition between managerial teams." While this may be an oversimplification, it does point up the fact that performance of the managerial group can make the difference between keeping the plant open and shutting it down. Naturally you will promote and hire the best available people to fill your supervisory and managerial positions. The purpose of this section is to help you provide an organization structure which not only does not get in their way, but actually gives them positive help toward top performance.

Exhibits 1 and 2 provide examples of the managerial structures of a typical small plant and large plant, respectively. Both plants operate twenty-four hours a day, seven days a week, and require four shifts (A, B, C, and D). The horizontal line across each chart separates hourly from salaried employment levels; in Exhibit 1 it was possible to include all the plant workers on the chart, but in Exhibit 2 they are merely indicated below the line.

The charts themselves offer a number of suggestions to the plant manager attempting to set up his line organization and provide it with adequate staff support. The simple supervisory structure of the production line organization in Exhibit 1 has been expanded to include general foremen, department superintendents, and a production manager in Exhibit 2. Personnel has been expanded to Industrial Relations, and Quality Control is part of a large Technical Department. A Materials Management function, which did not appear in the smaller plant, combines the activities of purchasing and inventory control. There is no specific point in increasing plant size when the more elaborate structures are needed; this must be decided for the individual case, and some smaller plants require a Technical Director or a Materials Manager because of the peculiar nature of the business. When structuring your managerial organization, take into account these factors:

1) Keep it lean. Provide no more than the minimum number of supervisors and managers you foresee will be needed. If you must add help later on, it is easier to increase the staff than to cut it back. You do not want to get into the position of one company, threatened with bankruptcy, which called in a management consultant. Among other strong recommendations, he advised the dismissal of half of the plant foremen; his advice was followed with disastrous results for a number of innocent people.

2) Provide unity of command. This is the principle that every man in the organization reports to and takes orders from one superior only. This is plain common sense and plant managers will be naturally inclined to follow it, but there are occasions when it must be violated to a degree. In Exhibit 1 the Shift Leaders are hired, trained, promoted, fired, and receive their primary work instructions from the Department Supervisors. When on shift, however, they are accountable to and take instructions from the Shift Supervisors regarding certain work situations and emergencies. The chart shows this by a dotted line. When "dotted line" relationships are necessary, it is essential to spell out clearly where the authority of one manager ends and another begins.

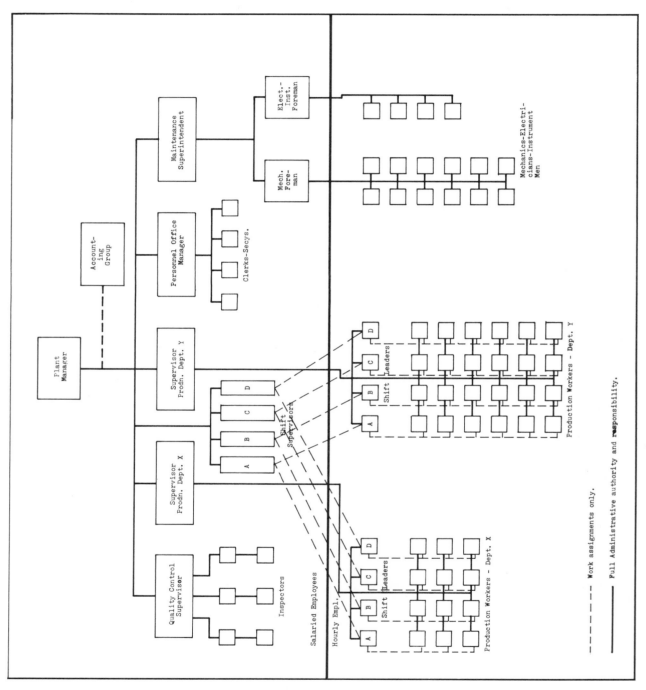

Exhibit 1. A Small Plant Organization

3) Determine span of control. An often used rule of thumb for the number of people one man can supervise is eight to twelve, but this number can be sharply reduced or increased by the conditions of the job. When the workers are spread out over a large area, or are engaged in complex operations, a smaller number may be in order. When they are all in the same room, or on the same floor, or handling relatively simple tasks, the supervisor may be able to handle 20 to 35 people or more.

4) Specify the line-staff relationship. At one end of the spectrum of thinking on this subject the philosophy is to hire strong, versatile managers, and give them whatever help they need within the line organization; the view at the other end is that the line organization should merely carry out the procedures and ideas generated by the staff groups, where the really creative work is done. In Exhibit 2, a line-oriented company might place the Director of Materials Management under the Production Manager; a staff-oriented company might have the Director of Industrial Relations reporting to a corporate vice-president instead of the Plant Manager. The author's experience leads him to favor a strong line organization; wherever your thinking or the philosophy of your company puts you on the spectrum, it is important that you determine exactly what you expect of line and staff, and build the organization accordingly.

Assign Responsibilities

The basic responsibilities of most of the plant departments and sections are self-evident from their titles—Screw Machine Department, Coil Winding Department, Powerhouse—and no elaborate schemes are needed to help a plant manager decide what these responsibilities are. The real contribution which the manager makes is to adjust the fine points of responsibility assignment to create a smoothly functioning organization:

1) Responsibilities must add up. The sum of the responsibilities assigned to the departments must equal the total carried by the plant, without a "dropped ball" somewhere in the organization. Major responsibilities are not likely to be overlooked, but minor ones can be troublesome. For instance, will the Shipping Department be responsible for receiving *all* supplies including those of the office and the Maintenance Department, or will vendors be required to deliver separately to those departments? Whatever your decision, you must make an adjustment in the organization of the affected department so that it can handle the work.

2) Put it in writing. Verbal instructions in a matter of this importance are totally inadequate; they are too easily confused, misinterpreted, or forgotten altogether. The most complete and elaborate format for the written assignment of responsibilities is the Plant Operations Manual, and the plant management should develop one as soon as possible. Usually made up on printed forms and distributed in bound copies, the manual is a complete statement of the procedures to be followed and the responsibilities assigned to the plant departments. Exhibit 3 is an example of one such procedure.

If you do not have the time, resources, or personnel to develop a full-scale Operations Manual right away, there is an alternative. Issue each supervisor and manager a looseleaf binder labelled "Procedure Manual." Each time you handle a problem or establish a new system involving department responsibilities, write a procedure memorandum and distribute it to all manual holders for insertion in the appropriate section. Exhibit 4 is an example of a procedure memorandum which could have been put on a dictating machine in less than fifteen minutes. As these memoranda are collected over a period of time, they will constitute a useful operations manual which can be easily coverted to a more formal volume when resources are available.

3) Match the responsibilities assigned to a group with its numbers, skills, and physical

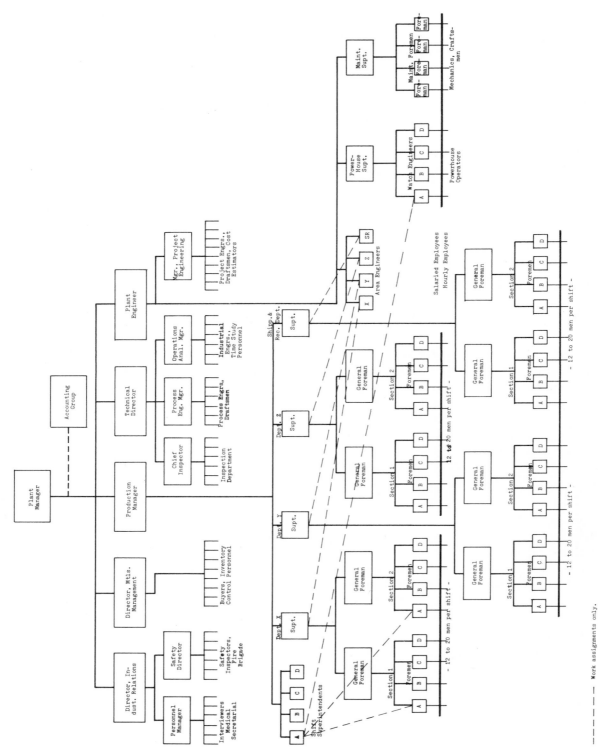

Exhibit 2. A Large Plant Organization

facilities. Don't over-assign, giving it more responsibilities than its resources can handle; there is no point in assigning the repair and maintenance of a new computer-controlled milling machine with elaborate electronic gear to a maintenance department having only the traditional electrical and mechanical skills. Either the organization must be changed so that it has the necessary skills, or the responsibility assigned elsewhere. It can be just as bad to under-assign, leaving the group with more equipment and people than needed for its mission; sloppy work practices and featherbedding are likely to be the results.

4) Keep up to date. Responsibilities must be reassigned as process methods, equipment, and available labor skills undergo change; these reassignments should be as clearcut and as formal as the original assignments, and made prior to or at the same time as the changes requiring them.

PLANT OPERATIONS MANUAL

SUBJECT Receiving Reports	PROCEDURE NO. SR-4 PAGE 1 OF 1
DEPARTMENT Shipping & Receiving	DATE ISSUED
OTHER DEPTS.	REVISES PREVIOUS ISSUE DATED None
CONCERNED Purchasing, Accounting	
WRITTEN BY S. Jones	APPROVED BY T. Vilani

Purpose of this procedure: To establish a method of and assign responsibility for the reporting of incoming shipments.

Background information: The standard Purchase Order form will contain one blue copy imprinted "Receiving Report." At the same time the Purchasing Department mails an order to a vendor, it will send the blue copy to the Shipping & Receiving Department (see Procedure PG-11, this manual).

1. When a shipment arrives, the Shipping Department Foreman will compare the Bill of Lading with the appropriate Receiving Report. If he cannot identify the Receiving Report concerned, he will seek assistance from the Purchasing Department.

2. The Foreman will compare the Bill of Lading with the Receiving Report. If they match exactly in type and quantity of material, he will instruct his personnel to unload the vehicle. If they do not, he will notify the Purchasing Department, who will provide instructions to unload all, part, or none of the shipment.

3. During the unloading, the Foreman will have a check made of the actual contents of the shipment against the Bill of Lading. If they do not match exactly, he will ask the vehicle driver to remain while he obtains a decision from the Purchasing Department concerning unordered material.

4. If the contents do match the Bill of Lading, the Foreman will have the material stored in the warehouse, and sign the Receiving Report in the space marked "Received By.."

5. When the material actually received differs from that listed on the Receiving Report, the Foreman will note the differences in writing.

6. When a shipment arrives for which there is no Receiving Report, the Foreman will notify the Purchasing Department. If their decision is to unload the material, they will make a Purchase Order immediately and send the blue copy to the Shipping Department. Under no circumstances is material to be unloaded without a Receiving Report.

Exhibit 3. Specimen Page, Plant Operations Manual

Coordinate Activities

The organization chart clearly shows the vertical structure of an organization, but it has one weakness—it says nothing about the horizontal relationships between people and groups

TO: Maintenance Foreman   Date
FROM: Plant Manager
SUBJECT: Procedure Memorandum: Minor Work Orders

1. Effective June 1, 19—— all requests for maintenance jobs estimated to cost less than $100 must be made in writing on a Minor Work Order form (except in bona fide emergencies).

2. A supply of Minor Work Order pads will be maintained in the office supply locker by the Office Manager. Worker orders are to be made out in two copies, with the originator keeping the pink copy and forwarding the white copy to the Maintenance Foreman.

3. Please assess the cost of completing each Minor Work Order you receive. If you estimate it to be more than $100, return to the originator requesting him to resubmit it on a Major Work Order form.

4. If you estimate the work to cost less than $100, please complete the job as soon as manpower and equipment are available. If it must be placed on the Maintenance Schedule, bring it up during our weekly scheduling meeting.

5. Please maintain files of completed work orders, and those awaiting action for my review. Notify me when there is a backlog of more than two weeks.

Distribution: All Production Foremen, Office Manager, R & D Section Leaders.

Exhibit 4. Typical Procedure Memorandum

within the organization. These horizontal relationships constitute the problem of *coordination,* which requires careful adjustment to keep the organization running smoothly. To make these adjustments:

1. Arrange the use of buildings, equipment, and vehicles to avoid conflict between groups trying to use them at the same time.

2. Spell out clearly the responsibility for the care, cleaning, and maintenance of equipment used by more than one group.

3. Specify exactly the condition in which materials completed by one department are to be passed on to the next department.

4. Settle materials handling problems. Who moves process material from Department A to Department B? Exactly where is it to be dropped off? How much materials is Department A allowed to accumulate before it must be moved to Department B?

5. Demand lateral cooperation. The plant manager must make it clear that he will not tolerate squabbling between departments and shifts, but that he expects full cooperation between them all of the time. Make cooperation a stated policy in operations manuals and written procedures.

6. Help the departments in their lateral communications. Verbal communications are often confused and misunderstood; a simple printed form, such as the Minor Work Order mentioned in Exhibit 4, can eliminate the difficulty. Other examples are requisitions for materials, samples, tools, quality checks, and transportation service.

HOW TO STRUCTURE THE HOURLY WORK FORCE

Although the hourly rated work force in the plant does not contain levels of authority and reporting relationships like those of the management structure, there is, nevertheless, a system of job levels associated with the difficulty of performing each job and the rate of pay which it commands. This structure deserves no less careful attention than the management organization; not only does it have major impact on the cost of operating the plant and the morale of the hourly employees, but once installed it may be very difficult to change at a later date. Choose from these four basic systems:

Flat Rate

Everyone receives the same rate of pay, and all do the same kind of work. While not found very often in industrial manufacturing plants, it does have application to specialized situations such as the assembly of novelties or the loading and unloading of freight in a truck terminal.

Advantages 1. The simplest system to administer.

2. The easiest to adjust in a tight labor market. The single rate can be raised to attract job applicants when necessary, in contrast to the difficulty of raising the bottom rate of a spread system to the same level and finding the top rate impossibly high.

Disadvantages 1. Very limited application.

2. No opportunities for advancement within the hourly ranks.

Merit System

In the most basic form of the system the new worker is hired at a standard beginning rate, and his performance reviewed semi-annually or annually by his supervisor. Any wage increase is based on the results of the supervisor's evaluation. In a modified form wage ranges are assigned to various classes of jobs, and merit increases awarded within the established ranges.

Advantages 1. The most management-oriented system. Management is in complete control of the individual's wage rate, and he is compensated entirely on the basis of performance.

2. The morale of the superior employee is kept high, since he is rewarded more than the less capable or industrious employee.

Disadvantages 1. The most vulnerable system to conscious or unconscious favoritism on the part of the foreman and supervisors.

2. Results in a very unequal wage structure after several years of operation.

Classification

This is the type of structure encountered in most industrial plants. The work content of each plant job is described precisely (see "Decide What Workers Are Needed" on page 37) and the job given a title descriptive of the work performed. The jobs are then classified in an ascending order according to a number of objective factors—skill and experience required, severity of working conditions, physical and mental effort called for, and the degree of responsibility for materials and machines. The higher rated jobs, of course, carry higher rates of pay. A typical classification system is shown in Part I of Exhibit 5.

The number of positions in each classification is firmly fixed; for example, the plant in Exhibit 5 may have ten Punch Press Operator positions. An employee in the Cutting Machine Operator classification must wait until a Punch Press Operator leaves his job before he can be promoted. This promotion will usually be awarded to the most senior Punch Press Operator who can perform the work. The frequency of advancement for any individual employee in this system depends, therefore, upon the chance openings which occur in the classifications above him.

I. Typical Classification System Job and Rate Structure

Production Department

	Step 1	Step 2	Maximum
Production Welder	3.66	3.76	3.91
Lathe Operator	3.46	3.56	3.71
Punch Press Operator	3.33	3.43	3.58
Cutting Machine Operator	3.18	3.28	3.42
Polisher	3.07	3.17	3.32
Helper	2.93	3.03	3.18

Maintenance Department

	Step 1	Step 2	Maximum
Machinist	3.86	3.96	4.11
Welder (Maintenance)	3.81	3.91	4.05
Electrician	3.76	3.86	4.00
Pipefitter	3.76	3.86	4.00
Helper	3.25	3.35	3.50
Lead Janitor	3.14	3.24	3.39
Janitor	3.00	3.10	3.25

II. Typical Operator Grade System Job and Rate Structure

Production Department

Grade	Qualification	Time Period (After Hiring)	Rate
Beginner	(Hired)	—	3.23
Operator D	Automatic	3 months	3.38
Operator C	Automatic	6 months	3.53
Operator B	Performance Review and Examination	12 months	3.78
Operator A	Performance Review and Examination	18 months	4.08

Maintenance Department

Helper	(Hired)	—	3.49
Mechanic C	Automatic	6 months	3.74
Mechanic B	Performance Review and Examination	14 months	4.04
Mechanic A	Performance Review and Examination	20 months	4.39

Exhibit 5. **Comparison of Classification and Operator Grade Systems (All figures in dollars per hour.)**

Advantages   1. The pay rate for each job is closely matched to the work performed; this should result in the lowest average rate of pay for the plant work force.

2. It is the system best adapted to organizations with a wide range of skills required between the top and bottom jobs. Because it is encountered so often, it is the sytem best understood by hourly workers and labor unions.

Disadvantages 1. Employees may resist being assigned to jobs or being asked to work overtime outside their job classifications. The result is an inflexible work force which cannot cope with absenteeism, labor shortages, or sudden changes in workload within specific classifications.

2. The new employee faces an uncertain schedule of advancement; when jobs are plentiful he may become frustrated and leave if he cannot foresee his next move up.

A further note about the classification system shown in Exhibit 5. Within each classification three rates are shown—Step 1, Step 2, and Maximum. Progression to the higher steps can be made either after the passage of a fixed period of time of satisfactory performance, or preferably, after a fixed time and formal merit review. In this way some of the advantages of the merit system can be retained in the classification system.

Operator Grade System

This system is not encountered as often as the classification system, but it is found in smaller plants and those which require a high degree of flexibility in the work force. A typical progression and rate schedule is shown in Part II of Exhibit 5.

The work tasks are not combined into "jobs" in the usual sense, to be held indefinitely by a particular person. Instead they are combined into work areas, and any employee can be assigned to any work area at a given time. Each employee is expected to learn to perform in all of the work areas and, after several automatic raises, his promotions are based upon performance reviews by his supervisor, and the administration of a written examination to be sure he knows the job content. At the Operator B level he is expected to know the routine procedures of each work area and to be able to perform them with normal supervision. At the Operator A level he is expected to demonstrate his ability to handle unusual or complicated situations and to perform the job with a minimum of supervision. The opportunity to take the examination and undergo the performance review are offered each employee at a stated time interval after hiring. The supervisor has an obligation to train and rotate every new employee through the work areas so that he will be prepared to meet these tests. The end result is a highly flexible work force, in which any man can do any job. No limit is place upon the number of men who can reach the top grade.

The way in which work areas are constructed from basic tasks is discussed on pages 40-41.

Advantages 1. Maximum flexibility. Training each employee in all of the jobs in a department produces a strong work force, capable of meeting the problems of absenteeism, sudden separations, or shortages of help. Plant process and equipment can be changed with less upset, since no "jobs" are eliminated, only work activities. There are no arguments about work assignments or ability and obligation to perform overtime work.

2. Maximum opportunity. Since there is no limit on the number of men who can reach the top grade, the individual employee does not have to wait until someone in a higher grade leaves *his* job. Promotion is attained on a definite time schedule, and on his own merits.

Disadvantages 1. This system can result in a higher average wage rate. When every man has reached the top rate (as in periods of low labor turnover), the simpler tasks will be performed at wage rates higher than might be the case in classification or merit systems.

2. Once an employee reaches the top rate in his department, his incentive for further personal development is minimized and only based on transferring to other departments or the hope of promotion to salaried ranks.

Supervision Within the Hourly Work Force

Some companies establish a first level of supervision within the hourly work force, designating a "Shift Leader," "Leadman," or "Chief Operator" at the top of the hourly rate structure. This employee takes charge of the work performed by his group, including the assignment of tasks to other workers. He does not have the right to hire or fire, or to discipline; his supervisory relationship is of the "dotted line" type shown in Exhibit 1, where the hourly work groups are headed by Shift Leaders.

This method has the advantage of providing supervision at lowest possible cost, but there are some major disadvantages. One is the problem of split loyalty, which confronts this employee when he is called upon to report an operating error committed by one of his fellow workers. A second is the tendency for the post to be filled by the most senior man in the group, as opposed to a candidate carefully chosen for his supervisory ability. And some plant managers hold as a basic philosophy that all supervision should be within salaried management ranks.

MEETING SOME SPECIAL CHALLENGES

Upgrading an Existing Organization

The plant manager who has had the opportunity to design and staff his own organization from the very beginning is fortunate; he is also very rare. In most cases the plant manager inherits an organization set up by others.

He may be dismayed by what he finds. Years of neglect in the procedures for hiring, training, and weeding out substandard employees can produce an organization incapable of efficient performance or future progress. When you are faced with this situation, use these tools to improve the caliber of the organization:

1) Raise the hiring standards. Decide what levels of education, experience, and quality of previous work record you need, and insist that those doing the hiring meet them. Require the foreman to interview every applicant coming into his department; if he approves, he has a commitment to help the employee make good. If he disapproves, the chances for success are low, and the employee should not be hired.

2) Separate the inadequate employee. This can seem like a formidable task, especially when a union is present to challenge your moves. But you have two basic factors working to your advantage:

a. Attrition itself. The inept and unconcerned employee tends to drift from job to job. When he leaves, replace him with a better one.

b. Enforcement of plant rules. Incompetent employees usually have bad absence and lateness records. By enforcing the plant rules rigidly in these areas, you can weed out some of the ineffective people. In some plants you can apply established rules for work output and quality performance in the same way. (Of course, you must apply all these rules fairly to all your employees, and you run the risk that once in a while a "good" employee will have to be discharged. It is a small risk, and well worth taking.)

3) Salvage what you can. Many substandard employees got that way because management permitted sloppy and careless habits to develop. With firm handling and close attention, these employees can be restored to a higher level of performance, and the advantages of upgrading an employee you know over hiring a new one you don't are many.

4) Start training programs. If you take over an organization which seems incapable, it may be that its people do not know what they are expected to do, or how they are expected to do it. Training is the answer. The most effective training is accomplished with compulsory, in-house programs using instructors recruited from the plant staff. When it is not possible to set up such a program, company-sponsored off-hour courses are another way of filling the need. An especially thorough treatment of company training programs appears in *Executive's Desk Manual For Profitable Employee Handling* (Englewood Cliffs, N.J.: Prentice-Hall, Inc., 1972).

Preserving the Organization During Slow Periods

Temporary layoffs can result from a number of conditions beyond the plant manager's control—a protracted sales decline, disabling fire in all or part of the plant, shortage of essential raw material, major change in product line. Such layoffs can do violence to the manager's achievements in building a capable organization, especially when employees can find permanent jobs in other companies in the area. Take these steps to lessen the impact of a temporary slow period on your organization:

1) Forecast the length of the slow period. You will need an accurate estimate to make sound decisions on the cost break-even point between retaining and laying employees off and to plan the interim programs listed below. Make your own estimate, then compare it with those of the sales department, corporate planners, engineers, purchasing department or any appropriate corporate group.

2) Compare the cost of layoff with the cost of retention. It will be simple to calculate the cost of keeping any given number of employees for the duration of the slow period, but don't forget that there are direct dollar costs incurred by laying off. Unemployment insurance rates go up, severance pay may be involved, and there will be the cost of hiring and training the replacements for the predicted number of laid off employees who will be lost to the company for good. When these costs are calculated you will be able to establish a break-even point in time; how long you retain people beyond that point depends on the dollar amount you convince yourself and your superiors should be spent as an investment in the organization.

3) Find other work to do. During periods of high production a number of useful jobs may have to be postponed because of the press of business. Performing these jobs during slow periods can provide the economic justification needed to keep the organization intact. Here are some suggestions:

(a) Take inventory—finished goods, raw materials, capital equipment, fixtures and furnishings.

(b) Use production personnel to assist with equipment repairs and preventive maintenance activities.

(c) Paint equipment and buildings.

(d) Housekeeping.

(e) Training. Train or retrain workers in plant procedures, equipment care, safety, quality procedures, new technical developments, or general background of the company and its products.

(f) Try to find substitute operations. A top quality printing house may offer to print cheap handbills when business is slow. A processing plant with a tunnel dryer does contract drying for outside firms. A plastics manufacturer supplying industry makes toy novelties.

4) Take vacations. Employees may be willing to take their vacations at odd times of the year rather than go on layoff.

5) Use the "key man" concept in layoff. This requires establishing a procedure which protects some proportion—say one-third—of the employees in the top classifications of any department from being bumped out during a layoff. The idea is keep the more qualified and ambitious employees who have sought the top jobs from being pushed out by less able employees who happen to have more seniority. If you operate a non-union plant, you should carefully establish and annouce this provision well ahead of time; if the plant is unionized, press for a contract clause at the next collective bargaining.

Shift Operations

When the plant operates a second or third shift, some special problems of coordination, assignment of responsibility, and communication arise. The daytime managerial staff wants to maintain as much control as possible, but must relinquish some of its authority to shift supervision. Department foremen become uneasy when it appears that instructions from the shift superintendent conflict with those of their daytime superiors. And the separate shifts, using the same buildings and equipment and frequently working on the same materials, can fall to bickering over who left what in poor condition.

The plant manager can minimize these problems by taking pains with the following aspects of shift operation:

1) Spell out the shift supervisor's duties and responsibilities precisely and in writing. Exhibits 1 and 2 depict plant organizations with four shifts for 24-hour, seven days per week operation. Consider the small plant organization in Exhibit 1. The B Shift Supervisor is shown having a dotted line relationship to the Shift Leaders of B Shift in Departments X and Y, although these shift leaders normally report to the day supervisors of the two departments. Of course the Shift Supervisor will have the authority to keep order, to react to emergencies, and to maintain a smooth flow of production materials through the plant. But does he have the authority to shut the plant down when quality is off? Can he fire an hourly worker on the spot? Can he order the shift leaders to switch product lines? Does he give the shift mechanic routine assignments, or only emergency work (leaving the routine work to be assigned by the daytime maintenance foreman)? At exactly what point in process difficulties is he required to call the daytime supervision? Unless his position and authority in such matters are clearly understood by everyone involved, confusion and conflict are inevitable.

2) Clarify lines of communication. In the small plant organization of Exhibit 1 it is feasible to require that the Shift Leaders make no calls outside the plant (to day supervision) except through the Shift Supervisor; in the organization of Exhibit 2 with eight foremen and a watch engineer on each shift it may not be possible to have every question about the technical details of shop orders passed on through the Shift Superintendent. If the foreman is allowed to call his General Foreman directly, what matters is he allowed to refer in this way, and which ones must go through the Shift Superintendent? Technical questions only? Shutdown decisions when quality is poor? Alternate production when raw materials are not available for scheduled runs? To whom does the foreman refer when he feels that he cannot carry out the General Foreman's night instructions? Even if the plant manager does

nothing these questions will be answered somehow; the results will be far better if he answers them in advance with clear procedures.

3) Require the keeping of Shift Logs. The Shift Leaders or Foremen, and the Shift Supervisors or Superintendents, should be required to keep a written log of all significant events occurring on the shift, the condition of plant and materials at the end of the shift, and precautions and warnings for the oncoming shift. Attempting to transfer this information orally can only lead to misunderstanding, contention, and denial. On the positive side, written records are not only important to the oncoming shift, but can serve to keep the daytime supervision fully informed of plant conditions.

4) Beware of "Shift Wars." It is a common phenomenon for the operating shifts to begin criticizing each other. Complaints and perhaps sarcastic comments will appear in the shift logs, or tales carried personally, that "D Shift left the plant dirty," or "A Shift did not set up materials properly," and so on. This kind of bickering can be the result of simple competition—the foreman feels he can get ahead by running the other man down. When this is the case, the plant manager can correct the situation by stating directly that he wants cooperation, not contention, and by rewarding those who cooperate and censuring those who do not.

But the problem may not be one of simple competition. It may be the result of poorly conceived procedures, or no procedures at all, or misunderstandings about responsibilities and authority. When organizational principles have been neglected, the symptoms may very well be the complaints and bickering mentioned above. The cure is to straighten each confused situation out with a well-defined procedure.

The Job of Organization Summarized

The process of building a plant organization structure consists of successive interrelated phases. In the first phase the manager establishes the goals and criteria which he wants his organization to meet. In the next phase he lists the tasks to be performed, and combines them into workers' jobs. The third phase includes the establishment of sections and departments, and providing them with an effective managerial and supervisory structure. Responsibilities are assigned to the groups and their activities coordinated in phase four. In the fifth phase the plant manager gives special attention to the way in which the hourly work force is structured, aware that there are a number of kinds to choose from and the advantages and disadvantages of each. And finally, the manager faced with particular problems in shift operations, upgrading his organization, or trying to hold it together in slow periods, applies the special techniques suited to these problems. The end result of all this effort is a well-designed, carefully adjusted organization capable of meeting its goals.

Organizations Change

The conditions which lead a manager to build his organization in a particular way are not static, and he must be prepared to revise his organization as changes occur. Some changes are so obvious and dramatic that they cannot be ignored: a new product is introduced, new equipment is purchased, and a new building erected to house them. But there are many gradual, subtle changes which also affect organization: employees leave and are replaced; sales competition requires higher quality and better service at the same or reduced cost; the supply of skilled people in the labor market expands and contracts. When the plant manager begins to see symptoms of organizational trouble—production delays, missed schedules, departmental squabbling—it is time to review his organizational structure, adjusting it to the new conditions.

CONCLUSION

This chapter began with a reference to "people," and so it will end. No part of the management cycle is more closely concerned with human values than organization. It is the process by which the manager brings his people into harmony with the work they do, the place they do it in, the results they are trying to achieve, and with each other. When he does it well, he offers them maximum opportunity for success.

Chapter 3

Improving Industrial Relations, Union or No Union

A plant manager's work with people is far from done when he has created jobs for them, placed them in an organization, and set them to work making the company's products. Industrial workers have come to expect far more from their employer than the simple opportunity to trade a day's work for a day's pay. They want security, advancement, physical safety, fair treatment, and financial protection from disability and old age. In fact, the Stanford Research Institute identifies employees as "stakeholders" in the corporation (along with customers, suppliers, stockholders, creditors, and the community)—persons whose interests are affected by the company's actions and who have a stake in its success or failure.

The total relationship between employees and the company is the subject of industrial relations—not just the administration of fringe benefits or the negotiation of a union contract. That is why every plant manager has a vital interest in the state of industrial relations in his plant; if his expectations of employee performance and output are to be met he must be deeply involved in the satisfaction of the employees' expectations in wages, fringes, and working conditions. This involvement persists whether the plant manager has complete charge of industrial relations activities or whether he is assisted by a department or section which reports elsewhere.

Pervading the whole situation is the question of unionism. Employees have the option of entrusting the satisfaction of their expectations to the management of the company (the non-union plant), or of banding together, calling in a third party for guidance and assistance, and using their collective economic strength to enforce their demands (the unionized plant). The approach to industrial relations is necessarily different in these two cases, and in this chapter we will deal with the special problems of both the union and non-union plants. In addition, important facets of industrial relations in both types of plants will be covered from the plant manager's perspective.

THE NON-UNION PLANT

The Question of Unionism

The ambivalence of some managers who wonder whether "a union might be a good thing" for their plants is surprising. Perhaps they are tempted to think that by the presence

55

of a union and a union contract the scrambled mix of personnel problems requiring management policy decisions will somehow be codified and taken care of. They may feel that a union will help shoulder the responsibilities of controlling absenteeism and dealing with complaining workers. Or they may be lured by the prospect of having to deal with the adjustment of wages and fringe benefits only at the formalized intervals of contract renewal—from one to three years.

These can be dangerous delusions. No union will (nor should it be expected to) handle any portion of management's responsibilities; it has serious and important responsibilities of its own which it frequently considers as opposing those of management. Personnel problems do not lie dormant during negotiation intervals; management has the job of administering the contract, and its administration is continually probed and challenged by the union's complaints, grievances, slowdowns, and even work stoppages. Not only will the benefits of having a union in the plant prove illusory, but there will be three major areas of disadvantage in addition:

1. Strikes. When the union chooses to use its economic weapon, the plant is shut down and its output reduced to zero while many of its costs continue, customers look for other sources of supply, and employees are stirred to a bitterness against the company which may have long-lasting effects.

2. Interference of a third party. The direct, one-to-one relationship between a company and its employees end when a union enters the picture. A third party, which has no interest in the success or even continuation of the business, must now be consulted on every major matter affecting employees. Union headquarters may decree that settlements at your plant must conform to some regional or national pattern which has nothing to do with your company's particular situation. The union has its own regulations and discipline for employees, and demands that they split their loyalty. Politics and factionalism within the union can create unwanted tension and divisiveness among your employees. And they may be promised benefits by the third party which the company has no ability or intention to grant.

3. Diversion of managerial effort. Huge amounts of managerial time at all levels of the company are devoted to preparing for and handling union negotiations, demands, and grievances. The difference between this effort and that required to do a good, responsible job of labor relations in the non-union company could be better devoted to improving operations and conditions for all concerned. The ultimate security of the plant's employees rests not with the union, but with the combined efforts of management and labor to improve those factors which make their product competitive: quality, cost, and output.

Special Problems

Let's assume that you are manager of a non-union plant which you would like to keep that way. You will be faced with three special problems:

1) Irresolution at other management levels. Consider the men at lower management levels—the foremen, supervisors, and superintendents who report to you. They may have lingering feelings that a union isn't too bad an idea, and it might get us all another holiday or two. You will want to call these people together, and explain carefully the reasons for your position with emphasis on what is at stake for them—the constant challenge to their authority, the necessity of handling every situation so that it will later stand up under the grievance procedure, strike duty, and the deterrent to higher management's placing new or

expanded facilities at the unionized site. And you will want to drive home the point that the union can't grant anything; only the company can grant additional benefits from the income generated by the business.

With higher levels of management, your best persuasive powers are called for. If you present the same reasons which led to your position in a cogent manner, you can usually win support; in most cases it will be there anyway. One thing is certain: without that support, your task is virtually impossible.

2) The temptation to take employees for granted. Managers, especially those in older plants, can falsely assume that there is a mystical bond of loyalty between themselves and their employees that a union can never break. This is the "old Joe would never vote for a union," or "our employees are perfectly happy," school of thought.

Look out.

"Old Joe" may never have heard the word *paternalism,* but he'll support a union if he thinks you feel you own him. And those "happy" employees may be harboring a nest of hidden grievances and frustrations just waiting for a chance to come out in the open.

Your employee relationships in the non-union plant should never reflect a feeling on your part that your employees will support you no matter what you do. And your entire management team must be constantly sensitive to hidden complaints and grievances which do not come out in the open as quickly as in the unionized plant.

3) Sensitivity of the work force to major moves in industrial relations. When wages are increased, fringe benefits expanded, layoffs carried out, or major disciplinary action taken, the plant communications to its employees should be handled in such a way that they will not feel that they would have come out better with a union. If they are working in an area where they can easily make comparisons with practices in nearby plants, the reasons offered for such moves should take account of these comparisons.

Keeping the Union Out*

Maintaining your plant's non-union status cannot be left to chance. A conscious, sustained effort to prove to the plant employees that their needs and expectations can best be met by the plant management, without the interference of a third party, must be mounted.

The first phase of this effort, and by far the most important, consists of everything you do to establish sound industrial relations before a particular union knocks on the door, claiming to represent the plant employees. Concentrate on these aspects to give the union organizer as little as possible to work with:

1. Wages and fringe benefits. Keep them at least equal to and preferably ahead of the surrounding plants in your labor market. If your workers feel that they are enjoying greater rewards than unionized plants can provide, you have a long head start.

2. Job security. People want two things: Continuity of employment, and fair treatment when layoff becomes inevitable. The manager of a non-union plant ought to do everything he can to avoid layoffs (see "Preserving the Organization During Slow Periods," page 51) which, at best, upset employee morale. If layoff cannot be avoided, each employee will want to know exactly where he stands and

---

* This title is not meant to imply that there is something inherently evil about all unions, or that they are to be kept out of the plant by any means, legitimate or not. Current labor law in the United States gives the employer the right to vie with the union for the confidence of his employees, with the result to be determined by a secret ballot election. I believe that an enlightened, progressive, truly professional plant management can do better for its employees (and all its stakeholders) without a union, and that it should try to convince its employees that this is so by every legal means available.

why. Meet his expectations by establishing and publishing a detailed layoff procedure well before the need to use it arises.

3. Individual self-respect. Your employees want to feel that they are doing important work, that opportunities for advancement exist for them, and that they will be treated with respect. Management has sole control over these areas, and therefore has unique opportunities to reach its people which are not open to the union. Use all appropriate means of communication to show each employee the importance of the company's products, and where his contribution fits into the larger picture. Promote from within whenever possible, interview all qualified employees, explain to all the reasons for the final decision. Ensure that employees are treated courteously by their supervision and in their dealings with personnel, insurance, and payroll departments.

4. Complaint handling. There must be an active, trusted, and workable grievance procedure.

Phase two begins when one of your employees seeks out or is contacted by a union representative. This marks the start of a union campaign which should eventually end in a secret ballot election to determine whether your employees want that union or no union. To survive this phase plant management must:

1. Be alert for the first signs of organizing activity and prepare to deal with it calmly and effectively.

2. Take advantage of all legal means open to it to win the campaign. In general, management has the right to communicate with its employees, to present its case under certain rules of fairness, and to challenge illegal conduct by the union.

3. Avoid handing the election to the union by the commission of unfair labor practices. You cannot offer rewards or promises of benefits to "buy off" the employees, nor threaten, discipline, or discriminate against those attempting to organize.

Grievance Handling—The Toughest Problem

The employee who works in a plant where there is no set procedure for handling complaints, where the foreman's word is "law," or where his complaints go unanswered for long periods or are forgotten altogether, is fair game for the union organizer. Plant management, busy with its production problems, perhaps uneasy about dealing with such a negative feature of its employee relations, and possibly feeling that complaints only come from "troublemakers" anyway, may hang back from establishing a definite grievance procedure. The result is a big gap in the relations between the company and its employees, a source of frustration to the latter, and a golden opportunity for the organizer.

Setting up a grievance procedure which employees of a non-union plant will really trust is not easy. But you must do it if you would hope to have your employees vote "No union" in a representation election. Meet these key requirements for your complaint system:

1. Make it formal. Every employee should have the right to have his complaint heard in a succession of explicit steps, starting with the first-line supervisor and proceeding up through the management chain to the personnel department, the plant manager and on to the highest level included—perhaps the president of the company. The procedure should spell out his right to have another employee accompany him and present the case, the point at which the complaint is reduced to writing, and the number of days allowed for an answer at each level before the complaint automatically goes to the next level.

2. Publish it widely. Give a copy to every new employee, and make it part of the introduction procedure. Make copies available to all in the personnel office. Post it on the bulletin boards. If there is an employee handbook, this will be one of its most important sections.

3. Train foremen, supervisors, and department managers to use the procedure effectively. Not only should they be thoroughly familiar with each step of the procedure, but they must be more sensitive to real or imagined complaints than their counterparts in unionized plants. Make it clear that unless they handle this part of their jobs well, a union will soon do it for them. And they should understand that you will rate their skill in grievance handling in your reviews of their performance.

4. Avoid token provisions and insincere statements of the "my door is always open" type. Your door isn't always open, and obviously can't be. Tell the employee how he really can get in contact with you—what levels of the complaint procedure must be previously exhausted, whom to see to make the appointment, who else must be notified. He can understand and accept these provisions without feeling that he has been fooled by a bland statement which really means nothing.

5. Make sure it is legal. Labor law forbids setting up company-dominated, quasi-union organizations. For instance, it may be illegal to have employees in the non-union plant elect representatives to handle their grievances. Let your labor attorney review the procedure before you publish it.

Employee Handbook

Publish an employee handbook in about the same size and format as a union contract. Make it more attractive in appearance, and less legalistic in language. Involve line management as well as the industrial relations department in writing its sections. In it explain the wage system, fringe benefits, holiday schedule, sick leave provisions, plant rules, disciplinary action, and the grievance procedure. Not only is this a good way to communicate such important matters to employees, but it will give them a sense of security to see them spelled out in a printed book with the company's name on it. And it can be an important psychological offset when the union organizer arrives brandishing his copies of union contracts from other plants.

Wages and Benefits

A baffling problem. If we have to pay wages and benefits above those of the area, why don't we just forget the whole thing and have a union? Because you can afford to use some of the money which having a union will cost. Keep the situation under control by handling it this way:

1. Find out exactly where your plant stands in wages and benefits. Exchange detailed information with other plants in the area, and participate in surveys conducted by employers' associations. See "Sources Outside the Company," Chapter 4, for additional ways to gather information.

2. Decide how far above the prevailing level you can afford to go. Remember that if you have a union you will have to pay for hourly workers' time consumed in union business or for their replacements when they are absent but unpaid, for managerial time spent on union matters, for strikes, for expenses of contract negotiations—hotel rooms, secretaries, recording, printing of contracts, for grievance arbitration and the legal help you will need in them. Your colleagues in

union plants can help you estimate these costs; you can then decide how much can be allotted to keep wages and benefits above surrounding levels.

3. Beware of attempting to match the wages of every plant in town. If you are assembling electronic components, you probably can't afford to pay the wages offered in an oil refinery. You will have to be honest in explaining to your employees that wage levels are different from industry to industry, and that there are usually compensating factors for these differences.

Keeping Communications Open

Nothing can hurt a plant management more than to be unaware of the problems and issues on the minds of its employees. It must know exactly where the rough spots are in its employee relationships; which of its moves work well and which do not; when organizing activity begins; what the issues are between the pro-union and anti-union groups among the employees.

How are communications kept open? Start with the first-line supervisor who, of all management people, is closest to the work force and in the best position to know what questions and problems are on employees' minds. Train him to be sensitive to issues affecting plant workers, to be a good listener, to pass information upward without bias or editing. The upward flow of communication will stop, of course, unless higher levels of management—department heads, superintendents, assistant plant managers and the plant manager himself—are interested in what the foreman has to say, and are available for him to say it. These people should be seen frequently in the plant, and available to employees for informal chats. Continue the flow of information by including a discussion of the state of employee relationships in the daily production meetings.

What to Do When the Union Appears

Sooner or later you can expect the union organizer to appear, either on his own or in response to a call from some of your employees. His arrival marks the start of the campaign, and it calls for these actions by you:

1. Make no moves in panic, rashness, or from emotion. Your actions are now covered by a complicated body of law, and a wrong move can hurt your cause in any legal battles to follow. (If you don't have a labor attorney or consultant it is very late; hire one immediately.)

2. Report the organizing activity to other concerned elements of the corporation—headquarters, other plants, industrial relations, your immediate superior.

3. Call together your management people, including first-line supervisors. Bring them up to date on the facts of the situation. Instruct them on what they can and cannot do; tell them you will meet with them later to outline the campaign and their part in it in full.

4. The union representative may present you with authorization cards signed by a majority of your employees, and ask you to recognize his union without an election conducted by the National Labor Relations Board. You should refuse this request for two reasons: if pressure was brought to bear on some of your employees who signed them, the cards may not really represent a majority, and if the union really does have a majority you will be better protected against intrusion by other unions if yours is certified rather than recognized.

It is possible that two or more competing unions will be trying to organize your plant at the same time. Both names will be on the ballot, along with "No Union."

5. Plan the campaign you will conduct. Working with your attorney or

consultant, develop the arguments you will use to convince your employees and the message you want to convey to them. Outline the means of communication open to you—employee meetings, letters home, the line organization, industrial relations department, and the company newspaper. Set a timetable for the moves you want to make. And be sure to decide in advance what the tone of your response will be to the various types of union criticism of you and the company which are sure to be a part of the campaign.

6. Put the plan into effect. Remember that you cannot intimidate, coerce, threaten, or make promises of rewards to keep a union out. But you do have the right to communicate with your employees, to state your case, and to challenge the union when it commits unfair labor practices. The legal details will have to be answered by your attorney; you will be asking him such questions as these: Can I prohibit union organizers from entering plant property? Can I prohibit distribution of union literature by my own employees inside the plant? How far am I, my managers, and the first-line supervisors allowed to go in discussing the campaign with individual employees? What information am I required to supply to the union?

THE UNION PLANT

The basic principles of good management and effective industrial relations do not suddenly change when the plant becomes unionized. Employees continue to want the same returns from their employment as their non-union brothers; they will still respect good leadership from the plant management. What is different is the formality of a written contract, the intervention of a third party, and the threat of strikes to enforce employee demands.

The Union Contract

This document is a statement of the agreements reached by company and union negotiators during collective bargaining, on such subjects as wages, fringe benefits, grievance procedure, and may cover a wide range of industrial relations topics. Frequently there is a "management rights" clause and very often a preamble recognizing the duty of both parties to establish peaceful labor relations and to operate the plant safely and economically. Remember these points when you must deal with a union contract:

1. It is a legal agreement. You should expect to live up to the company's commitments under it, and should expect the union to do the same.

2. It does not cover every detail of industrial relations. When the contract is silent on a given matter, an opportunity exists for management to establish its own practices.

3. It does formalize the relationship between you and your employees, and you will have to live by the letter of its provisions even when it seems eminently fair to do otherwise.

Example: One of your hourly men has been out sick for a long period, and today is his first day back at work. You require four hours of overtime in that department. The contract says that overtime must be offered to the man with the lowest accumulated hours, and charged against his total if he refuses it. Operating from common sense, you would prefer not to offer this overtime to a man just returned from sick leave, nor to penalize him for refusing it. But you must offer it. If you don't, the next man in line may object to having the hours charged against him, and file a grievance. Even if you get by with it, the union can use the incident as precedent for some future case which you might want to handle differently.

Grievance Handling

The typical union contract defines a grievance as "any dispute or controversy arising out of the meaning or interpretation of this agreement," and then proceeds to spell out a series of steps involving ever higher levels of authority within the union and the company through which the complainant can take his case. If agreement is not reached in one of these steps, the dispute may ultimately go to an outside arbitrator whose decision is binding upon both parties.

The situation differs from that of the non-union plant in two significant respects. The first is that the question may be ultimately settled by an outside authority, and therefore every management decision on it must be judged on how it will stand up before that authority. The second is the extreme formality of the procedure, which creates a dangerous pitfall: that management will tend to ignore those employee complaints which do not technically qualify as grievances.

>   Example: An hourly employee doesn't like and doesn't get along with the employee working next to him. He complains in a general way to his foreman, who realizes that the complaint hardly qualifies as a "dispute . . . arising out of this agreement," and may be inclined to ignore it rather than resolve it. Therein lies the danger. The unresolved complaint may be followed by a request for transfer to another department. If that is denied, the employee and his shop steward may find all kinds of grounds for filing a grievance—interpretation of the seniority clause, contract clauses regarding transfer, preferential assignment, what the company has done in previous cases. If the company should lose such a grievance, the whole system of work assignment in the plant could be badly undermined.

Follow these fundamental principles for handling grievances and complaints in the unionized plant:

>   1. Train the entire managerial staff to recognize the difference between a complaint and a formal grievance, and to understand the importance of each. Make sure that first-line supervisors do not ignore complaints simply because there is no contractual basis to consider them grievances.
>   2. Prepare the first-line supervisor to handle his part in the grievance procedure. When a grievance is presented, he should know how long he has to answer it, what form his answer should be in, and who should be present when he gives it. It is essential that he review his decision on the grievance and the way he will present it with you before replying to the employee and the union.
>   3. Do your homework on each case. Obtain all of the "facts" available; challenge their validity until you are satisfied they will stand up as facts. Then assess your chances of winning the case if it should go to arbitration. Consult your labor attorney, check up on "past practice," review the grievance files for decisons on similar cases, study current publications.
>   4. If you can't win, get out early in the grievance procedure. Fighting a losing grievance through the higher levels, "as a matter of principle," simply makes it harder for management people, especially first-line supervisors, to accept the inevitable defeat gracefully.

5. Insist that the union follow the rules. If the contract states that the grievance must be taken to Step 3 within four days after the decision in Step 2, don't accept it six days later. If the contract limits the number of union representatives who can leave their jobs to attend grievance meetings, don't allow the limits to be exceeded. To do so is to jeopardize the handling of future cases, and to introduce a great deal of uncertainty in the procedure.

The First-Line Supervisor

The management man who feels the impact of a union in the plant most consistently is the foreman; that is to be expected because he works at the point of contact between management and the hourly work force. It is he who sometimes must make decisions in a hurry, only to have them become the source of union grievances and possibly second-guessing from his own management. Every move he makes comes under the scrutiny of union stewards who may only be waiting for him to make a mistake. Take these steps to keep your first-line supervisor effective while operating under a union contract:

1) Don't let him become intimidated. He can be plagued into almost complete inaction by fears—the fear of losing a grievance, the fear of organized opposition, the fear of having to defend his action in formal proceedings, the fear of being criticized by his superiors for having "too many" grievances. Faced by opposition from below and second-guessing from above, he may simply decide it is easier to avoid decisions than to make them.

You can help him. Make sure he understands that all of the agencies concerned with the development and administration of labor law—managements, unions, the National Labor Relations Board, arbitrators, the legislative bodies which passed the laws—all expect the foreman to assert and use his authority to manage his operation. Of course he runs into trouble when he makes a mistake but he will run into more trouble by failing to make decisions and to take consistent, authoritative action.

> Example: A foreman who has repeatedly failed to enforce the rules on lateness now realizes the situation is getting out of hand, and wants to apply a disciplinary penalty to the last man in a long line of violators. If the case goes to arbitration, he may be in for a difficult time; the arbitrator will be much more likely to support the position of a foreman who has clearly and consistently enforced the lateness rule from its beginning.

2) Make sure that he knows the union contract thoroughly, and understands your interpretation of any of its unclear provisions. Require him to review the decisions he makes under it with you whenever possible, especially if those decisions have plantwide implications.

3) Keep him informed. When you have negotiated a new contract, made a supplementary agreement on an existing one, or simply held a meeting with the union to discuss problems, inform your first-line supervisors immediately. It is essential to their morale that they hear the results first from you, rather than from their employees or shop stewards. When you settle a grievance in one department, notify the supervisors in all the other departments—one of them may have a similar case. And if you have changed your interpretation of some part of the contract, or know of new developments in state or federal labor law which affect supervisory functioning, you should explain the situation to them.

4) Be realistic with him. Don't tell him you will "always back him up." You can't do that. Tell him you will back him up when he is right, will help him to be right, and will help him get out of trouble gracefully when he is wrong.

Past Practice

No matter what the union contract says, if both parties to it have permitted a particular practice to prevail over the life of the contract, that practice may become the rule. For instance, a company which had always permitted its employee to leave their work place five minutes before lunch time to wash up would probably find that it cannot withdraw that privilege even though the contract is silent on it. The union might have a great deal of trouble in requiring the company to follow contract rules on overtime assignment if it has consistently looked the other way when the company awarded overtime outside those rules.

Although this is a tricky area legally, the message is clear: Be sure that those plant rules and contract provisions which are important to you are regularly enforced. If you don't, they may turn out to be ineffective when you do decide to enforce them.

Probationary Period

Under most union contracts new hourly employees are hired for a probationary period lasting anywhere from thirty days to six months. During this period the employee can be discharged at the discretion of the company, without recourse to the grievance procedure.

Train your supervisors to observe the new employee very carefully during this probationary period. He knows he is on probation and his performance will be as good or better than at any later time. If there are latent signs of trouble—incipient absenteeism, lateness, not getting along with other employees, inability to learn the work—it will be better to discharge the employee than to live with a host of troubles generated by him later on. Once he gets past the probationary period he becomes a full union member and cannot be discharged except for cause, and that is subject to challenge by the union.

You can help the supervisor in two ways. Have the personnel department send him a written notice of the expiration of the probationary period in time to make a deliberate judgment of the employee. Then require him to fill out a rating form which covers all the qualities you consider important in a new employee.

Role of the International Representative

Sometimes called the "business agent," this man is a paid professional probably working out of a regional headquarters of the international union of which your unit is a local. He is the "third party" in your industrial relations; he will advise your shop stewards on matters at issue between them and the plant management, he will help them decide whether or not to file a grievance over a given management action and you will be dealing with him when either the company or the union has a special request to make of the other. He will be a key figure in collective bargaining, and in any strike situation which may develop. The grievance procedure usually calls for him to enter the discussions at the third or fourth step. Most contracts give him the right to enter plant property "for purposes of administering the contract."

Here are three key points to cover in your relationship with the international representative:

1. Assess the degree of his influence with your local union leaders. If it is strong, he may be able to make agreements for the local on his own. If his position is weak, he must constantly refer decisions to the local leaders, who will challenge and sometimes reject his ideas. If you are not sure where he stands on this scale of control, test the situation on some relatively unimportant matter at the first opportunity.

2. Try to estimate his position within the international union. He may aspire to

higher office. He may be fighting the loss of his job because of a union merger. He may be part of a faction pressing some particular point of view within the international union. He may be trying to negotiate uniform clauses on a specific subject into all the contracts in his area. This kind of knowledge will explain many of the moves he makes, and allow you to predict his future positions and actions.

3. Insist that the formalities of the contract be observed regarding visitation. If it states that he must obtain permission of the plant manager before entering the plant, be sure that he does. You will always want to know when he is in the plant, and if possible, whom he is talking to and why.

IN ALL PLANTS

Downward Communications

The company is continuously communicating with its employees. Verbal communications include instructions and information from the first-line supervisor; meetings with personnel or industrial relations people on safety, insurance, pensions, etc.; and occasional meetings with higher plant management to receive information on the progress of the plant and company. Written communications take the form of bulletin board notices, employee handbooks and union contract booklets, operating procedures and plant regulations, the house organ, and letters sent to the employee's home.

There are two vital requirements for all these communications. First they should be straightforward, and mean what they say. I have always been puzzled by the ability of some railroad unions to stage a slowdown by following all the regulations in the book of rules. If a rule isn't meant to be followed, it shouldn't be in the rule book at all; if it is important enough to be in the book, it should be followed all the time. Second, communications must be consistent. A loyal employee will soon turn into a cynic if he attends a safety meeting to learn a safety practice and then is told to ignore that practice when he returns to his work area.

Performance Appraisal

To meet the need of employees to know how their work is rated, most plants use some form of performance appraisal. The method may range from simply having the foreman call in the employee once or twice a year and "tell him how he is doing," to the use of an elaborate printed form which is filled out by the foreman and reviewed by one or more higher level of supervision. Whatever system you use* include these characteristics: Choose rating factors which can be measured in terms of results, such as quantity and quality of work, and attendance. Avoid rating factors which are subject to bias on the part of the supervisor, such as "personality" and "judgment." Review the results of the rating with the employee, with emphasis on how it can help him to improve performance.

Work Environment

The company says more about what it thinks of its people by the way it builds and maintains its plants than in almost any other form of communication. A good foundation for industrial relations is established when work areas and personnel facilities are clean, attractively painted, well-maintained, and properly lighted and ventilated.

---

*For a thorough treatment of the various types of rating systems see *Executive's Manual for Personnel Handling* (Englewood Cliffs, N.J.: Prentice-Hall, Inc., 1965), pp. 5301f.

Safety as an Industrial Relations Tool

The prime objective of any safety program is the prevention of accidents but the plant manager should also be aware of its immense value in developing and maintaining good industrial relations. Employees will be favorably impressed by the willingness of the company to spend time and money to protect them from injury; despite some initial grumbling, they will respect the company for insisting on obedience to safety rules. And the company which has a good safety record and reputation for safety in the community has a valuable edge in hourly recruiting.

Employee Suggestions

There are two basic approaches to handling employee suggestions. One is to establish a formal suggestion system, in which the employee writes his idea on a printed form and drops it in a suggestion box. It is reviewed by a committee, and if accepted, the employee is given a lump sum cash award, or a percentage of the cost savings for a fixed period.

The second approach is informal. Supervisors are trained to be alert for employee suggestions, and to communicate them upward. Suggestions are given as careful consideration by all levels of management as in the formal system; the reply to the employee is more personal and direct. Rewards for accepted suggestions are in the form of praise, recognition, and the employee's satisfaction in seeing his idea actually applied in the plant.

I favor the second approach. I believe that, when properly handled, it establishes a deeper sense of involvement of the employee in his company than can be achieved by cash awards. And it avoids some of the unpleasant side effects I have observed in cash award systems: dissatisfaction with the size of an award, suspicion that another employee was rewarded for one's own idea, claims that the company used the suggestion without paying for it.

Disciplinary Action

In either the union or non-union plant, keep the disciplinary system as simple as possible. Here is a simple three-step progression of disciplinary action for a repeatedly offending employee:

   1. Verbal warning. The first-line supervisor tells the employee what he has done, why it is wrong, and what may happen if he does it again. A written record of the warning is placed in the employee's personnel file, and the union is notified of the action (if there is a union).

   2. Disciplinary letter. Written over the foreman's signature, with copies to personnel file and union. Refers to the verbal warning, states what has happened since then, and warns the employee that the next step will be discharge.

   3. Discharge. The third infraction represents a serious challenge to the rules of the plant or the authority of the supervisor, and discharge is usually called for. It should always be carried out by the supervisor—no one else. To avoid embarrassing reversals, have the supervisor put the offending employee on suspension as a matter of policy. The discharge can then be reviewed the next day by all concerned to be sure that the facts of the case warrant termination.

Such a progression is clear to everyone involved, and will stand up under an arbitrator's scrutiny.

Two essential points: While it is a good idea to publish a set of plant rules which you expect employees to observe, don't let the list become too long or picayune. If it does, a rule which is not listed may be unenforceable. Avoid writing long lists of punishable offenses into the union contract. Arbitrators and courts expect employees to know the basic rules of industrial conduct on their own. Above all, don't publish a rule unless you mean it; if you publish it, enforce it impartially.

Disciplinary layoff is sometimes added to the disciplinary progression shown above. It is being abandoned by more and more companies for two reasons: It always penalizes the company, which has to replace the absent employee at overtime rates, or by some rearrangement of work schedules. And it is downright silly to attempt to penalize a chronic absentee by giving him days off; the penalty is the same as the offense.

Absenteeism

To tolerate a high rate of casual absenteeism (as opposed to legitimate absences such as sickness and funerals) is inexcusable on the part of any management. Using the disciplinary procedure in the previous section, you can control casual absenteeism this way:

1. Publish the absenteeism rule—on the bulletin boards if it is not already in your employee handbook. If you have a rule but have not been enforcing it, restate your intention to enforce it.

2. Enforce it rigidly. You can't penalize one worker and ignore the absenteeism of another. Don't buy the "he's a good worker when he's here" approach—the man who doesn't show up for work is worth zero to you that day.

3. Keep good records. A special absence record book can be kept by the foreman or by the personnel office, with a separate page for each employee. When a disciplinary case comes up, you don't want to have to search through a stack of old time cards.

Unions are usually reluctant to press an absenteeism case through the grievance procedure if the record is unassailable and the rule has been impartially enforced.

4. What is an acceptable rate of absenteeism? There is no pat answer for your organization. A plant with an excellent attendance record would not want to loosen its control to allow absenteeism to come up to some "national average." A manager who is bringing the rate down would not want to relax his efforts simply because he has achieved such a level. But it is valuable to have a statistical reference point by which to judge whether the overall rate in your facility requires stronger enforcement action.

These figures, which originally appeared in *Monthly Labor Review* (July, 1973), are discussed critically in Prentice-Hall's *Personnel Management—Policies and Practices,* Report Bulletin 7, Volume XXI, July 31, 1973, pp. 3-5:

For a Typical Week in 1972

Industry	Percent of Employees Absent for Part of Week	Percent of Employees Absent Entire Week
All Nonfarm Wage & Salary Workers	4.3	2.3
Manufacturing	4.7	2.7
Service	4.5	2.3
Finance	3.7	1.7

Transportation and Utilities	3.4	2.6
Construction	4.3	2.2
Retail & Wholesale Trade	3.7	2.1
Public Administration	4.8	2.3

CONCLUSION

The plant manager must be prepared to deal with a central fact of today's industrial life—that there is much more to an employee's relationship with his company than simply coming to work and being paid for it. Many of his human needs—security, safety, a sense of usefulness, personal progress—will be met by specific programs and actions of his employer. When these programs are well communicated and their execution lives up to their promise, the company has gone a long way on the road to good industrial relations. When the employee feels that these needs are not likely to be satisfied by the company, he may turn to a union to help him.

Nine-tenths of the effort made by the plant manager and his staff to ward off unionization is completed before the union organizer appears. Once the campaign begins, however, a legally complicated phase is entered and professional advice is needed. This chapter offers an outline of the campaign and management strategy, with some "what to do until the labor lawyer arrives" advice.

Once the plant is unionized, the approach to industrial labor relations is put on a more formal plane by the introduction of a third party into the relationship and the specifications of a union contract. But the plant manager must realize that the responsibility for the state of industrial relations remains with him, and that a union can only partly fulfill the needs of employees.

Chapter 4

Successful Collective Bargaining: Ready, Set, Go

In the unionized plant, such matters as wages, working conditions, fringe benefits, and the manner of settling complaints are not determined by the management alone, but are specified in a union contract which is produced by collective bargaining. Bargaining teams (or sometimes individuals) representing the management and union sides meet to exchange proposals and counterproposals dealing with these and other issues. This exchange normally takes place in the sixty days prior to the termination of the present union contract, but many companies start the process earlier, and some make arrangements to continue the bargaining process throughout the life of the contract. Most plants come under state and federal laws requiring participation in the collective bargaining process, and managements or unions which refuse to meet and consider proposals and make counterproposals are subject to charges of unfair labor practice.

Each side comes to the bargaining table with its own weapon to coerce the other side into agreement. For the union, the weapon is the strike; for the company it is the lockout, but it is rarely used, and the company's real weapon is its ability to withstand a strike longer than the union can carry it on. Both the strike and the lockout, when resorted to, represent a breakdown of the collective bargaining process.

In this chapter, all phases of the collective bargaining process from the management side will be presented, beginning with the responsibilities of the plant manager and organization of the company bargaining team, proceeding on to preparation for and conduct of the bargaining sessions, and ending with actions to be taken in the event of a strike. Followed closely, it will be an effective guide to the conduct of a successful collective bargaining campaign.

RESPONSIBILITIES OF THE PLANT MANAGER

As Chief Negotiator

By the very nature of his job, the plant manager is intimately associated with the matters concerning both sides in collective bargaining. His ability to meet responsibility for the profitability of the plant is directly tied to the cost of wages, fringes, and work practices specified by the union contract. For these reasons the plant manager is very often chosen to be the chief negotiator for the company, and the remainder of this chapter is written from this point of view. As chief negotiator, he will have the multiple jobs of recruiting, organizing, and directing the management bargaining team; preparing for and conducting bargaining sessions; and developing and executing plans for action in the event of a strike.

As Supporting Member

In some companies a member of the industrial relations department is designated as chief negotiator, and the plant manager joins him as a supporting member of the team. In very large companies, when multiplant bargaining is conducted at company headquarters, he may be asked to participate as a team member. In these situations the plant manager is in a unique position to supply valuable information about the day-to-day operations of the plant, and the effect of union proposals on product cost, customer service, and management control. Even as a supporting member, he will want to become familiar with bargaining techniques and strategy developed in the remainder of this chapter.

Not on the Team

In some situations the plant manager will not be present in the bargaining room at all; this usually happens when a lawyer or labor consultant is hired or assigned to negotiate alone for the company. Such a professional negotiator will look to the plant manger for much of the information he uses in the bargaining sessions. He should be required to maintain close contact with the plant manager, keeping him informed of the progress of negotiations.

ORGANIZING THE MANAGEMENT TEAM

Size of the Team

A bargaining team of four or five members represents the best compromise of the conflicting factors which affect team size. Smaller teams may not be able to provide sufficient coverage in depth of all the subjects which will be discussed in the bargaining sessions. Individual members may become overloaded in attempting to handle larger shares of the bargaining work in addition to their regular duties. If one or more members are lost to the team during the negotiations (illness, transfer, separation), it may become too small to handle the load. Hasty recruitment of new members during the course of the negotiations is not likely to produce the desired results at the bargaining table.

Larger teams may have the undesirable effect of diverting too much of the plant staff from its regular duties. They may prove unwieldy in reaching strategy decisions when meeting alone, and difficult to control in the bargaining room.

Selection of Members

Because the results obtained by the bargaining team cannot be expected to surpass the combined capabilities of its members, their selection requires great care. Failure may not always be the fault of the team, but success cannot be obtained without a highly capable group. Look for these qualities:

1. Enthusiasm for and an interest in collective bargaining.
2. General knowledge of the plant and detailed knowledge of one of its operational or administrative functions.
3. A stake in the outcome.
4. Good health.
5. Ability to function as part of a team.
6. Alertness and sensitivity.

Once his selections are made, the plant manager often finds he has one more hurdle to clear: some of the men he wants may not report to him, and he has to convince another executive that it is in the company's best interests to detach a man from part or all of his regular duties for a period of time. Presented with the consequences of a bad contract or a strike, the executive will usually respond favorably; when this is not the case, the help of higher management should be sought immediately.

Department Sources

The departments from which the team members are chosen is a matter of great importance. In its proposals and bargaining discussions the union will bring up a wide variety of issues requiring thorough analysis by the company representatives. It will often raise specific points requiring immediate rebuttal for best effect. In these situations the company needs bargainers who can respond from a close association and detailed knowledge of the topics at issue.

Several of the members will be selected from the manufacturing department, since their knowledge of plant operations is essential in evaluating union proposals on work rules, shift assignments, distribution of overtime, seniority in work assignments, and the like. They should come from as many different sections of the manufacturing operation as possible—production, maintenance, shipping—to have the widest coverage available in the bargaining room.

The plant which has a personnel or industrial relations department will invariably place a member from that group on the bargaining team, because of their close contact with grievances, insurance, transfers, seniority lists, pensions, and many other matters directly governed by the union contract.

Less obvious is the very important need to have a member of the accounting department on the bargaining team, and many companies overlook the two essential services he can provide: 1) More quickly and surely than anyone else, he can develop cost information supporting the company's position on wages, fringes, vacations, insurance, sick leave, etc. 2) He can be of immeasurable help in quickly and accurately determining the impact of the union's proposals on plant finances, especially those proposals which may contain hidden costs. All too often a company will sign a union contract without fully understanding how much it will cost. And it is a depressing sight to watch a company negotiator who has failed to bring a good cost man with him, and armed with vague, incomplete, and possibly inaccurate cost information, attempting to maintain his position against the onslaughts of a union negotiator who detects the weakness.

First-Line Supervisors

It is a good idea to bring the first-line supervisors into the bargaining sessions. They do not need to be assigned as permanent members, but can attend in rotation. In the bargaining room they can be very helpful in preventing the union's representation of what goes on in a particular department from becoming too one-sided (it is valuable to have the maintenance foreman at the bargaining table the day the discussion turns to problems of overtime distribution in the maintenance department), and they will develop a greater appreciation of the problems faced by the management in negotiations and a more positive identification with management positions on various issues. Once back in the plant, they will be less subject to distorted rumors about the course of the bargaining.

Keep Out

Who should *not* attend the bargaining sessions? In a word, all outsiders. When the bargaining is conducted by a union team consisting of workers from the local plant (and perhaps an international representative), the introduction of strange faces into the bargaining room simply forces them into a period of suspicious waiting. Avoid the temptation to have a lawyer sit in on or conduct the negotiations; the union team may conclude that the company is trying to fool them with tricky legalistic maneuvers, and become impossible to convince of anything.

In the branch plant or subsidiary company the idea may be advanced that a representative of headquarters management should come and sit in on the bargaining sessions. The local negotiator should hold out against this idea as long as he can. The message to the union here is that there is a higher authority it can appeal to, and its best strategy is to bypass the local management team and bring in higher management as soon as possible. If the union is successful in this ploy, the local management team will have great difficulty in ever conducting serious bargaining again.

MAKING TOUGH MANAGEMENT DECISIONS IN ADVANCE

Hard Questions

Union contract negotiations are going to force the company to make some very hard decisions sooner or later. How much money can it afford to grant in wage and benefit increases? At what wage level will it take a strike rather than go higher? How far is it willing to go in yielding management rights to the union? Will it accept a strike rather than grant another holiday?

All too often the chief company negotiator finds it harder to obtain early decisions on these questions from his own management than it is to bargain with the union. While the reluctance of top management to contemplate the worse is understandable, the chief negotiator must make clear to higher management that his position is badly weakened unless he has these answers. The union will be probing the company bargainers all through the negotiations for signals—what they say, tone of voice, facial expressions—telling it where the company really intends to draw the line. The company negotiator who doesn't know whether his company will take a strike rather than grant another holiday is unable to put it convincingly that another holiday isn't possible. Both sides can blunder into an unnecessary strike under these conditions.

Lost Time

The company which makes its final decisions under the pressure of a contract expiration in a few days or hours, or worse yet under the pressure of a strike, is putting itself at an unnecessary disadvantage. It has forfeited the time needed to make a thorough examination of the consequences of yielding on a particular issue. If the issue is of such importance to both sides that a strike is inevitable, the company is far better off knowing this early in the negotiations.

PREPARATION FOR BARGAINING

Success at the bargaining table (either in terms of obtaining a contract acceptable to the company or obtaining a contract at all) cannot be achieved without extensive preparation by the management team. There are no shortcuts, no quick and easy methods. And the ill-prepared team in the bargaining room is headed for certain disaster.

Start the Day After

Preparation for the next contract starts the day after the previous contract is signed. The first order of business after a contract completion is for the chief negotiator to write a critique of the just-finished bargaining while it is still fresh in his memory. His report will contain a narrative history of the negotiations, and an objective evaluation of the company's strategy. What was done right? What features of the company's approach should be retained and enhanced in the next negotiations? What features should be dropped? Improved? What were the union weaknesses and how can they be turned to the company's advantage next time?

Negotiating File

The second step is to establish a bargaining file labelled with the date of the next negotiations. Over the life of the contract material on such subjects as cost of living, contract settlements in other companies, reports of strikes, changes in union leadership, National Labor Relations Board rulings, and court decisions can be collected from newspapers, trade magazines, and government publications. As plant situations occur which suggest new or improved contract provisions, they should be written up and inserted in the file. Incidents of this kind are easily forgotten over a two or three year contract period; reduced to writing and collected in one place, they perform valuable service in developing company demands at the next negotiations.

Team Meetings

Start holding private meetings of the company bargaining team about six months before the expiration of the contract. A quiet location and freedom from interruptions is required; since these ideal conditions are hard to come by during the regular business day, some committees have found a solution in having dinner together at the end of the day and meeting for several hours in the early evening. Once a week is a good frequency for these meetings. Each meeting should have an agenda prepared by the chief negotiator, and cover a specific topic such as company goals, anticipated union demands, information needed and assignments for collecting it, company demands, location and timing of the bargaining sessions, bargaining room strategy, and strike preparation. While a definite agenda is used (to avoid wasting the time of the committee members), an atmosphere of free and open discussion should be maintained. It is in these meetings that the most valuable ideas for company strategy will be developed, and the team shaken down into a well-disciplined and smoothly functioning unit.

Essential Steps in Preparation

Some of the required steps in preparing for bargaining have already been discussed, and others will be covered later in this chapter. The essential steps to be taken in the period preceding actual bargaining are listed here for convenience:

1. Select the management bargaining team members.
2. Arrange for legal aid.
3. Begin regular management team meetings.
4. Collect factual data needed—cost of proposals, other contracts, general economic information.
5. Draw up company demands.
6. Develop bargaining manual.
7. Obtain higher management decisions on strike issues.
8. Notify union of intention to amend contract.
9. Notify Federal Mediation and Conciliation Service and appropriate state agencies of expiration of contract.
10. Make arrangements with union representatives for the first bargaining session.

This list is roughly in order of the sequence to be followed, but should be changed to fit individual situations.

WHERE TO OBTAIN INFORMATION

The company bargaining team will need to have at its fingertips full and accurate information on a wide variety of subjects. Before it can adopt sound bargaining positions on wages, fringe benefits, and working conditions, it must have complete cost information. Not only will this information be required to convince higher management of the correctness of the team's position, but it will also be used to back up the company's position in the bargaining room. Here the data presented by the company will be subject to challenge by the union, and will have to stand up to adverse examination. (There is a reverse benefit to be gained here: if the company's information is repeatedly found to be accurate and complete, the union will spend correspondingly less time in challenge.)

The gathering of this information cannot be left to chance. It should be the subject of an early bargaining team meeting at which a list of the required data is developed, and individuals assigned the responsibility for collecting it.

Data Required

While it is not possible to list every conceivable type of information which may be required in a particular bargaining situation, these items represent the major proportion of the cost data which will be needed:

Wages: Total annual dollars paid in total payroll, straight time, overtime, and shift differential. Average individual hourly rate, straight time and overtime.

Hours Worked: Total annual straight time and overtime hours. Average hours per man, straight time and overtime. Overtime hours as a percentage of total hours.

Fringe Benefits: Total annual dollar cost *and* cents per hour cost of holidays, vacations, insurance, sick leave, pensions, funeral leave, jury duty, military leave, special bonuses, work clothing and safety equipment.

Economic Background: Cost of living index for the area, with recent trends; business outlook for the year ahead for the company and industry; recent contract settlements in major industries; average wages paid and hours worked in your specific industry.

Other Companies: As much detailed information as can be obtained on wages, fringe benefits, and contract provisions and work rules from companies in your area and in your industry. This information should be collected for the categories shown above.

Lost Time and Absenteeism: Fifty-two weeks times forty hours per week amounts to 2,080 hours. Deduct holidays and vacation time; then compare the average straight time hours worked per man with this figure. The difference is lost time from all sources, and it can be broken down into sick leave, jury duty, etc. Casual absenteeism can be derived from these calculations, or worked up from the individual time records. Calculate Monday and Friday absenteeism as a percentage of the total.

Sources Within the Company

Plant Time Records: Many companies prepare daily or weekly compilations of actual time worked and time lost by hourly personnel in each section of the plant. Records are often kept of overtime worked and overtime refused by each man. Individual summaries of time worked and lost may be kept for each man on an annual basis.

Such records will provide the information required in the "Hours Worked" category. If they are not available, however, the bargaining team must fall back on the one basic time record—the individual time card. Abstracting the desired data from them can be a time-consuming job, and must be started early if the information is to be of any use. It will usually pay to assign clerical personnel to perform the job.

Cost Reports: The monthly cost report, issued in some form in virtually all manufacturing plants, contains a great deal of information useful to the negotiator. It will provide much of the basic data on wages, overtime, and fringe benefits, and will show the time trends for these items. Caution must be exercised in deciding how much and in what form this data can be revealed to the union during the negotiations.

Accounting Department: The accounting department can provide a great deal of help in assembling and analyzing the data discussed so far. More importantly, it can handle the more complicated calculation projects such as determining the future cost of anticipated or actual union proposals (what will it cost in the coming year to raise holiday overtime pay from double time and a half to triple time?), the total cost of various settlement packages, and the effect of a total settlement on company profits and prices. The chief negotiator will want to establish a close working relationship with the accounting department early in his preparations; this task will be made easier if a member of the accounting department has joined the bargaining team.

Personnel Department: Much of the discussion at the bargaining table will concern aspects of the work force which cannot be measured in dollars and cents. The files of the personnel department will give the average age of the work force, distribution of seniority among its members, labor turnover, interdepartmental transfers, number and size of insurance claims, and safety statistics. Managers in this department can offer valuable insights into the morale and attitudes of the plant work force.

Sources Outside the Company

Other Companies: It is essential that the company bargaining team enter the negotiations with full, up-to-date information on wages, fringes, and work practices of other companies in the same labor market area. Exchanges of union contracts are relatively easy to arrange with neighboring plants. The non-union plant may be more reluctant to divulge information about its pay practices. In either case, a personal visit is the most effective way of establishing a good mutual information exchange. The personnel department may be perfectly capable of handling area surveys but it is a good idea to assign some of the contact work to members of the bargaining team to give them a better perspective on the local labor picture.

Regional and Trade Associations: Regional groups such as the local Chamber of Commerce, Management Council, or state Association of Manufacturers frequently act as statistical collection agencies for their members, and may issue reports on wages and fringe benefits paid in the area. Often these groups will provide forums for personal exchange of experiences and discussion of problems of common interest. Trade associations, made up of companies engaged in a specific industry, perform similar services for their members, but application of their data requires caution because of the wide geographical area covered.

Publications: Every plant manager sooner or later finds himself on the advertising mailing list of a number of periodicals covering continuing developments in the labor relations field. It is a good idea to subscribe to one or two of these bulletins, and to pass them on to all members of the bargaining team.

Of special interest is a monthly magazine published by the United States Department of Labor called *Monthly Labor Review.* The editorial content consists of articles about such subjects as employment outlook in various industries, developments in insurance and pension plans, union conventions, and reviews of decisions by the courts and the National Labor Relations Board. The Bureau of Labor Statistics uses the magazine to publish about forty pages of data on hours worked, earnings, labor turnover, and employment in various industries, as well as the familiar cost of living index. Subscriptions are obtainable from the Superintendent of Documents, U.S. Government Printing Office, Washington, D.C. 20402 for about ten dollars.

The National Industrial Conference Board has published two very good studies of collective bargaining based upon extensive surveys conducted among several hundred companies. The companies answered extensive questionnaires on every facet of the bargaining process, and the results are compiled with a running editorial interpretation of the statistics. The reports are entitled *Preparing for Collective Bargaining* and *Preparing for Collective Bargaining-II.*

Several publishing firms offer continuing services in the labor relations field. Prentice-Hall publishes a two-volume series called *Labor Relations Guide.* The purchaser pays an annual fee in addition to the original purchase price. He receives a current set of volumes in looseleaf binder form, and periodic replacement sheets to keep the books up to date. These volumes cover labor law changes, NLRB and court decisions, arbitration awards, government executive orders, cost of living statistics, and changes in state labor laws. Similar services are offered by Commerce Clearing House in *Labor Law Guide* and the Bureau of National Affairs in *Collective Bargaining and Negotiation of Contracts.*

LEGAL AID

The management bargaining team should have at its disposal the services of an attorney skilled in labor law and contract negotiations. Often the choice of an attorney is made by higher management; if the chief negotiator makes the choice he will look for a man who not only has sound legal qualifications, but is currently active in the labor field. Plus values would include a knowledge of the industry, international union, and possibly the international representative.

It has already been recommended that the attorney not be present in the bargaining room. However, he should be available by telephone on very short notice once the bargaining sessions begin. It is wise to have him review all contract clauses before they are included in the final document. He should check the completed contract before it is signed for possible conflict between the various articles and clauses. A very valuable orientation session can be provided for the entire negotiating team by having him come to one of the preparation meetings and giving his views on bargaining in general and the upcoming negotiations in particular. If legal complications develop during the negotiations, such as charges and countercharges of refusal to bargain or unfair labor practices, his services will be indispensable.

THE INTERNATIONAL REPRESENTATIVE AND THE SHOP COMMITTEE

Just as a baseball team scouts the opposition before an important game, it will pay the company bargaining team to learn as much as it can about the work-related factors affecting the thinking of the representatives on the other side of the bargaining table. Such factors as age, education, seniority, pay, ratings by supervisors, and jobs held within the company and prior to employment by it, may help to explain or predict the thinking of various individuals on the bargaining issues. Any information which can be obtained about the political situation within the union and the aspirations of the union bargainers will be of assistance in understanding their motives in the bargaining room.

Scouting the international representative is a more difficult task. If anyone in the company has previously negotiated with him, this person would be the first to contact. Talk to bargainers from other companies who have bargained with him; they will be able to discuss his style of bargaining, weak points, issues he gives priority, objectives in recent negotiations, and political aspirations in the international union. Your labor attorney may be able to supply similar information.

NOTIFICATION OF CONTRACT EXPIRATION

If the plant is covered by federal labor law, either party to the union contract must notify the other party sixty days before contract expiration of its desire to amend or change the contract. The party taking this action must notify the Federal Mediation and Conciliation Service *and* any state mediation service which may exist, thirty days later if a settlement has not been reached, that a dispute exists.

The services of the federal mediator are available at no cost to the parties on a completely voluntary basis. He will usually meet separately with the parties, try to find the causes of deadlock, and search for areas of agreement. He may then make suggestions to both sides of the ways in which they might move toward agreement. He may then call the sides together in a joint meeting to get the bargaining going again. He will not assume the role of an arbitrator or try to judge the merits of the dispute. The company negotiator will make his decision to accept or reject the services of the mediator on a number of local factors: ability of the mediator himself, confidence of the union side in him, nature of the issues at stake, and the degree to which communication between the parties has broken down. Mediation can be a very valuable tool in reaching a contract settlement; it should not be rejected without the most careful consideration.

CONDUCTING PRODUCTIVE BARGAINING SESSIONS

Physical Arrangements

The first step is to decide where the bargaining sessions are to be held—on company property or away from it. The union may insist on meeting off the company premises; in any case the advantages lie with making arrangements for meeting rooms at a local hotel, motel, or other facility. The management team will be better able to concentrate on the job at hand free from the many interruptions which seem inevitable when they are on the plant site. The union team will feel freer to involve themselves in the give and take of bargaining if they are not subjected to questioning by their own membership every time they emerge from the bargaining room.

If bargaining arrangements are not already determined by long practice, it is worthwhile to discuss with the union sharing the cost of the rooms. One survey has shown that the union pays some portion of the room cost in about twenty-five percent of the bargaining situations studied.

Have at least two rooms available—one for meetings, the other for team caucuses. The furnishings need not be elaborate, but the rooms should not be so small as to be crowded, and should be provided with a large table, water pitcher and glasses, pads and pencils, and a blackboard or chart pad.

Take Charge

In many bargaining situations, especially when union personnel are relatively new to negotiating, the chief company negotiator may be able to assume a kind of informal chairmanship of the meetings—open them, adjourn them, call for breaks, determine the order in which topics are discussed. While this isn't quite the same thing as being elected president of the local Rotary Club, it does offer some opportunities to guide and control the course of the negotiations, and the company negotiator should go as far as he can in this direction.

Businesslike Tone

Insist that the negotiations be conducted in a businesslike manner. Emotional outbursts should be minimized and must never come from the management side. If the union takes the occasion to go back over all of the individual complaints which have come up during the life of the contract, they should be reminded that such matters are not the subject of the negotiations and should be handled by the grievance procedure.

The company negotiator should present the arguments for his proposals and the responses to the union's proposals in a straightforward, unruffled manner. If he can develop a reputation early in the negotiations for complete honesty and having his facts straight, it will pay off handsomely in the latter stages of the bargaining. This is the point where exhaustive preparations begin to pay back the time and effort invested in them.

Above all, the management team should never allow itself to become the target of personal abuse or profanity. If faced with this kind of behavior the chief company negotiator should remind all present of their obligation to conduct themselves in a civil manner; if this fails, he should postpone further negotiations until a calmer atmosphere can be restored.

Team Discipline

The management team should operate under a tight discipline in the bargaining room, with the chief negotiator controlling the management strategy. Team members can unwittingly cut the ground out from underneath the chief negotiator with casual remarks or side conversations which have not been thought out carefully in advance. Set up a system of signals for the team members to get the attention of the chief negotiator when they wish to speak. Simply passing written notes is one system, and has the advantage of notifying the chief negotiator of what the speaker wants to say.

Good use can be made of the caucus as a strategy device. When tempers are rising across the table, or the management side seems boxed in, or a question of fact needs to be researched, or the management team is divided on a subject, simply call a caucus to get the time needed to adjust the situation.

Late Hours

Avoid late-hour bargaining. Physically tired men cannot give the full, careful scrutiny to contract changes which they require. Whenever possible, schedule negotiating sessions during regular business hours; a fully rested management team will do a better job, and if it does need additional review and strategy meetings, the evenings are left open for them.

KEEPING RECORDS OF BARGAINING SESSIONS

It is important that a complete and accurate record of the bargaining sessions be kept. As contract language is agreed to during the progress of the sessions it may later become the subject of controversy if an unassailable record is not kept. The management team will often want to refer to exact statements made by either side in earlier sessions. And if a dispute arises during the life of the contract as to the intent of a particular clause, an arbitrator may decide the issue on the basis of what was said during the negotiations. The company having an accurate record of the bargaining sessions can approach such a problem with confidence that the record will support its position, or if this is not the case get out of the situation gracefully at an early stage.

Stenographic Reporter

The best method of obtaining a complete record of the proceedings is to hire a stenographic reporter or stenotypist, who will take down everything that is said word for word, and return a transcript of the sessions in as many copies as desired. This written record will not only be valuable in the current negotiations, but will be extremely useful to the team which must take over in a year or two at the next negotiations. It is the most expensive method, and the cost for ten bargaining sessions can run over a thousand dollars. If the company pays for the entire cost of the transcript, the record belongs to it. If the union wants a copy, it should be asked to pay half the total cost of hiring the stenotypist.

Tape Recordings

The tape recorder is sometimes used to make a record of the proceedings. It is cheaper than stenotype and still gets every word preserved. However, it does have several disadvantages: It is difficult to locate a particular subject or passage in a long reel of tape, and they are difficult to index. If the tape is months or years old, it may be difficult to identify the person speaking. If it must be played back in the presence of union representatives, any heated exchanges or emotional outbursts are all revived exactly as they occurred.

Take Notes

A third (and often used) system is to have one of the management team members take notes of the sessions. This method is the least satisfactory because the man assigned to note-taking is so preoccupied with that job that he will not be able to function effectively as a bargainer. His notes may be incomplete, or unconsciously edited. And they are certainly subject to challenge by the union as a complete, accurate, and unbiased record of the proceedings.

UNION DEMANDS

The end product of all collective bargaining is a new or revised union contract, a document which is written in precise, matter-of-fact, and often legal language.

The demands submitted by the union at the first bargaining session may look like anything but formal contract language. They may be delivered verbally. They may be delivered in a variety of written forms ranging all the way from carefully typewritten, precisely worded clauses down to crudely scrawled pencil lists. The first job of the company negotiator in the bargaining sessions is to review them one by one with the union, translating them into specific contract clause changes. When this is completed, ask if these are all the demands the union has—no surprises are wanted later in the negotiations.

The union list is likely to be long and to include many items which will not be included in the completed contract. The company bargaining team will meet alone shortly after the union demands are in to try to determine which are important to the union and which are not. This evaluation necessarily contains a large element of guesswork, and will be subject to continuing review as the negotiations proceed.

The team now proceeds to assess the union's demands from the company's point of view. It will decide, or seek decisions from higher management, which union demands are acceptable, which can be tolerated, and which are completely unacceptable. If all of the information needed to make these decisions is not at hand, assignments can be made to the team members to research the proposals in terms of their effects on cost, management rights, conflict with corporate policy, ability to serve customers, and impact on salaried personnel. Then the company team will be ready to prepare its counterproposals.

COMPANY DEMANDS

Counterproposals

Many of the union proposals will deal with sections of the contract which the company would also like to see changed. In some cases the company will go in the same direction as the union, but not quite as far. In others, it will want to go in the exact opposite direction. Rather than confuse the issue by stating its position in brand new proposals, the company submits counterproposals to those put forth by the union. For example, the union may have proposed that the new contract provide for two additional holidays. The company, desiring to grant only one additional holiday, would submit a counterproposal calling for a single holiday addition.

Own Demands

The company should *never* enter collective bargaining without a set of demands of its own. In most contract settlements the company ends up giving a great deal; it should get something in return. Without company demands, the bargaining takes on a one-sided atmosphere. With them, the company team has some points to trade off against union proposals. If the union unexpectedly accedes to some of them, the company is that much farther ahead.

The company's demands will find their sources in the overall corporate objectives, future plans for the plant whose contract is being negotiated, and experiences—good or bad—with the existing contract. In drafting the company demands, exercise caution on two points: 1) Be sure that the company demand will have real value to the company if the union agrees to it; otherwise you may wind up trading an important concession to the union for a worthless gain for the company. 2) If either side bargains for a contract change, but fails to achieve it, its position on the subject may be weaker than if it had never been mentioned (with respect to law and arbitration proceedings). For example, if the contract is silent on interdepartmental transfers, and present practice favors the company, it would be unwise to bring the subject up in collective bargaining. If the company demand is not included in the final contract, the union may be able to restrict the company's right to administer transfer, by showing that the company had failed to gain its right in the collective bargaining.

BARGAINING MANUAL

As the negotiations proceed, the bargaining team will find that it has been amassing a large amount of information. Cost data, area surveys, economic background, company demands and the supporting reasons for them, union proposals and the arguments supporting the company's position on them—all are being gathered in the company's file. The entire bargaining team will need to have instant access to all of this information in the bargaining room.

This objective is met by developing a bargaining manual, which contains the collected information in readily accessible form. While in some very large companies it may reach the proportions of a fully bound and printed volume, in most medium-sized plants it will be in typewritten looseleaf form, with a copy for each permanent member of the bargaining team. Work should begin on the bargaining manual as soon as the negotiating team starts its regular meetings. Cost data and other factual background information can be included before the actual negotiations begin.

THE JOHN DOE MANUFACTURING COMPANY
Union Contract Negotiations
Bargaining Manual

BASIC COST DATA

I. Actual Wages and Fringe Benefits, Previous Year

	Cost in Dollars	% of Total	Dollars per Hour
A. Wages			
1. Straight Time	430,481	62.5	3.23
2. Overtime	63,858	9.3	
3. Shift Differential	2,453	.3	.02
Total Wages	496,792	72.1	3.25
B. Fringe Benefits			
1. Holidays	17,969	2.6	.13
2. Vacation	22,929	3.3	.17
3. Sick Leave	8,567	1.2	.06
4. Funeral Leave	473	.1	.003
5. Break & Washup Time	45,187	6.6	.33
6. Attendance Bonus	9,239	1.3	.07
7. Group Insurance	21,453	3.1	.16
8. Social Security, Unemployment Tax	26,925	3.9	.20
9. Workmen's Compensation	20,294	3.0	.15
10. Work Clothing	19,255	2.8	.14
Total Fringes	192,291	27.9	1.413
Grand Total	689,083	100.0	4.66

II. Useful Cost Data

A. Average Hourly Rate	3.23
B. Average Overtime Hours	324
C. Cost of an Additional Holiday	
1. Total Dollars	1,912
2. Cents per Hour	1.4
D. Annual Cost of Increases	
1. 1%	$49,654
2. 1¢/hr.	1,539
3. 5¢/hr.	7,695
4. 10¢/hr.	15,390
5. 15¢/hr.	23,085
6. 20¢/hr.	30,780

Exhibit 1. Sample Bargaining Manual Page—Cost Data

Exhibit 1 is a sample page from the bargaining manual of a fictitious corporation preparing for collective bargaining. Actual cost data for the entire payroll costs for all the previous year are shown in terms of dollars paid, dollars per hour worked, and the percentage which each item represents of the total. Another section provides handy cost factors which can be used for quick mental or written calculations. The negotiator with this book at his fingertips can quickly respond to union arguments and avoid costly pitfalls. Without this kind of help he must grope through his files hoping to locate the needed information or recess the negotiations while the information is collected.

As the union demands are received and evaluated, a separate bargaining manual page should be devoted to each one. Exhibit 2 is an illustration of how John Doe Manufacturing decided to handle Union Proposal No. 11. Most of the entries on this page are self-explanatory, but the section "Company Reasons" deserves comment. In it are shown the fundamental reasons for the company's position. They may or may not be reasons which the company wishes to expose to the union. The section "Bargaining Arguments" gives the points which can be used in the bargaining room, and are worded for maximum persuasive effect.

THE JOHN DOE MANUFACTURING COMPANY
19__ Union Contract Negotiations
Bargaining Manual

UNION PROPOSALS

UNION PROPOSAL No. 11. Article V, Section D 4.

Work performed on a holiday or on the day on which the holiday is celebrated shall be paid for at twice the regular rate in additon to the holiday pay.

COUNTERPROPOSAL: None

COMPANY POSITION: Retain present contract provision.

COMPANY REASONS:

Labor cost becomes prohibitive if future developments in customer requirements or process changes should require holiday work on a regular basis. Triple time rate would become $9.69 per hour—$3.23 for straight time, plus $6.46 for the premium.

BARGAINING ARGUMENTS:

1) We do not work holidays often. Keep contract on those items which have more meaning.

2) Proposed language tends to benefit only a few people, and of course, would have to come out of the total economic package granted by the company. It is better to provide benefits in which everyone can share.

3) Object of the business is to run at a profit. If we have to operate the plant on a holiday to accomodate a customer, we cannot triple the cost of labor and still make a profit. The company is therefore left with two very poor choices: Fail to serve the customer, or, serve him at a loss. Neither of these choices is good for anyone.

SECOND LINE OF DEFENSE:

If it becomes necessary to grant this proposal, be sure to eliminate the words "... on a holiday ..." Otherwise, if the 4th of July falls on a Sunday, and is celebrated on Monday, we will have to pay triple time for hours worked on both days.

AREA PRACTICE: Of 9 local companies:

2 pay triple time.
5 pay 2½ time.
2 pay double time.

Exhibit 2. Sample Bargaining Manual Page—Union Proposal

CONTRACT LANGUAGE

The completed union contract is a document which attempts to set forth the intentions of the parties which agreed to it. During its life it will be subjected to interpretation by people who were not present when it was drafted, and to the strains of grievance and arbitration procedures. While it is definitely recommended that the contract not be studded with legalistic "whereases" and "wherefores," the wording of each clause accepted or proposed by the company should be carefully considered. For instance, an incomplete street address in the very first sentence of the contract may mean that the new plant being built on the other side of town is automatically unionized the day it opens. Many clauses can be strengthened or weakened from the management point of view by simple changes in the wording. Use these techniques to obtain the best wording:

Compare Contracts

In the course of bargaining preparations copies of union contracts will have been obtained from a number of other companies. When preparing wording of a vacation clause change, review the vacation clauses in all of the other contracts. Then select the best combination of phrases for your clause.

Get a Book

Obtain a published contract language guide. Several publishers in the labor relations field have one or more books on this subject. They point out pitfalls in drafting contract language, and offer specimen clauses designed to maximize management rights. Of special interest is a booklet published by the Research Institute of America called "Protecting Management's Rights Under a Union Contract," and Prentice-Hall's *Manual for Drafting an Employer's Union Contract.*

Legal Help

The company's labor attorney should review every clause change before it is written into the final contract. During preparation he will be able to suggest or obtain good clauses on the subjects you anticipate dealing with. He should review the entire contract before it is signed to be sure 1) that the various clauses do not conflict with each other, and 2) that the contract does not violate any federal or state laws.

ROLE OF THE FIRST-LINE SUPERVISOR

The plant manager should decide exactly what he wants from his first-line supervisors during contract negotiations, and explain their part in the proceedings to them in a clear, unmistakable manner. It is a serious error to neglect these men during the bargaining period; not only will their positive contributions be lost, but since they are in continuous contact with union members it could not be considered unhuman of them if, hearing nothing from their management, they come to agree with the union's point of view on some issues. No serious company negotiator wants to hear from the union side of the bargaining table, "Your own foremen agree that we should have two more holidays."

The first-line supervisor's participation as a member of the bargaining team has already been discussed. Here are some additional ways in which he can contribute:

Company Demands

Because he operates at that point in the organization where the union contract provisions are translated into action, the foreman is in a unique provision to discover what parts of the contract are unworkable or detrimental from a management point of view. Solicit his ideas when drawing up the list of company demands.

Calm Shop

Plant operations can be seriously affected by the high degree of excitement which can develop among the hourly workers at contract negotiation time. There will be discussion, disagreement, and arguments among the workers and between them and their union leadership. If this activity is allowed to become a major occupation of the work force, production output may suffer at a time when it is most needed. The first-line supervisor should be instructed to do all he can during this period to maintain a calm, businesslike atmosphere in the plant. Since plant management is likely to be tied up in negotiating sessions, the supervisor often finds himself very much alone in carrying out this responsibility; he needs all the prior guidance he can get.

This is a period when the rumor mill is at its most active, and the wildest versions of what the company wants and is doing in the negotiations will not only circulate among the plant workers, but will pervade the lower salaried ranks as well. One of the company's best weapons against the most outrageous misrepresentation is a well-informed foreman, who can scotch a wild story before it gets started. Clearly, it is to the advantage of the company to keep the first-line supervisor well-informed.

Upward Communication

His closeness to the union membership puts him a very good position to collect scraps and bits of information which may be of value to the bargaining team, and a means by which he can pass this information along should be provided for the first-line supervisor. While the law forbids his engaging in spy-like activities designed to intimidate the workers or interfere with their right to organize and run a union, in the normal course of his work he will hear and see things about union politics, relative importance of union demands, and the mood of the membership which can help the plant management chart a better course for all involved.

STRIKE PREPARATION

The plant manager can do a great deal to minimize the effects of a strike on his company by careful preparation in advance of the contract expiration.

Sales

At least six months prior to the strike deadline, he should work out a program with the sales department to protect the company's customers. The sales people may want to contact their customers, informing them of a possible strike situation, and asking them to place protective stock-up orders early in the negotiation period. A plan to stock outside warehouses might be developed, so that deliveries to customers could still be made if the plant is struck. Whatever system is devised, the plant manager will have to measure the difference between normal production and total capacity, and start early enough so that the difference can be used to amass the desired protective stock.

Operation Decision

The company must decide whether it will attempt to operate the plant if a strike occurs, either with non-union personnel, or by replacing the strikers (get legal advice on this move). The factors involved in this decision are very well discussed in John G. Hutchinson's *Management Under Strike Conditions* (New York: Holt, Rhinehart and Winston, Inc., 1966). If the decision is to run the plant during a strike, plans must be made to move raw materials in and finished goods out, to provide and assign personnel to production jobs, and arrange for their food and rest if passage in and out of the plant is not feasible.

If the decision is not to operate the plant, plans must still be made for protecting plant property and communicating with municipal agencies, employees, and the public. Personnel arrangements must be made for final payments due the strikers, and decisions reached on whether to grant vacation pay for any part of the strike period and whether or not to continue insurance benefits.

WHEN A STRIKE OCCURS

The plant manager carries very heavy responsibilities when the plant goes on strike, and the nature of his duties will vary widely with the size of the plant, the degree of higher management involvement, and the way in which the union chooses to conduct the strike. In any strike he will be concerned, at a minimum, with the following factors.

Communications

As soon as he knows he has a strike on his hands, the plant manager will advise his higher management of the situation, and continue to keep them informed of developments. The next move is to put the communications plan for plant supervisory personnel into effect, so that all non-union personnel can be instructed to assume their strike duties.

Suppliers will need to know of any cancelled deliveries, or, if it has been decided to keep the plant in operation, of problems they may face in making deliveries. Customers must also be notified, but in most companies the sales department will handle this job.

If contact with the union representatives has been broken off, it should be resumed to establish new meeting dates for resumption of bargaining. The strikers themselves must be notified when and where to pick up the last paycheck, and informed of the status of their fringe benefits.

When the impact of the strike is likely to be heavy upon the local economy or the issues are of concern to the community, it may be advisable to establish contact with the news media and important public leaders. The plant manager will usually look to the industrial relations department for assistance in this area; the important point is that only one person should be authorized to speak for the company.

Protection

Protection of plant and personnel is a major concern requiring immediate attention. Local police and fire authorities should be notified as soon as the strike starts. Special instructions in writing should be given to the plant guard force, and to any supervisory teams working in or patrolling the plant. A responsible, accurate person should be designated on each shift to keep a written log of all incidents as they occur, including date, time, and names of people involved. This log may be very valuable to your attorney in any later legal action.

Operations

If the plant is to be shut down, non-union personnel will have to complete any unfinished production operations which might result in spoiled material or damaged machines. If the plant is to run, the plant manager will be heavily occupied with putting the operations plan into effect. Arrangements may have to be made with railroads, truck lines, and utility companies for special services. In either case, the plans for housing and feeding personnel remaining in the plant will be put into action.

Aftermath

The immediate aftermath of the strike requires careful handling by plant management to minimize any bitterness or tension which may have arisen, and to keep them from becoming long-lasting effects. Instruct first-line supervisors to establish a business-like, get-back-to-work approach quickly, avoiding any tendency for groups to gather and go over recent events. The supervisors themselves should be cautioned against discussing the strike or showing their personal feelings about any of the individuals involved in it.

Chapter 5

Helping the First-Line Supervisor to Be First-Rate

This employee occupies a truly unique place in the plant organization: he is the only member of line management who deals directly and continuously with the hourly work force. Because he is the focal point of communication between the plant workers and management, he is worthy of a great deal of special attention by that management.

More than any other plant employee, he has a problem of identification. He spends most of his time with the hourly workers; he shares their place of work, their working hours, their overtime, their problems and successes. He is praised with them, and criticized with them. He has probably risen from their ranks. No wonder he identifies with them, and the question of whether he is a "company man" is one he gives considerable thought—a question which never arises at other management levels. More than any other employee, he needs to be reminded that he is a manager, that all levels of management are interested in, and indeed dependent on, him.

Why? Because he is always present (and often the only management representative) at critical moments in the life of the plant—emergencies (fire, flood, power outage, wildcat strike), and the startup of new processes and equipment, sudden developments in labor relations. His ability to meet and handle these situations can mean the success or failure of carefully developed plans and of the management moves which must follow them.

The importance of the first-line supervisor to industrial relations (Chapter 3) and collective bargaining (Chapter 4) have already been developed. In this chapter we will deal with recruiting, motivating, and evaluating the performance of this influential employee.

Recruiting

The plant manager has two basic questions: What are the qualifications for this job, and where will I find the men to fill them? First, let's look at qualifications:

1) Education. While a high school diploma is not an absolute must, especially when older men are being considered, you will want communications and mathematical skills at least equivalent to that level of education. A year or two of college would be a real plus. If your industry is highly technical in nature, you may have to require special training in the candidate's background.

2) Experience. At least five years of industrial plant experience is indicated, and most promotees have considerably more. Don't deprive yourself of good potential candidates by

requiring experience in too narrow a range; a bright man with good leadership qualities will pick up all but the most difficult technology very quickly.

3) Leadership. This is the key quality, and it must be present in demonstrated or clearly potential form. You should be able to visualize the man you promote or hire giving orders, training people, organizing work, applying plant rules or a union contract, correcting substandard performance, supervising former co-workers, and handling emergencies. If you can't find these qualities in the man, don't put him in the job.

Resist the temptation to promote the "best lathe operator," the "best millwright," or the "best darn machinist in the county." The qualities which make a superior plant worker may or may not be combined with the leadership qualities required of a foreman. An employee with those leadership qualities may be performing at less than full capability in the plant out of simple frustration. And many a promotion to supervisory ranks has been based on demonstrated leadership in the union. Now, for sources of candidates:

1) Within the company. Typically, a foreman is promoted from the hourly ranks of the plant work force, and for good reasons. He is familiar with the company's products, the manufacturing processes, quality requirements and problems, the people and the rules under which they work. Training requirements will be limited to developing an understanding of the managerial process and familiarization with some administrative procedures. You will want a substantial proportion—at least fifty percent—of your foremen to have this background.

If *all* of the first-line supervisors are recruited from the hourly ranks, there is a danger that the organization will become too ingrown and unable to generate or cope with new ideas and approaches. Broaden your search within the company to include potential candidates from quality control, the drafting room, accounting department, materials management department, and the pilot plant. You may be able to offer attractive opportunities to younger men in these departments, while achieving diversification of background and viewpoint in the foreman group.

2) Outside the company. When the supply of candidates within the company is exhausted, or foremen with specialized backgrounds are needed to start new manufacturing processes, or the decision has been made to broaden the field from which candidates are selected, you will be looking at the qualifications of candidates from outside the company. The risk is great, because you will be placing a new employee in a very sensitive position without having seen him at work. Two hints to help make the selection process successful: limit the candidates to those who have already attained foremanship elsewhere; it is too chancy to assume that a man can make the vertical move to supervisory ranks at the same time he is making a lateral move to another company. Second, examine the reasons for a candidate's change of companies very closely; if they don't make sense to you, don't hire him. He may be covering up an inability to get along with those who work with him.

3) Transfers. Foremen have generally been regarded as creatures of their local communities, and transfers to distant plants have been uncommon. As the American population becomes more mobile, however, geography is less of an inhibiting factor to putting a man in the job best suited to him and to offering him the maximum opportunity to develop his abilities. Don't overlook transfer from a remote plant when you have a supervisory slot to fill.

4) College graduates. See the closing section of this chapter.

Recognition of Status

The comments made at the beginning of this chapter concerning the foreman's problem of identification constitute the rationale for taking deliberate steps to recognize his status as a management employee. Here are some ways in which you can further this recognition:

1) Uniforms. When the plant supplies its hourly force with work clothing, distinctive uniforms should be provided for the foremen. (Some companies have their foremen wear shirts and ties.) Most commercial laundries will supply dress shirts and attractive slacks for this purpose.

2) Office and desk. Every manager should have a place where he can answer the phone in privacy, a desk to work on and keep important papers in, and a place to discuss individual matters with his employees. The foreman is no exception. If a fully walled-off office cannot be included in building plans or added to an existing structure, a good-looking partition-type office (complete with ceiling) can be inexpensively installed in the work area.

3) Secretarial help. Notices posted over his signature, and the occasional report, letter, or memorandum which the foremen writes, should be professionally typed. While he does not need a secretary of his own, the foreman should be able to call upon this kind of help when he needs it.

4) Foreman's Club. An organization sponsored and usually subsidized by the company exclusively for first-line supervisors. It can be the focus of training activities as well as a social program. Some companies provide a special building on the plant property for this purpose.

5) Training programs. Of course the essential purpose of conducting in-house training programs or sending foremen away to seminars is to develop better supervisors. But the very fact that the company is devoting time and money enhances the status of those enrolled in them, and announcements of these programs should be made in such a way as to make the most of this aspect.

6) Department dinners. In smaller plants the entire production department and in larger plants the individual departments may hold dinner meetings to discuss broad problems, review progress, or to make important announcements. The first-line supervisors should always be invited to these functions.

·7) Compensation. Nothing the company does says more about the value it places on its foremen than the salaries it pays them. If their compensation falls below that of the surrounding area or that of the most highly paid hourly workers in the plant, their status will fall with it.

An especially difficult problem arises in payment for overtime. From the management point of view, it is preferable not to pay the foreman directly for overtime, thus avoiding his having a direct financial interest in overtime. The best method is to include enough money in his base compensation to cover anticipated overtime activity. If that is not possible, an alternative is to pay nothing for casual overtime (short, unscheduled periods), but to pay a fixed rate for scheduled overtime (sixth and seventh days, or a week of ten-hour days).

8) Subscriptions. Many companies buy subscriptions to bulletins and magazines published for foremen; receiving such a publication enhances the foreman's own view of his job.

Motivation

By the time an employee has reached the level of foreman, the simple needs of food, clothing, and shelter are no longer prime motivating factors; he has advanced to a level of need for recognition, accomplishment, belonging, and self-realization. The plant manager can move to meet those needs in the following ways:

1) Keep score. To use a baseball analogy, your players are not likely to be motivated to give their best at the right moment in the game if they don't know what inning it is, the score, and the number of outs. The leaders of your production team in the plant should

know when production quotas are met or missed, and by how much; what level of quality is being maintained; what their cost performance is compared to standards and budgets; and the frequency and severity of accidents in their departments. Be sure to make available to them reports of all these statistics.

2) Teach him management principles. The first-line supervisor can hardly be expected to motivate himself to become a professional manager if nobody takes the trouble to teach him what management is. Nothing that you do to make him feel a part of management will have more effect than instructing him in the fundamentals of planning, organizing, and controlling, and expecting him to apply these principles.

3) Involve him in plans and decision-making.

—Let him make as many of the plant operating decisions as he can successfully handle.

—Share corporate plans with him, and bring him into management conferences at the highest appropriate level.

—Let him review blueprints for engineering projects which affect his work, and consider his suggestions.

—Ask him to write the operating procedure for the newly completed project or process.

Every corporation has its policies, its customs, and its style of operation which may limit the degree to which you can involve the foreman in these activities. Our purpose here is not to conflict with such policies, but to obtain the greatest allowable participation by the foreman in plant management.

4) Reward his efforts. Of course you will think of salary increases and promotions as rewards for jobs well done, and as incentives for greater achievement. But don't neglect the motivational value of sincere commendation for good work, and above all, the satisfaction of seeing his own ideas adopted in the plant.

Compensation

The plant manager's problem in setting salary ranges for first line supervisors breaks down into three components: what factors to consider in setting base pay, how to find out what others are paying for similar services, and what to do about premium pay such as overtime and shift differential.

1) Factors affecting base pay:

a. Highest paid worker supervised.

b. Number of workers supervised.

c. Value of equipment and materials handled, and criticalness of operation to overall plant production.

d. Allowances for overtime and shift differential, if not paid separately.

e. Degree of supervision exercised. This can range from that of a working foreman who does little more than assigning work to his fellow employees, to that of a foreman exercising full administrative control over several assistants and an hourly group with a wide range of pay rates and skills.

2) Where to get salary information.

a. National Surveys. The Executive Compensation Service of the American Management Association issues to its subscribers an excellent statistical survey of base and fringe compensation for supervisors and foremen, on a national basis. Another very good source of information is a study published by the National

Industrial Conference Board entitled "Compensating First-Line Supervisors in Factory and Office."

b. Local surveys. Regional employers' associations, chambers of commerce, and management councils often publish local surveys which include supervisory salaries.

c. Want ads. The salaries mentioned in want ads can be misleading, because the full job content is not always revealed by its title, but when the same job title is advertised with salaries by a number of companies, a reasonably good estimate of the range being paid will emerge.

d. Other plants. Personnel departments and your counterpart manager in other plants may be willing to trade supervisory salary information with you. Expect more reluctance to reveal this kind of information than hourly rates, which are usually published in union contracts and employee handbooks anyway.

e. Employment agencies. Reputable firms which place large numbers of foreman can give you very current information on salaries being paid at hiring. Beware of misunderstandings about job content in evaluating their data.

3) Special problems.

a. Overtime. This is the most difficult compensation problem, and companies have adopted a bewildering variety of schemes to handle it. Ideally, the foreman's base pay should be adjusted to compensate him for the average amount of overtime he works, for two reasons: first, it removes any personal benefit to him when his group works overtime, and second, surveys have shown that when this is the case the amount of overtime worked by the group drops sharply.

Other methods include calculating the foreman's hourly rate, and paying him under the same rules as the workers; paying a flat rate of so many dollars per eight hours accumulated overtime; paying only for overtime scheduled in advance; and giving no pay, but allowing the foreman to take equal time off at a later date.

b. Shift differential. If shift differentials are paid to the hourly workers, then the foremen should be paid a premium or have it included in their base pay when assigned to a night shift or placed on rotating shifts.

c. Fringe benefits. Vacations, holidays, insurance plans, pensions, and sick leave are taken for granted by most industrial workers today, and you will have to offer them if you are to maintain an effective supervisory force. On the other hand, they are not likely to have much impact on the recruitment and motivation of foremen unless their provisions are exceptionally good or bad. When stock options and bonus plans are offered to management employees, make sure that first-line supervisors are included; the extent of their participation is not nearly so important as the fact that they are included in the managerial group in the eyes of the corporation.

Training

Industrial progress inevitably brings more complicated processes to the plant, and higher performance standards for the managerial team which operates it; plainly, the need for training to acquire, improve, and update skills pervades the entire plant organization. Nowhere is this need more intense than at the level of the foreman, who must now be able to perform as a professional manager while supervising employees who carry out a wider variety of more technical tasks.

1) Technical Training

a. In-house. If your corporation is large enough to have a training department capable of conducting technical courses you have the best possible situation, because those courses can be tailored to the technology and equipment you are using. In the smaller company you may be able to recruit very effective instructors from the engineering staff and line management who can use operating procedures and suppliers' manuals as the basis for course content.

b. Outside. Local colleges, technical institutes, and adult education courses at public high schools all offer training in the basic sciences and mathematics. Where there are many manufacturing plants in the area, such courses may be designed especially for first-line supervisors.

Companies which supply highly technical equipment, such as instruments, computers, and power plants, often conduct training schools in the use of such equipment.

2) Managerial Training.

a. Remote. The non-profit American Management Association as well as a growing number of private consulting firms are offering workshops, seminars, and training courses on various aspects of foremanship at regional centers throughout the United States (New York, Chicago, Dallas, Atlanta). The programs usually last from two to five days, and cover such topics as the management cycle, training new workers, discipline and grievances, administering a labor contract, and motivating and evaluating hourly employees. These courses offer well-thought-out programs led by excellent instructors, and give the foreman a chance to talk over common problems with his peers in other companies.

b. Local. Employers' associations, YMCA's, and colleges may sponsor and conduct seminars similar to those mentioned above, or regular semester courses meeting for one or two evenings a week. These programs are usually inexpensive, and are often tailored to local needs.

c. In-house. Again, if you can call upon the services of a professional training department within your company, a very important function can be handled with very little effort on your part, yet with full assurance that the company's management philosophy is the one being taught to your foremen.

The best system of all (though perhaps better suited to the smaller plants) is to teach the course on management techniques yourself, possibly with another senior line manager as co-chairman. While the demand on you is heavy—probably requiring two nights a week for a period of three months—the rewards are very great. The foreman no longer wonders whether the material he is being taught is really meant to be applied in the plant; he is hearing it from the plant manager himself. You will develop a very deep rapport with your supervisory group, and you will learn things about your organization from the comments and discussions in the training sessions that you would never have gleaned in any other way.

Information to Pass On

The alert, interested supervisor wants as much information about his company as he can get; he wants to know about personnel changes, new product developments, corporate plans for the future, and union-management relations above his own level. The plant manager has rightful concerns of his own about releasing confidential information, or simple giving more information than the recipient can wisely use. Use these guidelines:

1) Some things he must know to perform his job, and you have no choice but to pass them on. When information could be dangerous if lost, there are ways to make it harmless.

For instance, one company uses code numbers for raw materials on its process instruction sheets; if the sheets were lost, the new owner would have no idea of what went into the product. Another company issues cost reports to the foreman, but not in terms of dollars; his copy shows man-hours of labor, kilowatts of electricity, and pounds or units of supplies consumed per unit of product.

2) Some information can be revealed without harm to the corporation or anyone in it; examples are new engineering projects, high level personnel changes, new developments in parent or subsidiary companies. Make it a habit to be the first to communicate this kind of news to your first-line supervisors.

3) Some information can be revealed only in confidence, and you will have to make this clear when you disclose it. Whether you dare release such information depends upon the ability of your group to keep a secret. Test them by releasing some innocuous information as confidential, and see how long it takes to get around the plant.

4) There are kinds of information which carry such great risks to the company's competitive position, or to the reputations of individuals, or might cause needless worry to groups of employees, that they simply cannot be revealed. Withholding this information is not likely to cause resentment among your foremen, especially if you have been forthright on other subjects.

Follow two cardinal rules: They must be the first to hear information which affects them personally, and it must come from the immediate superior. Second, don't equivocate. The foreman's communications problems are difficult enough, and the last thing he should have to contend with is unreliable or misleading information from you.

Job Descriptions

This handbook will not subject you to the tedium of examing a job description taken from the files of a particular company; corporate styles, nomenclature, and ideas of what should be in a job description vary so much that the exercise would not be helpful to your situation. What we will do is examine the fundamentals of constructing a job description—its uses, its content, and some of the pitfalls to avoid.

1) The uses of job descriptions:

a. Training. Nothing can be more helpful to a man learning a job than a clear statement of its responsibilities and duties; when the statement is written he can refer to it as often as he needs to.

b. Recruiting. The personnel department, an outside employment agency, or anyone assisting in the recruiting process can do a better job when they know exactly what is wanted. The prospective employee can measure his abilities against its requirements, arriving at a sounder decision on acceptance.

c. Performance appraisal. The first step in measuring a man's performance is to compare it to a statement of the responsibilities he is expected to meet.

d. Job evaluation. A complete job description furnishes an objective basis for determining its salary, and its relation on the salary scale to other jobs in the organization.

2) What job descriptions should contain:

a. Objectives. The first section should contain a broad statement of the job's responsibilities and the objectives it is designed to fulfill.

b. Reporting relationships. State the titles of all individuals reporting to the job holder, as well as the title of his superior. Be sure to include dotted line relationships in the job description if they are shown on the organization chart.

c. Lateral relationships. No job description is complete unless it specifies the other organizational groups—both line and staff—with which the incumbent is expected to relate, and his cooperative responsibilities to them.

d. List of duties. Often the attempt is made to condense a long list of duties into a brief summarizing statement; while the objective is commendable, it is nevertheless true that a detailed statement of all of the duties performed is necessary if the full dimensions of the job are to be revealed. The following list of categories of foreman's activities can be used here and in the preceding paragraph on objectives to be sure all duties are included:

Production	Communications	Administration:
Quality	Employee Relations	Production Reports
Cost	Improvement Ideas	Time Records
Safety	Maintenance	Inventory Reports
Housekeeping	Materials Movement	

What to avoid:

a. Responsibilities too generalized.

b. Responsibilities too narrow—statement leaves no room for short-term growth of the job.

c. Personality requirements. You are describing a job, not a person. By putting personality requirements ("eager, responsive, friendly") in the description you may eliminate some very capable candidates for the job, or wind up with a frustrated incumbent who can get the work done, but doesn't match a personality profile.

d. Impossible performance requirements. Statements like "Must meet all production schedules," or "Plant must be neat and orderly at all times," in his job description will cause the foreman to shrug his shoulders, hope for the best, and conclude that the cards are stacked against him from the beginning.

Conducting Performance Appraisal

Plant managers all too frequently surrender their control over format and content of the performance appraisal interview to those of a printed form sent around by the personnel department. The foreman, on the other hand, often finds the performance review a stilted procedure which has little relationship to his performance or future with the company. Make use of these principles to build an effective appraisal system:

1) Decide what you want from the performance appraisal; it will be a combination of some or all of these factors: a) performance improvement, b) basis for salary increase, c) ranking of a number of individuals performing the same job, d) an opportunity for upward communication, e) counseling of employees, and f) warnings to substandard performers.

2) Establish the content. Even if you are sent a printed form to use, you can add appraisal factors to it, and minimize those which do not meet your needs. When devising your own form, be sure to:

a. Relate the categories of appraisal to the job description, the performance objectives of the department, and the fundamentals of the management cycle.

b. Avoid subjective or personality-oriented criteria. One rating form identifies "enthusiasm" as an appraisal factor, with "works enthusiastically" near the top of the scale, and "matter-of-fact attitude" near the bottom. I see no value and some danger in this. In my industrial experience the "enthusiastic" man sometimes accomplishes very little, while the "matter of fact" or even dour individual gets the work done. You are after results, not happy faces or sunshine personalities.

c. Use as many measurable criteria as possible. The foreman will understand more clearly and you will have a more objective basis for rating when you include performance statistics on production quantity, quality percentages, frequency and severity figures on safety, and cost information.

3) Handle the interview.

a. Notify the employee in advance of the interview, and give him a blank rating form to fill out. During the interview compare his estimate of his performance with yours.

b. Do not announce a salary adjustment during the interview. You want the employee's full attention on his performance; you won't get it if he is expecting you to announce a raise.

c. Give the employee a chance to tell you how he sees the factors affecting his performance. There may be conditions beyond his control of which you are not aware.

d. Act on your reviews. Promotions, raises, transfers, bonuses—these and other rewards should be given on the basis of performance. When this is not done, foremen will soon lose interest in the appraisal procedure, and it becomes a meaningless exercise.

4) Determine the timing. Annual reviews are the most common, and the year is a long enough time period to fully evaluate a foreman's performance. Some companies adhere to a semi-annual schedule, but more frequent reviewing is not recommended. The shorter schedule is useful for recently appointed foremen, or when there are frequent transfers and new assignments.

College Graduates as Foremen

A number of companies recruit a proportion of their foremen from young college graduates coming into the company who aspire to a career in production management or engineering. The benefit is twofold: The young professionals can learn the manufacturing operation, its products, and its capacity to produce and deliver, from the actual experience of helping to manage it. What they learn will be of value to them and the company in any future job they may hold. In return, they bring a fresh point of view and an analytical frame of mind to the manufacturing process, helping to keep the permanent foremen's thinking stimulated and the organization from becoming too ingrown.

Two points: You can't expect to keep these men as foremen permanently. Within two to three years you will have to move them laterally or up, or you will probably lose them. And don't recruit all of your foremen from this source; you need the stabilizing effect of the long-service non-technical foreman. Fifty percent is a good ratio—it provides equal balance of both points of view, and prevents one group from dominating the other by weight of numbers.

CONCLUSION

This chapter identifies the first-line supervisor as key employee in the plant organization because of his position at the interface between plant management and the work force. He reveals to the workers what the company thinks of itself and them by his attitude and the things he says and does. His ability and motivation have powerful impact on the success or failure of many of the plant's plans and programs.

   The thrust of the chapter's counsel to the plant manager is to involve himself deeply in the recruiting, training, motivation, and evaluation of the first-line supervisory group; neglect of this obligation, or excessive delegation of it, carries high risks of performance failure for the entire plant organization and alienation of the work force from the plant management.

   Much of the chapter's content, especially the sections on training, passing information on, job descriptions, and performance appraisal will be useful in the development of salaried personnel other than foremen.

PART 2

Plant Operations

Chapter 6

Getting into Operation Smoothly: Schedules, Shifts, and Procedures

Plant managers preside over an incredibly large variety of process operations; their plants produce everything from toy dolls to mammoth presses, from potato chips to petrochemicals. Some operate continuous flow processes, others produce assembled units for stock, some manage custom job shops. Yet within this multiplicity of processes there are problems common to all—how to schedule the plants most efficiently, how best to utilize manpower, how to handle start-ups and shutdowns, how to meet emergencies, how to keep track of materials produced.

It is with these universal concerns of production operations that this chapter deals, offering an analysis of each problem and a choice of solutions.

Scheduling the Plant

The scheduling problem is conveniently broken down into three parts: what scheduling is trying to do, what information goes into it, and the methods of handling it.

1) Objectives of scheduling:

      a. Meet customer delivery requirements.

      b. Satisfy inventory requirements.

      c. Minimize cost by maximizing plant efficiency:

            (1) Load the plant even as possible with long production runs.

            (2) Hold to a minimum the interruptions of production for setups and cleaning of equipment.

            (3) Realize the highest possible return on capital investment by fully utilizing machinery and equipment.

2) Informational inputs:

      a. Known customer orders. They should take precedence over all other scheduled production, and can be scheduled farther in advance with confidence that the production will actually be needed.

      b. Sales forecasts. They vary widely in accuracy. If your sales department provides consistently reliable projections, you can safely schedule production on them. If not, you can still use them as guides for scheduling, but make periodic adjustments based on the accumulation or depletion of inventory—perhaps on a weekly or monthly basis.

c. Inventory requirements. When stock levels have fallen below minimum levels, or when distribution pipelines must be filled for a new product, some of the plant's production is scheduled for inventory. There is usually enough flexibility in these requirements to permit scheduling the plant for maximum efficiency; the one danger is that inventory production delayed too long may suddenly become a customer requirement which has to be produced hastily.

d. Crisis events. When a strike is impending in his own plant, or in suppliers' plants, or in local or national transportation systems, the plant manager must adjust production schedules to minimize the effects of these emergencies. Calculate the maximum number of production units the plant can turn out in a week, and deduct from it the normal weekly production expected for the period in question; the difference is the production which can be devoted to emergency stock. Divide this into the total emergency stock required, and you have the number of weeks prior to the deadline at which you must start emergency production. Allow for the fact that production scheduled in the last week may not be of much value; workers in your plant or other industries may slow down considerably as the strike deadline nears, and time will be needed to make transportation arrangements for the last production units to leave the plant.

Fire, explosion, bad weather, flood, earthquake—all can affect suppliers' operations or public transportation systems. These events come with little or no forewarning, and scheduling is reduced to reaction to late deliveries and insertion of substitute work or clean-up activities into the production schedule.

3) Scheduling techniques:

a. Put the schedule on paper. Have it typewritten or mimeographed for distribution; if a larger size is required for posting it can be reproduced on blueprint or electrostatic copiers. Blackboards or peg boards which are changed as the schedule is completed are good for display purposes, but they leave no permanent record. Such a record can be very helpful to the plant manager who must make plant capacity calculations and needs data about machine loading at his fingertips.

b. Use the schedule as a control device. Next to every increment of production shown leave a blank space for entry of the actual increments produced. This method gives management a daily indication of whether production is on schedule, and if not, how far it is off.

c. Communicate the schedule to all who need it. Maintenance, purchasing, order departments—these and many others will benefit from knowing what the plant is planning to do. See that they get copies of the schedule and are kept up to date on changes.

d. Match scheduling technique to the type of production operation.

(1) Continuous process. One product is produced in a continuous stream, as in a food processing plant, petroleum refinery, or chemical plant. Make up a simple printed sheet, with the days of the month listed vertically in the left-hand column. Next to this draw four vertical columns one each for the day's scheduled production, for its actual production, for the month-to-date scheduled production, and the month-to-date actual production.

(2) Series operations. Material produced in one section of the plant become the raw material for the next section, and so on until a number of steps yield a completed product. This schedule is essentially a flow diagram of material through the plant. Establish a time scale across the top of the schedule. Draw a horizontal bar for each machine (similar to a Gantt chart) and show inside the bar the number of units that machine is scheduled to produce in the time period covered by the bar. Arrows connecting the bars show the flow of materials from one machine to the next. Observe these precautions: In a series operation the entire plant has to be scheduled around the slowest production unit, or else in-process inventory will pile up in the faster units. Allow time between production operations for material transfer and quality inspection.

(3) Single unit manufacture. One large unit is manufactured by or assembled from a series of production operations as it moves through the plant. The simplest schedule is the Gantt chart, with a horizontal time scale across the top, and each operation represented by a single horizontal line whose length indicates the time period it is scheduled to cover. Operations which overlap each other or can be carried on concurrently are readily shown on this chart, permitting the scheduler to choose an arrangement which gives the shortest manufacturing time. Further refinements of this technique are critical path scheduling, and its more sophisticated cousin, Program Evaluation and Review Technique (PERT). (See Chapter 13.)

Changes in Schedule

Once the schedule has been established, materials ordered or work begun, sudden changes can have the following negative effects on plant operation:

1. Crowding of operating floor with materials assembled for prior orders, which must now wait while the rush order is processed.
2. Overtime costs.
3. Increased chance of production and quality errors.
4. Reduced plant efficiency in output per man-hour.
5. Wasted time of schedulers, foremen, and managers.
6. Worker resentment of sudden changes in assignment, especially when they result in waste of previous work.

The plant manager bears a double responsibility when schedule changes are demanded of his plant. It is his duty—and that of everyone in the company—to serve legitimate customer needs. On the other hand, it is also his duty to point out the additional costs of the negative effects listed above, and to probe the reasons for schedule changes. Often the reasons are poor—someone "forgot" an order, "lost a paper," or a clerk was absent and no one did his work. When such cases occur frequently, the plant manager can rightfully demand that these deficiencies should not be redeemed by increased plant costs.

Use of Overtime

Premium rates charged for overtime range from one and one-half to three times the base hourly rate, making a prima facie case for very close control and even elimination of overtime. Nevertheless, practicing plant managers know that they cannot simply do away with overtime by issuing an edict, and that the cost decisions are not as simple as they first appear. Here are some guidelines to use in making overtime decisions:

1) Use overtime to keep the organization lean. When your man-hour calculations call for 9.5 men to staff a section, hire nine and make up the difference with overtime. Assuming that you pay for the 0.5 man at time and a half, your cost liability is 0.75 at straight time rates, rather than the 1.0 you would have paid had you hired the tenth man. Equally important, you will avoid hiring more people than you need, a practice which inevitably leads to loose work habits and hidden costs much higher than the overtime incurred.

2) Base overtime decisions on hard economic facts whenever possible. If holding a freight car another day will cost $25.00 but four man-hours of overtime at $3.50 times 1.5 can get it unloaded, then the decision is in favor of the overtime. If it will require a thousand dollars worth of overtime to meet a deadline on a job which will only return seven hundred dollars in profit, the economic decision is against the use of overtime.

3) The cost of fringe benefits affects the economics of overtime decisions. Often the cost of these benefits, such as vacations, holidays, work clothing, and insurance, will total thirty percent of the base hourly rate, but does not increase because of overtime. Thus when a choice must be made between having the existing force work overtime or hiring new workers at straight time, it is really between 1.5 times the base rate for the overtime work, and 1.3 times the base rate for the new workers.

4) Budget impressed overtime. Sometimes the plant manager is required by forces beyond his control—sales policy, clerical mistakes in order handling, bad weather, orders to clean up for important visitors—to use overtime work. Although individual incidents cannot be predicted with accuracy, the total costs tend toward an annual figure which can be foreseen. The plant manager should insist that his budget cover these costs.

Plant Start-Ups and Shutdowns

Throughout the year the plant manager is faced with a number of occasions requiring the planning of a shutdown or a start-up: holidays, slow production periods, vacations, maintenance turnarounds, and bringing new facilities on stream. It is imperative that these operations be carried out from written procedures, not only to prevent the omission of an important step, but also because the mere act of planning will uncover problems of coordination which must be answered ahead of time.

1) Shutdowns. Use this checklist of special preparations for a plant closing:

a. Building security—windows and doors locked, heating and ventilating systems adjusted properly.

b. Electrical systems—switches off, fuses pulled, breakers locked out.

c. Fluid systems—valves closed, vessels and pipes drained, depressured, or vented.

d. Sprinklers and other fire protection systems—in working order, provisions for last-minute checks.

e. Freeze-ups. Special protection not only for outdoor equipment, but for pipes which pass through or run close to cold walls.

f. Preparation for maintenance work—if equipment repairs and overhauls are planned for the shutdown, be sure that it is cleaned up, process materials removed, and potentially dangerous conditions countered by safety measures.

2) Start-ups. The object is to get the plant running again quickly and smoothly. Consider these points in planning the start-up:

a. Bring maintenance and utility crews in early—to have buildings, machines, and services ready when the production personnel start work.

b. Coordinate material flow—plan operations, especially in continuous and series-type production, so that production crews are neither idle nor swamped by excessive work coming from previous steps in the process.

c. Beware of pressure systems—steam, gas, and water lines may be carrying unusually high pressures because of zero demand during the shutdown period; valves must be opened more slowly and carefully than usual.

d. Expect equipment problems—lubricants will have drained from metal surfaces, pumps lost suction, fluid systems become airbound, and instruments off calibration or stuck in one position.

Emergency Procedures

As in the case of start-ups and shutdowns, emergency procedures must be thought out ahead of time, reduced to printed form, and widely disseminated to those who will actually put them into practice. It is an excellent idea to conduct drills and problem exercises in the use of power failure, flood, and fire emergency procedures to be sure that plant personnel will react promptly and effectively when actual emergencies occur.

1) Power Failure. (Loss of electricity or steam)

a. Prior to any actual emergency examine all instruments and control devices to be sure that they are set for *fail-safe,* that is, when they are deprived of power they will cause cooling rather than heating, low rather than high pressure, to occur.

b. Shut off electrical start-stop switches. Some types of electrical equipment can be damaged by a partial return of electric power, and in any event, the main breakers may cause a second power failure if they are overloaded with all equipment on when the power returns.

c. If the failure is in the steam system, take steps to protect the building against freezing—close windows and doors, turn on emergency electric heaters if electricity is available. Decide at what building temperature workers will be sent home. Close steam valves at points in the system where process materials can be drawn into the pipes by vacuum, and where air can be drawn in.

d. Provide for emergency cooling. If your plant has a cooling tower for heat removal from process equipment, its fans and pumps will be shut down in an electrical failure. Arrange for emergency tie-ins to city water mains to accomplish enough cooling for safety purposes.

2) Fire.

a. The first step in preparing an emergency procedure for fire is to decide what you want your employees to do first. Turn in the alarm? Evacuate the building? Fight the fire with hand equipment until it is out or too big too handle? The answers to this question will vary with the type of plant you operate and the prevailing safety philosophy in your company. The important point is that the decisions be made ahead of time and incorporated into well-rehearsed procedures.

b. Shutdown decisions can be more complicated than they first appear. If there is a fire in one section of the plant, it would seem sensible to shut down operations in all other sections until the situation is under control. But if a part of the plant is handling flammable liquids or gases, a sudden shutdown can cause venting of these materials, or perhaps spills, increasing the danger of fire. It may be safer to keep a department of this type running unless the fire is very close to it.

c. The fire procedure will contain a description of the plant alarm system, its signals, and what to do if it fails. It should also spell out who is authorized to deal with the press and public in an emergency situation.

3) Flood.

a. Flooding usually gives more warning of its arrival than other types of emergencies, and the decision process can be spread out over a longer period of time. If your plant is in the flood plain of a river your state flood control agency or the U.S. Army Corps of Engineers can probably give you detailed data on the depth of water to expect and the frequency of flooding in the area.

b. Develop the procedure for evacuation. The primary questions are who makes the shutdown decisions, on what criteria, which sections shut down first, and the composition and duties of emergency crews, if any.

c. Provide for protection of property. Doors and windows are closed, and if there is time, sealed. Electrical equipment is de-energized, delicate apparatus moved out of danger, materials which can catch fire when exposed to water relocated.

4) Snow Emergency.

a. The decision-making process is the key to a successful procedure, and should be detailed carefully in advance. Who makes the final decision on running or shutting down? With whom must he consult? Who feeds the first information and warnings to him? How will the information be disseminated to employees?

b. Beware of hourly pay squabbles. Some union contracts (and even non-union plant rules) require that prior notice be given of a cancelled shift, or the workers are paid for the day anyway. Situations can arise in which one worker stays home and gets paid, while another reports, does a day's work, and gets the same pay; obviously the second worker will feel he is owed some kind of premium. To avoid such situations, one plant stays open if at least one supervisor can make it to the plant to assign workers; those who do report get paid for the work they do, while the absentees are not paid.

c. Communications. If the plant is to be shut down, employees must be notified in advance. Make arrangements with one or more local radio stations to broadcast your emergency announcements. Each fall post a notice telling employees which stations to listen to for emergency instructions.

Holiday Operations

Some operations must run on holidays, either because their outputs cannot be stored or because they are too costly or complicated to shut down. Others which have the option of shutting down will usually do so unless urgent customer needs or exceptional economic conditions dictate keeping the plant open. In either case, give special attention to these points when considering holiday operations:

1) "Double time and a half" is not what it seems. You pay an employee eight hours straight time pay whether he works the holiday or not; therefore, when he works the holiday your incremental cost is at time and a half.

2) In prosperous times employees will generally resist holiday work, unless the nature of the operation obviously requires it. If the entire plant does not have to operate, it may be wiser to recruit a skeleton crew from among those who wish to volunteer for holiday work.

3) Holidays may bring increased incidence of drinking, sleeping on the job, and absenteeism; at these times the rules need to be firmly announced and impartially

administered. Plant rules or the union contract should provide that an employee must work the day before and the day after the holiday in order to receive holiday pay.

4) Prepare for a lack of supporting operations both inside and outside the plant. The office is closed, clerks are gone, truck terminal dispatchers and railroad agents not available, fuel and food deliveries may not take place.

Shift Operations and Schedules

The problems encountered with shift operations will usually deter the plant manager from resorting to them unless the need is compelling. In this section we will examine the needs and the problems, as well as how to set up shift operations.

1) Reasons for establishing shift operations:

a. Utilization of capital equipment. When the cost of a machine is very high compared to profit realized on each unit of production, the machine may have to be operated for more than eight hours a day in order to justify its cost.

b. High sales and production levels. When they exceed one-shift capacity the work day must be extended to second and third shifts. Because it is time-consuming to recruit and train supervision and operating personnel for additional shifts, this decision is usually made to run on more than a short-term basis—at least a matter of months.

c. Processes which cannot be shut down easily or economically. High heat furnaces, which take several days to reach operating temperatures, and complicated chemical processes in which a raw material does not emerge as the finished product until a week after it has entered the process, are examples of operations which require shift work. Plant personnel will be more receptive to the idea of working shifts when the process itself makes the need obvious.

d. Products which cannot be stored. Transportation terminals and electric power plants are examples of plants whose "products" must be used at the instant they are created, and their need for shift work is obvious. Plants which make products for a daytime market—such as bakeries and dairies—are similarly affected.

2) Management problems with shift operations:

a. Communications. Direct contact between the upper levels of plant management and personnel of second and third shifts is limited to brief periods in the early morning and late afternoon; with some shift schedules direct contact can be almost non-existent. To overcome the problem written communications are used to a greater extent; the daytime superintendent or general foreman may leave a handwritten "night sheet" in which he gives detailed instructions for the work to be performed that night, any safety hazards he foresees, and minor notices of interest to the shift personnel. The shift foremen, in turn, keep a written log of their acitvities for the use of daytime supervision.

b. Management control. It is much more difficult for daytime plant management to be sure its procedures and plant rules are being observed when its members are not physically present to see what is going on. The use of rotating rather than fixed shift schedules can help management to overcome this problem.

c. Labor shortages. When employment rates are high in the surrounding area, it becomes difficult or impossible to staff night shifts. It may be necessary to offer very high wages and shift differentials to attract workers, and even these are not guaranteed solutions.

d. Cost of shift premiums. When shifts are instituted the cost of labor rises through the payment of a shift differential. Five percent of base wage is a typical level, but premiums in excess of 10 percent are not unheard of.

e. Reduced worker efficiency. Many third shift workers do not get full, satisfying rest; there are too many daytime household noises and distractions to permit uninterrupted sleep. The second shift worker fares better, but he is tempted to take a second job or become absorbed in home projects during the day, showing up for work with a day's activity already behind him. In either case the worker may not be inclined or able to work with as much efficiency as the daytime worker.

3) How to set up shift operations.

a. Assign workers. This can be the knottiest problem of all. Workers usually feel that they should be allowed to choose their shift assignments on the basis of seniority, while management feels that it should have the right to assign workers so as to give each shift a balance of experience, skills, strengths and weaknesses. One answer is to set a schedule of rotating, rather than fixed, shifts so that each group takes its turn at night work.

b. Assign supervision. When shifts must be added, the problem of finding adequate supervision can be acute. Most plants promote from within, feeling that it is easier to train an employee familiar with the company's products and procedures to be a foreman than it is to hire a foreman from outside and teach him new operational techniques. Whichever plan is chosen, the new foreman will need at least four to six weeks break-in period on days under the eyes of the plant superintendent or manager.

Rotating shifts can be used to achieve supervisory balance on the night shifts as well as worker balance. Some companies use different schedules for supervision from those of the workers; the idea is to have each supervisor work with all of the shifts over a period of time, avoiding the "ingrown" effect of having the same workers and supervisor together for long periods of time.

c. Keep operations at a minimum. The fewer tasks carried out on the night shift, the smaller the problems of staffing, communications, and management control. Unit cost of production may be higher on the night shifts because of shift premiums paid to employees.

d. Provide support services. When the combined cost of lost production and maintenance call-ins caused by equipment breakdowns on the night shifts approaches the wages of a maintenance man, it is time to assign a shift mechanic to each of the night shifts. This employee should report administratively to the daytime maintenance supervisor, but should receive work assignments on breakdowns from the night superintendent.

Provision must be made for emergency food service. While employees will generally bring their own lunches to the night shifts, depending upon the plant only to provide vending machines for beverages, candy, and cigarettes, a problem arises when a worker stays over from one shift to another and has no opportunity to provide himself with a lunch. There are three solutions to the problem: 1) send the employee out to a restaurant, 2) arrange for a caterer to bring the required number of meals in on each shift, or 3) maintain a stock of frozen dinners and a quick-heat oven at the plant so that employees can serve themselves. The last mentioned method offers the best combination of employee satisfaction and management control of the situation.

e. Establish shift schedules. There are two basic types—fixed and rotating:

(1) Fixed shifts. Personnel are permanently assigned to either the first shift (7 A.M. to 3 P.M. or 8 A.M. to 4 P.M. are typical hours), second shift (3 P.M. to 11 P.M. or 4 P.M. to 12 M.), or third shift (11 P.M. to 7 A.M. or 12 M. to 8 A.M.). Advantages of this system are that it is easier to follow for both workers and management, and is probably less fatiguing to personnel than the rotating shift system. Disadvantages are that the night shifts are out of contact with daytime supervision, and there will be heavy pressure on the plant manager to award preferred shift assignments on the basis of seniority. The latter can lead to a serious unbalance in shift capability.

Five-day week. Simply assign personnel to the first, second, and third shift. The one basic question to be answered by the plant manager concerns the start and end of the work week: should it begin at 11 P.M. Sunday night and end at 11 P.M. Friday night, or should it begin at 7 A.M. Monday morning and end at 7 A.M. Saturday morning? In the absence of any overriding technical information which affects starting time, choose the former system because it avoids having two full shifts in operation after daytime supervision has left for the week.

Seven-day week. When the plant operates twenty-four hours per day for seven days per week, four shifts are required, usually designated by the letters A,B,C, and D. A typical fixed-shift, seven-day schedule is shown in Exhibit 1. The three lettered shifts A, B, and C have permanent assignments on the first, second, and third shifts, respectively. D is the "swing shift," which fills in on the days off of the other three shifts, and therefore has a rotating schedule of its own.

	M	T	W	T	F	S	S
1st Shift (7-3)	A	A	A	A	A	A	D
2nd Shift (3-11)	B	B	B	B	D	D	B
3rd Shift (11-7)	C	C	D	D	C	C	C

Exhibit 1. Fixed shift, 7-day schedule.

The seven-day schedule has a basic problem: four groups working five days per week can only cover twenty shifts, but there are twenty-one shifts in the calendar week. There are two ways to make up the difference. One is to schedule one of the groups to work six days per week on a regular basis, and in Exhibit 1 Shift A was chosen for this assignment. Another is to train one "relief" worker to handle the jobs of each group of five men on the shift, and let him relieve them a day at a time.

(2) Rotating shifts. Personnel are assigned to lettered shifts—A, B, C, and D—which take turns working the first, second, and third shifts. Advantages are that each shift shares equally in the inconveniences of night work, making assignment of personnel to the various shifts far less controversial; and daytime management personnel are assured of meeting each shift regularly for a series of full days. Disadvantages are more complex work schedules, and the greater difficulty experienced by workers in adjusting to the constantly changing hours of work.

Five-day week. Assign personnel to three lettered shifts (A, B, and C), and schedule each group on first, second, and third shifts in weekly rotation. Some plants prefer to rotate every two or three weeks to give employees a better chance to become acclimated to the different working hours.

Seven-day week. The most complicated of all the schedules. Four lettered shifts are needed (just as in the fixed shift seven-day schedule), but there is no "swing shift." There is an almost endless variety of rotating shift schedules in use (cf. *Shift Problems and Practices,* Studies in Personnel Policy No. 118, New York: National Industrial Conference Board, Inc., 1951), with cycles ranging from four to twenty weeks.

Jul				1	2	3	4	5	6	7	8	9	10	11 Jul
Jul	26	27	28	29	30	31	1	2	3	4	5	6	7	8 Aug
Aug	23	24	25	26	27	28	29	30	31	1	2	3	4	5 Sep
Sep	20	21	22	23	24	25	26	27	28	29	30	1	2	3 Oct
	M	T	W	T	F	S	S	M	T	W	T	F	S	S
12-8	C	C	D	D	D	D	D	D	D	A	A	A	A	A
8-4	A_1	A_2	A_3	A_4	A_5	A	B	B_1	B_2	B_3	B_4	B_5	B	C
4-12	B	B	B	B	C	C	C	C	C	C	C	D	D	D

Jul	12	13	14	15	16	17	18	19	20	21	22	23	24	25 Jul
Aug	9	10	11	12	13	14	15	16	17	18	19	20	21	22 Aug
Sep	6	7	8	9	10	11	12	13	14	15	16	17	18	19 Sep
	M	T	W	T	F	S	S	M	T	W	T	F	S	S
12-8	A	A	B	B	B	B	B	B	B	C	C	C	C	C
8-4	C_1	C_2	C_3	C_4	C_5	C	D	D_1	D_2	D_3	D_4	D_5	D	A
4-12	D	D	D	D	A	A	A	A	A	A	A	B	B	B

Exhibit 2. Rotating Shift, 7-day schedule, with calendar superimposed. Subscripts indicate "relief days" for each shift position.

Exhibit 2 shows a four-week, seven-day, rotating cycle. Each lettered shift is scheduled for an extra day when it comes on the 8-4 shift, but a "relief man" can be set up for every five positions on the shift to avoid having anyone work overtime. Note that although the other three shifts work only five days in the calendar week, they actually work seven days in a row; because of this their days off keep advancing through the week until they finally achieve a long weekend. For example, C shift is off Sunday of the third week and Monday and Tuesday of the fourth week. The calendar for three months of the particular year has been superimposed on this schedule to show how a printed card or mimeographed sheet can be made up to help employees keep track of their assignments.

Production Reporting

Every manufacturing plant needs a system for reporting its production activities; the variations in form are wide, and you will want to develop your own system to meet your particular needs. Use these fundamental concepts:

1) Objectives of production reporting. To record for a specified time period:

  a. The quantity of material produced.

  b. The quantities of finished goods produced which are salable, require rework, or must be scrapped.

c. The total quantities of raw materials consumed, and the rate of consumption per unit of production.

d. The process conditions prevailing at stated intervals—pressures, temperatures, flow rates, number of lines operating, number of machines in use.

e. Inventory levels of raw materials, finished goods, and supplies.

f. Usage of man-hours, supplies, and utilities per unit of finished goods produced.

The need to collect this data to determine plant operating costs and performance levels is obvious, but the plant manager sees further applications for the collected reports:

g. Using the reports as raw data, a clerk with an adding machine can soon give him valuable information on trends in costs, productivity, quality, and inventory levels.

h. They can be used as control devices—that is, they supply information on the difference between what is desired and what is actually happening in such a way that the plant manager can make decisions on what to do. Example: The supervisor of Department A claims that Machine X is down for repairs too often and ought to be replaced. If good plant operating reports are available, either he or the plant manager can have a study made to determine exactly how often the machine is down, for what lengths of time, for what reasons, and can then make a decision to repair it, replace it, or even eliminate it altogether.

2) Techniques of production reporting.

a. Job ticket (or batch card, work ticket, job order, batch sheet, and many other names). A printed form which accompanies the work as it is processed from stage to stage through the plant. It carries the lot, job, or batch number and gives instructions on what raw materials are to be used and how they are to be processed. It becomes a production record when spaces are provided for the operators to sign off operations as they are completed, and to enter the quantities of material used, the time spent in each operation, and the quality results at each step.

As job tickets are collected from the end of the process, clerks tabulate them to build a picture of the plant's production rate, quality record, and cost performance. Once filed, they can be used at any time later for tracing the history of any production lot—especially when customer complaints arise.

b. Shift log. At the end of each shift, the foreman makes a written record of its activities—the routine (units produced, machines in operation, people present), the unusual (absences, equipment breakdowns, late raw materials), and problems he foresees for the relieving shift.

Have your printer make up a log book with perforated pages and carbon paper. Two copies are made of each log; one is forwarded to the production superintendent or plant manager, and the other is left in the book to become a valuable reference for the foreman who has been away on vacation or a long shift changeover.

c. Operator's log. Ask the print shop to make up an eighteen by twenty-four-inch sheet. The horizontal lines will be for each hour of the day; the vertical columns will represent various pieces of equipment or instruments to be read. As the shift progresses, readings are taken of process conditions by the hour, and the completed sheet is sent to the production manager in the morning. This method is especially well adapted to continuous operations.

Utilization of Manpower

Chronic shortages of labor and the high cost of available people make compelling reasons for any manager to avoid wasting manpower in his operations. Follow these lines of action:

1. Keep the work force flexible. The more kinds of work each man can perform, the better the manpower utilization.

2. Have plans ready for slow periods. Cleanup, painting, repairs, scrap rework—all can be used to utilize manpower effectively when production operations are at an ebb.

3. Develop and maintain the attitude that all employees are expected to be engaged in useful activity during working hours.

4. If flexibility is not a prime consideration, then be sure that all plant work is performed at the lowest possible skill level.

5. Consider the use of manpower pools for the entire plant, rather than duplicate reserves of men within each department.

6. Provide sufficient supervision. When the ratio of supervisors to workers drops too low, even the best motivated worker wastes time trying to find someone to give him a new assignment or to whom he can report a production holdup.

7. Provide effective support services. Materials on time, machines in good repair, tools and supplies readily available.

Outside Personnel Working in Plant

It is inevitable that there will be people working in your plant who do not belong to your organization—truck drivers, utility company workers, sales and delivery men, cleaning service personnel. While deliberate hostile acts—theft, industrial spying, disturbing regular employees—are rare, there is a significant danger from outside personnel not knowing the safety hazards and precautions required on the premises. Use these methods to keep control of the situation:

1. Designate one of your supervisors to be responsible for each kind of outside employee—maintenance foreman for utility workers, project engineer for contractors' personnel, personnel supervisor for vending machine servicemen. Your employees should know when outside personnel enter the plant, when they leave, and what they do while in it.

2. Identify visitors clearly. Use special visitor's badges; if safety hard hats are required in the plant, use a special color for visitors.

3. Issue written instructions to outside personnel. One company has a printed card—about eight by ten inches—which the gate guard hands to every truck driver and picks up from him as he leaves. It tells the driver where he can and cannot go in the plant, what facilities (lunchroom, rest room, smoking area) he may use, whether he can leave his engine running, and any safety precautions he must take. A one-page mimeographed sheet is handed to *and reviewed with* each contractor's employee.

CONCLUSION

In this chapter we have dealt with the problems common to all manufacturing plants—production scheduling, the use of overtime, start-ups and shutdowns, emergency procedures, holiday and shift operations, the utilization of manpower, and outside personnel working in the plant. Throughout the techniques developed to handle these varied problems runs the basic theme of the management cycle: the need to make plans and prepare for contingencies, to organize the work group and assign its members to the mutual advantage of themselves and the company, and to establish reliable methods of monitoring and controlling the operation.

Chapter 7

Structuring the Maintenance Department for Maximum Effectiveness

The maintenance department performs a number of important functions for the plant: it repairs defective equipment, maintains equipment so as to prevent failure, completes small to medium-sized capital projects, keeps track of the capital equipment inventory, provides some utilities and monitors the receipts of others, provides or purchases painting, cleaning, and other upkeep services. Its activities affect the performance of the plant in five of its major responsibilities—production, quality, cost, safety, and housekeeping.

Once he has established an organization which can do the work assigned to it, the plant manager's chief concerns with the maintenance department center around efficiency and control—ensuring that manpower is used efficiently, that the cost of supplies is carefully controlled, and that its costs are charged out to the other departments which use its services. This chapter is designed to help the plant manager understand and control the maintenance function.

Organization of the Maintenance Department

Depending upon the size of the plant and the nature of its operations, one or more of the following crafts and skills may be needed in the maintenance group:

Riggers	Insulators	Firemen
Pipefitters	Electricians	Painters
Millwrights	Instrument Mechanics	Janitors
Machinists	Motor Vehicle Mechanics	Welders
Mechanics	Carpenters	Tool Crib Attendants
Mason-Plasterers	Tool & Die Makers	Oilers
Air Conditioning-Ventilating Mechanics		

The principles of organization outlined in Chapter 2 should be applied by the plant manager as he structures the maintenance organization. It is especially important that he strive for the goal of flexibility—the right to assign a single maintenance employee to a number of different jobs. One method is shown in "Operator Grade System," p. 49, and Exhibit 5 of Chapter 2. Of equal importance in maintaining flexibility is the right of the plant management to use outside contractors when it is more efficient to do so; this right should be established as early as possible and defended in collective bargaining.

The selection and training of foremen for the maintenance department should be handled according to the principles of Chapter 5. When the department becomes large enough to break up into two or more sections, the composition of each section will be based in part on the ability of the foreman to supervise the various crafts within it. The crafts listed above could be broken down into four sections, each having related skills so that it can be supervised by one man:

Group 1	Group 2	Group 3	Group 4
Riggers	Insulators	Electricians	Machinists
Millwrights	Pipefitters	Instrument Mech.	Mechanics
Masons	Firemen	Welders	Oilers
Carpenters	Janitors	Air Cond. Mech.	Motor Vehicle Mech.
Painters	Tool Crib Attend.		Tool & Die Makers

Maintenance Scheduling

Routine scheduling of the maintenance department's work is a must for the plant manager who wants to control this important function. Here are the reasons for and the advantages of maintenance scheduling:

1) The maintenance foreman is required to think through his work activities in advance—the assignment of personnel, arrangements for materials and tools needed, and the methods he will use to accomplish the work in the allotted time. His planning skills will improve automatically.

2) Supervisors of departments in which work is to be performed are notified ahead of time, and can have equipment shut down and prepared for maintenance work at the proper time. They can also schedule their production activities around the predicted equipment outage.

3) By participating in the preparation of the maintenance schedule the plant manager can be sure that his own order of priority is used in programming the work. He is aware of the man-hours planned for each job, and can keep track of the backlog of jobs awaiting action. The file of completed schedules is an excellent source of information for the manager's reports, and studies he may want made of long-term trends in maintenance activity.

4) Planning maintenance work is an essential part of a program of preventive maintenance. The regular removal of equipment from service for preventive maintenance overhaul can hardly be accomplished without a maintenance schedule.

Follow these steps to get a maintenance scheduling system started:

1) Convene a weekly meeting (Thursday or Friday) of the plant manager, maintenance superintendent and foremen, and appropriate production supervisors.

2) Schedule all maintenance work for the following week which requires more than one-half man-day to complete. List all the jobs to be performed in a left-hand column opposite five columns for the days of the week. Show the number of men assigned to each job on each day that it is scheduled. For a man assigned for a half day use the symbol "1/2." For two men assigned for a half day, use the symbol "2/2."

3) Add to the schedule a backlog list of the jobs waiting to be performed but which cannot be included in the following week's schedule.

4) Have the schedule typed up, duplicated, and distributed to foremen, supervisors, and managers of interested departments—production, engineering, shipping, office, and laboratory.

Minor Work Order System

The first step in keeping track of the work performed by the maintenance department is to establish a work order system and insist that every job performed be covered by a major or minor work order. The term "minor" indicates a job estimated by the originator to cost less than $200 (or any appropriate figure set by the plant manager).

Exhibit 1 shows a minor work order form which can be printed and bound in pads, with alternate white and yellow copies. The originator uses a carbon, forwards the white copy to the maintenance foreman and keeps the yellow copy for follow-up. Have the printer number the forms serially; it will help the originator, the maintenance department, and the accounting department (if the completed form is used for charging out costs) locate filed orders more easily.

The plant manager should have the maintenance supervisor bring the file of uncompleted work orders to the weekly schedule meeting. In this way he can keep himself informed of the size of the maintenance backlog and the priorities observed by the maintenance supervision.

THE XYZ CORPORATION
Beaver Falls Plant

No. 89463

MAINTENANCE JOB ORDER (MINOR)

Date Written _____ Date Required _____ Charge Account No. _____

Describe Work to be Done _____

_____

_____

_____

Signed_____

(Originator)

Exhibit 1. Minor Maintenance Work Order

Major Work Order System

The major work order form shown in Exhibit 2 is used for projects whose cost falls between the maximum allowed on a minor work order and the minimum for which a special capital appropriation request is required. (Some plants use the major work order form even when a capital request is submitted, as a means of keeping track of the work in a uniform filing system.)

The originator of the major work order form is asked, in keeping with the large expenditure of money, to supply more information about the project he is requesting. A more complete description of the work is required, as well as a statement of the reasons for doing it and the economic justification. He must obtain a series of approvals, and is asked to outline the requirements of equipment preparation, downtime, and safety permits. The maintenance supervisor or the project engineer estimates the cost of the job before the approvals are given, and inserts the actual costs when it is completed.

The basic form can be made up by a printer in serially numbered form, but because of the larger number of copies required, carbons are not practical. The filled out form can be duplicated on the office copier; if one is not available the printer can make up the form on a duplicator master (such as Ditto) which can be written on by the originator and signers. When completed, sufficient copies can be run off to supply each signer, the originator, others who may have duties related to the work, and the central maintenance file.

THE XYZ CORPORATION
Beaver Falls, Pa.

No. 3649

MAINTENANCE JOB ORDER (MAJOR)

Date Written_____Date Required_____Dept. _____Page _____ of _____

Building _____Location_____ Ref. Maps & Dwgs. _____

Charge Costs to: Account No. _____Capital Approp. No._____

DESCRIPTION OF WORK (Include sketch of equipment.)

REASONS FOR WORK (Include economic justification when appropriate.

Signed_____
(Originator)

COSTS	ESTIMATED	ACTUAL	REQUIREMENTS	APPROVALS
Matls.			Equipment Downtime	Dept. Supv._____
Labor				Maint. Fmn._____
Contr.			Equip. Preparation	Plant Engr._____
				Proj. Engr._____
TOTAL			Safety Permits	Plant Mgr._____

Exhibit 2. Major Work Order Form

Preventive Maintenance

The objective of the preventive maintenance (PM) program is to service a piece of equipment *before,* rather than *after,* it causes damage in quality, production output, safety or cost. The program can be as simple as the handwritten reminders in a foreman's notebook and as elaborate as a computerized record system programming the activities of a separate preventive maintenance section of the department. But a preventive maintenance program appropriately matched to the size and complexity of the plant operation is a must if the plant manager expects to meet his performance goals. Here are the specific reasons for establishing a PM program:

1. Curtail unplanned outages of equipment. Sudden breakdowns interfere with timely delivery to customers, waste managerial time, impair employee morale.

2. Control repair costs. Emergency breakdowns are usually repaired on overtime, and may involve expensive transportation arrangements and high prices for repair parts and services. Production overtime and extra transportation costs to serve customers must be added to this bill.

3. Improve safety conditions. The sudden collapse of operating equipment may be accompanied by severe safety hazards—flying debris, overheating, high pressure, discharge of flammable or hazardous material, high electrical currents, fire, explosion.

4. Extend equipment life. Equipment which is routinely inspected, lubricated, and overhauled can be counted on to sustain a longer operating life.

5. Protect product quality. Process equipment which has gotten out of adjustment but is still running can cause a high quality reject rate. This is especially true of equipment with cutting edges, closely calibrated mechanisms, and control instruments. The preventive maintenance program can be designed to insure that critical equipment is kept in top operating condition.

Carried to its logical extreme, the idea of preventive maintenance would involve periodically shutting down and overhauling everything from the office pencil sharpener to the largest hydraulic press. This is neither physically possible nor economically optimum. Instead, use these guidelines to determine the selection and timing of PM activities:

1. Decide what is critical. Will downtime on a given piece of equipment subject the plant to severe safety hazards? Shut down other processing departments? Seriously delay customer deliveries? Cause product spoilage? If so, preventive maintenance is clearly indicated; if not, it may not be worth the expense.

2. Include PM in purchasing decisions. Consult present owners of proposed brands of equipment to determine incidence of breakdowns, frequency and extent of preventive maintenance required, and whether it is subjectable to PM procedures.

3. Make use of manufacturer's recommendations. They can be especially helpful for new equipment on which there is no plant history.

4. Conduct inspections. Periodic inspection of equipment will not only reveal whether it needs to be taken out of service for repair of expected defects, but the nature and extent of unexpected defects as well.

5. Use plant experience and history. If a pump bearing in rough service repeatedly wears out between twelve and fifteen weeks, schedule it for preventive maintenance once a quarter.

Operational details of a particular preventive maintenance system will be tailored by the individual plant to meet the needs of its equipment, service position with customers, economics, and safety hazards. These operating pointers are fundamental to all systems:

1. Tie it in with maintenance scheduling. At the weekly scheduling meeting the plant manager should always include on the agenda a review of upcoming PM activities. Those which are not planned for the week immediately following can

be put in the backlog list to give the longest possible notice to those concerned. The maintenance foreman will be thus encouraged to make early preparation of manpower and materials to handle the job.

2. Establish a reliable record-keeping and follow-up system. In the very small plant the foreman's files and perhaps a notebook with a time schedule will suffice. Somewhat larger plants use a card system in which each piece of equipment has its own card with punched holes around the edges for sorting into various classifications. On the card is a timetable for preventive maintenance action, brief instructions on what is to be done, and a record of all maintenance activities. One commercial version of this card system is the McBee Keysort.

Follow-up is a control function of the plant manager. At the beginning of the year he can request a PM schedule from the maintenance department, and periodicially check to see that it is being followed.

3. Get maximum yield from the equipment downtime. Train mechanics to recognize and look for signs of major wear which must be scheduled for a longer repair period at a later date. If downtime and labor are expensive, it may pay to change all the minor, inexpensive parts of the machine even if they appear to be in good condition; the price of a ten dollar part may be worthwhile insurance against a fifteen hundred dollar outage.

Shop Facilities

From the plant manager's point of view, the key to successful development of maintenance shop facilities is to be sure that they match the needs of the plant precisely—and no more. He should require that requests for maintenance equipment be accompanied by economic justification just as cogent as he would require for production equipment. The cost of production losses must be carefully weighed against the cost of specialized maintenance equipment with full consideration of an important third factor: the availability and cost of outside repair services in the plant area.

There are three distinct steps to take in the design and specification of maintenance facilities:

1) Lay out the functional areas. Work benches, storage, machine groupings, welding and painting facilities will each claim separate areas of the shop.

The storage area will need suitable shelves and racks to hold minimum inventories of parts and supplies—pipe and fittings, fasteners, sheet metal, gaskets, seals, lubricants, wood, and electrical parts.

Welding and painting areas will require curtains, partitions, and ventilating equipment to protect the safety and comfort of workers using them and those in the general area.

In my opinion work benches should not be assigned to individual employees, but should be functional for the type of work performed—one for mechanical work, another for electrical work, sheet metal operations, and so on. In this way attention is focused on the work performed, and no one lays a claim to a particular part of the shop.

2) Select the major shop tools. Your shop may need highly specialized tools for maintaining the particular equipment of your industry; in additon the typical shop will need grinders, pipe threaders, bench saws, lathes, welders, and drill presses. The number, size, complexity, and degree of automation of each should be economically justified.

3) Provide auxiliary equipment. Hydraulic lift tables, automatic hoists, roller conveyors, and lift trucks for easy handling of equipment to be worked on. Wheeled tool boxes, motorized carts for moving individuals quickly to and from jobs in the plant. Pickup truck

or station wagon for moving small loads and making trips to hardware stores and supply points outside the plant.

Time Records and Charging Out Costs

The maintenance department is a service department, and all of its expenses should be charged out to the plant departments which use its services (except for small expenditures to maintain the shop itself). The major and minor work order forms provide the most convenient means for distributing maintenance costs. The originator of either document is required to include the operating account expense number or the capital appropriation number to which the cost of the work is to be charged. (Maintenance supervision should be instructed not to accept a work order without a suitable account number, and to raise questions if they doubt that the originator has the authority to charge costs to the account number given.) When the job is completed the total costs of labor and materials can be entered on the work order, which is forwarded to the cost department for posting to the proper accounts.

Individual time records have a dual purpose—they record the proportion of a mechanic's time applied to each of the jobs he works on, and therefore provide a way of costing out all of his time. They are also used to compare the time expended on a particular job with established standards or previous executions of the same job.

There are several ways of keeping individual time records. One is to print a form on the back of the work order, and each mechanic who works on the job enters his name or clock number, the time he spends on the job, and any materials he uses. A maintenance department clerk or someone in the accounting department can cross-total the hours listed to be sure each mechanic's time is fully accounted for.

Another way is to have each mechanic fill out a separate card for each day's work, showing the time he spent on each job. Maintenance supervision collects these cards at the end of each day, checks to see that each man's time is fully accounted for, and forwards them to the cost department for posting to the appropriate account numbers.

No matter what system is used, the collected papers—completed work orders, time cards, and material requisitions associated with the job—should be forwarded to the originator after they have been through the accounting department. He has a right to check out the charges, to see that they have been properly allocated, and to discuss with maintenance supervision any question he may have about the costs charged to his account.

Maintenance Supplies

The plant manager needs to assure himself of three results from his maintenance stores program: 1) that supplies are purchased at the lowest available price; 2) that they are used economically in the plant with little waste, and that they are charged out to the jobs and departments which actually use them; 3) that critical supplies are available when needed.

Use these techniques for stores purchasing:

1. Obtain competitive bids before choosing suppliers. There is an understandable tendency for maintenance supervision to buy from the nearest suppliers and those which offer the most convenient service. Usually, however, competitors can be found who will match the best service available in order to get the business.

2. Write annual contracts to get the largest discounts.

3. Whenever possible have the supplier, rather than your storeroom, maintain inventories.

4. Involve the purchasing department in the stores program; they can offer professional assistance in dealing with suppliers on the three previous points.

These are the basic principles in the control of stores usage in the plant:

1. Keep small, valuable, and "popular" items in specially locked compartments.

2. Very inexpensive items (nuts, bolts, small pipe fittings) may not be worth the expense of cataloguing and following with paperwork. They can be declared "free stock" and kept in bins in the shop for general usage without requisitions.

3. Conduct periodic inventories and audits, just as you would for production materials and supplies.

4. Control the issuance of supplies:

a. The large plant may use several storerooms, with a trained storekeeper manning each one. All items are listed in a printed catalogue with a control number suited to electronic data processing. Stores are issued only by written requisition showing the job or account number to be charged. Information from the requisition slips is fed into a computer to charge out costs, keep a perpetual total inventory in dollars, and remind the storekeeper when a reorder point is reached for any item.

b. Medium-sized plant. One storeroom with a full-time storekeeper. May not have printed catalogue, but requisitions are required; posting of charges to job numbers and accounts is done manually, as well as the monitoring of inventory for reorder.

c. Small plant. Storekeeping may be part-time job for maintenance foreman, clerk, or other maintenance department employee. Requisitioner may be simply required to sign out for materials in a log book. Reordering is based on visual charges out costs periodically from log book. Reordering is based on visual inspection.

To be sure that supplies will be on hand when needed:

1) Classify all stores items into critical and non-critical categories. Critical items are those which would result in unacceptable production delays or safety hazards if they are not on hand.

2) Establish maximum and minimum stock levels and reorder points for the critical items. The reorder point is set far enough above the minimum level to allow for anticipated usage during the period between reorder and delivery of the material.

Outside Contractors

All manufacturing plants use outside contractor services for various maintenance and project jobs from time to time, for these reasons:

1. They can handle peak loads without disrupting the normal work of the regular plant maintenance staff.

2. They complement plant forces, supplying skills which the latter may not have.

3. They can do some (or possibly all) of the maintenance work more cheaply.

Outside contractors are used to supply these services:

1) Maintenance operations which are sporadic, seasonal, or require specialized skills: painting, cleaning, window washing, vermin control, landscaping, testing and adjustment of scales, servicing control instruments, boiler cleaning, and railroad track repair.

2) Major equipment overhauls and capital projects.

3) All or part of regular mechanical maintenance operations. This is the famous "contract

maintenance" question, and in determining your answer to it keep these points in mind: If yours is a new plant you can start out with all contract maintenance and change to regular maintenance forces later, but you can't do it the other way around. The cost charged per hour of contract labor will seem high compared to the base rate of your own workers, but the cost of fringes, supervision, and other types of overhead must be added to your workers' base rates. And there is a high cost penalty for having permanent personnel on the payroll during slack periods. A mathematical method for determining the optimum ratio between permanent and contract maintenance forces is given by J.H. Jordan in "How to Evaluate the Advantages of Contract Maintenance," *Chemical Engineering,* Vol. 75, No. 8, March 25, 1968, pp. 124-130.

When outside help is being considered or is actually in the plant, take these precautions:

1) If either his shop or yours is non-union, and the other unionized, iron out any possible problems with all parties concerned before any outside forces report to work.

2) Make sure that all outside personnel are trained in, understand, and actually follow plant safety rules.

3) There is a natural tendency for outside personnel to use or borrow your tools and supplies, Clarify the question of who supplies these items beforehand, and instruct your people to refuse requests outside of those arrangements.

Measuring Maintenance Performance

This is a more sophisticated task than the measuring of production performance in units of output in a given time or percentage of first quality production. There are two fundamental steps in establishing a system for measuring maintenance performance:

1) Establish work standards. This can be as simple as the foreman estimating that it will take two men a half day to perform a certain job—in fact, the mere act of scheduling requires him to make just such a judgment. When the same job is repeated many times through the course of a year (such as the replacement of filter elements in a dust collection system), a standard number of man-hours for the completion of the job can be readily established, and all future executions of the job measured against standard. When it is undesirable to wait until a substantial history can be built up, or when there are too many tasks and not enough people to gather the past history, standards can be obtained from outside sources, such as the U.S. Navy Department Maintenance Standards.

2) Set up a numerical index and follow its trends. Some simple indexes might be total dollars spent per month in maintenance, total dollars for maintenance labor, cost of supplies, or hours of overtime. Even more useful indexes can be developed by taking the ratio of these factors to relevant plant variables—for instance, total maintenance dollars divided by units of plant output, or maintenance man-hours. There is no one index which is right for every plant; establish one or more which reveals conditions in your maintenance operation which you want to control.

A large selection of useful indexes is given in G.W. Smith, "Maintenance Planning/Scheduling-Measuring the Results," *Plant Engineering* Vol. 23, No. 3, February 6, 1969, pp. 57-59, encompassing such areas as maintenance productivity, coverage, backlog, level of maintenance, and cost of maintenance.

CONCLUSION

The plant manager looks to the maintenance department to provide vital and unique services for the attainment of the overall operations goals, but he also recognizes that maintenance costs can quickly escalate unless close control is maintained. He begins by setting up an organization with maximum flexibility in the assignment of personnel and with the most efficient worker-supervisor teams. Then he supplies shop facilities which are economically justified and closely matched to the true needs of the department.

Operational control of the maintenance function is achieved by setting up major and minor work order systems for initiation, approval, and follow-up of jobs; by establishing a program of preventive maintenance so that only a minimum amount of work is done on a "crash" basis; and by scheduling all maintenance activities so that they can be properly planned. When outside contractors or contract maintenance are employed, special steps are taken to forestall the problems which can arise in their relationships with plant personnel.

Tight control of costs is maintained by requiring time records of the work performed, and by charging out maintenance expense to the using departments. Maintenance supplies are purchased competitively, issued under control, and charged to the jobs on which they are used. Finally, performance of the entire department is measured by the trends of indexes devised to relate costs to activity level.

Chapter 8

Applying Quality Control Techniques to Improve Overall Performance

In no other aspect of manufacturing operations is the interlocking nature of the plant manager's responsibilities more clearly illuminated than in that of quality control. His achievements in plant output are meaningless if the material produced is defective and cannot be shipped to the customer. His battle with costs cannot be won if the plant must repeatedly bear the expense of rework and scrap. Employee relations are certainly not enhanced by the recrimination that often follows off-grade production, and safety itself may be jeopardized in the handling of off-grade material which is structurally, mechanically, or chemically unstable.

Certain returns are expected by the plant manager from his expenditure of effort and money on the quality function. Of course he requires testing of finished goods and a monthly report on plant performance. But he also wants quick resolution of quality problems, effective investigation of customer complaints, and an overall approach to quality which prevents, rather than merely corrects, quality problems. And all of this at a cost which the price structure of the product can support.

The plant manager looks at quality, therefore, in its broadest phases—not just the testing of output, but a whole array of concerns, values, and activities which will keep him ahead in the endless race for better quality at lower cost.

Where to Start on Quality

The broad view of quality requires the plant manager to involve himself with these critical stages in quality development:

1) Product design. If the blueprints, formulas, or job orders are so drawn that the plant manager believes the products made from them will not meet specifications, he must register his objection before production begins.

2) Raw material purchase. Often raw materials are purchased without any specifications, or so loosely specified that there is no assurance that finished goods specifications can be met. The plant manager must assure himself that raw material quality is capable of producing required finished goods quality.

3) Equipment procurement. When manufacturing tools and equipment are purchased the plant manager must satisfy himself that the materials of construction will not detract from

product quality, that there will be no contamination of product by lubricants, that designs for sampling devices are included, that control instrumentation is adequate for quality needs, and that the performance warranty covers quality of finished product.

4) Sales vs. manufacturing specifications. As illogical as it may sound, cases have occurred in which the sales literature for a product contains specifications different from those used by the manufacturing department in making it. When manufacturing specifications are tighter than sales specifications, money is wasted in producing unnecessarily high quality; when the situation is reversed customer complaints and rejection of shipments are the inevitable result.

5) Operating procedures. General shop orders and plant operating procedures should not only spell out the steps for carrying out process operations, but should also instruct the operator in the precautions he must take to protect product quality.

How to Organize the Quality Control Department

Smaller plants may require only a basic testing group; larger plants and those with more complicated technology need more elaborate quality organizations. These are the basic considerations for setting up a quality control department:

1) Establish the basic testing group. It is the nucleus of the department, and in many plants is the entire department. It consists of inspectors or quality control technicians who perform a series of standard tests on raw materials, in-process work, and finished goods. They pass or reject the material tested on the basis of objective, predetermined specifications; display test information for the benefit of the plant operators; maintain sample files; and report the results of accumulated quality records to the plant manager.

2) Specialize and add. As the plant grows, the basic group can be divided into sections which specialize in raw material, in-process, and finished goods testing. But more fundamental changes come when the department branches out by establishing sections for Statistical Methods, Value Analysis, Vendor Evaluation, and Quality Engineering.

3) Choose between salaried and hourly personnel. The present trend in industry is toward salaried personnel for inspectors and quality control technicians. While some economies may be realized by the use of hourly employees, there is a problem of split loyalty and peer pressure when they are called upon to reject material produced by their associates.

4) Fix reporting relationships. The quality control department usually reports to some level of production management for two reasons: quality of line product is the responsibility of production management, and the speed and accuracy with which testing is performed affects the flow of production material through the plant.

How to Develop Test Procedures

The results produced by the quality control department can be no better than the tests it uses to measure quality. Test methods must be carefully chosen to ensure that the customer is getting the properties he is paying for, and to uncover processing errors in the plant. They must be accurately performed on representative samples if the true status of quality is to be known. And to be sure that differences in the way individual technicians perform the tests do not give a false impression of product variability, publish a detailed test procedure manual and insist that its instructions be rigorously observed.

1) Sampling techniques. Because tests must be performed on a very small sample of the product it is essential that the sample be *representative* of the entire lot. To get representative samples, a) select material at random from various parts of the batch, b) if the

system to be sampled is fluid, be sure it is well mixed before sampling, c) if the process is continuous, sample it at intervals spread throughout the production shift, and d) have a well-trained, responsible person take the sample and label it clearly. The design of sampling techniques can be further refined by the application of statistical mathematics to the sampling problem.

2) Raw materials.

a. Get agreement with the supplier, not only on the specifications, but on the test methods to be used. Much fruitless debate will result if he is using a different test than yours.

b. Reliable suppliers will often perform quality tests and report the results at no additional expense to you. When these services are used, verify the results with an occasional spot check.

c. When the plant cannot afford to test all of the raw materials received, select on the basis of quantity, value of each shipment, and importance to the quality of finished product.

3) In-process materials. The minimum contribution of in-process testing is to remove defective material early in the production process, before money is wasted on subsequent steps. Beyond that it provides a basis for corrective action, so that material which is off-grade at an early stage can be processed to a successful quality conclusion. Economy can often be achieved by training process operators to perform some of the tests, and there is a growing trend to instrumentation which monitors the process—beta ray thickness gauges, in-line pH meters, chromatographs, and viscosimeters.

4) Finished goods. These are the most important tests of all because they offer the last opportunity to prevent defective product from getting to the customer. Ordinarily the quality control department is empowered to release finished goods for shipment if all test results are within specification limits.

The principle of *product integrity* must not be forgotten at the time of final qualification of product (see Chapter 1). If any foreman or supervisor knows of any significant processing deviation or adverse quality attribute, he should be empowered and encouraged to suspend shipment of the material until the plant manager can render a decision, *even though it meets standard quality specifications.*

5) Sources of test methods.

a. Suppliers and customers. When you buy from or sell to a large organization, its technical staff may have standard quality tests which they will make available to you. Besides being an inexpensive way to acquire test methods, it eliminates disagreement over what tests are to be used in quality evaluation.

b. National organizations. The American Society for Testing and Materials (ASTM) publishes a wide variety of quality standards and test methods. A catalog can be obtained by writing to the society at 1916 Race Street, Philadelphia, Pa. 19103. The American National Standards Institute (formerly the United States of America Standards Institute) at 1430 Broadway, New York, N.Y. 10018, offers similar services.

c. Manufacturers' associations and technical societies. The National Electric Manufacturer's Association (NEMA) is an outstanding example of the many industrial associations which develop and publish quality standards for their products. The American Society of Mechanical Engineers (ASME) and the American Society of Heating and Ventilating Engineers (ASHVE) are examples of technical societies which publish product codes and test methods for materials and equipment.

d. Develop your own. Employees of the quality control department should be encouraged to devise test methods where none exist, and to suggest simpler and cheaper versions of existing tests.

Statistical Techniques: The Normal Distribution

The science of statistics has placed in the hands of the quality control manager very powerful tools for the analysis and interpretation of quality measurements collected in the plant. The most important of them is the curve of the normal distribution, shown in Exhibit 1.

When a large number of measurements of a single attribute are made (the weights of a thousand children in the seventh grade, the diameters of six hundred shafts turned out in a plant, the viscosities of nine hundred resin batches made in a chemical plant), a graph of the individual measurements against the frequency with which they occur often approximates the bell-shaped curve known as the normal distribution, one example of which is shown in Exhibit 1. Measurements are plotted along the horizontal axis, and the frequency with which they occur on the vertical axis. The average value is at the center of the curve and occurs most frequently. The spread of the data around the average is measured by the value of σ, which is the distance from the average to the point of inflection of the curve. 68.3 percent of all the values will fall within the span of σ on either side of the average, known as the "one sigma limits." 95.4 percent will fall within the two sigma limits, and 99.7 percent within the three sigma limits, as shown on the graph.

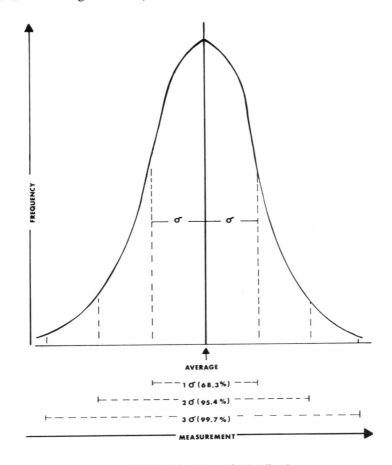

Exhibit 1. The Normal Distribution

In statistical terminology, when all of the individuals in a population are measured and plotted in the frequency distribution, the average is designated by the Greek letter mu (μ), and, as we have seen, the spread of the data, or the *standard deviation* by the Greek letter sigma (σ). It is seldom possible to measure all of the individuals in a population, and the average and standard deviation are often estimated from a sample of the population; when this is done they are designated as $\overline{X}$ (pronounced "X-bar") and s respectively.

The way which the average and standard deviation is calculated is shown in Table I. In this case twenty measurements from a manufacturing process are listed in the left-hand column, headed "X."

Table I.

X	X - $\overline{X}$	(X - $\overline{X}$)^2
2.935	-.063	.003969
3.083	.085	.007225
3.082	.084	.007056
3.086	.088	.007744
3.003	.005	.000025
3.003	.005	.000025
2.998	.000	.000000
2.972	-.026	.000676
2.965	-.033	.001089
3.006	.008	.000064
2.903	-.095	.009025
2.958	-.040	.001600
2.968	-.030	.000900
3.095	.097	.009409
2.928	-.070	.004900
2.981	-.017	.000289
3.024	.026	.000676
2.919	-.079	.006241
3.022	.024	.000576
3.038	.040	.001600
ΣX = 59.969		$\Sigma(X - \overline{X})^2$ = .063089

Table I.

The twenty measurements are added up, and their total indicated at the base of the left hand column by the symbol ΣX (the upper case Greek letter sigma, Σ, denotes summation, and can be read "sum of"). The average is the sum of the measurements divided by their number, N, and in statistical notation becomes

$$\overline{X} = \frac{\Sigma X}{N}$$

In our example, ΣX is 59.969 and N is 20. The average is therefore

$$\overline{X} = \frac{59.969}{20} = 2.998$$

The standard deviation is calculated by the formula

$$s = \sqrt{\frac{\Sigma (X - \overline{X})^2}{N - 1}}$$

In Table I the figures in the column marked X - $\overline{X}$ are obtained by subtracting the average from each of the individual measurements. In the third column this quantity is squared, yielding $(X - \overline{X})^2$. By adding the figures in the third column we obtain $\Sigma (X - \overline{X})^2$, or in the example given, .063089. Since N - 1 = 19, the standard deviation becomes

$$s = \sqrt{\frac{.063089}{19}} = .0576$$

Using this sample of twenty measurements as an approximation of the entire population from which it is drawn, we would expect the process to yield an average measurement of 2.998, and that 99.7 percent of the output will fall within $\pm$ 3 x .0576 or $\pm$ .173 of the average. The larger the number of measurements N in the sample, the more closely $\overline{X}$ will approximate the true average μ, and s the true standard deviation, σ.

Statistical Techniques: The Quality Control Chart

If the quality measurements of the output from an industrial process follow the normal distribution, the parameters of that distribution can be used to develop a very useful monitoring device called the Quality Control Chart. The straight-line axes of the normal distribution (see Exhibit 1) are rotated ninety degrees to the right, and the average line becomes a horizontal solid line, while the 3 σ limit lines are drawn above and below it (as dotted lines). The measurement axis is now vertical rather than horizontal. As samples are taken from the process they are numbered successively, and the quality result for each sample plotted on the chart.

This process is illustrated in Exhibit 2, which depicts some of the important features of an industrial quality control chart. In this case the solid center line is the average line, but on some charts the center line is placed at the quality target rather than the actual average of the process. The positive and negative 3 σ dotted lines are labeled "Upper Control Limit" (UCL) and "Lower Control Limit" (LCL) in control chart terminology. The samples are numbered consecutively, and the quality measurement for each represented by a round circle; the circles are connected by straight lines to aid in visualizing what the process is doing.

One very important benefit to be derived from the control chart is the intelligent setting of product specifications. If they are set at the upper and lower control limits, the process can be expected to produce 99.7 percent acceptable quality. If they are set narrower than the control limits, plant personnel are doomed to struggle indefinitely to satisfy quality standards which the process is incapable of meeting. If specifications are set too far outside the natural limits of the process, sloppy production practices will begin to appear in the plant; in addition, a competitive advantage is lost in the marketplace if the product specifications are set at a wider range than the process can normally produce.

The use of the control chart in monitoring the production process is shown in these interpretations of the quality patterns in Exhibit 2:

1. From points 1 through 10 the process is in good control. The points fall above and below the average line in random pattern (if seven points fell on one

side of the line it would indicate a shift in process average), and there are no disturbing trends.

2. Point 11 and the seven points following constitute a trend; the chart is telling us that something has happened in the process to push quality measurements toward the high side, and if left unchecked, will eventually result in off-grade quality.

3. Point 18, labeled "P," lies above the upper control limit and is the culmination of the trend which we saw starting at Point 11. But even if point P were not at the end of a trend it would still be significant. We expect that 99.7

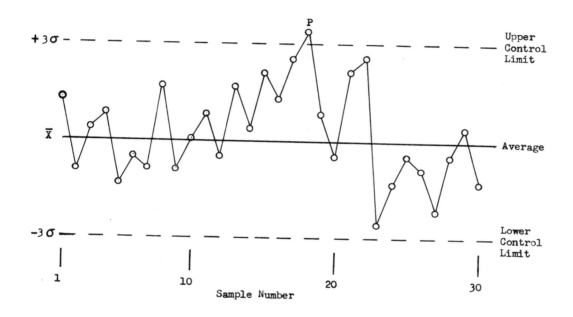

Exhibit 2. Industrial Quality Control Chart

percent of the material produced will lie within the 3σ limits, or that only 3 measurements out of 1,000 will lie outside. Another way of putting it is to say that the odds are 333 to 1 that point P is not part of the normal variation of the process, but is the result of an *assignable cause*—some factor which changed the process. Whatever the factor turns out to be, it may or may not affect the points on either side of P.

4. The spread between points 22 and 23 could be a case of "overcontrol." Someone became nervous when point 22 approached the upper control limit (even though it may have been part of the normal process variation) and ordered a major adjustment of process controls. The result was a sudden shift to the low

side, with seven of the last eight points falling below the normal process average; it will probably require another adjustment to bring it back up to desired levels. Had the process been left alone at point 22 the second adjustment would not be necessary, and a more satisfactory quality level would have been achieved.

Many industrial quality control departments use a refinement of the quality control chart called the Shewhart chart for averages and ranges. In this system individual measurements from the process are not plotted as in Exhibit 2; instead the measurements are grouped together in samples of n̲ individuals. The average of each sample is plotted as one point on a chart for averages; the range, that is, the difference between the highest and lowest measurement in each sample, is plotted on another chart. Special statistical tables are used to find the control limits for each of these charts. The Shewhart system offers these advantages: 1) When averages of samples are plotted in a frequency distribution the resulting curve is closer to a normal distribution than if individual measurements are plotted, 2) both the level of quality (average chart) and the variability (range chart) of the process are constantly monitored, and 3) upward or downward trends in either level or variability stand out more clearly.

Statistical Techniques: Assorted Useful Methods

The following methods of statistical analysis will be of value in solving specific industrial quality problems:

1. The *Student t* test is used to determine whether the average of a sample (say a week's quality measurements) is significantly different from the averages of the total population (overall plant output).
2. The *F test* is used to determine whether the variances of two samples are significantly different so that it can be assumed, at a given level of probability, that they did not come from the same population.
3. A number of techniques under the general heading of *Analysis of Variance* are used when it is desired to design experiments to reveal the effects of a number of variables on a process result. Not only do these techniques cut down the number of experiments needed to determine the effect of the variables, but they also reveal interactions between the variables.
4. *Regression* and *Correlation* techniques are used to study the relationship between two process variables, and to draw the best straight line through a plot of the data.
5. *Evolutionary Operation* (EVOP) is an elaborate statistical technique which is applied in the plant on regular process operations. Small changes (so as not to risk off-grade production) are repeatedly made in the process, and the results analyzed to indicate the directions in which process variables should be changed to give the best possible quality and yield.

Quality Control and the Cost Function

The value of the overall quality operation must be measured in terms of its impact on production costs; it is no more privileged in this respect than any other phase of plant operation. Costs incurred must be weighed against the benefits they produce. Use these factors when making judgments:
Cost benefits:

1. Reduce or eliminate the cost of material which must be discarded, reworked, or sold at distress prices because of poor quality.

2. Reduce or eliminate costs incurred because of customer dissatisfaction, lawsuits, or warranty replacement of goods.

3. Competitive advantage and increased sales resulting from improved quality performance.

Reduction of quality control costs:

In attempting to strike a balance between the benefits derived and the dollars spent on quality control, the plant manager will be constantly searching for ways to reduce its cost of operation. Look for opportunities in these areas:

1. Keep the number of tests performed on each product at a minimum. Perhaps measuring four attributes will serve as well as measuring six.

2. Keep each test as simple as possible. Avoid complicated or delicate test apparatus when there is a simpler way.

3. One hundred percent testing is not always necessary. Often statistical techniques can be applied to allow testing a fraction of the output while still maintaining a reliable evaluation of quality.

4. Wherever possible install process instruments to eliminate testing.

CONCLUSION

Quality control is not an end to be served in itself, but an interrelated function which must make its contribution to the overall operation, and the plant manager looks for specific economic returns from the financial investment which he commits to quality control. In developing the quality control organization he starts with the basic product and raw material testing group, and adds specialized units as the size and complexity of the plant operation increase. He seeks technical help from every available source to minimize the amount of testing and to obtain the best test methods. He acquires a basic training in statistical techniques so that he can understand, or even take the lead in their application, ensuring that the powerful analytical tools available from this source will be used. Above all he develops respect for product integrity in his organization, and a pervasive concern with product quality in the related areas of product design, raw material procurement, capital equipment purchases, the setting of sales specifications, and the drafting of operating procedures.

Chapter 9

Meeting Higher Standards for Safety and Housekeeping

The attitudes of plant managers and their seniors toward safety and housekeeping have been maturing over the past several decades, and they have come to understand the impact of these responsibilities on each other and on the remaining plant functions of production, cost, and quality. No longer are safety and housekeeping ignored in the evaluation of plant manager's performance. And the managers themselves increasingly recognize the value of these important tools for improving employee relationships. Overlying these aspects is a stringent new federal law requiring adherence to detailed safety standards.

In this chapter we will consider all aspects of safety at the plant manager's level, including responsibility, impact on costs, the plant safety program, safety procedures, accident statistics, fire prevention, sources of safety information, and the Occupational Safety and Health Act. The second section deals with the reasons for and techniques of carrying out an effective housekeeping program.

SAFETY

Responsibility for Safety

There is no escaping the basic principle: Safety is a *line* responsibility. Staff people can offer assistance in a variety of important ways, but accident and property loss prevention is the job of the foremen, superintendents, managers, and their superiors in the manufacturing line organization. Any safety program which is based on delegation or dilution of this responsibility is doomed to failure.

Foremen especially must understand that they are responsible for all aspects of safety performance in their departments—observance of safety rules, training of new employees, and accident prevention. Above all they must not be allowed to develop the notion that safety performance is the concern of the personnel department, the safety department, or "someone else" in the corporate organization.

What Accidents Cost

The humanitarian aspects of a good safety program are obvious, and any responsible manager and his corporation would find them sufficient justification for the program. But neither can afford to lose sight of the impact of accidents on one of their most important performance criteria: costs.

In 1972 workmen's compensation payments to injured employees averaged $400 for transitory lost-time accidents, $2,900 for cases involving permanent injury, and $24,200 for fatalities.* Although these are "insurance" payments, they may be charged back to the company almost dollar-for-dollar under some compensation insurance arrangements. These payments have been rising at an average rate of 7.5 percent per year, but more than that, they represent only the money paid for medical costs and wages. The hidden costs of an accident are estimated to double the figures given. Here are some of those hidden costs which add to the dollar toll of a plant accident:

Time lost by other workers—to help injured, discuss accident, etc.

Downtime; lost production; off-grade production.

Cost of overtime to replace injured worker, or train a new employee.

Legal costs, if lawsuits follow.

Time spent by supervisors and managers on investigations and reports.

Damage to machines and equipment—repair costs and replacement rental.

Special costs to meet shipping commitments—phone calls, telegrams, air freight, other special arrangements.

Establishing the Plant Safety Program

There are four basic elements to the plant manager's safety program:

1) Provide safe buildings and equipment. When new equipment is designed or proposed for purchase, or when new buildings are to be constructed, potential safety problems should be considered at the earliest stages of design. Safety features are of two kinds: those designed to *prevent* accidents, such as machinery guards, non-slip walking surfaces, electrical grounding, automatic cutoff devices, spark suppression, pressure relief, etc., and; those designed to *minimize injury and damage* after an accident occurs, such as fire extinguishers, sprinklers, hose houses, safety showers, eye baths, fire doors, first aid equipment, emergency lights, alternate exits, fire alarm systems, etc.

2) Formulate rules for safe practices. Publish the rules in writing, and cover these points:

a. Personal protective equipment. Specify equipment which must be worn all the time in work areas, such as safety shoes, hard hats, and safety glasses. Then specify equipment which must be worn for special operations—welding masks, goggles, face shields, acid suits, rubber gloves, rescue harness.

b. Plant conduct. Forbid running, sudden loud noises, horseplay. Require attendance at safety meetings, cooperation with fire drills and training exercises. Call for reporting of hazards and unsafe conditions.

c. Performance of work. Spell out the safety precautions to be followed in the operation of machinery and the transportation of materials through the plant.

d. Handling of hazardous materials. Identify raw materials and in-process work which poses special hazards to personnel, tell what the hazards are, and the safe methods of avoiding them.

e. What to do in case of accident or emergency. Instruct personnel to report all accidents to foremen. If fire, power failure, flood or other emergency occurs, employees should be well rehearsed in the procedures you want followed— whether to leave equipment running or shut it down, whether to fight fire or evacuate immediately (see Chapter 6).

3) Train personnel. When safe equipment has been provided and plant rules established, the never-ending job of safety training begins. It starts with the first-line supervisor, who

---

*As reported by National Safety Council in *Accident Facts,* 1972 Edition.

should carefully instruct all new employees in safe work procedures. He should also be required to hold regular, short safety meetings with his group, accenting topics relevant to its work assignment. Safety meetings for larger groups should be conducted by the plant personnel manager, safety engineer, or line superintendents and managers. These meetings can cover more general topics, and can be livened by the use of motion pictures and guest speakers. Regular drills to practice evacuation, fire-fighting, and rescue techniques should be held. The program can be rounded out by the use of safety contests, posters, and awards as means of keeping employees' attention focused on the subject.

4) Enforce regulations. The quickest way for the plant manager to measure the degree of compliance with safety rules is to walk through the plant and make his own visual observations. If he discovers violations, he brings them to the attention of the foreman of the area for correction; he never attempts to correct the erring employee himself. Accident investigations are another source of information on the degree of compliance. It is important to keep in mind that if an individual accident report is used primarily as an enforcement tool, it can lose its effectiveness; however, if a large number of accident reports reveal repeated employee failure to follow rules, the manager knows he must step up his education and enforcement programs. Another useful enforcement tool is the periodic safety inspection conducted by a plant committee which files a formal written report. Inspections can be made competitive among the departments as a way of stimulating interest.

SAFE WORK PERMIT

Date_____

_____ is authorized to
(Name of person performing work)
_____ on _____
(Work to be performed)   (Equipment to be worked on)
                                                PM
in Department _____, Section (Floor or Building) _____, between _____ AM and
AM
_____ PM . The equipment to be worked on has been prepared (circle one or more: shut down, drained, cleaned, depressurized, disconnected, locked out, fuses removed, other _____) for maintenance work. The following safety precautions are to be observed by persons performing this work:

☐ Tank entry permit required.
☐ Fire permit required.
☐ Other _____.
☐ Other _____.   Signed _____

Exhibit 1. Safe Work Permit

Issue Safety Procedures

Provide each operating department with its own set of safety procedures. They can be written by department superintendents (or even foremen with an aptitude for it) but should be reviewed and approved by the plant manager. Publish them in typewritten form, with the pages inserted into acetate envelopes and bound in sturdy covers. Distribute them throughout the operating areas of the plant for easy access to all operating employees.

Contents should include the general plant rules and then go on to cover the special safety hazards of the individual department—dangerous materials, precautions in the use of tools and equipment, safe handling of heat, electrical, or radioactive energy, use of vehicles, and instructions for emergencies. The procedures should not fail to set forth the safety requirements for work performed in the department by outside agencies, such as the maintenance department or contractors.

Exhibit 1 is an example of how the safety conditions surrounding outside work can be controlled. It is issued by the foreman of the department where the work is to be done after he has seen that the necessary precautions have been taken. It authorizes the mechanic to begin work at a certain time, and limits the period in which he may work. Since the foreman's authority does not extend beyond his shift, the authorization automatically terminates at the end of the shift, and the oncoming foreman countersigns or re-issues it for an additional time period. The safe work permit can be made up in pads of printed forms; some plants find it handy to have it printed on the back of the Maintenance Job Order (Exhibit 1, Chapter 7).

The issuance of separate safety procedures is not the end of the plant's effort to specify safe work practices. Every shop order and operating procedure should contain a brief statement of the safety hazards which will be encountered in the work it describes, and the precautions taken to offset them. Required safety steps should be matter-of-factly included in the detailed instructions for performing the operation.

Investigate Accidents

Zero accidents is the goal of the plant safety program; therefore, when an accident occurs it represents a failure of the program in some aspect to some degree. The only way in which these failures can be studied and remedied is through thorough accident investigation. Use these guidelines:

1. It is essential that the investigation be reported in writing. Your insurance company will provide printed forms—or you can design your own. Exhibit 2 is an example of a supervisor's accident report form.

2. Include the names of the injured and any witnesses, the date, time, and place of the accident, degree of injury sustained, a narrative report of exactly how the accident happened, and what machinery, tools, equipment, or vehicles were involved.

3. The investigation report should be filled out immediately following the accident by the foreman of the area in which it took place.

4. The investigation is not a witch hunt. Its objective is not to fix blame as much as to find preventable cause.

5. The report form should ask for a statement by the foreman as to why the accident happened and how it can be prevented in the future.

6. Include near misses, especially where the injury could have been serious or fatal.

7. File reports in a central place where they can be tabulated and studied. Use them as a basis for devising safety rules, and for deciding where to put emphasis in safety training.

Safety Statistics

A system of scoring safety performance is needed so that managers can observe trends, compare plants, and measure the results of steps taken to reduce accidents. Two statistics are widely used in the United States—*frequency* and *severity*. Both are calculated according

SUPERVISOR'S ACCIDENT REPORT

☐ Injury ☐ Near-Miss   Date of report _____

Accident location _____ Date _____ Time _____ AM
                                                                                               PM

Describe how accident took place, including personnel, machinery, tools, equipment, and vehicles
involved _____

_____

_____

_____

Name of injured _____ Dept. _____ Badge/Clock No. _____

Describe injuries _____

☐ First Aid   ☐ Treated by doctor   ☐ Taken to _____ hospital

Lost time _____ days (☐ estimated ☐ actual). Was injured wearing or using required
safety equipment? Explain _____

_____

What action can be taken to prevent this accident from happening again? _____

_____

_____

Action ☐ has been completed ☐ will be competed by _____ (date).

Supervisor's signature _____

Exhibit 2. Supervisor's Accident Report Form

to American Standards code Z 16.1, Method of Recording and Measuring Work Injury Experience.

Frequency is a numerical index of how often accidents are occurring in the plant, without reference to how serious they are. It is the number of disabling injuries divided by the number of employee-hours of exposure multiplied by one million. A plant which has had three lost-time accidents after working 500,000 man-hours has a frequency of

$$\frac{3 \times 1,000,000}{500,000} = 6.0$$

Severity is a measure of the seriousness of the accidents which do occur. It is the number of man-days lost because of injuries divided by the number of employee-hours of exposure multiplied by one million. In the example give above, if the three accidents had resulted in the loss of a total of fifty-seven man-days, the severity would be

$$\frac{57 \times 1,000,000}{500,000} = 114$$

These statistics are usually calculated on both a monthly and an annual basis. A detailed explanation of the rules used in defining disabling injuries and employee hours can be found in the American Standard code, or in an excellent presentation in *Accident Prevention Manual for Industrial Operations* (5th ed., Chicago: National Safety Council, 1964) pp. 9-11 to 9-22.

Sources of Safety Information

The field of industrial safety is a highly developed technology, and much of the work involved in making a manufacturing process safe requires the application of specialized information. The plant manager and those whom he designates to assist him in the development of the safety program can turn to these sources for this information:

1) The National Safety Council. A non-profit national organization chartered by Congress, and dedicated to the prevention of accidental injury by the gathering and dissemination of safety information. It publishes six safety periodicals, annual compilations of accident statistics, and several accident prevention manuals. It also conducts safety training courses at its Chicago headquarters, and sponsors the annual National Safety Congress. It welcomes industrial corporations as members.

2) Trade Associations. These industrial groups, formed to promote the general interests of their respective industries and member companies, often supply very good safety information. An outstanding example is the Manufacturing Chemist's Association, which publishes an extensive series of *Chemical Safety Data Sheets* covering the properties, hazards, and safe handling methods for specific chemicals. There is almost sure to be a trade association offering safety information relevant to one or more of your plant's operations, as indicated by this very small sample: Steel Plate Fabricator's Association, American Welding Society, Milk Industry Foundation, Adhesives Manufacturers Association of America, Portland Cement Association, and Printing Industry of America, Inc.

3) Government Agencies. A number of departments of the Federal Government issue publications on various safety topics. The Superintendent of Documents, Government Printing Office, Washington, D.C. 20402, publishes Price List No. 78, which is a compilation of the government publications on health, hygiene, safety, and compensation.

State agencies and the federal Occupational Safety and Health Administration deal specifically with the issuance and enforcement of industrial safety codes and health regulations. You should be familiar with these regulations, since they represent the minimum legal standards for conditions in your plant. (See the section on the Occupational Safety and Health Act in this chapter.)

Regulations concerning the storage and transportation of flammable liquids are promulgated by the Department of State Police in many states, and are detailed in the OSHA standards.

4) Insurance Groups and Special Organizations. If your workmen's compensation insurance carrier is a large company, it probably provides a wide range of inspection, advisory, and educational services. It may also offer help through the American Mutual Insurance Alliance in Chicago or the Association of Casualty and Insurance Companies in New York; both offer a variety of safety manuals on specific topics. Your fire insurance carrier probably provides inspection and fire protection services through the Factory Insurance Association (FIA) in Hartford, Conn. or the Factory Mutual Engineering Division (FM) in Norwood, Mass. The National Board of Fire Underwriters in New York, Underwriter's Laboratories in Chicago, and the National Fire Protection Association in Boston all conduct research and issue publications on a wide variety of fire protection topics.

Fire Prevention

Three ingredients are required to start a fire: an accumulation of combustible material (solid, liquid, or gas), oxygen, and a source of ignition. Industrial fire prevention consists of the steps taken to preclude these three elements from coming together at the same time.

1) Accumulations of *solid* combustible material are controlled by engineering design which minimizes the use of wood and cloth in industrial buildings; by housekeeping practices which prevent the accumulation of combustible trash; and by limiting to 2,500 cubic feet the storage of empty boxes or similarly combustible materials in any one building

(Fire Prevention Code of the National Board of Fire Underwriters). *Liquids* and *gas* accumulations are forestalled by the proper venting of storage tanks, by rigidly controlled methods of transfer from vessel to vessel, by adequate ventilation of confined spaces, and by diligent maintenance of tanks, fittings, and pipelines to avoid spillage.

2) Oxygen is much more difficult to eliminate because it is present in air at a concentration of 21 percent by volume. Sometimes it is swept from the vapor space above flammable liquids in tanks by the introduction of gaseous nitrogen or carbon dioxide (neither of which supports combustion).

3) Much attention is given in industry to the elimination of sources of ignition. In many plants smoking or the carrying of matches and lighters is forbidden in working areas. Electric motors are of the totally enclosed type; electric and gasoline driven lift trucks are purchased with spark suppression systems. Electrical ground straps are used to dissipate a possible static potential difference between metal containers when flammable liquids are poured from one to the other. Tanks and vessels used for the storage and processing of flammables are electrically grounded to a copper plate buried in the ground. Static collector combs are installed to draw off static potential created by moving belts. Process operations which require the use of flame, or which repeatedly produce sparks, are carried out in isolated buildings or behind fire walls.

CLASS B FIRE PERMIT
(For spark-producing tools only. Not good for
welding or open flame work.)

Date_____.

_____ (is) (are) authorized to use the spark-producing
(Name of workmen)
tools or equipment checked:

☐ Steel hand tool. Specify_____ .　　☐ Electric tool. Specify_____ .

☐ Air-driven tool. Specify_____ .　　☐ Electric appliance or extension cord.
　　　　　　　　　　　　　　　　　　　　　　　Specify_____ .

☐ Other _____ .

in Building_____ at _____ between _____ AM
　　　　　　　　　　　　(Specific Location & Equip.)　　　　　　　　　　PM

and _____ AM. These precautions must be observed.
　　　　　　　PM

☐ One man must be assigned as fire watch.　　☐ Notify these persons before starting work:
　Name _____ .　　　　　　　　_____ , _____ , and _____ .

☐ Flammable vapor concentration test re-　　☐ Keep tool contact area wet with water.
　quired. Meter reading: _____ .

☐ Other _____ .　　　　　　　☐ Stop work at request of any employee.

Signed _____
　　　　　　　(Foreman)

Exhibit 3. Class B Fire Permit

A significant danger of ignition arises from sparks inadvertently produced by routine maintenance and welding operations in the plant. Exhibits 3 and 4 illustrate the way in which this danger is controlled. Exhibit 3 is a Class B Fire Permit, which must be filled out by the production foreman of the department before any work involving the use of spark-producing tools, such as hammer and chisel, star drill, hack saw, etc., is allowed to begin. The Class A permit shown in Exhibit 4 is used for welding and open flame operations, and should require the signature of a department superintendent or the plant manager himself. In both cases the conditions under which the work is carried out are carefully controlled. The forms can be printed up in pads; the fire insurance organizations may provide standardized versions at no charge. (Smaller plants may find it convenient to combine the two forms into one.)

CLASS A FIRE PERMIT
(Required for open flame work and welding.
Must be signed by Dept. Supt. or Plt. Mgr.)

Date _____.

_____(are) (is) authorized to use the open flame and welding de-
(Names of workmen)
vices checked below:

☐ Cutting torch.   ☐ Blow torch.
☐ Gas welder.   ☐ Electric welder.
☐ Lead or tar furnace.   ☐ Burn debris.
in Building _____ at _____ between
            AM   AM   (Specific location & Equip.)
_____PM and _____PM. These precautions must be observed:

☐ Foreman must sign before work is started   Lay out:
_____.   ☐ Fire hose, fully pressured.
☐ Stop work at request of any employee.   ☐ Fire exting. Type _____.
☐ Notify these persons before starting work: ☐ Names of men assigned as fire watch:
_____, _____, and _____.   _____, _____, and _____.
☐ Flammable vapor concentration test re-   (Must patrol floor above and below ½ hr.
quired. Meter reading: _____.   after completion of welding.)
☐ Remove combustible materials within 35   ☐ Other _____.
ft. radius of work.
                                               Signed _____.
                                                      (Dept. Supt. or Plt. Mgr.)

Exhibit 4. Class A Fire Permit

Occupational Safety and Health Act (OSHA)

The Williams-Steiger Occupational Safety and Health Act of 1970 applies to almost any conceivable manufacturing plant by defining an employer as "a person engaged in a business affecting commerce who has employees . . ." It establishes in federal law a wide-ranging set of safety requirements, including detailed safety and health standards, maintaining records of accidents and employee exposure to harmful materials, plant inspection by federal agents, and civil and criminal penalties for violations. Here is what you must do to comply:

1) Provide a work place free from recognized hazards and which meets specific safety and health standards put forth by the Act. These standards are contained in a government publication, *Occupational Safety and Health Standards,* Federal Register, Volume 37, No. 202, Part II, October 18, 1972. It is available from the Government Printing Office, North

Capitol and H Streets, N.W., Washington, D.C. 20401 for 20¢. The standards include these categories:

Walking-Working Surfaces

Occupational Health and Environmental Control

Personal Protective Equipment

Fire Protection

Machinery and Machine Guarding

Special Industries (Paper, textiles, bakery, laundry, sawmills, logging, and agriculture.)

Means of Egress

Hazardous Materials

General Environmental Controls

Compressed Gas and Compressed Air Equipment

Hand and Portable Powered Tools and Other Hand-Held Equipment

Powered Platforms, Man-lifts, and Vehicle-Mounted Work Platforms

Medical and First Aid

Materials Handling and Storage

Welding, Cutting and Brazing

Electrical

The standards are revised form time to time. You can obtain current information from the nearest Department of Labor office, or subscribe to a commercial newsletter service, such as the *Occupational Safety and Health Reporter* (published by The Bureau of National Affairs, Inc., Washington, D.C. 20037).

2) Post notices and keep records. You must post a notice supplied by the Occupational Safety and Health Administration informing your employees of their rights and the general provisions of the law. You must also post a copy of any violation citation received after an inspection (but you can post next to it a notice of your intent to contest the violation).

There are three types of records which must be kept at the plant site: 1) a log of occupational injuries and illness, 2) a detailed record of each injury and illness, and 3) an annual summary of occupational illnesses and injuries which must be posted by February 1 for the preceding year.

3) Undergo inspections. Your plant can be inspected at any time by a federal inspector, or a state inspector empowered under a federal-state agreement. The government may initiate the inspection, or be responding to a request by one of your employees. In either case, you must allow an employee representative to accompany the inspector. It is unlawful for anyone to give unauthorized advance notice of an inspection.

The inspector will look for generally recognized hazards, nonobservance of accepted industry standards, and violations of specific OSHA standards. The inspection may last for hours, days, or weeks. It will cover general health conditions (heat, noise, toxic fumes) as well as physical safety hazards.

The inspector will classify violations he finds in one of these categories:

Imminent danger. Immediate likelihood of death or serious injury. Labor Department will seek a court injunction to close down the plant.
Willful or repeated violations.
Serious violations. Substantial probability of death or injury.

Non-serious violations. Lower probability of death or injury, but still affects safety and health.

De minimis violations. No immediate risk to safety or health.

4) Face up to penalties. Civil penalties and fines of up to $1,000 can be assessed for serious and non-serious violations, giving advance notice of inspections, and violation of posting requirements; up to $10,000 for willful or repeated violations, willful violations causing death, and filing false documents. Criminal penalties of up to six months or a year of imprisonment can be imposed for willful violations causing death, giving advance notice of inspections, and filing false documents.

An employer who wishes to contest a citation or penalty must notify the Department of Labor within fifteen days of receipt of the notice of violation. He will then have a hearing before the Occupational Safety and Health Review Commission, which may affirm, modify, or vacate the citation and penalty. Further recourse is to the Federal courts.

SUCCESSFUL HOUSEKEEPING PRACTICES

The rationale for an agressive housekeeping program is not always apparent to plant managers and their subordinates in operations management. The pressures of fulfilling production schedules and meeting shipment deadlines often seem to overwhelm the available manpower, leaving no time for "cleanup." The absence of any reference to housekeeping practices in the standard operating procedures and shop instructions implies to plant personnel that housekeeping can wait until some spare time is available, and, since that spare time never seems to appear, the job is indefinitely postponed. The reasons for a thorough housekeeping program will be established in the next two sections; the remaining section will offer some ideas for implementing the program.

Tie-in with Safety

A warehouse employee (actual case), while walking in the concrete aisle of a storage area looking for some material stored in an upper rack, stepped on a piece of wood which had broken off a shipping pallet. A heavy man, he twisted his ankle so badly he was out of work for three weeks.

Variations of this accident are needlessly repeated thousands of times each year in American industry. People will fall and injure themselves over solid pieces of debris left lying about a plant. They will slip and injure themselves on liquid spills which are not immediately cleaned up.

The threat to personnel posed by careless housekeeping readily extends to fire prevention. Accumulations of combustible trash (even small ones) provide a fuel bed for sparks which would otherwise expire on a bare surface. Lubricating oils and grease spilled on or exuding from machinery will feed a fire; if the wiping rags used to clean them are not disposed of promptly they can start a fire by spontaneous combustion. Dried films resulting from spills of plastic emulsions or solutions, while not easily ignited, will burn fiercely once started.

Further Reasons for Good Housekeeping

1) Quality control. Not every industrial process requires a "clean room," with filtered air and controlled humidity, but it is increasingly true that products made under standard conditions, and the instruments and tools used in their manufacture, will not tolerate exposure to dirt and dust.

2) Employee morale. Employee attitudes toward their work and toward their company are significantly affected by the cleanliness of the place they work in.

3) Higher management impressions. As discussed in Chapter 1, corporate officers and directors often are not experts in the process the plant is using, but get their impressions (and the basis for investment decisions) from its general appearance.

4) External relations. Customers who have occasion to visit the plant will be favorably impressed by a high state of cleanliness and order; conversely, they will become alarmed about the integrity of your product and service if the plant is dirty and unkempt. Community relationships are also enhanced by a clean plant, and it assists the recruiting effort if your plant is known as "a good clean place to work."

Implementing the Housekeeping Program:

Use these methods to achieve and maintain a clean plant:

1. Establish housekeeping standards for each department and section—in writing. Your organization will never satisfy your demands for cleanliness if they don't know how clean you want the plant to be.

2. Train foremen and workers. Start with the employment interview. Continue in early indoctrination. Use housekeeping as a safety meeting topic. Incorporate housekeeping steps in the detailed operating procedures.

3. Conduct regular inspections. The most important is your own; they should be done frequently, and your impressions—good or bad—made known to the supervisors of the departments you visit. Set up a formal committee (rotate assignments) of foremen, supervisors, and superintendents to conduct monthly inspections and report their findings in writing to you. Hourly employees, when appropriate, can be included on this committee. Invite higher management to inspect the plant periodically and demonstrate their interest.

4. Use competition. The inspection report can be used to rate the departments competitively, and the winners awarded prizes and publicity in the house organ.

5. Provide auxiliary services. If your employees get the impression that housekeeping is simply a form of drudgery for them, without any contribution from management, the program will fail. You must provide routine painting of buildings and work areas, effective trash removal services, tools and machines for housekeeping, prompt repair of oil, steam, and process leaks, and consideration for housekeeping problems in the engineering design of new buildings and equipment.

CONCLUSION

Safety and housekeeping are essential contributors to the plant's overall performance; without excellence in these areas the plant organization cannot fully succeed in meeting its goals for production, quality, cost, and employee relationships. Both functions require support from higher management, steady attention from the plant manager, and incorporation in the regular procedures for accomplishing the work of the plant. This chapter has presented the fundamental steps the plant manager must take to mount safety and housekeeping programs, and the specific techniques and sources of information for filling in the details of their operation.

Chapter 10

Developing
Efficient Materials Movement
from Basic Principles

Every plant is faced with the problem of how best to receive and store its raw materials, move them from step to step in the manufacturing process, store and ship them as finished goods. In many plants a critical review of the materials movement methods used will open up major opportunities for cost reduction; in every new plant design logical planning for material movement is essential to maximum efficiency.

This chapter is designed to provide the plant manager with a broad view of the choices of method and equipment which are available. It opens with a review of the fundamentals of material movement, covers the movement of solids and liquids in bulk, the types of containers available, the movement of containers and large single items, and finally deals with the problems of external traffic.

FUNDAMENTALS OF MATERIALS MOVEMENT

Apply these principles when evaluating existing systems of materials flow or those proposed for a new installation:

1. Adopt a wide perspective. Consider the movement of materials not as a series of discrete steps between processes, but as one integrated flow system from the receipt of raw materials to the shipment of finished goods. You will then be in the best position to undertake the elimination of unnecessary steps and backtracking, the maximum utilization of space, and the best adjustment of the physical layout of the plant to all the requirements of processing and materials movement.

2. Combine movement with processing whenever possible. If a material must be dried, baked, coated, wetted, oiled, sorted, sealed, labeled, steamed, heated, or cooled, consider carrying out the operation while the material is in transit from one work station to another. If successful, you can telescope the time and space required for movement and processing.

3. Make the trips short. Arrange plant layout so that material moves directly from one processing step to the next, and reserve the shortest moves for the most

difficult material conditions (the heaviest, most viscous, most fragile, most laborious), while saving the longest moves for the easiest material conditions to handle.

4. Adjust speed of movement to the capacity of the process. There is no point in moving material from Step A to Step B faster than Step B can use it; it will simply pile up and require storage space.

5. Make full use of vertical space. When material can be moved overhead, the floor space below becomes available for process.

6. Move and store materials in bulk form whenever possible; bulk handling offers the cheapest and fastest movement.

7. Whenever practicable, handle material in fluid form. Fluid systems offer speed, safety, convenience, and low labor cost. Particulate solids can sometimes be converted to fluids by slurrying them in water, or suspending them in a moving gas stream. Viscous solids often can be made thin enough to handle as fluids by raising temperature.

8. Utilize gravity. Look for situations where a material can easily be transported in bulk form to the upper levels of a process building and then passed downward by gravity through the process steps, using ramps, chutes, conduits, and large pipes.

MOVEMENT OF MATERIALS IN BULK

Liquids

A liquid handling system has four components: pumps, piping, flow measurement and control devices, and storage tanks. The job of the system designer is to select the least expensive combination which will handle the physical properties of the liquid to be moved.

1) Liquid properties. These are the important properties which must be taken into account in the design of a fluid transportation system: *Density* (water has a density of 8.33 pounds per gallon at 20° C.). Usually not critical in the selection of equipment, but must be taken into account in pressure and energy calculations. *Viscosity* (the consistency of a fluid—at 20° C. water has a viscosity of 1 centipoise; molasses has a viscosity of 100,000 centipoises). Significantly affects pipe size and pump selection. *Vapor pressure* (the degree of volatility—at 20° C. water has a vapor pressure of .34 pounds per square inch, while that of ethyl alcohol is .85 psi). Important to the design of the system on the suction side of the pump, and to the type of tank selected. *Corrosiveness.* If the fluid is very acid or alkaline, or if it contains suspended solids whose particles are abrasive, the designer will have to choose materials of construction which can withstand these conditions. Special construction materials may also be required for fluids which might become contaminated by the system. *Temperature.* As the temperature at which a fluid is handled goes up, viscosity and density usually go down. Vapor pressure rises, and corrosiveness is likely to as well. *Shear sensitivity.* Some liquids, especially colloids and emulsions, are permanently damaged by violent mechanical action, such as that created by a centrifugal pump impeller. Viscosity of some fluids is reduced by mechanical action.

2) Tanks. The important considerations are: *Materials of Construction.* Carbon steel is the standard of cost and availability. Wooden tanks can be cheaper, and offer inexpensive corrosion resistance to a variety of chemicals. More expensive metals used to meet special service requirements are aluminum, stainless steel, copper and its alloys. When it is desirable to combine the low cost and strength of carbon steel with the corrosion resistance of more expensive metals, stainless-, nickel-, and monel-clad steel is used. Steel tanks are also lined

with rubber, glass, and plastic. *Shape*. Vertical cylindrical tanks occupy less floor space and make good use of overhead space, but require carefully laid, level foundations. Horizontal cylindrical tanks can be supported on concrete saddles. Spherical tanks are often used for liquids with high vapor pressure. Rectangular tanks are available in smaller sizes. *Pressure rating*. Under most government and insurance codes (be sure to check local regulations) a tank becomes a pressure vessel when it is designed to operate at 15 psi gage or higher, and strict design, construction, and inspection rules apply. *Location*. Most often at ground or floor level. Can be elevated to conserve space or gain static pressure, or buried underground to conserve space, or for safety reasons.

3) Pumps. *Centrifugal pumps* are the workhorses of industrial liquid systems. They are inexpensive to buy, convenient to install, economical to run, and easy to maintain. They are available in capacity sizes from less than ten gallons per minute to as much as one hundred thousand gpm, and will develop pressures in excess of two thousand pounds per square inch. While there is no theoretical design limitation for viscosity, centrifugal pumps are not often used for liquids over several thousand centipoises because special design features are required. Flow rate decreases in a centrifugal pump as the pressure head it pumps against increases. *Positive displacement pumps* offer steady flow rates against varying pressure heads, will handle higher viscosity liquids, and can generate pressures up to and in excess of ten thousand psi. Important types are piston pumps, plunger pumps, diaphragm pumps, and rotary pumps.

4) Piping. *Materials*. Mild steel (0.2% carbon) is the most widely used, with cast iron, stainless steels, aluminum, brass, bronze, nickel, and a wide variety of specialized alloys also available. Glass, rubber, and several types of plastic are used to make pipe and as linings for steel pipe. Wood, concrete, and graphite pipe is obtainable. *Choice of pipe size* is an economic compromise: small pipe is cheaper to buy and install, but requires more energy to pump a given amount of liquid through it. The pipe designer balances these factors to achieve minimum overall cost. *Joints* are screwed (preferred for smaller sizes, and not generally available over 12"), flanged (larger sizes and higher pressures), and welded (cheaper installation for long, permanent runs). *Basic fittings* are couplings, elbows, tees, reducers, nipples, plugs, and caps. *Valve types* are globe (up to 2"), gate (larger sizes), ball, plug cock, check (for one-way flow), butterfly (for gases), and diaphragm (for corrosive fluids and slurries).

5) Flow measurement and control devices. *Displacement meters* include piston, wobble plate, and nutating disc types; they are usually equipped with digital counters which indicate total accumulated flow. *Differential pressure* meters depend on an orifice or venturi tube installed in the flow path; the differential pressure created is transmitted to a manometer, flow indicator, or recording instrument. In *rotameters* (a type of *area meter*) all the fluid is passed upward through a vertical glass tube with an etched scale. A metal float inside the tube rises to a position on the scale corresponding to the flow. All of these devices can be connected to mechanically-, pneumatically-, or electrically-operated valves to throttle or cut off flow.

Solids

The designer of a solids transportation system evaluates the properties of the materials to be handled, and selects the most economical components for storage, movement, and flow control.

1) Solids properties. *Particle size*. Measured in inches (for particles over ½ in. in diameter), mesh (the number of openings in one linear inch of screen; used for measurement of particles ranging from 2 mesh down to 400 mesh), and microns (one micron is equivalent

to 0.001 millimeters). With most bulk solids, the larger the particle the more free-flowing is the material. *Bulk density.* The weight in pounds of a cubic foot of the material in the state in which it will be handled. Required for the calculation of material flow rates and for the design of bin structures. *Hardness.* Measured on the Mohs scale—talc is a hardness of 1 on this scale, and diamond 10. Higher hardnesses and larger particle sizes combine to create more *abrasive* materials. *Cohesiveness* is the tendency of the particles to stick to each other; it is aggravated by *hygroscopicity,* which is the tendency of the material to absorb moisture from the air. *Angle of repose* (the angle made with the horizontal by the edge of a cone-shaped pile freely built up) is important to the design of bins and conveyors, and to capacity calculations for yard storage. *Corrosiveness* requires more resistant (and therefore more expensive) materials of construction; *toxicity* can require enclosing the handling system or the addition of elaborate ventilation equipment; *explosibility* may have to be dealt with by the use of inert atmospheres and explosion-proof electrical equipment.

2) Storage of solids. *Outdoor storage piles* offer the most economical method of storing large-volume bulk solids, but are limited to those which are not affected by sunlight, rain, snow, heat and cold. Heavy-duty trucks, cranes, and conveyors are usually needed to move material to and from the pile. *Storage bins* can be constructed in any convenient shape (round, rectangular, cone-bottom, horizontal, vertical), and from a variety of materials (metals, wood, concrete, and brick or block walls). Bin design must take into account the angle of repose and the *angle of slide* (the minimum angle of an inclined surface which will cause the material to flow); because solids tend to "bridge" at the outlet opening, various vibratory and aerating devices are used to keep the material flowing at that point. *Silos* are vertical cylindrical containers with flat bottoms which rest on the ground or an indoor floor. They can be built of the same construction materials as bins, and are relatively inexpensive, useful for storing materials with high angles of repose, and take advantage of overhead space.

3) Movement of solids. *Horizontal and inclined conveyors* include the following types: *Vibratory.* Usually reserved for short runs, but can be used up to 150 ft. with loadings of over 400 tons per hour. Very useful for handling hot material. *Screw.* Will handle loadings in excess of 250 tons per hour and can be used up to 300 ft. Can double as mixers for the material being transported. *Continuous flow.* Allowable distances and flow rates vary widely; manufacturer of equipment should be consulted for each application. Totally enclosed, protecting the material transported. A single system can have both horizontal and vertical legs. *Belt.* Loads up to 5,000 tons per hour and distances exceeding 1,000 feet. High first cost, but can be very economical for long runs and high flow rates. *Vertical conveyors* include these types: *Bucket elevators.* Widely used for vertical lift. Low first cost. Standard capacities to 150 tons per hour. Can handle large lumps, operate at high temperatures. Subdivided into *continuous discharge, positive discharge,* and *centrifugal discharge* types. *Vertical screw.* Very good in specific applications. Capacities to 150 tons per hour. Requires only a minimum of floor or ground space and support structure. *Skip hoist.* A single large bucket (up to 150 cubic feet) alternately raised and lowered on a hoisting mechanism. Useful for high lifts (75-150 ft.)

4) Pneumatic conveying. Based on the principle that a fast-moving stream of air in a pipeline can suspend and transport solid particles. A pneumatic conveying system consists of the bins or other storage containers to and from which the material is moved; one or more air blowers which generate the gas velocity; the pipelines through which it moves; cyclones, filters, or other devices for separating solid particles from the air at the end of the transport; and airlock valves for separating the pressurized parts of the system from the non-pressurized.

CONVEYORS

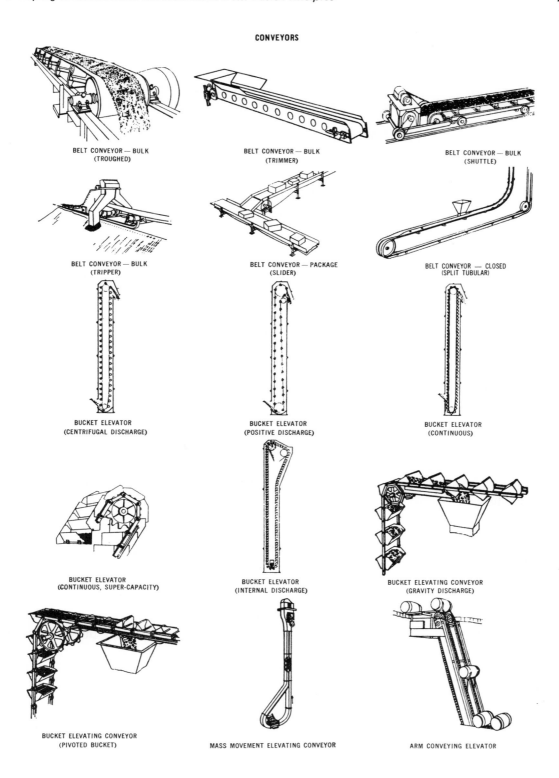

BELT CONVEYOR — BULK
(TROUGHED)

BELT CONVEYOR — BULK
(TRIMMER)

BELT CONVEYOR — BULK
(SHUTTLE)

BELT CONVEYOR — BULK
(TRIPPER)

BELT CONVEYOR — PACKAGE
(SLIDER)

BELT CONVEYOR — CLOSED
(SPLIT TUBULAR)

BUCKET ELEVATOR
(CENTRIFUGAL DISCHARGE)

BUCKET ELEVATOR
(POSITIVE DISCHARGE)

BUCKET ELEVATOR
(CONTINUOUS)

BUCKET ELEVATOR
(CONTINUOUS, SUPER-CAPACITY)

BUCKET ELEVATOR
(INTERNAL DISCHARGE)

BUCKET ELEVATING CONVEYOR
(GRAVITY DISCHARGE)

BUCKET ELEVATING CONVEYOR
(PIVOTED BUCKET)

MASS MOVEMENT ELEVATING CONVEYOR

ARM CONVEYING ELEVATOR

**Exhibit 1. Solids Conveyors (Courtesy of *Modern Materials Handling*
and Conveyor Equipment Manufacturers Association.)**

Practical design limits are up to 1½ in. particle size, 75 tons per hour carrying capacity, and 1,000 feet length, but every one of these "limitations" has been exceeded by wide margins in specialized installations. Pneumatic conveyors are especially useful in situations where twists and turns are required in the flow path which could not be negotiated by mechanical conveyors. They can also be used for heating, cooling, and drying the solid. If it must be protected from oxygen, an inert gas can be used as the carrying stream.

CONTAINERS FOR MATERIAL STORAGE AND MOVEMENT

When shipments to customers or the handling of materials within the plant takes place in quantities too small to justify the use of bulk equipment, a large variety of containers is available for packaging both solid and liquid materials. These are the basic types:

1) Steel drums. Used for handling both solids and liquids. Most popular sizes are 55, 42, and 30 gallons, but other capacities are available. The *open head* type has a solid disc cover sealed at the perimeter with a gasket and a metal ring whose ends are held together by a quick-locking device or a threaded bolt and nut. The *closed head* drum cover is not removable, but has one or more threaded bungs. *Basket* drums have a bung in the sidewall, usually close to the bottom. The normal steel thickness is 20 gauge for the body and 18 gauge for the heads, but heavier gauges (down to 12) may be required for corrosive liquids and lighter gauges (up to 26) can be used for solids. The cheapest drums have a bare steel interior, but fused linings of plastic, rubber, stainless steel and other metals are used for special service, as well as disposable plastic liners.

The steel drum is used when the package is exposed to the weather, requires unusual physical sturdiness, or contains hazardous materials. Its first cost is higher than that of other packages, but it has a reclamation value—it can be cleaned out and re-used, or sold to a drum reconditioner. The purchase of reconditioned drums is a way of achieving lower first cost.

2) Fiber drums. Cheaper than steel, they can be used for solids or liquids. Available in almost any desired capacity up to 75 gallons. The sidewall consists of glued layers of heavy paper; bottoms and heads are made of steel, wood, fiberboard, and plastic. Drums to be used for liquid shipments have a sprayed plastic interior lining, or they can be lined with a disposable plastic sheet.

In addition to their lower first cost, fiber drums offer lower costs for handling and shipping because they are lighter. However, there is usually no reclamation value.

3) Paper bags. The most economical small package of all. Capacities up to 100 lbs., with 50 and 80 lb. sizes the most popular. Bags are rated by the weight of the paper used (50, 60, and 70 lb. kraft), and the number of layers of "plies" (ranging from two to seven). Special plies of treated kraft, aluminum, or plastic are used to protect sensitive materials. More plies are needed when the material shipped is expensive or dangerous, when the distances are longer, and the number of handlings greater.

When the bag is filled its top can be closed by sewing, pasting, heat sealing, taping, or tying with wire, or a combination of these methods. A large choice of machinery for automatically filling, weighing, and closing paper bags is available.

4) Portable Bulk Containers. Manufacturing industries have experienced an expanding need for containers larger than the steel drum but smaller than tank cars and trucks. This need has been met by a variety of containers used for both intra-and interplant shipment.

The most common of these is a rectangular metal bin, ranging in capacity from four to ten 55 gallon drums. It can be made of carbon steel, stainless steel, aluminum, or other metals, is provided with legs so that it can be picked up by a forklift truck, and if used for liquids is likely to be equipped with a standard 55 gallon drum lid for the top opening, and a short length of pipe and valve for the bottom opening. These bins and tanks can be constructed so that they can be stacked on top of each other without additional rack support. While they represent a convenient labor-saving method of storing and transporting "semi-bulk" quantities, their cost of purchase, cleaning, and freight for return trips must be compared to the cost of conventional packages.

Another form of portable container for solids is a large fabric bag capable of holding 4,000 pounds of material. It has a metal ring at the top which allows it to be picked up by a forklift truck. When collapsed, it fits into a shallow metal pan for easy storage and shipment. For liquids, a deflatable rubber bag (roughly resembling a large air mattress) can be strapped to the bottom of an ordinary truck. For the return trip, it can be rolled up into a small space.

HOW TO MOVE CONTAINERS AND BULKY ITEMS

Seldom can an industrial plant move all of its materials in bulk form, and almost every plant is at some time faced with the need to transport containers and bulky single items too large to be carried by hand or too inconvenient to move by conveyor. Use these tools for such movements:

1) Dollies, carts, and hand trucks. Dollies are simple rectangular, triangular, or circular frames mounted on fixed or swiveled wheels or casters. (One type of circular dolly is used to support a 55 gallon drum, making it a mobile package.) Carts are made by adding bodies of wood, metal, or plastic or simple platforms to the basic wheeled structure; they can be provided with racks and shelves or fittings to hold special types of loads.

Two-wheeled hand trucks may have a wood or tubular steel framework, with handles at the top, and short forks, a platform, or other device at the bottom for supporting the load. Specialized adaptations are available for handling bags, cartons, 55 gallon drums, gas cylinders, wire reels, beverage cases, and appliances. Users of 55 gallon drums can buy a combination hand truck and tilting rack, which allows the drum to be stored indefinitely in a horizontal position for withdrawal of material.

2) Pallets and skids. Used for moving more than one container or item at a time. Pallets are low, flat platforms which rest directly on the floor and have enough space between top and bottom layers for insertion of the forks of a lift truck. They may have a solid surface or one constructed of cross-members, and are made of boards, plywood, steel, wire mesh, and paper board. Skids are wood or metal platforms raised on metal legs at the four corners.

Bags and cartons are stacked on skids in an interlocking pattern to give load stability. Loads which will not ride well can be banded to the pallet or skid. A recent development is *shrink-wrapping*, in which the palletized load is enclosed in a sheet of plastic film and passed through a heated tunnel. The plastic shrinks, tightly enclosing the load. The unitized package is not only more structurally stable, but the plastic protects its contents from weather, dust, and pilferage.

3) Power trucks. When the load exceeds 1,000 lbs., the distance of movement 50 ft., and the height of lift more than a few inches, powered industrial trucks must be considered. A profusion of styles and features are available; these are the selections you can make:

a. Rider position. *Sit-down rider* trucks provide a cushioned seat for the driver, and are used when the driver's sole assignment is to operate the truck. *Stand-up rider* trucks have a small platform at the center or rear of the truck for the driver, and are used when the driver is expected to leave the truck and assist with the removal of the load. *Walkie* trucks do not carry the driver at all; he walks behind the truck, guiding it with a drawbar handle on which the controls are mounted.

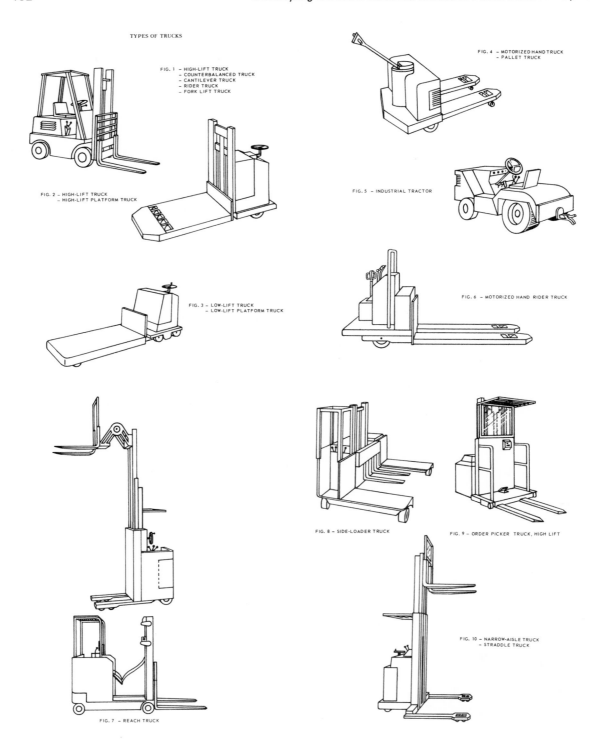

TYPES OF TRUCKS

FIG. 1 – HIGH-LIFT TRUCK
   – COUNTERBALANCED TRUCK
   – CANTILEVER TRUCK
   – RIDER TRUCK
   – FORK LIFT TRUCK

FIG. 2 – HIGH-LIFT TRUCK
   – HIGH-LIFT PLATFORM TRUCK

FIG. 3 – LOW-LIFT TRUCK
   – LOW-LIFT PLATFORM TRUCK

FIG. 4 – MOTORIZED HAND TRUCK
   – PALLET TRUCK

FIG. 5 – INDUSTRIAL TRACTOR

FIG. 6 – MOTORIZED HAND RIDER TRUCK

FIG. 7 – REACH TRUCK

FIG. 8 – SIDE-LOADER TRUCK

FIG. 9 – ORDER PICKER TRUCK, HIGH LIFT

FIG. 10 – NARROW-AISLE TRUCK
   – STRADDLE TRUCK

Exhibit 2. Power Trucks [Extracted from USA Standard Safety Standard for Powered Industrial Trucks (USAS B56.1-1996) with the permission of the publisher, The American Society of Mechanical Engineers, United Engineering Center, 345 East 47th Street, New York, N.Y. 10017.]

b. Load capacities and load centers. Forklift and platform trucks are commercially available with maximum load capacities from 1,500 to 120,000 lbs. Because the lift truck carries its load outside the wheelbase, the distance between the front wheels and the center of the load must also be specified. The most common distance is 24 inches, but models with load centers ranging from 14 to 48 inches are available. *Counterbalanced* trucks have a heavy weight mounted in the rear to keep the truck from tipping forward when the load is raised; *straddle* trucks have two protruding arms which remain in contact with the floor outside the forks while the load is being lifted.

c. Power source. *Electric* lift trucks are quiet, fumeless, smooth-operating. They are powered by large storage batteries which must be recharged after 8-12 hours of operation. *Gasoline* and *diesel engine* trucks are used for heavier loads and outdoor work. *LP Gas* trucks are used for both indoor and outdoor service, require only minimum downtime for changing gas cylinders, and can be very economical in areas where liquefied petroleum gas is inexpensive.

d. Explosion proofing and spark suppression. If the truck is to be used in areas where flammable gases and vapors or combustible dusts are likely to be present, one of the safety-rated types of trucks must be used. Underwriters' Laboratories, Inc. sets the standards for and puts its label on those trucks which meet the standards. The type designations, in ascending order of safety rating, are: Electric trucks—Types E, ES, EE, and EX. Gasoline trucks—Types G and GS. Diesel trucks—Types D, DS, and DY. Liquefied petroleum gas trucks—Types LP and LPS. Type EX is the only truck with a true explosion-proof rating, that is, suitable for use in a Class I, Group D, Division 1 atmosphere as described in the National Electrical Code. See Exhibit 3 and these publications: *Power Operated Industrial Trucks,* UL 583 (Chicago: Underwriters' Laboratories, Inc. Revised periodically), and *Use, Maintenance and Operation of Industrial Trucks* (Boston: National Fire Protection Association. Revised periodically).

e. Other design features. *Maximum height* to which forks can be raised, and *speed* with which they can be raised and lowered. *Height of telescoping mast* raised and lowered, and *free lift,* the height to which forks can be lifted before telescoping mast begins to rise. *Forward speed*—loaded and unloaded. *Turning radius* and *minimum aisle width* for right angle stacking. *Mast tilt* (measured in degrees), backward and forward. *Wheel types* and *sizes. Gross weight*—important on upper floors and in box trailers. Don't forget to include weight of battery or gas cylinder and payload. *Special attachments*—carton clamps, drum tilters, vacuum holders, load rotators, drum and crate grabs.

EXTERNAL TRAFFIC

The plant manager's relationship to the external traffic function may range from complete control, in which the traffic department reports to him as part of the plant organization, to no control at all, in which a centralized traffic department arranges for all external movements, and the plant manager's responsibility ends at the plant door. In either of these positions, or in some intermediate relationship, the plant manager will be concerned with these aspects of external traffic:

Integrate with Internal Handling Systems

The cost of a great deal of labor can be saved when raw materials and outgoing shipments can be handled in exactly the same condition as they arrive at the dock—for instance, when bags and drums do not have to be palletized or removed from pallets. The plant manager who has discovered cost advantages in the use of semi-bulk containers within his plant

TABLE I
SUMMARY TABLE ON USE OF INDUSTRIAL TRUCKS IN VARIOUS LOCATIONS
(For full details see PART A of this Standard)

Class I Locations

Classes	Unclassified	Class I Locations
Description of Classes	Locations not possessing atmospheres as described in other columns	Locations in which flammable gases or vapors are, or may be, present in the air in quantities sufficient to produce explosive or ignitible mixtures.
Groups in Classes	NONE	A — Acetylene; B — Hydrogen; C — Ethyl ether; D — Gasoline, Naphtha, Alcohols, Acetone, Lacquer solvent, Benzene
Examples of locations or atmospheres in classes and groups	Piers & Wharves Inside and Outside, General Storage, General Industrial or Commercial Properties	—
Divisions (Nature of Hazardous Conditions)	NONE	**1** — Above condition exists continuously, intermittently, or periodically under normal operating conditions. **2** — Above condition may occur accidentally as due to a puncture of a storage drum.

AUTHORIZED USES OF TRUCKS BY TYPES

Groups in Classes	(Unclassified)	Div. 1 — A	B	C	D	Div. 2 — A	B	C	D
Types of Trucks Authorized	NONE								
Diesel Type D	D**								
Type DS							†	†	DS*
Type DY							†	†	DY*
Electric Type E	E**								
Type ES							†	†	ES*
Type EE							†	†	EE*
Type EX						EX		†	†	EX*
Gasoline Type G	G**							†	†	GS*
Type GS							†	†	GS*
LP-Gas Type LP	LP**								
Type LPS							†	†	LPS*
Paragraph Ref. in No. 505	210, 211	201(a)				203(a)	209(a)		204(a),(b)

**Trucks conforming to these Types may also be used — see Paragraphs 210-212.

TABLE I
SUMMARY TABLE ON USE OF INDUSTRIAL TRUCKS IN VARIOUS LOCATIONS
(For full details see PART A of this Standard)

Class II Locations / Class III Locations

Classes	Class II Locations	Class III Locations
Description of Classes	Locations which are hazardous because of the presence of combustible dust.	Locations where easily ignitible fibers or flyings are present but not likely to be in suspension in quantities sufficient to produce ignitible mixtures.
Groups in Classes	E — Metal dust; F — Carbon black, Coal dust, Coke dust; G — Grain dust, Flour dust, Starch dust, Organic dust	NONE
Examples of locations or atmospheres in classes and groups	—	Baled waste, cocoa fiber, cotton, excelsior, hemp, istle, jute, kapok, oakum, sisal, Spanish moss, synthetic fibers, tow.
Divisions (Nature of Hazardous Conditions)	**1** — Explosive mixture may be present under normal operating conditions, or where failure of equipment may cause the condition to exist simultaneously with arcing or sparking of electrical equipment, or where dusts of an electrically conducting nature may be present. **2** — Explosive mixture not normally present, but where deposits of dust may cause heat rise in electrical equipment, or where such deposits may be ignited by arcs or sparks from electrical equipment.	**1** — Locations in which easily ignitible fibers or materials producing combustible flyings are handled, manufactured, or used. **2** — Locations in which easily ignitible fibers are stored or handled (except in the process of manufacture).

IN GROUPS OF CLASSES AND DIVISIONS

Groups in Classes	Div. 1 — E	F	G	Div. 2 — E	F	G	Class III Div. 1	Class III Div. 2
Types of Trucks Authorized							NONE	NONE
Diesel Type D								
Type DS					†	DS*		DS
Type DY					†	DY*	DY	DY
Electric Type E								E*
Type ES					†	ES*		ES
Type EE			EE		†	EE*	EE	EE
Type EX	EX*	EX*	EX*	EX	EX	EX	EX	EX
Gasoline Type G					†	GS*		GS
LP-Gas Type LPS					†	LPS*		LPS
Paragraph Ref. in No. 505	202(a)			205(a)		206 209(a),(b)	207(a)	208 *208(a)

*Permitted with approval of the authority having jurisdiction.
†Type authorized to be determined by the authority having jurisdiction.
Type letter inserted indicates authorized use.

Exhibit 3. Permissible Areas of Use for Various Safety-Rated Trucks. (Reproduced by permission from "Type Designations, Areas of Use, Maintenance and Operation of Powered Industrial Trucks (NFPA No. 505)," copyright National Fire Protection Association, Boston, Mass.)

should ask his sales department to explore the possibility of shipping to customers in the same container. These are merely two short examples of the way in which intra-and interplant movements can be integrated to the financial benefit of all concerned.

Go for Bulk

The cost incentives for handling material in bulk within the plant apply to external movement as well, and water, rail, and motor lines all provide cargo carriers fully adapted to the needs of particular commodities. *Compartmented vehicles* allow several different materials to be shipped at the same time, even though no one of them is in sufficient quantity to qualify for a bulk rate on its own. All three modes of transportation offer open vehicles for the shipment of bulk solids, covered vehicles for shipment of solids which must be protected from the weather, and tanks for the shipment of liquids. There are many variations within each type of equipment, and the carriers should be consulted for specific applications.

Specialized Shipments

When materials in transit must be refrigerated or heated, domestic rail and motor carriers offer equipment which will maintain the required temperatures. For rail shipments of easily damaged cargo, the carriers offer *damage-free* (DF) freight cars which have special shock-absorbing suspensions and internal braces for stabilizing the load within the shipping compartment. In *piggy-back* shipments a truck semi-trailer is loaded, taken to a rail terminal and placed on a railroad flatcar on which it rides to a point near its destination, is removed and driven as a truck to the customer's plant. In *containerized shipments* a box mounted on a semi-trailer frame is loaded and sealed, hauled to a terminal where it is removed from the trailer frame, and loaded on a ship or rail car. Upon arrival at its destination terminal it is reloaded on a truck frame and delivered to the customer.

Hazardous Materials

Both the shipper and the carrier are responsible for the proper packaging, labelling, and handling of flammable, corrosive, toxic, or otherwise hazardous materials. In 1967 responsibility for establishing and enforcing safety regulations was transferred from the Interstate Commerce Commission to the newly formed Department of Transportation. These regulations are set forth in *Code of Federal Regulations,* Title 49–Transportation, Parts 1-199, for sale by the Superintendent of Documents, U.S. Government Printing Office, Washington, D.C. 20402.

CONCLUSION

In developing his approach to the problems of material movement, the plant manager looks for cost reduction opportunities in the fuller use of space, conversion to bulk handling, conducting process operations while material is moving, and in the application of the basic principles of materials movement to the overall flow through the plant. He then chooses the equipment most suited to the properties, quantities, and hazards of the materials to be moved. Finally, he integrates internal and external movements for the greatest cost benefit. In the review of engineering design and in the selection of equipment he challenges proposed concepts until he is satisfied that the optimum selections have been made.

PART 3

Costs, Budgets and Cost Reductions

Chapter 11

Perfecting Cost Systems and Budgets to Measure Plant Performance

The corporate profit and loss statement is like the scoreboard at a baseball game—it tells the local team how well it is doing against the competition, when it has scored successes, and when it has made errors. If the scoreboard is to be of any value the information on it must be accurate, up to date, and contain all the facts the manager needs to make winning decisions.

P & L statements are not cast in terms of hits, runs, and errors; instead they deduct costs from income to show profit. This chapter is designed to help the plant manager who will design his own cost system as well as the manager who operates under a cost system framed by others. It identifies the cost elements manufacturing people must deal with, methods of collecting and reporting costs, and the cost systems into which the information can be constructed. Ways of predicting future costs are developed, and the problems of preparing annual expense and capital budgets are explored.

COST ELEMENTS

The starting point for any cost system is the choice of types of expenditure which will be reported and charged to the plant, department, or other cost center for which the system is devised. Choose from this list of manufacturing cost categories:

LABOR
  Production
  Shipping
  Materials movement
  Quality control
  Fringe benefits
  Training
  Supervisory and administrative
UTILITIES
  Water

RAW MATERIALS
  Purchase price
  Freight in
  Handling and yield losses
CONTAINERS FOR FINISHED GOODS
SUPPLIES
  Production
  Shipping
  Maintenance
  Janitorial

Fuel
Electricity
Telephone
DEPRECIATION
   Buildings
   Equipment
   Vehicles
CUSTOMER RETURNS OF
   DEFECTIVE GOODS

Office
TAXES AND LICENSES
INSURANCE
SUPPORT SERVICES
   Fire protection
   Guard service
   Waste disposal
   Lunch/Cafeteria
   Cleaning

Not all of these costs will be included in every report used throughout the company. A cost report which will be used for making decisions about product pricing or plant location should be all-inclusive. Another report intended for cost control by general foremen would omit items like depreciation, taxes, and insurance in order to focus their attention on items over which they have more control.

How to Collect and Report Costs

Any cost system is meaningless unless all the expenditures made by the plant, department, or other cost center are recorded and charged back to it on the periodic cost report. This is a complicated job, and requires use of the following techniques:

Labor

The hourly time card is the base record. A space should be provided for the account number to which the employee's wages are charged; several spaces will be needed if he works for different cost centers. (This arrangement will be useful for the man who completes a day in one department and then works overtime in another.)

Salaried personnel do not ordinarily punch time cards, but may keep time sheets; account numbers can be inserted as for hourly time cards. If the time distribution of either type of employee is very complicated, a separate card (suitable for computer processing) can be used for time distribution alone. The time card may also be used to record the employee's output, such as number of pieces produced.

Raw Materials and Containers

Purchase price and freight charges are readily available from suppliers' invoices and freight bills. Handling and yield losses are determined by charging the quantities of material delivered to a cost center and comparing them to the amount in inventory and consumed in finished goods at the end of a fixed time period. Use job tickets, shift logs, and intra-plant receipts to keep track of material consumed and transferred. (See Chapter 6.)

Supplies

Purchase orders and suppliers' invoices are the key records. Establish a policy that nothing is to be bought without a written purchase order; then insist that the originator furnish the account number to which the material is to be charged.

Utilities

Monthly bills make it easy for the accounting department to keep track of the total sums spent; the difficulty lies in distributing the charges among the various cost centers within the plant. The most accurate method is to put meters on steam, air, and water lines and distribute the charges according to usage. Often this is prohibitively expensive and offers no overall return on the investment. Many plants, therefore, have their engineers estimate the proportion used by each department, and charge the costs out on a percentage basis.

Depreciation

Tax regulations require precise segregation of funds spent for current operating expenses from those spent on capital investments. The best place to start is with a Capital Expenditure form (also called Appropriation Request, Project Justification, etc.) which must be filled out by the originator of the project before any purchases are made. On it he is required to show the cost of the capital acquisition, its classification (land, buildings, fixtures, machinery, vehicles, etc.) and its depreciable life. The accounting department will need this information to apportion depreciation charges properly, from both a legal and a cost analysis standpoint.

Support Services

If these services are supplied by plant employees the methods of allocating labor and supplies charges already shown will suffice; if the services are obtained outside the company, purchase orders or service contracts will be the basic documents used for cost distribution.

Taxes, Licenses, and Insurance

These charges are billed annually or less frequently, and are usually handled by the central accounting office without special documentation from the plant.

Building a Cost System

The purpose of a cost system is to display the collected cost information in the best form for managers who must make economic evaluations and decisions. Any system devised for a particular manufacturing operation should be adapted to its peculiar problems, but in general the choices are between these major types of approach:

1) *Job order* and *process* costing. The job shop produces "one-of-a-kind" products to specific customer order; if it is to know whether a given order was profitable or not, it must keep track of and charge all the costs to the job. Material and labor usages can be recorded on the job ticket (see Chapter 6). Manufacturing overhead is often apportioned on the basis of the number of hours of labor consumed, or the hours of machine time allotted to the project. This is called *job order* costing.

When the plant operates a continuous process or produces discrete items which are all alike, the costs of labor, materials, and overhead are collected for a definite time period (usually one month) and divided by the number of units produced in that period to find the unit cost. This is called *process* costing.

Job order costing provides detailed, up-to-date information on each order turned out, and identifies inefficiencies and cost overruns early; it may be required on cost-plus contracts. It has the disadvantages of being costly to operate. Process costing is cheaper to administer, but local deviations tend to be hidden in the "average" cost of production.

2) *Actual* and *standard* costing. The difference between these two lies in the way inventories are valued. In an actual cost system all of the expenses actually incurred in making the product are collected and charged to the in-process and finished goods inventory. In a standard cost system these inventories are valued at a predetermined standard cost, and any deviations incurred in manufacture are reported in the P & L statement as variances (raw material price variance, material usage variance, labor variance, and overhead variance). Either method can be used with a job order or process cost system.

Actual costing gives the most accurate value of goods produced, and is valuable in industries whose raw material (or other) costs fluctuate rapidly, and which tend to produce a variety of custom-made items. It has the disadvantage that costs are not known until the work is finished and the costs have been collected and tabulated. Standard costing allows much earlier valuation of goods (even before they are made), and gives the manager a yardstick with which he can measure the cost performance of his operation.

3) *Absorption* and *direct* costing. The distinction is based on the difference between *variable* and *fixed* costs. *Variable* costs are those which fluctuate with the amount of product turned out; the acid test of a variable cost is that it goes to zero when no product is produced. Variable costs can be in materials, labor, *and* overhead. *Fixed* costs do not fluctuate with the amount of product made, and include such items as depreciation, taxes, insurance, and some utility and support services. In absorption costing (sometimes called conventional costing) all of the fixed and variable manufacturing expenses are included in inventory valuation and reported on the cost center's statement. In direct costing only the variable expenses are included, and the fixed expenses are listed as a separate item on the overall P & L statement.

Absorption costing gives an all-inclusive cost of goods produced, and assures that fixed costs are not forgotten. Direct costing, by focusing on the variable cost elements only, is more useful for cost control by managers, for judging profitability of alternative products, and for make-or-buy decisions.

There is no reason why elements of these cost systems cannot be combined in the construction of a cost system for the individual plant, and they are seldom found applied in their pure forms. The options are numerous in the development of a cost system, with the exception that government tax and securities authorities may require that certain bookkeeping practices be observed when direct costing is used.

Allocate Service Department Costs

Every plant has operating departments which produce no product, but supply services to the departments which do. Examples are the maintenance department, power house, water treatment plant, storeroom, and materials handling department. Some of these departments are users of services themselves—the power house, for instance, requires maintenance services.

There are two reasons why it is important to collect the costs of these service departments and charge them back to the manufacturing sections: 1) the true cost of manufacturing a product will never be fully known unless the costs of services which it requires are charged to it, and 2) intelligent decisions about discontinuing an operation or relocating it require a good historical record of service costs as well as direct costs.

Follow these steps to develop the allocation system:

1. Establish a cost account number for the service department.

2. Charge all of the costs which the service department incurs to its account number.

3. Establish a method of assessing the proportion of the service department's output which each using department consumes. A method for the maintenance department has already been suggested (see Chapter 7). In the case of a power plant producing steam or electricity, meters can be installed at each of the consuming departments. If such installations are too expensive, or the service cannot be measured, a standard percentage allocation can usually be arrived at from basic engineering information.

4. At the end of each cost period (one month is typical) charge back *all* of the costs of the service departments to the consuming departments.

How to Predict Operating Costs

Every time the plant manager is asked to submit an expense budget he is, of course, called upon to predict operating costs for some period in the future. Between budgets he must often predict costs for proposed new processes, or estimate the cost effects of important changes on existing processes. Draw from these sources of information for cost predictions:

1) Activity Forecasts. The amount of material which is to be manufactured in a given period is the most significant determinant of the total costs which will be incurred. Furthermore, the level of activity is likely to have an effect on the unit cost of production—a product which costs $0.83 per hundredweight to manufacture at a level of ten million pounds per year may cost only $0.69 per cwt. to make at an annual activity level of twenty million pounds. The figures for next year's production rate may come in the form of an assignment from higher headquarters, be based on the sales forecast, or derived from historical production data by the plant manager and his staff.

2) Cost history. Any cost item for which records have been kept over a period of years can be plotted on a sheet of graph paper to see if a trend is discernible. Projections into the future should be limited to 20 percent of the base time period; beyond that they tend to become unreliable. A refinement of the graphical technique is to use a sheet of semilogarithmic paper—plot years or months on the arithmetic scale, and the cost to be studied on the log scale. If the points fall along a straight line the cost is rising or declining at a fixed percentage rate.

Price fluctuations can often obscure trends in usage, and it is better for some purposes not to plot dollars but units consumed. Consider the case of an operating department in which the consumption (and therefore the conservation) of electric power is important. A graph of kilowatt-hours consumed per unit of production may show a definite trend over a period of years which will allow a reliable projection; if the same data were plotted in terms of dollars spent on electricity the curves could be seriously distorted by rate raises granted to the utility company, or by the kilowatt-hour charge dropping into a lower bracket because other departments are consuming more electricity.

3) Foreseeable Effects. When major factors affecting manufacturing costs are known in advance they can be added to or substituted for the trends of historical data. Look for predictable changes in these areas:

Labor rates. If the plant has a union contract, labor rates can be predicted with great precision for as long as three years. If the contract expires in the current year, the size of wage settlements in other companies can be used as a guide. The non-union plant can use wage surveys of its area and its industry to foretell the labor rates it will have to pay to remain competitive.

Materials and supplies. The plant which uses only a few materials can have its purchasing department research possible price fluctuations intensively, usually with accurate results. If a large variety of materials and supplies is consumed it may not be feasible to fully probe the cost future of each of them; historical plots of total costs (especially the semilog type) can be a reliable substitute.

Utilities. Applications for rate increases by public utility companies usually must be filed well in advance of the effective date, and are covered in the local news media; the utility companies themselves, or even the commission to which they must apply, may be willing to answer inquiries about pending rate increases. *Depreciation* charges for new equipment can be predicted from the capital budget; proposed changes in *taxes* at all levels of government are usually known well in advance of their enactment and are covered in the news media.

4) Cost reduction efforts. Projects which are fully defined and certain of implementation can be included in cost predictions; it is dangerous, however, to include overall goals or "blue sky" savings in budget preparation.

*Annual Expense Budget**

The annual expense budget and its corollary, the monthly budget report, are the culmination of the expense reporting methods selected, cost systems chosen, and predictions generated according to the previous sections of this chapter. Its appearance and final form will depend upon the choice between absorption and direct costing, job order and process costing, the way in which service department costs are allocated, and so on. But there are two basic elements in any budget, no matter what its form, for it is a plan for spending money on specified items for a definite period in the future, and its monthly report is a device for measuring how close to the plan the actual spending comes.

Beyond that there are variations in the way companies use their operating budgets. For some, they are general guides to plant spending, and the only requirement is that major variances be explainable. For others they are a very closely followed control tool, and the manager's performance rating is closely tied to his control of budget expenses. In some situations the budget is the authorization for the manager to spend funds, and he is not allowed to exceed its limits without prior approval.

Exhibit 1 is an example of an expense budget monthly report, and a detailed examination of its features will shed light upon the ways in which a budget can be constructed:

1) Choice of cost center. A cost center is a collection of personnel and equipment to which charges are assigned and which generates a measurable output. In this example Department Z is the cost center; it could have been a subsection of a department, or could have been the whole plant.

2) Production level. This plant's experience had been that the cost of producing a unit (100 lbs. in this case) varied with the total amount produced in a month; therefore budgets were developed for 1.0, 1.5, 2.0, and 2.5 million pounds. Because the actual production fell at 1,603,410 lbs., the budget standards for 1,500,000 (the closest budgeted figure) were used. The use of different production level budgets explains why the budgeted cost of Raw Material A is $2.23 for March, but only $2.18 for the year to date.

3) Figures reported. The designers of this budget chose to report in terms of dollars spent per 100 lbs. of product. Thus the figure of $1.50 in the Actual column for Raw Material B means that $1.50 x 1,603,410 lbs./100 lbs. = $24,051.15 was spent for this raw material by the department. They felt that since production fluctuates from month to month, ratio reporting would iron out the effects of the fluctuations. If the production rate were constant from month to month, they might have chosen to report total dollars. If the price of the raw material fluctuates widely, they might have preferred to report pounds of Raw Material A consumed rather than dollars.

4) Cost system. This is a budget for a process cost system, with only one product produced by this department. If the department manufactured a great number of products during the year, separate budgets might have been developed for each product, or a job order cost system devised.

The report is designed for both direct and absorption costing. It is broken down into sections marked "Variable Costs" and "Fixed Costs." In a pure direct costing system only the variable cost section would be shown, and only the costs shown in it would be used to valuate finished good inventory. In absorption costing, the fixed cost section would be added, and included in value of inventory. "Fixed Costs" might even be included on a direct costing report as a matter of interest and guidance to the managers using it.

---

*The term "expense" has different meanings in cost accounting, some of them quite restricted. It is used here in its broadest sense—to include all of the recurrent charges to an operating cost center, and to differentiate the expense budget from the capital budget.

MANUFACTURING COST REPORT. Dept.: Z Product: Y Month: March 19___						
Budget Quantity: 1,500,000 lbs. Quantity Produced: 1,603,410 lbs.						
Cost Basis: 100 lbs. Figures in: Dollars						
Cost Category	This month			Year to date		
	Budget	Actual	Var.	Budget	Actual	Var.
Variable Costs						
Materials						
Raw Matl A	2.23	2.20	.03	2.18	2.19	(.01)
Raw Matl B	1.49	1.50	(.01)	1.47	1.40	.07
Containers	2.37	2.37	—	2.36	2.35	.01
Scrap Reworked	.27	.32	(.05)	.29	.28	.01
Scrap Discarded	.01	—	.01	.01	.03	(.02)
Labor						
Straight Time	.98	.96	.02	.95	.95	—
Overtime	.14	.17	(.03)	.11	.13	(.02)
Fringe Benefits	.21	.21	—	.20	.18	.02
Variable Supervision	.09	.08	.01	.08	.09	(.01)
Supplies	.74	.78	(.04)	.72	.75	(.03)
Variable Maintenance	.16	.17	(.01)	.15	.13	.02
Quality Control	.12	.12	—	.12	.11	.01
Variable Utilities	.07	.06	.01	.06	.04	.02
Subtotal	8.88	8.94	(.06)	8.70	8.63	.07
Fixed Costs						
Fixed Supv. & Admin.	.08	.07	.01	.07	.07	—
Fixed Utilities	.03	.03	—	.02	.03	(.01)
Depreciation	.83	.85	(.02)	.81	.80	.01
Fixed Maintenance	.04	.04	—	.03	.05	(.02)
Taxes & Insurance	.11	.12	(.01)	.10	.10	—
Subtotal	1.09	1.11	(.02)	1.03	1.05	(.02)
Grand Total	9.97	10.05	(.08)	9.73	9.68	.05
( ) indicates unfavorable variance.						

Exhibit 1. Expense Budget Monthly Report

A word about "variable utilities" and "fixed utilities:" Let's say that a process uses steam to manufacture its product. The steam used for actual manufacture would be costed under "variable utilities." If the plant were shut down, however, the steam used to keep the building warm would be classed under "fixed utilities." Similar comments apply to "variable maintenance" and "fixed maintenance." The former would include the cost of maintenance work to keep the production machinery going; the latter would include the building repair work or any other maintenance services required even when there is no production.

Capital Expenditures Budget

Just as the company formalizes its plans for operating expenditures in the expense budget, so must it establish a definite program for spending on capital projects. Here are the reasons why:

1. The company's financial managers need to be informed in advance of the dates on which they will have to supply the very large sums of money required for capital projects.

2. The capital budget is a planning tool. It requires the responsible managers to clearly define their projects, estimate their costs accurately, and predict their times of completion.

3. The capital budget is a control tool. When issued in a periodic (monthly, quarterly, or even annual) report form, it highlights the comparison between the actual progress of a project and its original goals, offering the manager a first basis for corrective action. Combine it with the post-completion audit discussed in Chapter 13, to achieve beginning-to-end control of capital projects.

4. It provides a method of first approval. Most companies require detailed cost estimates and economic justification calculations before *final approval* of capital projects. But the manager with a capital proposal can submit a *budget estimate* for his project; if the proposal is not approved for inclusion in the budget, he need spend no further time and money on detailed analysis.

Exhibit 2 illustrates one way in which a capital budget and its report form can be constructed. The report is issued quarterly, this one covering the first quarter of the year. Each project is listed by title with a project number (which can also be used as the engineering department's project number) followed by a letter suffix indicating whether the capital item is an addition of new equipment or replacement of old.

The cost and expenditure columns are divided into "Estimated" and "Known" or "Actual" categories. In project 803R the exact cost was known at the time it was included in the budget, so no estimate is given. Project 804A was estimated at $23,500, but actually cost $24,900 when built; both figures are shown in the "Total Cost" section.

Spending projections for the current year are shown in the "Expenditures" section. There are no entries in the "1st Quarter-Estimated" column because the period is ended, and any money spent would be shown in the "Actual" column. Taking Project 801A as an example, we find that $33,000 was spent in the first quarter, $100,000 is planned for the second quarter, $41,000 for the third and $6,000 for the fourth quarter. The last column shows that completion of the project is anticipated by November 1 (projects already completed are marked "Compl." in this column). As new reports are issued through the year the figures are updated to reflect the latest cost information.

This report has been held down to a simple one-page affair, but there is no reason why it could not be expanded to show additional information needed by those who use it. For instance, columns could be added showing the capital appropriation number, whether or not the project has final approval, salvage value of old equipment, anticipated cost overruns, depreciable life of new equipment, and financial criteria such as percent return on investment and payback period.

Depreciation

When the plant buys a piece of equipment which costs $50,000 and is expected to last ten years, an accounting problem is created. If the $50,000 is charged as an expense in the year the equipment is purchased, profits will be low (or non-existent) that year, but

ZZZ Corporation.   **Denver Plant.**   CAPITAL BUDGET QUARTERLY REPORT   Date Issued: March 31, 19___

Proj. No.	Title	Total Cost Est'd.	Total Cost Known	Spent to Date	1st Qtr Est'd.	1st Qtr Act.	2nd Qtr Est'd.	2nd Qtr Act.	3rd Qtr Est'd.	3rd Qtr Act.	4th Qtr Est'd.	4th Qtr Act.	Est'd. Compl. Date
803R	Replace Lift Truck #3	—	9.4	-0-			9.4						5/15
801A	Warehouse Expansion	180	—	33		33	100		41		6		11/1
796A	Welding Machine-Maintenance Dept.	—	1.5	1.5		1.5							Compl.
800A	New Screw Machines-Fastener Dept.	122	126	95			31						6/30
802A	Land Acquisition (Parcel "C," South side of Plant)	117	—	-0-					117				9/15
799A	Fire Alarm System	—	36	12			24						4/23
798A	Warehouse Racks	18	—	-0-					18				8/31
804A	New Electrical Service to Main Building	23.5	24.9	24.9		24.9							Compl.
806R	Replace Boring Machine-Gear Housing Dept.	31.6	—	-0-							31.6		12/15
805A	New Press Brake-Sheet Metal Dept.	14.5	—	-0-							14.5		11/30
	TOTALS	506.6	197.8	166.4		59.4	164.4		176		52.1		

NOTES: 1. All figures in thousands of dollars.

2. Project Number Code Letters: A = Addition   R = Replacement

Exhibit 2. Capital Budget Quarterly Report

unrealistically high in succeeding years. It would make more sense to distribute the cost of the equipment over its expected lifespan.

Depreciation is an accounting system which does just that—it provides a method of charging some portion of the cost of capital equipment to expense in each year of the equipment's life. It is a fictitious charge—after all, the $50,000 really was expended the first year—and because it is fictitious it is *added* to annual income to calculate cash flow. To fully understand the profitability of capital projects the plant manager must understand the basic principles of depreciation.

Because depreciation is an annual charge to expense, and is therefore deducted from total income, the federal government (which taxes net income) has established definite rules for the calculation of depreciation. Land cannot be depreciated at all, nor can raw material and finished goods inventories. The Internal Revenue Service of the U.S. Department of the Treasury publishes allowable depreciable life spans for equipment in various industries.

These are the methods used for calculating annual depreciation charges:

1) Straight-Line Depreciation. The original cost minus anticipated salvage value is divided by the years of depreciable life. In our example, if the salvage value is $5,000 the annual depreciation is ($50,000 - $5,000)/10 years. = $4,500.

2. Declining Balance Method. A multiple (usually 2.0) of the straight-line annual percentage is used to obtain the first year's depreciation, which is then deducted from the first cost and the multiple percentage applied to the balance to get the second year's depreciation. The process continues until the last year, or until a switch to straight-line depreciation is made (otherwise the balance would never reach zero). This method and the one which follows gives higher rates of depreciation in the early years of the equipment's life, coming closer to the actual profile of its value than the straight-line method.

3. Sum-of-digits method. To find the depreciation cost for any year, multiply the depreciable value by the number of years remaining in the depreciable life, and divide by the sum of the digits representing the total number of years in the depreciable life. In our example the depreciable value is $50,000 - $5,000 = $45,000. At the start of the first year there are ten years remaining. The sum of the digits representing the numbers one through ten is 55. The first year's depreciation cost is $45,000 x 10/55 = $8,182. The depreciation cost for the seventh year (four years remaining) is $45,000 x 4/55 = $3,273.

CONCLUSION

The first step in the management of plant spending is the development of a plant cost structure. Whether he uses a format developed by someone else or is required to build his own system, the plant manager is closely concerned with the way in which basic cost data is collected, displayed, and built into cost systems. He can make important contributions to the decision process which chooses between job order and process costing, actual and standard costing, and direct and absorption costing.

Once the cost system is chosen, the plant manager goes on to the preparation of capital and expense budgets for future periods of time. With these important activities in full swing, he is ready to dig deeper into the problems of cost control and cost reduction.

Chapter 12

Implementing a Cost Control and Cost Reduction Program That Boosts Financial Returns

Cost systems and budgets are control tools, and the name itself locates their position in the management cycle (planning, organizing, and controlling). In themselves they accomplish nothing, and only come to life when the manager uses them to measure the deviations from his spending plans and takes action to close the gaps.

But even that is only a first step toward true cost control. In a plant where careless labor habits are permitted or material wastage is ignored, the cost of these poor practices insinuates itself into the standard costs, and budgets and cost reports no longer serve as tools for removing it. The only antidote is a management team which steadily applies all the available techniques of cost control and cost reduction. This chapter will deal with both of these functions, showing how to get results in the major areas of cost control, how best to utilize cost reports, what to do when costs get out of control, and how to set up and operate a permanent cost reduction program.

COST CONTROL

How to Get Results in the Major Areas of Cost Control

The corporation is interested in controlling the costs of many items—everything from the salesmen's expense reports to the consumption of office supplies. For the plant manager, however, there are four basic areas where his efforts will do the most good, and in this section we will identify those areas, discuss aspects of their routine control, and tell how to go beyond routine surveillance to get maximum effect.

1) Labor. First decide how much of a variance* from standard you are willing to accept; then request an explanation of each deviation beyond that amount from the foreman or supervisor involved. It helps greatly to have the labor account broken down into its component parts—as is the case in Exhibit 1, Chapter 11, where costs are reported for straight time, overtime, fringe benefits and supervision—because the corrective action for a deviation in any one of these components will be quite different from the others. If you find recurring variances in a particular category, set up additional routine reports which

---

*Difference between actual cost and standard cost.

highlight the problem area. For instance, if overtime charges repeatedly exceed standard on the monthly budget report, establish a weekly overtime report so that all managers and supervisors concerned can follow the situation more closely.

But control of labor costs requires much more than checking monthly reports. Walk around the plant. Are employees habitually late in returning from breaks and lunch periods? Are there obvious labor-saving operational changes which could be made? Have someone above the level of foreman review the weekly time-clock cards. Are there strike-overs, erasures, and write-ins of missing time punches? If so, dishonest and illegal practices may be getting started; they must be controlled immediately. Absenteeism is a prime cause of excessive labor and overtime costs; insist that each foreman keep an absentee log on each of his employees (rather than rely on distant personnel department files) so that he can quickly identify overtime problems arising from that source and take the required action.

2) Materials. Detailed knowledge of the cost of materials going into the finished product is essential to the running of any business, and every manufacturing plant will have some kind of materials accounting system. The plant manager will want to satisfy himself that these costs are reported in sufficient detail for item by item control; this point is illustrated in Exhibit 1 of Chapter 11, where the materials used by the department are broken down into raw materials, containers, off-grade material reworked, off-grade material scrapped, and supplies. A significant negative variance for any one of these items will put the investigating supervisor on the right track quickly; a large positive variance (if it is not a record-keeping error) may lead to an important cost reduction.

Even that cost breakdown may not be detailed enough; for instance, the "Supplies" category may be too broad to be of much use to the investigator when costs are out of line, and he would be greatly helped if all the individual supplies used were listed separately. The growing use of computers for turning out cost reports makes a detailed breakdown more feasible, but if the list is still too long try breaking out the top 20 percent of the supplies ranked in order of money spent on them; you will probably find you have accounted for 80 percent of the total supply costs.

Visual inspection by the plant manager will be as rewarding in this cost area as it is in that of labor. Are raw materials and supplies carelessly handled by employees? What is going into the sewer? What is going out of the plant in trash containers? Again poor practices, if accepted or ignored by management, wind up in "standard" costs.

3) Equipment. Cost control with respect to major pieces of equipment makes two demands upon the manager: to prevent costly unplanned breakdowns, and to keep the capital investment fully utilized. The first is achieved by an active preventive maintenance program whose operational details and cost implications are described in Chapter 7. The second is met by the use of utilization reports which compare the actual hours of operation and downtime with established standards; they can be developed for any time period from one shift up to a month—for most plants one week is a good choice.

Put equipment costs in perspective. Find out how much it costs per hour to keep a critical piece of equipment in operation—the sum of depreciation, repairs, and electrical or other energy to run it. If it costs $20 per hour for the equipment and the cost of labor is $4 per hour, you can sacrifice labor efficiency to keep the equipment running. If the equipment costs $2 per hour, you can sacrifice its utilization to gain labor efficiency.

4) Utilities. Be sure that utilities are included on the cost reports that first-line supervisors receive; without their knowledge and cooperation control of utilities usage is impossible. Many companies turn their utility bills over to commercial claim services which verify the accuracy of the charges in return for a percentage of any savings achieved.

Budget Cost Reports

A great deal of work goes into the preparation of periodic cost reports, but they are not always used as effectively as they could be. Cover these points to get the most cost control from them:

1) Distribute to first-line supervisors. Just about every decision they make affects costs; their ability to take cost factors into account depends on their knowledge of the plant's cost standards and its current performance in relation to the standards. Merely handing them the cost reports will not be enough—they will need the plant manager's counseling and direction in applying the information to cost control.

2) Frequency of issue. One month is the most common, but don't hesitate to issue them more frequently, or to abstract especially important sections and publish them at shorter intervals, when quicker response to deviations in certain costs is called for.

3) Special editions for supervisors. A dilemma is created when the decision is made to pass cost reports on to the first-line supervisor: much of the information on it is either confidential, or sensitive, or both. Supervisors frequently have desks and offices in locations where it is hard to keep papers concealed, and the company may not want its hourly employees to know the cost of producing Product A or how much money was spent on overtime last month.

One way out is to publish a version of the report in terms of units consumed, rather than in dollars. In Exhibit 1 of Chapter 11, for instance, raw materials could have been reported as pounds, tons, or number of pieces; labor as man-hours; and quality control in terms of units of test work.

4) Action on deviations. The cost report is just another interesting piece of paper until it becomes the basis for action taken on cost deviations. The plant manager's goal is to be sure that his supervisors and managers know why the cost deviations occurred and have plans for correcting or taking advantage of them. He does this through personal contact, holding cost meetings, or even requiring written cost control reports.

Cost Control by Purchasing Practices

The purchase of raw materials and supplies accounts for a very large share of the cost dollar in most companies, and is the logical place for intensive cost control efforts to begin. Whether he supervises the purchasing function directly or it is a staff service to him, the plant manager will want to be familiar with the application of these purchasing cost controls:

1) Economic order quantity. It costs money to process an order, and the fewer raw material orders processed the lower this cost. But if fewer orders are placed, more material must be purchased, and it costs money to carry inventory. This formula gives the optimum balance between the two factors:

$$Q = \sqrt{\frac{2AC}{I}}$$

Where Q is the economic order quantity in dollars, A is the annual requirement in dollars, C is the cost of processing an order in dollars, and I is the annual cost of carrying inventory expressed as a decimal fraction of the purchase price. Note that this formula does not take into account discount prices for larger orders; for a more elaborate treatment of this and other variables involved in determining order quantity see W. Evert Welch, *Tested Scientific Inventory Control* (Greenwich, Conn.: Management Publishing Corp., 1956).

2) Special arrangements with suppliers. You may be able to obtain more favorable pricing and delivery arrangements from a supplier if you offer to contract for a whole year's needs. With or without a contract, he may be willing to take on the job of maintaining inventory in order to get your business.

3) ABC analysis. Make a list of all the materials and supplies purchased, ranking them in order of total dollars spent on each per year. Chances are that you will see a distribution somewhat like this: The top 10 percent of the items will account for 60 percent of the money spent (Class A), the next 25 percent will account for 30 percent of the money spent (Class B), and the bottom 65 percent will account for only 10 percent of the total expenditures (Class C). Class A materials offer the greatest rewards for effort in price reduction and inventory control; Class B materials should be carefully watched; and Class C items can be managed with less control because they have so little impact on total cost.

Cost Control by Payment Authorization

This is a simple, effective device for cost control, but somehow ignored in many companies. It consists of having the appropriate supervisor, superintendent, or manager initial each invoice or bill for purchases ordered by his department before the accounting department makes payment. Although it adds some "paperwork" to the jobs of each of these men, it has the following advantages:

1. It keeps the manager informed of expenditures as they occur, rather than having him confronted with an accumulated total of bills too numerous to investigate.

2. It helps him to recognize differences between what he was told an item "would cost" and what is actually charged for it.

3. Because of his special knowledge of the department and the circumstances surrounding the purchase, he may be able to correct erroneous charges.

4. As the manager monitors the incoming bills, he can caution his subordinates and put the brakes on his own spending if he sees the totals climbing too high.

What to Do When Costs Go Out of Control

Despite the most carefully designed cost control systems and the best efforts of the people who use them, the plant manager will eventually receive a cost report showing large unexpected deviations from budget. When this happens, use these guidelines to discover the causes and to develop corrective action:

1. Inform everyone concerned. You will need their observations, knowledge, and opinions to arrive at the causes. Ask for help from outside the production department—engineering, accounting, purchasing, and inventory control personnel may have valuable insights into the problem. It is especially true of cost problems that the more eyes and ears focused on the investigation, the better its chances of success.

2. Temporarily shorten the intervals of reporting. If the normal reporting period is one month and you are in trouble with high raw material usage, have inventory counts and usage reports issued weekly or every two weeks until the trouble is cleared up.

3. Attack a complex cost problem with a priority system. If it is not possible to investigate several out-of-control cost components at once, an obvious method is to take the costliest ones first. Or, it may result in quicker payoff to handle first those which appear easiest to solve.

4. Look for unrealistic cost standards. If the standard cost of manufacturing an

item is based on 1,000 pieces per day, but the process is actually run on a machine which can only produce 500 pieces per day, there is little hope of meeting the standard, and it must be changed. Newly developed standards are more suspect than older ones.

5. Look for cost reporting errors. If labor charges, material requisitions, or vendors' invoices are charged to the wrong accounts, the cost report can be seriously unbalanced. There is a clear-cut trail leading back from the cost report through ledgers and postings in the accounting department to the original cost documents; following it can be a time-consuming job, especially in the larger companies.

COST REDUCTION

A Continuing Program

Peter Drucker has aptly stated the situation in many companies: "The annual cost reduction drive . . . is as predictable in most businesses as a head cold in spring. It is about as enjoyable."*

In fact the annual cost reduction drive is really not cost reduction at all; it is usually an attempt to get people to do what they should have been doing all along—exercise proper cost *control. Cost reduction* is something far different—it is the continuing development and application of *ideas* which eliminate or favorably modify specific cost-generating activities. To be effective, it must be as formal as the cost reporting system, i.e., it must have stated objectives and a means of measuring actual performance against those objectives.

The Formal Cost Reduction Program

Ideas, of course, do not implement themselves, and the purpose of the formal cost reduction program is to provide a climate in which each proposal is clearly stated, its sponsors committed to a time schedule for completion, and its results monitored. The mechanism for achieving all this has these two elements:

1) The project approval form. Exhibit 1 is an example of the way in which a cost reduction proposal can be reduced to specific terms, approved for implementation, and entered on the program's books. This particular form assumes that the plant is divided into departments, but any cost center designation could be used instead. The sponsor is asked to describe his project, show the savings it will produce, and commit to a date for the savings to begin. He is also asked to quantify the investment required, and to describe it briefly. When the project is approved it is given a number, and copies sent to the originator and the Cost Reduction Program Coordinator.

2) The period report. Exhibit 2 shows how the actual savings achieved by each project can be summarized into a performance report for the entire program. A supervisor or manager from the production organization (preferably, or from the accounting department) is appointed as Cost Reduction Program Coordinator, and it is his job to prepare the performance report from data supplied by the cost centers themselves or the accounting department. Its frequency of issue is determined by the needs of the individual plant—the level of activity in the program, the importance of reporting its accomplishments, and keeping motivation and interest at a high level. This report happens to be issued quarterly; some plants would prefer a monthly report.

This exhibit is made up for a Production Department and a Maintenance Department; most plants will have more than two cost centers, and the report would be enlarged to

---

*Peter F. Drucker, *Managing for Results* (New York: Harper & Row Publishers, Inc., 1964), p. 68. Used by permission.

THE RTZ CORPORATION
Dudley Plant

COST REDUCTION PROJECT

DATE_____

PROJECT TITLE_____

DEPARTMENT _____   PROJECT NO._____

DESCRIPTION OF PROJECT:

EXPECTED SAVINGS: $_____ PER _____(UNITS OF PRODUCTION)

                                PER _____(MONTH OR YEAR)

                    BEGINNING_____(DATE)

INVESTMENT REQUIRED: $_____ CAPITAL (APPR. NO._____)

                       $_____ EXPENSE

                       DESCRIPTION OF INVESTMENT _____

                                  APPROVALS: _____ (SUPERINTENDENT)

                                             _____ (PLANT MGR.)

Exhibit 1. Cost Reduction Project Approval Form

include all of them. Each project is identified by the cost center sponsoring it, and by project number and title. The forecast savings are taken from the project approval form, and the actual savings and capital spent during the period reported by the cost centers. Project 932 illustrates the point that cost reduction projects should have a finite life (one year is a common choice), after which it is marked "expired" and included in the basic cost structure of the plant.

THE RTZ CORPORATION
Dudley Plant

COST REDUCTION PERFORMANCE REPORT

4th Qtr., 19___

Dept.	Proj. No.	Project Title	Forecast Savings	Actual Savings	Capital Spent
A	931	Improved Scrap Recovery Method	$11,623	10,136	24,235
A	932	Steam Condensate Return System		— Expired —	
A	933	Consolidation of Second Shift	1,623	1,623	—0—
A	934	Replacement of Wooden Storage Pallets with Steel	439	474	3,212
A	935	Use of Smaller Size Grinding Wheels	118	118	—0—
		Total	13,803	12,351	27,447
Maint.	1026	Motorized Tool Carts for Remote Jobs	563	762	2,493
Maint.	1027	Use of Pre-cut Pump Packing	186	179	—0—
Maint.	1028	Open Stock Issue of Small Fittings	57	57	—0—
Maint.	1029	Automatic Pipe Threader	228	217	1,214
		Total	1,034	1,215	3,707
		Grand Total	14,837	13,566	31,154

Exhibit 2. Cost Reduction Program Period Performance Report

Not only does the use of these two forms accomplish the goals set forth in the first paragraph of this section, but it builds into the program a key motivating factor—that of competititon between the departments to achieve the highest savings totals on the period report.

Selection of Projects

Exhibit 1 identifies the plant manager as the final approving authority for projects submitted; in the very large plants this function may have to be delegated further down in the line organization. In either case the approving authority and those participating in the program need a set of criteria for judging proposed projects. Use these guidelines for establishing your own standards:

1. Set a minimum level of cost savings to keep the program from being bogged down in the "we saved twelve paper clips per week" type of project. Fifty dollars

per month is a suggested level for a plant doing ten million dollars per year in sales, but local factors may require raising or lowering this figure.

2. Each project must have a definite, demonstrable financial return. "We should spread salt on the sidewalk in winter because it may save the cost of an accident," while a worthy idea, is not a cost reduction project.

3. Avoid confusion between cost reduction and cost control. "We will put the lights out every night and save $700 per year," is not a cost reduction project; it is a form of cost control which should have been exercised right along.

4. Don't hesitate to accept projects which depend wholly or largely on labor savings. Some managers object to this on the grounds that a project which saves two man-hours per day doesn't allow a reduction in the number of people employed, and therefore doesn't really save money. The answer is threefold: the saving of two hours per day may immediately reduce the use of overtime; although one project saving two hours does not permit a reduction in force, several projects totalling eight hours do; and the cost center which has been working at labor savings for a period of time can handle additional duties or expanded production capacity without adding people.

Role of the Purchasing and Accounting Departments

These are staff functions, and it must be remembered that the primary responsibility for cost reduction in the production organization is not theirs—indeed, they have major responsibilities for cost reduction in their own departments. But they can offer assistance to the production group in its search for cost reduction opportunities:

1) Purchasing. Because of their continuing contacts with the outside world of suppliers and salesmen, the personnel of this department are in a good position to collect and transmit suggestions for improved operating methods and reduced costs to the operating departments. Those departments should inform the purchasing people of the areas in which they are seeking improvements, no matter how vague the requests might be in the early stages, so they can be alert for solutions to the cost problems.

2) Accounting. These people are in the best position to discern trends in costs, to identify the cost categories which offer the greatest opportunity for cost reduction, and to make specific suggestions for cost reduction projects. Their ideas should be solicited; in return they will usually work very hard to help the cost program. They may also provide important staff services in evaluating cost reduction proposals—gathering cost data and calculating rates of return.

Sources of Cost Reduction Ideas

The whole program depends upon the number and quality of the cost reduction ideas generated, and when the program is first announced plant personnel will need some coaching in where to look for possible projects. Here are some ideas they should examine:

1) All capital appropriation requests. Capital improvements are most often justified on the basis of a financial return which comes from expanded capacity or reduced costs. The latter type are very legitimate projects for inclusion in the cost reduction program.

2) The major cost categories. Production departments control costs in four major areas: labor, materials, supplies, and utilities. They should be encouraged to search each of these areas methodically for cost reduction opportunities.

3) The highest cost elements. When studying supplies, for instance, list the individual items purchased in order of the dollars spent on them annually; those at the top of the list offer the greatest opportunities for cost reduction.

4) Ongoing efforts. Production departments characteristically strive to make their work easier, more productive, and less costly. Many of these efforts will meet the criteria for cost reduction projects, and should be included in the program. Encouraging department heads to develop projects out of these routine efforts can be a big help in developing their enthusiasm for the program, particularly when it is first being organized.

5) Purchases and activities which can be eliminated altogether. There is no surer way of achieving a cost reduction than to eliminate the activity which generates the cost; although the rewards are great, it is the most difficult kind of cost reduction for most department heads.

CONCLUSION

Having made his contributions to the choice of a cost system and the development of budgets, the plant manager moves on to the problems of cost control. He looks at the major areas of plant expense, establishing reporting systems which inform his subordinates and himself of the status of cost control, and urges them to effective action when deviations are unacceptably large. In his constant effort to keep costs at a minimum, he applies the special techniques available in purchasing practices, and requires payment authorization by department managers.

He identifies cost reduction as a continuing responsibility of his organization, rather than a sporadic effort, by establishing a formal cost reduction program. That program encourages competition between the cost centers of the plant, gives them recognition for the projects they propose and implement, and reports periodically on the progress and achievements of the cost reduction effort.

PART 4

Plant Equipment and Facilities

Chapter 13

Managing Plant Projects from Concept to Post-Completion Audit

The capacity, effectiveness, quality, and reliability of the plant's physical equipment are fundamental factors in the achievement of its manufacturing goals. Equipment does not remain static—as the plant's assignments change, so must its equipment to maintain product output and quality, and the safety and efficiency of the process. These changes are accomplished through the execution of engineering projects which modify the physical plant.

The plant manager is always involved in these projects, and he needs to understand the successive stages of their development. This chapter starts with the early conceptual and engineering design phases; goes on to economic justification, awarding of the contract, and control of work progress; and ends with the post-completion audit.

CONCEPTUAL STAGE

This is the phase in which the most basic questions about the project must be answered:

1) How big will it be? If a building, square footage and height; if process equipment, output rating; if material transport facility, carrying capacity per unit time.

2) What will it be made of? The choice of construction and engineering materials has a significant effect on the cost of the project. Any possible corrosion or contamination effects of the product on the equipment or of the equipment on the product must also be considered.

3) Where will it be placed? This decision is usually made on the basis of cost, and in turn hinges on the expense of moving materials to and from the new equipment, and the cost of running utility services to it. Movement of labor can also be a cost factor. Noneconomic considerations such as safety, sensitivity of the product to contamination, and pollution may weigh heavily in the final decision.

4) Should provision be made for future expansion? The present cost of providing space and capacity not immediately required is weighed against the probability of its being needed in the foreseeable future and the increased cost of providing it at a later time. The answer is influenced by the circumstances surrounding the individual project and the company's

general philosophy on capital expenditures; the important point is that the question be consciously considered and resolved in the planning stage of the project.

5) Are there special requirements in safety, reliability, housekeeping, utility supply, pollution control, or maintenance? Any of these considerations may influence the original design concepts and can cause unwanted delay and expense if they are ignored until the project is in its late stages.

In this stage develop as wide a range of thinking as possible—new ideas should be encouraged, a search for the latest equipment and methods undertaken, and if the project entails the duplication or expansion of existing facilities, improvements based on the experience gained with the old facilities incorporated. The conceptual stage can be handled by the plant's engineering staff, by outside consultants, or by a corporate central engineering department, but it should always involve the higher levels of plant management who may have original ideas of their own to contribute and who can help evaluate new ideas developed by others. It ends with the issuance of sketches and blueprints showing the major components of the project, their physical location, and the flow of materials through the process; and a written report stating the objectives of the project, the basic design philosophy, and descriptions of the equipment and process which cannot be conveniently shown on the prints.

ENGINEERING AND DESIGN STAGE

The object of this phase is to define the project sufficiently in blueprints and specifications so that it can be submitted to contractors for firm bid prices, and once the winning bidder is selected, actually constructed. Adequate detailing at this point will prevent misunderstandings later on—in cost, in what is expected of the contractor, in performance requirements of the equipment.

Let us assume that the project in question consists of erecting a new building on the plant site to house several new pieces of production equipment. The engineering department (or outside engineering firm) will prepare the following types of blueprints:

1) Plot plans. Essentially large scale maps of the plant area, they show existing and proposed buildings, roads, fences, utility lines and poles, railroads, streams and ditches, parking lots, sheds and pumphouses, any other significant external feature, and the property boundary lines.

2) Architectural drawings. One or more of these drawings will be prepared as determined by the size and complexity of the project:

   a. Foundation plans. The subsurface structures, including piles and footings, required to support the building and construction details of the basement or first floor slab.

   b. Floor plans. They show how each floor is divided into production areas, warehouse and storage, offices, lavatories, lunch rooms, locker rooms, elevator shafts, stairways, aisles, and passageways.

   c. Elevations. Views of the front, sides, and rear walls of the building, showing doors, windows, and decorative features.

   d. Wall sections. Vertical cross-sectional drawings of one or more of the walls of the structure. They start with the underground footings, and show the construction details of the basement and upper walls, including innner and outer facings and the intersections with the several floors and roof.

3) Structural drawings. They depict the structural framework which supports the

building. Most modern industrial buildings have a structural skeleton of steel beams and columns, and the drawings are likely to be entitled "Steel Framing Plan."

4) "Mechanicals." This is a term used by many engineering firms to include drawings showing the following types of building appurtenances:

Electrical (Power supply, wiring, circuit breakers, controls, receptacles, lighting fixtures)

Fire Protection (Sprinkler piping, cut-off valves, hose reels, hose houses, foam units)

Piping (Steam, water, compressed air, gases, and process fluids)

Heating and Ventilating (Air ducts, blowers, fans, radiators, space heaters, air conditioning equipment)

Instrumentation (Indicators, recorders, controllers for temperature, pressure, and liquid level; alarms interlocks, and cutoff devices)

5) Detail and Shop Drawings. The drawings described so far usually cover too large an area to permit showing the many details of construction. In the case of a building, the front and side elevations cannot effectively show the manner in which doorcases are affixed to the walls, or the exact position of the hinges. This is done in a *detail drawing,* on which may be shown the details of several items, such as doors, windows, steps, etc.

Shop drawings are usually supplied by contractors and equipment vendors, and submitted to the owner and the architect for their approval before construction is begun. On them these suppliers show, in great detail, how their sections of the building or equipment are to be constructed.

Specifications are prepared by the architect or engineer (usually in the form of an 8½ x 11 in. mimeographed booklet) to accompany each set of drawings. They give all the design details and construction procedures which cannot be described adequately on the blueprints. For instance, the specification for concrete defines the quality of the raw materials used to make it, the manner in which it is to be mixed, delivered to the site and poured, and the laboratory and field tests which it must pass. The electrical specification on transformers gives the required current capacity, the voltage stepdown, the manner of wiring, miscellaneous electrical characteristics, and the accessories which must be supplied with them. It may also specify the manufacturer whose product is to be used, or give a list of acceptable suppliers, any of which may be chosen by the contractor.

Blueprint Checklist

The plant manager is often asked to review a set of blueprints and specifications and give his approval before the project proceeds into the construction stage. Unless he is very familiar with engineering practice the task can be a confusing one, because blueprints seem to present the large and the small, the important and the unimportant in equal focus.

A useful tool in this situation is the blueprint checklist, an example of which is shown in Exhibit 1. This particular list covers most of the major areas of interest to a plant manager working with a project involving plant building or equipment, and can be used as is. Or it can be used as the basis of an individualized checklist developed by the manager to cover his special needs.

In the small plant the plant manager may be director of engineering as well; in this situation he can develop a whole series of checklists for reviewing each of the types of drawings mentioned in the previous section.

BLUEPRINT CHECKLIST

☐ Building and equipment meets size and capacity requirements determined in conceptual stage.

☐ Correct suppliers and model numbers for purchased equipment.

☐ Proper materials of construction used. No prohibited materials included.

☐ Has required ratings for pressure and temperature.

☐ Meets governmental zoning, building, health and safety codes. Meets insurance requirements.

☐ Physical arrangement—major components, controls, nozzles, feed and discharge ports, motor mounts arranged properly from right to left, top to bottom, front to rear.

☐ Equipment connections—lugs, bolt holes, clamps, support frames, piping and electrical connectors properly located for attachment to building and existing equipment.

☐ Lubrication. Grease fittings, oil ports and gauges, external lubricators, pressure cylinders, auxiliary pumps provided.

☐ Equipment and building layout designed for efficient materials movement and storage.*

☐ Allowance for future expansion in space allocation, structural design, and mechanical-electrical connections (if desired).

☐ Maintenance. Machine design allows for easy replacement of wear-prone parts. Building design provides vertical and horizontal room for removal of shafts, other large components.

☐ Required air, water, and noise pollution control devices included.

☐ Proper indicating, recording, and controlling instruments provided, along with needed quality control devices and sampling connnections.

☐ Specific safety devices, code and non-code, included. Coupling guards, safety brakes, shields, relief valves, shear pins, fusible links, lockout devices.

☐ Housekeeping. Building and equipment constructed with minimum crevices and corners for dirt to accumulate. Surfaces easily cleaned. Trash collection and removal systems adequate.

☐ Insulation. Provided where needed to conserve heat, prevent freezing, avoid injury to people.

☐ Machine controls, valves, instruments, sight ports easily accessible from floor to catwalk.

☐ Spare units (motors, pumps, etc.). Mounts, brackets, electrical and pipe connections uniform so that one unit is usable anywhere.

☐ Blueprints coordinated with specifications. No conflicts in requirements, no areas not covered by either.

Exhibit 1. Blueprint Checklist.
(For item marked * See Chapter 10, page 150 for detailed criteria.)

Economic Justification

As soon as the project has progressed to the stage where a firm price can be established (or very closely estimated) for its acquisition, it is ready for justification. And since it is the primary function of a business enterprise to return a profit on the money it is given to invest, nothing comes closer to the heart of the business than the way it decides to invest capital funds.

There are really two kinds of justification—non economic as well as economic. In *non economic justification* the business authorizes the expenditure of capital funds without a definite financial return for such reasons as safety, employee morale, governmental regulation, and community relations.

But the purchase of a new production machine or the erection of a building to house a new manufacturing process must be justified on purely economic grounds, and most companies have devised some kind of uniform system for evaluating the financial attractiveness of proposals for capital expenditure. In developing the following example we will try to show the three major elements of a financial justification and the most common methods of handling the financial data:

A) Statement of Project Cost. Assume that a major piece of production equipment is to be purchased and installed, and that an outside contractor will handle the installation. The project cost section of the justification will look like this:

1. Purchase Price of Equipment (Include freight charges and taxes.)	$42,019
2. Contractors' Charges (Include subcontractors' fees for rigging, piping, electrical work, etc.)	10,448
3. Auxiliary Equipment (Lubricators, instruments, scales, other items not included in basic purchase price.)	2,750
4. Engineering Services (Preparation of prints and specifications by outside or internal engineering groups.)	5,510
5. Contingency (10% of costs up to this point.)	6,073
Total Project Costs	$66,800

If the installation (Item 2) is to be carried out by the plant maintenance forces rather than an outside contractor, the costs should nevertheless be calculated and included in the project total.

B) Effect on Profit. New capital equipment can only be justified on the basis of additional profit which it generates in either or both of two ways: by providing additional production capacity or by reducing manufacturing costs. Both factors are included in the following table, which gives sales and operating cost figures for the depreciable life of the project (ten years in this case).

	Present	Proposed
1. Sales	$9,885,492	14,193,612
2. Operating Costs	4,853,313	7,373,636
3. Pretax Profit (Sales minus Costs)	5,032,179	6,819,976
4. Net Gain in Pretax Profit	____	$1,787,797

The profit gain from this project comes from additional sales made possible by increased production capacity. If it were a pure cost reduction project, sales figures might not be shown, and the added profit would result from lower operating costs. Although sales, cost, and profits are shown as simple line items in this example, individual companies may require extensive supporting data on their justification forms to back up these figures.

C) Comparison of Profit to Investment. A number of measures of profitability are used as criteria for judging capital proposals, and two of the most common—return on investment and payback period—will be demonstrated in this example.

1. Calculation of Total Investment. To the project cost which can be capitalized must be added non-capital investment required to keep the project going, such as raw material and finished goods inventories to fill the "pipeline" between plant and customer, and the cost of accounts receivable. In our example total investment becomes:

a. Capitalized Project Cost	$66,800
b. Working Capital	55,433
c. Total Investment	$122,233

2. Return on Investment

a. Net Profit (10 years; from B. 4.)	$1,787,797
b. Less Depreciation	66,800
c. Taxable Profit	1,720,997
d. Income Tax at 52% (Tax rates vary; obtain yours from accounting department.)	894,918
e. After-Tax Profit (c. minus d.)	826,079
f. Average Annual Profit (e. divided by 10 yrs.)	82,608
g. Return on Investment (Average Annual Profit divided by Total Investment expressed as percentage.)	67.6%

3. Payback Period. Its calculation requires use of the concept of "cash flow," which is the stream of money entering or leaving the project. The positive cash flow from a project such as this is the sum of the after-tax profit and the depreciation; the total investment divided by the average annual cash flow gives the payback period in years:

a. After-Tax Profit	$826,079
b. Total Depreciation	66,800
c. Total Cash Flow (a. plus b.)	892,879
d. Average Annual Cash Flow (Total Cash Flow divided by 10 yrs.)	89,288
e. Payback Period in Years (Total Investment divided by Annual Cash Flow.)	1.4

4. Commentary, With an ROI (return on investment) of 67.6 percent and a payback period of 1.4 years, this would seem to be an attractive investment in any company, and likely to be approved. Smaller investments which fill an immediate need tend to have high ROI rates and short payback periods; larger ones, such as the building of an entire plant, usually require longer payback times and yield lower returns on investment. The standard figures at which a project is rejected or accepted vary widely from company to company, and from time to time within a company, but some basic criteria against which a project might be judged include the cost of borrowing capital, the overall ROI of the company, and the ROI and payback periods of other capital projects under consideration or recently completed.

Individual companies may employ ROI or payback period alone as their criteria for capital decisions; they may use variations of the methods shown; or they may use entirely different methods such as venture worth and discounted cash flow. For a very good description and comparison of investment evaluation methods see James B. Weaver, H. Carl Bauman, and W.F. Heneghan, "Cost and Profitability Estimation," in *Chemical Engineers' Handbook* (4th ed.), ed. Robert H. Perry, Cecil H. Chilton, and Sidney D. Kirkpatrick (New York: McGraw-Hill Book Company, 1963), pp. 26-33ff.

Who Does the Work?

For the plant manager the choice is between utilizing his own maintenance forces to complete the project, or employing an outside contractor. Base the decision on these factors:

1. Skills needed to complete the work. If they are not readily available within the plant force, the outside contractor is a must.

2. Time available for completion. Maintenance forces must divide their time between the project and the normal maintenance needs of the plant. If the anticipated workload of the maintenance department is heavy, or the allowable completion time short, it may not be the best choice.

3. Cost. Usually, though not always, cheaper with in-house forces.

4. Union contract. It may limit your right to use outside contractors to projects above a certain dollar amount. If the contract is silent, you may want to place jobs outside regularly in order to preserve the right to do so. During delicate stages of negotiation or times of troubled union relationships you may wish to forego the use of outside contractors if their presence could be provocative.

How to Select a Contractor

If the decision is to use outside work forces, the next step is to find suitable contractors. If the plant has a history of outside contracting a number of suitable firms will be on its bidder list; if not, such sources as other plants in the area, contractors' and builders' associations, or even the telephone book must be used to develop a list of potential bidders. When evaluating a potential contractor, you should satisfy yourself on these points:

1. Does he have sufficient capacity and technical resources to complete the job—people, equipment, know-how, experience?

2. Has he done jobs similar in scope and complexity?

3. Is he financially sound?

4. Does he have a good reputation among clients for whom he performed work?

The answers to these questions can be obtained from bank references, credit information agencies such as Dun & Bradstreet, Inc., industry associations, and other plants. Develop a list of at least three or four bidders for every job; don't put any contractor on the list to whom you would not want to award the contract.

The project is now ready to send out for bid to the acceptable contractors. Because it will eventually become a part of the contract documents, use a bid form suggested by your lawyer. It should contain these elements: designation of the time and place deadline for submission of bids, scope of the work, surety bond provision, a sample copy of the contract the successful bidder will sign, insurance coverage requirements, designation of the architect or engineer (when outside consultants are used), how copies of the blueprints and specifications can be obtained, reservation of certain rights to the owner and the formal procedure for handling of addenda and interpretations.

Drawing Up the Contract

If your original bidder list contained only approved contractors, you should be able to accept the lowest bid with complete confidence. (If any of the bids received seems absurdly low or high, you may want to contact the bidder to see if he fully understands the project.) The next step is preparation of the contract:

1) Have your lawyer or legal department prepare the contract (it may be a very false economy to accept the bidder's offer to have the contract prepared). Standard forms for this purpose are sold by The American Institute of Architects, 1735 New York Avenue, Washington, D.C. 20006, under such titles as *Owner-Contractor Agreement—Stipulated Sum, General Conditions of the Contract for Construction,* and *Owner-Architect Agreement—Percentage of Construction Cost.*

2) Read the contract carefully to see if you agree to all its provisions. The plant manager particularly will want provisions which require the contractor to maintain access to existing buildings and work areas during construction, to observe plant safety rules, and to clean up thoroughly when the work is completed.

3) Be sure that the bid form and all blueprints and specifications are legally included as contract documents.

4) Require the contractor to submit evidence of required insurance coverage and surety bonds before the contract is signed.

5) Be sure that both signers of the contract are legally officers of their respective companies.

Control of Work Progress

Every contract will have a completion date, but it is fatuous to sit back and assume that the work will be completed on time without any further attention. Use these techniques to get the work accomplished on schedule:

1) Insert a clause in the contract requiring the contractor to submit a detailed time schedule for the work as soon as the contract is signed. Be sure to discuss the requirements of this clause with each bidder before he submits his bid.

2) Consider the use of bonus and penalty clauses, which require the contractor to pay the owner a fixed amount of dollars per day for every day the project is late, and the owner to pay the contractor a fixed amount (not necessarily the same) for every day the project is finished ahead of schedule. Beware of legal loopholes which invalidate the penalty side of these arrangements.

3) Designate an individual to take responsibility for the on-time completion of the job—usually the plant engineer or a project engineer. Require him to submit written reports periodically (weekly or monthly) stating what has been accomplished, where the project stands in relation to its schedule, and what he plans to do about any slippage.

4) Use diagrammatic representations of the work schedule to show progress against it. For smaller projects, a simple Gantt chart will do. (The Gantt chart is essentially a bar graph with a horizontal time line and each activity shown as a horizontal bar whose ends represent the beginning and completion times of the activity.) The Gantt chart is useful as a planning tool because it provides visual coordination of the activities which must be completed to get the project done; it is valuable as a control tool because at any given time it shows which activities should have been started, which should have been completed, and the percentage of completion of those in progress.

Larger projects may use more elaborate methods, such as Critical Path Programming or Program Evaluation and Review Technique (PERT). In the diagrams used for these methods important events, such as the start or finish of critical activities, are represented as circles, connected by lines which designate the activity required to reach them. A time value is given to each line, and when all the circles have been connected by lines in logical sequence, the longest time path through the network can be discerned. This is the critical path, and the succession of activities on it are those which must be closely controlled by management if the project is to be completed on schedule.

5) Frequent personal inspection of the work. If the contractor only has two men working on the job when he should have six, or if his materials are stockpiled in a disorganized mess, personal inspection is the quickest way to spot the problem and personal contact the quickest way to get him to correct the deficiencies.

THE POST-COMPLETION AUDIT

This function is usually performed by the accounting department, but there is no reason why the plant manager should not conduct his own. It has two objectives:

1) To compare the actual cost of the project with the predicted cost. This part of the audit can be completed as soon as the last bill is received or the last internal cost charge is made. If an economic justification form was used to gain approval for the project, the predicted cost can be taken from it.

2) To compare the actual cost savings or new profits derived from the project with those predicted by the economic justification. Completion of this part of the audit must wait for some time—a matter of months, or perhaps years—after the project is in operation for representative cost results to come in. (If the plant uses the Cost Reduction Performance Report shown in Exhibit 2, Chapter 12, the data needed for the post-completion audit are already at hand.) Once the actual cost and savings/profit figures are available, actual return on investment and payback period calculations, such as those shown on pages 185-186, can be made.

Post-completion audits have sometimes been given more lip service than actual implementation, but companies are taking them more seriously for these reasons: project originators tend to submit more careful cost and return estimates if they know their projects will be subject to performance audit; if the projects of a particular plant or department tend to be consistently over- or underestimated, higher management can use this fact in its decision making; unexpected deviations in the profit and loss statement may be explained by the actual performance of key projects.

CONCLUSION

The plant manager is vitally interested in any project which enlarges or modifies the physical equipment of his plant. He can make significant contributions to the conceptual stage, in which the fundamental outlines of the project are developed; to the engineering stage, in which the precise details of construction and equipment selections are spelled out; to the decision on whether inside or outside forces are to perform the work, the selection of a contractor, and the drawing up of the contract; and to the control of the work progress.

Underlying all these aspects is the question of cost. The plant manager is almost always required to prepare or approve the preparation of the economic justification, using the basic concepts outlined in this chapter. Finally, he participates in the post-completion cost review to measure actual performance against cost and financial return predictions.

Chapter 14

Designing Plants
to Meet Corporate Goals

The design and construction of a new plant can be viewed as simply another engineering project, and it is true that most of the concepts developed in Chapter 13 will be relevant to new plant projects. But because the decisions made in locating and designing such a large facility involve so many basic company policies and concern so many important manufacturing department goals, the special factors involved require separate treatment.

Corporations build new plants for a variety of reasons: to increase production capacity, to house new processes, to get closer to raw material supplies or finished goods markets, to eliminate or consolidate inefficient or obsolete operations, or to find a better labor market. The motives for deciding to build a new plant and its planners' forecast of changing conditions during its lifetime lead to the choice of specific design goals for the project, an area in which the plant manager can make significant contributions. This chapter will cover the development of design goals, location of the new plant, layout of the site, choice of building types, problems of materials flow, utilities, safety, and personnel facilities, and the refurbishing of older plants.

DESIGN GOALS

In many industries plant designers must face the fact that the plant they build will outlive the original products they were designed to produce by many years, to say nothing of the sales forecasts upon which production capacities are based. The two fundamental objectives of any plant design are to build a facility which can produce the required product at the lowest cost, but beyond them there are other goals which may require emphasis in any given project:

1) Flexibility. A must for plants in industries whose products have short life cycles. Keep building design simple, with large unobstructed floor spaces. Provide extra strength in steel construction for heavier upper floor loading at a later date.

2) Expansion. Design for expansion when there is a strong likelihood that future production requirements will exceed the design capacity which can be presently justified. Leave room on the operating floors for additional machinery, and leave space around buildings for expansion. Building design should lend itself to easy extension of steel framing, sidewalls, floors, and roof.

3) Adaptation to Transportation Modes. If shipments must be received or sent by water

or rail transportation, the plant design must adapt to the usually narrow range of choices for the location of the required facilities.

4) Minimum Capital Outlay. This goal is in direct conflict with the first two on this list—provisions for expansion and flexibility will have to be dropped if conservation of capital has higher priority. Look for opportunities to save on initial expense in these areas: *installing production equipment outdoors,* a method which is readily adapted to continuous processes, and in light of increasing emphasis on automatic controls, feasible even in the colder northern sections of the United States; *review of non-process items,* such as fencing, landscaping, building facades, paving; and *low-cost buildings,* which tend to be single-story, one unit (rather than several buildings), and pre-engineered.

Where to Locate the New Plant

The important thing to remember is that the location decision is an *economic* decision; although intangible factors like "labor climate" may seem to be paramount, the plant cannot succeed if it operates under substantial cost disadvantages.

1) Factors to Consider in Plant Location.

a. Nearness to raw materials. Cost of transportation for inbound materials, reliability of supply, reliability of transportation.

b. Nearness to markets. Cost of transportation of finished goods, ease of distribution, ability to serve customers compared with that of actual and potential competitors.

c. Labor market. Wages and fringe benefit costs. Availability of labor in numbers and required skills.

d. Availability of land. Is there enough for present *and* future requirements?

e. Local and state governments. Will they offer financial assistance? Tax rates. Zoning regulations—will they affect or limit plant operations?

f. Transportation facilities. Rail siding available? Good trucking service? Ship and barge facilities? Air transportation for technical and administrative personnel?

g. Utilities. Water, steam, natural gas, electric power. Fuels for power plants.

h. Local hazards. Flood, earthquake, tornado, hurricane. Effect of proposed plant on neighboring plants and vice versa.

2) Where to Get Information About the Location Factors.

a. Government agencies. All of the states, the District of Columbia, and the Canadian provinces maintain agencies which provide information and assistance to companies considering locations within their borders. The larger cities also have industrial development agencies, and most towns (even down to the very small ones) have a Chamber of Commerce which will supply local information. (See Section c. below.)

b. Railroads and utility companies. Many of these companies maintain lists of and will gather information on potential plant sites within the areas they serve.

c. Publications. Business and technical magazines (such as *Plant Engineering* and *Modern Manufacturing*) run articles from time to time on plant site selection problems and the methods used by various companies to solve them. Of special interest is the *Site Selection Handbook,* published annually by Conway Research, Inc., Atlanta, Georgia, which gives economic, demographic, and manufacturing data on the states and provinces, an index of industrial sites, and a listing of the state and local agencies and the kinds of help they offer.

d. Private consulting firms. A number of management, engineering, and industrial consultants will undertake detailed site selection surveys for proposed new plants. Although the cost of these services may seem high, such a firm may have a vast reservoir of information and experience to draw from, and usually can take a more dispassionate view of proposed sites than company personnel.

3) The Decision-Making Process

a. From the plant location factor list extract a set of characteristics which the site for the proposed plant *must* have; then develop a second list of characteristics which would be *desirable*.

b. Using the sources of information selected, develop as large a list as possible of potential areas and sites.

c. Screen out all those areas and sites which do not have the characteristics on the required list.

d. Screen out the remaining sites which have the least number of desirable characteristics.

e. Make a detailed economic study of the remaining sites, comparing annual operating costs, costs per unit of production, and return on investment for each. A very small number of sites will emerge from this comparison for final executive decision.

Develop the Plot Plan

Once the site has been selected, the next step is to lay out the arrangement of buildings and facilities on a plot plan. Most of the following considerations should be explored before the land is actually purchased:

1) Determine what zoning laws and building codes apply to the site. They will affect building setbacks from the property line, the uses to which the land may be put, and the types of buildings and facilities which may be constructed. Insurance safety regulations are also a factor, affecting the minimum distance between buildings and storage areas which contain flammable or otherwise dangerous materials.

2) Place storage areas and transportation facilities—especially railroad tracks—around the outer perimeter of the property. If placed in the center they may create difficult and expensive problems when later expansions of process buildings are desired.

3) Place process buildings in the center of the property, with the direction of future expansion clearly defined, and room for such expansion allowed.

4) Specify the final location of buildings and heavy structures only after soil bearing tests have been made to see if there are underground impediments to construction—soil so soft that expensive footings and piling would be required, or rock formations which would require blasting.

5) Storage areas for materials which can be cheaply transported (liquids which can be pumped or solids which can be handled in bulk) should be located farther away from point of use, while nearer locations are reserved for materials more expensive to move, especially those requiring hand labor.

Fix Plant Layout and Materials Flow

The object is to arrive at the arrangement of process equipment and material flow paths which offers the lowest production costs. Include these considerations in developing plant layout:

1) The ideal material flow path is straight through, with minimum handling, and no backtracking.

2) In a plant where the cost of moving materials is a large part of the overall production cost, the fundamental precepts of materials movement must be included in the design. See Chapter 10, pages 145-146, for the detailed list.

3) The basic groupings of buildings and equipment are determined by the choice between process and product orientation for the manufacturing operations.

In *process-oriented* plants each of the operations performed (boring, grinding, heat treating, plating, painting, etc.) is carried out at a given location for all of the products made. Process orientation is suited to plants which produce smaller volumes of a larger number of products, and which are subject to relatively frequent product changes.

In *product-oriented* plants each product is passed through its own production line or department, and all of the steps required to produce it are carried out in sequence. Product orientation is suited to plants which manufacture large volumes of a smaller number of products, and where products changes are infrequent. See Chapter 2, page 40 for a descriptive example contrasting product and process orientation.

4) Plant organization and plant layout have inescapable effects on each other; when one is dominant, the other must conform. See Chapter 2, page 40, for detailed considerations.

5) A pitfall in new plant design lies in the tendency to make provisions for later expansion of production capability without corresponding provisions for increased materials flow. Be sure to leave room for additional storage, conveyors, rail car spots, truck docks, and other material handling facilities.

Choose Building Types

1) Limitations on choice. Building codes, zoning regulations, cost of construction, appearance requirements, size and shape of equipment to be housed, safety requirements, insurance regulations, and time allowed for construction all affect the choice of building types.

2) Types of building construction.

a. Foundations and basements. Office and laboratory buildings may be constructed with basements to provide storage space, but manufacturing buildings are less likely to have them. The type of foundation support depends upon the load bearing strength of the soil and the weight of the building; supports include *concrete footings, pilings* of wood, concrete or steel, and in especially soft soils, *concrete mats* which spread the load over the entire area of the building.

b. Floors. Almost all modern industrial buildings have reinforced concrete floors, but in special cases they are covered with wood blocks, matting of rubber or plastic, and plastic-bonded aggregates to meet special needs of worker comfort, spark control, and resistance to corrosion.

c. Framing. Structural steel is most commonly used for the support framework because it is cheap, strong, adaptable to a variety of building styles, and can accomodate long spans. Reinforced concrete structural members are sometimes used when heavy floor loads are required in high buildings.

d. Walls. The conflicting requirements are cost, appearance, fire resistance, maintenance, and insulation against heat loss. Corrugated steel is inexpensive to install, but requires periodic painting, and in most locations, insulation. Concrete block is widely used, has reasonable insulating characteristics and good appearance, but still requires painting. When face brick is added to improve appearance, the cost goes up sharply. Pre-fabricated wall sections of steel or aluminum with factory-installed enamel coatings are low-cost and low-maintenance alternatives;

insulation can be installed on the inside, or a "sandwich" version can be obtained—inner and outer metal skins with insulation in the middle.

e. Roofs. Pitched roof construction is used when the architect or owner desires fast runoff of rain and melted snow. Flat roof construction is used when penthouses, ventilating and air-conditioning equipment, dust-collecting apparatus, or other superstructures must be mounted, and when it is desired to make fullest use of the building volume.

f. Number of stories. Multi-story buildings are used when unusual equipment configurations must be accomodated, or it is desired to take advantage of gravity flow to move materials, or when land for expansion is not available at a site and the only direction to go is up. But in the continuing debate among engineers and architects, the one-story building has been winning out on the basis of economy, even in high-cost land areas. (Of the "Top Ten" plants chosen by *Modern Manufacturing* magazine in 1970, nine had one-story production facilities.)

g. Pre-engineered. Available in both metal and concrete, these buildings offer the economies of standard structural design and maximum use of prefabricated components, and have been a favored choice for housing operations which do not require specialized building shapes.

Provide for Utilities

Time deadlines and the considerable effort which goes into the design of process equipment and buildings create a temptation to give only routine attention to ways in which steam, water, air, and electricity are supplied to the plant. But utility installations are not easily changed once the plant is built, and in many production operations the efficiency with which they are supplied can have a marked effect on the cost performance of the plant. Check out these facets of the design plans:

1) Water. Can the municipal supply provide the plant's full needs? Are there any flows which can be recycled? Is the plant's projected usage of water large enough to justify its own treatment plant? Are there any uses which do not require fully treated water—for instance, does the makeup supply to a cooling tower have to be drinking water grade, or would filtered or merely flocculated water do? Do the plans include acceptable devices for preventing contamination of the municipal supply with lower grade plant waters? Is there sufficient pressure and flow in the supply of fire-fighting water to meet foreseeable emergencies and to obtain the lowest insurance rates?

2) Steam. Should steam be purchased (if available) or generated? If generated, are two or more boilers included in the plan so that failure of one will not shut the plant down completely? Does the arrangement of buildings on the site minimize the length of distribution lines, and thereby losses? Have pressures at points of use been worked out so that contamination of the steam by the process (or vice versa, if that is worse) is avoided?

3) Electricity. Is it more economical to generate electricity than to buy it—especially if waste steam from the generator can be used by the process? If purchased, should standby units be provided to handle emergencies such as power outages? Should primary or secondary selective feeder systems be installed to provide backup power in case of failure in the main line? Have power factor losses been considered and capacitors provided (if needed) to minimize them? Should office and some plant space heating be electrical? Can interior lights supply part of the space heating load?

4) Air. Have all the uses for compressed air been considered in reaching the design capacity—instruments, tools, painting, pumping of liquids? Is air for any of these services required to be oil-free or moisture-free, and have separators, dryers, and separate distribution loops been provided where needed?

Design for Safety

The plant safety program starts with the plant design: failure to incorporate sound safety principles at this stage invites injuries to personnel and damage to property for the entire life of the plant. Use this checklist of important safety provisions:

1) Fire prevention and control. Minimum use of combustible construction materials. Highly flammable raw materials and finished goods stored in isolated areas with suitable fire prevention devices. Fully equipped hose houses, hose stations, and appropriate types of fire extinguishers strategically distributed throughout plant. Sprinkler sytem designed according to code; sprinkler heads not blocked by equipment; design based on adequate water supply.

2) Mechanical equipment. Moving parts covered with safety guards. Controls clearly labelled, within easy reach. Safety brakes and quick-cutoff controls on machinery likely to draw the operator in (such as a rubber mill). Automatic hand and arm withdrawal guards on machines which cut, press, or stamp.

3) Personnel movement. Pedestrian and vehicle traffic separated as much as possible. Walkways and stairs provided with non-skid surfaces. Ladders over twenty feet equipped with safety cages. Catwalks, platforms, and stairs edged with kickplates and double handrails. Outside walks, ramps, and parking areas designed with snow and ice melting devices, or at least constructed to minimize winter hazards.

4) Electrical. All equipment used in hazardous areas has the appropriate National Electric Code rating. Multiple lockout devices furnished for safe shutdown and maintenance work. Use of portable equipment and extension cords avoided wherever possible. Conductive belts and static collector brushes used on moving machinery; ground straps for transfer of flammable liquids through pipes and between containers. Distribution system grounded. Battery-operated exit and emergency lights installed for safe evacuation in power failure.

5) Piping and conduit. Labelled, showing contents and direction of flow. Color coding for remote identification, danger warning. Hot sections within reach of personnel insulated.

6) Ventilation. Adequate for comfort. Reduces concentrations of toxic, flammable, and irritating dusts and fumes to safe levels.

7) Housekeeping. Surfaces designed for minimum dirt accumulation and ease of cleaning. Floors sloped to drains. Floors sealed off to prevent spills from cascading downward.

8) All systems. Meet applicable municipal, state, and federal safety regulations. Meet insurance safety codes. Meet OSHA requirements. Follow published recommendations of trade associations (see Chapter 9).

Personnel Facilities

The number, size, and elaborateness of these facilities depend on the number of employees in the plant and the company philosophy of industrial relations. These are the minimum considerations:

1) Food service. Very large plants may elect to install a full-fledged cafeteria complete with its own food preparation staff. Smaller plants may provide a central lunchroom with vending machine service, possibly served by an attendant during rush periods. Very small plants may provide a simple lunchroom with few embellishments other than chairs and tables. Consideration should be given to snack areas scattered around the plant to cut down the time personnel spend getting to and from lunch and coffee breaks. Under no circumstances allow food to be taken into the plant working areas; it is subject to contamination by all sorts of substances, and, if spilled, creates an attraction for vermin.

2) Locker room, toilets, and showers. Be sure the locker room is built with plenty of allowance for expansion. Use lockers with sloping tops; otherwise they will collect an array

of personal effects. Follow local building codes on the number of persons to one water closet; in their absence provide one toilet for every fifteen people. Shower facilities may be required by state or local codes; if not, they should be provided for dirty, dusty, or odorous operations.

3) First aid room. The company doctor should decide what equipment is needed; he will probably base his decision on the speed with which an injured employee can be gotten to the hospital or a doctor's office. The first aid room, dispensary, or an elaborate medical facility should be cheerfully decorated, well-lighted, and placed as far from plant noise and odors as possible.

4) Instructional facilities. A "classroom" fitted with a blackboard, projection screen, and comfortable chairs will prove valuable for safety meetings and in-plant instruction.

Pollution Control

The new plant must be provided with adequate pollution control devices if it is to meet the twin objectives of earning a reputation as a good neighbor in the community and complying with the increasingly strict laws in effect in most communities. Review the adequacy of design features in these areas of pollution:

1) Air. *Smoke* and *sulfur dioxide* emissions from boilers, diesel engines, fossil fuel burning equipment, and incinerators. *Dust* and any other particulate matter from process operations. Noxious *odors* which can be unpleasant, or unhealthy, or both.

2) Water. Discharges into rivers and natural waterways are usually limited to storm drainage, clean once-through cooling water, and effluents of high quality from waste treatment systems. Discharges into municipal sewer systems are usually required to meet a long list of physical and chemical specifications. In both cases there is likely to be a limit on the temperature of the discharge.

3) Noise. Federal and state labor laws may limit the allowable levels of noise in the plant for protection of the work force, but some communities—especially in the suburbs—may place a limit on noise levels at the plant boundaries.

4) Land. Piles of trash, tailings, or other solid waste may be objectionable from a community relations standpoint, or actually forbidden by law, especially if the material gives off odors, is likely to blow around, creates unsightly views, or stands to contaminate a waterway.

Estimate the Cost

The cost estimates for new plant projects usually prove to be low, creating unpleasant surprises for those who must supply capital funds and often resulting in elimination or severe cutback of parts of the project. Be sure to include in the estimate the cost of these items: site surveys, land acquisition (including brokerage fees), general engineering design, detailed engineering plans and specifications, site preparation (including allowance for unexpected subsurface work such as blasting), building construction, utilities installation, landscaping, equipment purchase, operating inventory, startup expenses including operator training and the cost of suppliers' technician services for calibration and adjustment of new equipment.

Inclusion of all costs is one essential ingredient of an accurate estimate; the other is the use of the most reliable methods of estimation available. This list of cost information sources is arranged in descending order of reliability in the author's view:

1) Contractor's firm bid. The most accurate of all cost data is the bid submitted by a contractor after he has reviewed the prints and specifications for the project. To it must be added the cost of land acquisition, engineering services, startup expenses, and a contingency factor for unforeseen "extra" work which is not included in the contractor's original bid.

2) Company files on similar construction and equipment projects. The cost data they contain must be adjusted for differences in time, geographical location, and equipment used for the process. The first two can be handled by applying cost indices appearing in *Engineering News Record.* The third is best handled by obtaining supplier quotations for the exact type of equipment specified for the new project.

3) Outside consultants. Consulting firms in architecture, management, engineering, and even some contractors can be retained to develop a project cost estimate. For this method to be successful, it is important that the agency selected has no other interest in the project; otherwise there is a natural pressure on them to estimate low in order to keep interest in the project alive.

4) Cost literature. Technical and even some local libraries can offer a number of books on construction cost estimating and equipment costs in specific industries; be sure to check the date of publication, because cost data published in book form may be outdated. Periodicals are in a better position to publish current cost information; the journals of the engineering societies publish cost articles from time to time, as do such general industrial periodicals as *Plant Engineering* and *Modern Manufacturing. Cost Engineering* is a magazine devoted to industrial equipment costs; it is published by Industrial Research Service, Dover, N.H. Also of interest are *Building Construction Cost Data* by R.S. Means, published annually at Duxbury, Mass., and *Manual of Commercial-Industrial Construction Estimating and Engineering Standards* published by Richardson Engineering Services, Inc., Downey, California, and updated on a continuing basis.

REFURBISHING AN OLD PLANT

There are times when the corporation feels compelled to install a new process or continue an existing process in an obsolescent building, and decides to renovate the facility. Consider these factors when undertaking a refurbishment program:

1) Layout is a compromise. The arrangement of operating equipment, aisleways, and materials handling facilities is limited by the physical structure of the existing building, and the optimum arrangement desired is not always possible to achieve. Try out as many ideas for equipment layout as possible, to be sure that the best compromise has been reached.

2) Major physical features *can* be changed. Steel support columns can be moved provided adjustments are made in the surrounding steel structure; floors (even on upper levels) can be chopped out and repoured; mezzanines can be built, or floors chopped out to achieve a two-level bay; interior partitions and walls can be rearranged; so can exterior walls (unless, as in some older buildings, they support the structure). Changes in the basic structure of a building are expensive, however, and should be economically justified by demonstrable savings in processing or materials movement.

3) Look for the likely weaknesses in an old building. Modifications and repairs are often needed in these areas:

   a. Roofs. May be leaking, in disrepair, and inadequately insulated.

   b. Heating, ventilating, and air conditioning. Insufficient capacity, equipment obsolete or not functioning, heating not coordinated with ventilation, or ventilation not coordinated with air conditioning.

   c. Windows and doors. In older buildings they tend to be small by today's standards, and often are in disrepair or unattractive. Enlargement and repairs will often return a great deal on the money spent in the way of improved appearance and employee morale.

   d. Illumination. Insufficient light at working surfaces, obsolete types of illumination (such as incandescent lights), inadequate wiring, and broken or dirty light fixtures may all require attention.

e. Utilities. Steam boilers may be inadequate for the load, in disrepair, or in need of replacement. Electric power mains, substations, and distribution wiring may need to be increased in capacity. Pipes and conduits for distribution of services throughout the building may be unsightly. Remove those which are not needed, hide the remainder from view wherever possible, fix leaks, repair insulation, and paint those which cannot be hidden.

f. Decor. When the "battleship gray" and "seasick green" interior colors of older plant buildings give way to more interesting color schemes, much is done toward modernization. Exterior masonry walls can be pointed, painted, and upgraded with new facia treatments, marquees, and entranceways.

CONCLUSION

The development of a plant design is a logical step-by-step procedure which demands the accumulation and evaluation of a large mass of information. The basic corporate motives for building a new plant, an evaluation of the business forecasting upon which the design capacity is based, and the nature of the business to be conducted at the new site all contribute to the selection of basic design goals which must be included in the subsequent steps. Site selection is primarily an economic process, but affected by the availability of needed materials and facilities. Once the site is chosen, the plot plan is developed, material flow paths determined, and building types selected. Detailed design attention can then be given to provisions for utility supply, safety, and employee morale and comfort, but the design is not complete without early consideration of the steps which must be taken to control air and water pollution. Refurbishment of an old plant involves the same basic design techniques as the building of a new one, but compromises usually have to be reached between the ideal layout and those which are possible in the existing building.

Cost overruns are as common as they are disturbing in new plant projects, and if the cost estimate is to be reliable it must be all-inclusive, based on the most accurate data which can be obtained, and constantly subjected to critical review.

Chapter 15

Selecting, Specifying, and Acquiring the Best Buys in Plant Equipment

Throughout the life of the plant, management will be making equipment changes—replacing worn-out units, updating obsolete systems, installing new production lines and processes. Because these new pieces of equipment are complicated, expensive, and have long working lives, the skill with which they are selected has an important bearing on successful operation of the plant.

In the smaller plant the plant manager is intimately involved in the selection process, while in the larger plant the engineering staff and purchasing department assemble the information required to make a decision. In either case the plant manager will insist that the search for the best equipment be thorough and conducted according to standards he has set. In this chapter effective methods for evaluating general attributes, developing specifications, utilizing the purchasing department and obtaining competitive bids, making the final selection, and performance testing of new equipment are given.

Consider These Attributes

The choice of a major piece of equipment is a risky process; if it fails to do the job it was purchased for, plant performance is seriously threatened in critical areas. The manager who makes or approves selection decisions must take every action he can to push the probability of success toward certainty. That process starts with evaluating each proposed piece of equipment against these attributes, and including those desired in the formal specifications:

   1. Actual performance vs. design capacity. Will the equipment really produce at the "design" rate? Will capacity drop off with age, and how much? Should it be overdesigned with a factor of ten, twenty, or some other percentage?

   2. Reliability. How often and how long must it be down for scheduled maintenance? What is the likelihood of unscheduled outages?

   3. Simplicity of design. Fewer moving parts and fewer wearable parts (such as seals and gaskets) increase reliability.

   4. East of operation. Are operating controls clearly labelled, easy to understand, convenient to reach?

   5. Ease of maintenance. Are the parts most subject to wear easily accessible

201

with a minimum of disassembly required? Can repairs be made in your shop, or must unit be shipped back to factory?

6. Low cost. Be sure to evaluate the combination of first cost and operating cost for the life of the equipment.

7. Materials of construction. Are they the least expensive types which will meet the needs of the operation? Will they be subject to corrosion? Will they contaminate the product?

8. Standardized construction. Parts interchangeable, readily available?

9. Safety. Meets national codes, insurance codes, state labor department requirements?

10. Appearance. Very little in the way of performance can be sacrificed for appearance in the choice of industrial equipment, but an attractive design helps operator acceptance and increases the confidence of those who supply the capital funds.

Develop Specifications

Insist that a written list of specifications be prepared before the first potential supplier is contacted; that will force your organization to clarify its thinking about what is really wanted in the equipment, and will assure that the quotations you receive are comparable. The specifications should be:

1) Inclusive. They should cover dimensions, output capacity, materials of construction, type and size of power train, utility connections, controls, manufacturing techniques (such as heat treating), insulation, lubrication devices, equipment auxiliaries, delivery date, and methods of performance testing.

2) Clear. Present them in precise terms, using the language of the trade. Vague instructions may result in the supplier using (innocently) materials of insufficient quality or of too high quality. For example, to specify that a part be made of "stainless steel" is inadequate; both performance and cost will be quite different if "Stainless Steel Type 201" is specified rather than "Stainless Steel Type 316" or "Stainless Steel Type 316L."

3) Not overspecified. It is a common error to require more in equipment performance and construction than is really needed, especially when the project engineer is unfamiliar with the equipment being purchased, or uses specifications taken wholesale from published standards. The results are excessive cost, unnecessarily complicated equipment, and longer delivery schedules.

Exhibit 1, which presents a detailed list of specifications for the purchase of an electric fork lift truck, is an example of how extensive and complicated the development of specifications can be for a seemingly simple and relatively standard piece of industrial equipment.

Role of the Purchasing Department

As soon as the desired general attributes are translated into a definitive list of specifications, it is time to call upon the purchasing department to perform these important functions:

1) Canvass the field. No department is in a better position to develop an exhaustive list of the potential suppliers of the desired equipment.

2) Screen unsuitable suppliers. Purchasing people can weed out early in the search suppliers who do not understand the specifications, whose equipment clearly does not meet the requirements, and those with poor performance records in delivery and quality.

3) Define the conditions of purchase. Whether it is to be by purchase order or formal

contract; delivery times, method of payment, cancellation rights, payment of freight charges, and price (when it is not determined by competitive bidding and must be negotiated).

EQUIPMENT SPECIFICATION: ELECTRIC FORK LIFT TRUCK

STYLE:	Stand up end rider, counterbalanced.	OVERALL DIMENSIONS:	Underclearance: 2 in. min. Length, without forks: 65 in. max. Height (Inc. overhead guard) 90 in. max.
CAPACITY:	3,000 lb. @ 24 in. load center.		
FORKS:	Type: Standard pallet. Length: 42 in.	WHEELS:	Wheelbase: 30 in. Drive wheels, size: 11¼ in. Tires: 16¼x7 in. Steering wheels, size: 6½ in. Tires: 10½x5 in. Tire type: Solid, polyurethane.
MAST:	Type: Telescoping. Collapsed Height: 83 in. max. Extended Height: 215 in. max. Free Lift: 46 in. min. Extended Fork Height: 186 in. min. Lift Speed, Loaded: 45 ft. per. min. Lift Speed, Unloaded: 90 ft. per. min. Forward Tilt: 10 degrees Backward Tilt: 5 degrees	TURNING RADIUS:	Outside: 64 in. max. Must right angle stack in aisle of 170 in. width.
		BATTERY:	No. of cells: 18. Ampere-Hours: 576. Voltage: 36.
		CHARGER:	Type: Solid State Rectifer. Power Supply: 220 v., 60 cycle, 3 phase. Charge Time: 8 hrs max.
LEVEL SPEED:	Loaded: 4 mph, min. Unloaded: 6 mph, min.		
CONTROLS:	Silicon Controlled Rectifer (SCR) type.		
ELECTRICAL SYSTEM:	Voltage: 36. Safety Rating: Type EE. (Must have UL label.)		

Exhibit 1. Detailed Specifications for Purchase of Electric Fork Lift Truck

4) Obtain competitive bids. It is the only way to assure that the lowest possible price is paid, and should be standard practice for all major purchases. The purchasing department can handle this chore in a professional manner, relieving the line and technical organizations of the many details involved. No matter who handles the bids, be sure that these two important "don'ts" are observed:

a. Don't put any supplier with whom you do not want to do business on the bidder's list. If his turns out to be the low bid, you may have a great deal of explaining to do about why you want to reject it. By limiting the list to acceptable suppliers you can confidently accept the low bid and proceed with the purchase as soon as the bids are opened.

b. Don't be lured into changing the specifications for one bidder. The representative of XYZ Company may suggest that "we can save some money if this stainless steel section is changed to aluminum—why don't you let me bid it that way?" To let him do so, of course, is to lose any valid comparison between his bid and the others. If his suggestion is acceptable use one of these methods to take advantage of it: 1) send a formal specification change to all the bidders, 2) require all the bidders to quote on the original specifications, then invite the low bidder and the one who submitted the suggestion to rebid under the new specification.

HOW TO EVALUATE PROPOSED EQUIPMENT

At some point in the selection procedure a specific piece of equipment will be offered, either in the form of blueprints for a special design to meet your needs, or as a standard item from the supplier's product line. Use these guidelines to evaluate the proposed equipment:

1) Compare its design features with your process experience. If you have had repeated structural failures, wearing of moving parts (such as shafts, bearings, gears, pistons, seals, etc.), motor burn-outs or overload failures of any kind, check out the design details of the new equipment to be sure its parts are rugged enough to handle your service.

2) Ask for a performance trial. If the equipment is readily transportable the supplier may agree to a trial on your premises on a rental basis, with the fees to be credited toward the purchase price if you decide to keep the equipment. If it is too large to be moved easily, ask the supplier if he can arrange a visit to a plant where his equipment is in operation. Or, the supplier may be able to show you a test run in his plant, or allow your personnel to conduct trials on pilot-sized equipment in his laboratories.

3) Investigate the supplier's capacity to service the equipment at your location. Are replacement parts readily available from nearby stocks? If service personnel are required, can they reach your plant quickly and do they enjoy a good reputation for competent work?

4) Talk to other owners of the equipment. The supplier may be willing to supply the names of other corporations which have bought his equipment; telephone calls to these owners will give you a good perspective on the performance history of the equipment. Bear in mind that the supplier is likely to give you the names of satisfied customers; it will take some independent digging to find not-so-satisfied purchasers.

5) Ask for a copy of the operating manual. Advertising claims tend to emphasize the most favorable attributes, but the operating instructions for use of the equipment reveal all of the precautions which must be taken in its use, and its major service limitations. Thorough study of this important document will discover information not otherwise available.

Watch Out for Warranties

Equipment purchases are usually made on a tight time schedule, and in the rush to get the equipment specified and on order warranty provisions may be only considered casually, or ignored altogether. If the equipment performs perfectly no harm is done by this neglect; the purchaser's problems begin when the equipment fails to perform and he finds that the warranty does not give him the protection he assumed it contains. Be sure to consider these aspects of equipment warranty before signing the purchase order or contract:

1) The warranty is only as good as the reputation and integrity of the supplier; if he refuses to make good on defective equipment, the cost of forcing him to do so through litigation may be prohibitively expensive.

2) When does it start, and when does it end? Some suppliers start the warranty period when the equipment is delivered, others when it is first placed in service, still others when the purchase order is placed. It may end after a definite time period (such as ninety days or one year), after so many hours of operation, or a fixed number of production units. If the equipment is part of a large construction project, beware of the warranty running out while it is waiting to be installed.

3) What does it cover? The following list of items which might be covered by a warranty is arranged roughly in order of diminishing likelihood that the supplier will agree to them:

    a. Replacement of defective parts (material only).
    b. Labor costs for replacement.
    c. Freight charges to and from supplier's plant.
    d. Refund of purchase price.
    e. Protection against patent infringement claims.
    f. Damage to purchaser's process materials.
    g. Financial losses suffered by purchaser in overhead costs and lost profits if supplier's equipment is unable to maintain normal production rate.

4) Are all bidders providing essentially the same warranty? The supplier who agrees only to replace defective parts can submit a lower bid than the one who agrees to cover financial losses resulting from performance defects. To put all bidders on the same basis, require them to submit essentially the same warranty; when that is not practicable, be sure to take differences in their warranties into account when evaluating bid prices.

5) The buyer has responsibilities, too. Under most warranties the customer is required to install and operate the equipment according to the manufacturer's instructions; connect it only to approved power supplies; keep it lubricated; operate it only within design limits of output, speed, pressure, temperature, and other operating conditions; shut the equipment down and notify the supplier promptly if it does not run properly; and to allow repairs to be made only by the supplier or personnel approved by him. Even if the warranty language does not mention these points specifically, the buyer probably weakens the claims he might have if he does not observe them.

Performance Testing

There are three compelling reasons for conducting a formal performance trial on newly acquired equipment: to discover defects before they impair the plant operation, to prevent the original defect from causing further damage to the equipment, and to eliminate supplier's claims that the buyer contributed to equipment failure by improper operation. Include in the time schedule for equipment procurement a definite period for performance testing, and base the test procedure on this list of activities:

1) Inspect before testing. As soon as the equipment is delivered, go over it for missing or broken parts, and compliance with design specifications. Perform any non-operational examinations such as leak testing, X-ray and ultrasonic tests for thickness and structural flaws, metal identification, and electrical checking of coatings, insulation, and linings.

2) Have manufacturer's representative present. For large, expensive equipment purchases his presence at the performance trial will probably be arranged as a matter of course but it is a good idea to invite the supplier to send a representative even when smaller pieces of equipment are tested. He can assure his organization that test conditions were correct, foresee and prevent damage, and attest to the failure of the equipment to perform if that is the outcome.

3) Follow a planned testing procedure. It can come from three sources: the manufacturer's instruction manual, developed and written by the buyer (but approved by the

manufacturer), or a standard test from such organizations as the United States Government (federal and military procurement specifications), technical societies, or manufacturers' and trade groups.

4) Keep a written log of the test. Record all operating conditions and performance observations: speed, temperature, pressure, output, voltage, current, and flow rates—and the times at which they are observed.

5) Shut down the equipment if it is not operating properly. Overheating, tripping of electrical breakers, popping of relief valves, excessive noise, inability to operate at design speeds—all indicate defects which may cause serious additional damage if the equipment continues to operate.

6) Report defects promptly. The manufacturer is entitled to quick notification that his equipment is defective; if it is delayed, it increases his suspicion that the deficiency was caused by the customer's method of operation.

Use of Industry Standards

A wide variety of technical, trade, and insurance organizations publish equipment design and use standards, and performance test codes. In Exhibit 3 of Chapter 10 we have seen an excerpt from "Type Designations, Areas of Use, Maintenance and Operation of Industrial Trucks," published by the National Fire Protection Association. Among professional society publications the "Boiler and Pressure Vessel Code" and "Power Test Code for Steam Boilers" published by the American Society of Mechanical Engineers are well known. The American Institute of Chemical Engineers publishes "Equipment Testing Procedures, Centrifugal Pumps (E-5)," "Solids Mixing Equipment (E-8)," and "Heat Exchangers (E-15)," among others. Examples of industry group publications are "NEMA Standards for Motors and Generators" by the National Electric Manufacturing Association, and "Standards of the Tubular Exchangers Manufacturers Association." Contact the professional society or trade association of your industry to see if it publishes equipment specifications; your insurance carrier or a librarian can help you gain access to the many similar publications in other industries.

These technical and trade standards provide help in three basic areas of equipment procurement:

1) The industry standard can be used as one criterion for judging a proposed piece of equipment. If it meets the industry standards, a minimum level of quality is assured.

2) Specifications can be taken verbatim or adapted from the industry standards, eliminating the cost of researching and developing them independently; the purchase order or contract can quote them or simply refer to the numbered sections. But beware of copying blindly—standardized specifications may not cover all points of importance to you, nor handle them according to your operation's special needs.

3) Performance tests offer a neutral ground between buyer and seller upon which to measure and evaluate the functioning of the new equipment. If they are to be used, they should be mentioned in the purchase order or procurement contract.

CONCLUSION

The equipment selection process consists of three phases: determining what attributes are needed in the proposed equipment, and developing specifications to insure the equipment will have them; searching the marketplace to develop a list of candidates for selection; and evaluating the available equipment and suppliers to make a final choice. Once the equipment is delivered and installed, performance testing verifies condition and capability. Throughout the process, industry and technical society standards are used to insure minimum quality, meet safety requirements, and establish middle ground for agreement between purchaser and supplier.

Chapter 16

Choosing Electrical Equipment
for Cost Effectiveness

Because it is cheap, clean, and easily distributed, electricity is the universally used form of energy, and it is difficult to think of a plant in which it is not the prime source for driving mechanical equipment. The plant manager, therefore, has a vital interest in the reliability, cost, and safety aspects of the electrical systems in his plant.

Any plant manager depends upon experts—design and operating engineers, maintenance foremen, electricians—to handle the complicated technical details of building and operating an electrical system. This chapter, while not attempting to make him an electrical design engineer, will familiarize the plant manager with the ways in which electrical power is received, distributed, used, and conserved in the plant. It covers incoming power and plant distribution systems, the power factor problem, the main types of electrical equipment, protection against power failures, safety considerations, and lighting.

Incoming Power

Utility companies transmit electric power at high voltages for two reasons which are important as well to the transmission of power within the plant. The first is that in an electrical circuit,

$$Power = Voltage \times Current.$$

Therefore, the higher the voltage the lower the required amount of current to transmit a given amount of power. The second is that the amount of current which a wire can carry is roughly proportional to its cross-sectional area; the lower the current, the smaller the wire. Summed up, higher voltages require less current which requires smaller wires, cutting the capital cost of the transmission installation. You can expect that the utility wires arriving at your plant boundary will be carrying voltages between 1,100 and 100,000 volts; 12,000 to 14,000 volts is a very common level.

The transmission line voltage is stepped down to lower levels for plant distribution by transformers which may be mounted on utility poles (smaller plants) or placed on concrete pads in substations (larger plants). The transformers may be owned by the utility company, by the consumer, or they may be jointly owned. Plants with electrical systems rated at less than five million watts usually prefer to avoid the capital expense and maintenance costs of transformer ownership, and favor ownership by the utility company. Plants with higher rated systems are likely to have elaborate distribution systems of their own requiring a number of transformers, and may find it more economical to own the transformers rather than pay rental charges. The decision goes to the system which offers the lowest overall cost; to make it requires a working knowledge of what equipment the utility company will provide, rental charges and rebates, and allowances (if any) for transformer power losses.

Distribution Within the Plant

The most commonly used electrical devices—lights, appliances and instruments, motors— are rated at 110, 208, 220, 277, 440, and 550 volts. The distribution systems which supply these utilization voltages are usually designed to operate at slightly higher levels, such as 120, 240, and 480 volts. In-plant systems seek the same economies as long distance transmission facilities: lowest capital cost resulting from the use of high voltages and low current. Large plants which distribute major quantities of electricity to different buildings scattered around the site often use intermediate voltages between the incoming primary and equipment utilization levels; 2,400 and 4,160 are typical values. Some limitations on maximum voltages are the ability of local maintenance forces to handle them, safety and building codes, and available voltage ratings on the larger pieces of electrical equipment.

Consider these factors in the design and analysis of the plant distribution system:

1) Substation components. The typical substation consists of the incoming high voltage power cables, a disconnect switch, a transformer, a bus bar to which the outgoing wires are connected, and one or more circuit breakers or fuses to protect the system against overload currents. In the simplest systems there is only one substation, and the incoming voltage from the utility company is reduced in one step to the voltage at which it will be used in the various load centers of the plant.

2) The ways in which substations are interconnected. Plants which use intermediate voltage distribution levels and those which have scattered load centers (buildings and process units) require a number of substations. The simples and cheapest way of connecting them is the *radial* method in which a direct and separate connection is made from the low voltage side of the primary substation to each of the scattered substations. The problems with this system are a tendency toward voltage fluctuation in the isolated branch circuits, and the fact that if there is a cable or transformer failure in one of the circuits, all of the loads on that circuit are dropped. If it is important to avoid these difficulties, more expensive connection systems can be resorted to. In general they involve connecting the substations in loop circuits equipped with sophisticated circuit breaker arrangements which can isolate a defective component while the rest of the system carries the load. They go by such names as secondary selective, banked secondary radial, primary selective, and network.

3) Polyphase systems. In an alternating current circuit, the voltage starts at zero, increases to a peak positive value, decreases to zero, continues to decrease to a low negative value, and increases back to zero, completing one *cycle*. As the voltage changes in value, so does the current, which flows in opposite directions during each half of the cycle. The net result of all this is that power is fed into the circuit in pulses, much as a piston pump creates surges of pressure and flow in a pipeline. And just as the hydraulic engineer builds a triplex pump with three pistons operating on staggered cycles to even out the flow, the electrical engineer designs generators which produce staggered pulses of power in three phases carried by separate wires. Sometimes a fourth wire is added as a neutral to ground.

The three-phase, four-wire system is commonly used for secondary electrical distribution systems within the plant. Power loads, such as motors, are connected to the three phase wires and take the full voltage of the system. Smaller loads, such as lighting and appliances, are connected between one phase and the neutral wire and draw the full voltage divided by 1.73. For instance, in a 208/120V system motors and large loads are powered by three-wire connection, while lighter loads are connected across one of the phases and the neutral. In plants with large lighting loads the 480/277V system is popular; the 277V circuits are used for lighting, and transformers added to provide 120V circuits for office machines and small appliances. This method of plant wiring is illustrated diagrammatically in Exhibit 1.

What Transformers Do

Electricity is seldom generated at more than 20,000 volts, is mostly consumed at less than 600 volts, and yet is transmitted at levels ranging into the hundreds of thousands of volts. The job of stepping up the voltage at the generating plant and stepping it back down in the distribution system falls to the *transformer*, the most expensive device in the substation.

Construction of the transformer begins with an iron core, made up of rectangular sheets of steel with rectangular holes cut out of the center. The sheets are bolted together to form a laminated core. The alternating current wire whose voltage is to be changed is wrapped around one leg of the core to form a coil with a given number of turns; this coil which takes the incoming power is called the *primary*. The wire which is to carry the outgoing power is wrapped around the other leg of the core to form a coil called the *secondary;* it will have a different number of turns. The alternating current in the primary coil will cause a magnetic flux in the core which in turn induces a voltage in the secondary coil. The voltages in the two coils will have the same ratio as the number of turns in their windings. Thus, if it is desired to reduce the voltage from 2,000 to 200, and the primary winding has 1500 turns, the secondary winding must have 150 turns. (To cut down internal energy losses, many industrial transformers have both coils wrapped around the same leg of the transformer.)

The designer of a three-phase electrical system has a choice: he can put a separate transformer on each wire of the system, or he can use a three-phase transformer (which has three core legs, with the primary and secondary coils of one phase wound on each). Separate transformers were once preferred because if one failed the others could continue to supply partial power to the system. In recent years the reliability of three-phase transformers has increased to the point where they are preferred for their cost advantage.

Consider these important aspects of the design, application, and selection of industrial transformers:

1) Methods of connecting three-phase transformer coils. If the three coils of one side of a transformer are connected to a central point so as to (diagrammatically) radiate outward, this is called a Y (wye) connection. The phase wires are connected to the ends of the branches. If the coils are connected so as to form a triangle, it is called a delta (after the Greek letter Δ) connection. Other methods are the open delta or V, the T (tee) and a modification of it called the Scott connection. The remaining side of the transformer can be connected in the same or a different configuration. Exhibit 1 illustrates a transformer wired in delta connection on the primary side, and in wye connection on the secondary side.

Y connections are used where it is desirable to have a fourth neutral wire. Delta connections are sometimes chosen because if the coils on one side of the triangle fail, the other two can operate as a V connected system. All of the possible combinations are used—wye-wye, delta-delta, wye-delta, and delta-wye. The V connection allows a lower first cost because it requires only two sets of coils; later, when more power is required, the third coil can be added to complete a delta connection. The T connection also allows the handling of three-phase power with only two sets of coils. The Scott connection is used for transformation from a three-phase to a two-phase system.

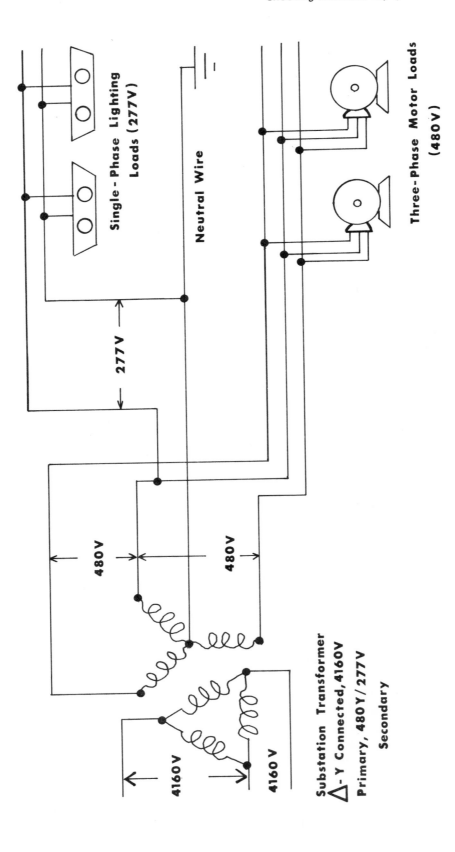

Exhibit 1. Three-phase, four-wire distribution system taken from secondary of substation transformer. 480V loads are connected across phase wires, and 277V loads are connected across one phase wire and neutral.

2) Energy losses and dissipation of heat. Of the power fed into the primary of an industrial transformer only 95-99 percent is realized as output from the secondary. The missing power is converted into heat in the core and coils and must be dispersed. In *dry* type transformers the heat is carried away by the surrounding air either by natural or forced convection; in *oil* type transformers the heat is transferred to mineral oil in which the core and coils are immersed and then dissipated to the surrounding air through fins or tubes; in *askarel* transformers the mineral oil is replaced with a synthetic transformer fluid. Fluid-filled transformers are used for higher power ratings and voltages; the fluids used are selected for their insulating properties as well as heat transfer.

3) Transformer ratings, installation, and special devices. Transformers are rated in terms of kilovolt-amperes (kva), and those used for primary and secondary power distribution in industrial plants range from 50 to 50,000 kva. Dry types are usually used for indoor installations; above 15,000 volts indoor transformers must be placed in a special vault, as must any indoor oil-filled unit. Askarel-filled transformers offer greater resistance to fire, but are heavier and more expensive. Outdoor units are set on concrete pads with wire enclosures to exclude all but authorized personnel.

As new electrical loads are added the voltage in the secondary circuit may drop to unacceptably low levels. To avoid this, a series of two to six *taps* are provided on the primary side at voltage intervals of 2½ percent above and below the rated voltage. As new loads are added, connections are changed from tap to tap to maintain the nominal voltage. Larger transformers may have special devices to accomplish tap changes without disconnecting wires. Some transformers have internal high voltage circuit breakers equipped with external operating handles.

Circuit Breakers for Protection

Very serious damage to electrical equipment and distribution systems can result from the excessively high current—known as *fault current* to the electrical designer—which accompanies the familiar "short circuit." To protect the system the designer selects circuit breakers, which are devices which open the circuit and stop the flow of power under adverse conditions; he selects breakers with ratings which will handle the normal current flow and the maximum fault current which can occur in a given section of the system (calculation of the maximum fault current is a complicated procedure involving resistance, reactance, and impedance of the system components).

1) Types. The simplest and cheapest type, with good reliability, is the *fuse*; it is available in thirty-five normal current ratings between 15 and 6,000 amperes. Despite their advantages, fuses should not be used if the time it takes to replace them represents an unacceptably long outage, or if equipment could be damaged by one phase being out while the other two still have power.

Mechanical circuit breakers usually have two elements: a *thermal* device which cuts out after a relatively low overload current exists for a period of time, and a *magnetic* device which trips instantaneously when a massive "short circuit" current occurs. Some are equipped with an *automatic reclosing* feature which restores the system to power if the fault has cleared quickly; after several unsuccessful attempts to close, it locks out permanently. Models are also available to protect against low current and low voltage. Equipment manufacturers often combine circuit breakers in package units with other devices, such as disconnect switches, alarm signals, and motorized lever actuators.

2) Application. On branch circuits serving a number of motors, the breaker is rated at the full load current of all the motors plus 125 percent of that of the largest motor. When breakers are selected for the main and secondary branches of a distribution system the choices represent a compromise between cost, continuity of service, full protection of the system, and the need to isolate branches with fault currents without disturbing the entire system. The three basic arrangements are the *fully rated, cascade,* and *selective systems.*

HOW MOTORS ARE DESIGNED, RATED, AND APPLIED

1) Basic principles. Engineers define the motor as a device for converting electrical energy into mechanical energy; it is based on the fact that if an electric current is passed through a conductor placed in a magnetic field, a mechanical force will be exerted on the conductor. Industrial motors are designed for operation on direct current (DC) or alternating current (AC); the most commonly encountered industrial type is the three-phase squirrel cage induction motor. At its center is the *shaft* (whose spin represents the output of mechanical energy) on which is mounted the *rotor* (a current-carrying device which looks like a squirrel cage). The rotor-shaft assembly fits inside a hollow cylindrical *stator* consisting of insulated iron laminations in which the magnetic field is produced. The stator, in turn, fits inside a steel cylinder called the *frame;* it is fitted with *end-bells*, each of which contains a bearing to support one end of the spinning shaft.

The important operating characteristics of a motor are torque, speed, and horsepower. *Torque* is the rotational force which the motor shaft is capable of applying to the attached load; it depends on the length of the conductor, the intensity of the magnetic field, and the amount of current. The basic reference point is full-load torque at full-load speed; starting torque is usually much higher, and is expressed as percentage of full-load torque. *Speed* is simply the revolutions per minute at which the shaft spins, but complicated design and selection problems arise in achieving desired speed, adjusting speed, varying speed, and finding the right combinations of speed and torque to accomodate different types of loads. Shaft speeds of 200 to 10,000 rpm are available in industrial motors; common shaft speeds for squirrel cage induction motors are 900, 1200, 1800, and 3600 rpm. *Horsepower* (which represents work done per unit time) derives from the combination of applied torque and speed; it is the primary characteristic used for matching a motor to a job. Available ratings range from ¼ to 5,000 HP, and special units have been built with ratings in excess of 100,000 HP.

2) Types of industrial motors available. AC motors are by far the most widely used because alternating current is the most common form of power distribution, they have good constant speed characteristics, and are relatively inexpensive and reliable. DC motors are used when high starting torque and variable speed control are important. To utilize DC equipment most plants have to convert AC power; this is done by means of motor-generator sets, mercury-arc rectifiers (such as the ignitron), semiconductor devices (selenium and silicon rectifiers), and static inverters.

DC motors are classified as *shunt* (the field coil is connected in parallel to the armature), *series* (field in series with the armature), and *compound* (both series and parallel connection). Shunt motors operate essentially as constant-speed motors; with appropriate control devices they are readily converted to controlled speed motors. They are used for compressors, machine drives, piston pumps, and building elevators. Series motors are used for variable speed loads requiring high starting torque, such as cranes and traction motors. Compound motors are used for similar applications as the shunt motor, with special application to machines whose loads are applied suddenly (cutters, punch presses, and stamping machines).

AC motors are *synchronous* or *induction* types. In the synchronous motor a rotating magnetic field is excited in the stator by a polyphase current. An electromagnet on the rotor is excited by a direct current. As the poles of the magnet follow the rotating field, the rotor is turned. Synchronous motors operate at constant speed, are cheaper than other types in certain applications, and have adjustable power factor. They are used in sizes above 25 horsepower to drive gas compressors, motor-generator sets, rubber mills, and pumps; very small sizes are used to drive electric clocks and instruments.

The induction motor is operated by the creation of a rotating magnetic field which induces a current in rotor winding. The *single-phase* induction motor is employed in sizes from fractional horsepower to 10 ph., and often has a 110 V. rating. The *polyphase induction* motor is the most widely used industrial motor, with standard sizes available from ½ to 5,000 hp., and much higher ratings as special designs. It is durable, inexpensive, essentially constant-speed, and can be modified to obtain high starting torque. The *squirrel cage* motor is the most common version; when high starting torque is required *wound-rotor* and *double squirrel cage* types are used. (All these polyphase motors are three phase; two phase motors are available but rarely used.) The chief disadvantage of polyphase motors is the difficulty of achieving speed control electrically, and mechanical speed reducers must be used when speed adjustment is desired.

Choosing a Motor

Once the basic type has been selected, the designer has further choices to make which are of interest to the plant manager:

1) NEMA design types (applies to squirrel cage motors). The National Electric Manufacturing Association has developed electrical design standards for squirrel cage motors involving various combinations of starting (or breakaway or locked rotor) torque, and maximum (or breakdown) torque (the highest torque developed by the motor as it picks up the load), both expressed as percentages of the full load torque. Type B is the standard used for most motor applications, and has starting torques from 105 percent to 275 percent of full load torque, depending upon speed and horsepower. Breakdown torques range from 200 percent to 300 percent of full load torque. Type A motors have similar starting torques but higher breakdown torques. Type C specifies higher starting torque but lower maximum torque; they are used for conveyors and compressors. Type D motors have high starting torque and high "slip" (the difference between the speed of the rotating magnetic field and that of the rotor); they are used to drive machinery with high inertia and sudden load changes, such as punch presses and shears.

2) Frame types. In ascending order of cost and protection from water and dust: *Open-frame*—including drip-proof and splash-proof types. *Totally enclosed*—including weatherproof, totally enclosed non-ventilated (TENV), totally enclosed fan-cooled (TEFC), and explosion-proof types.

3) Frame sizes. Through NEMA manufacturers of motors have agreed to standardize the dimensions of motors, and for each NEMA frame designation there are twenty-nine dimensions specified. Before replacing a motor or selecting one for installation on existing machinery be sure to check frame sizes and critical dimensions carefully. Equipment makers will be glad to supply detailed information; bear in mind that standard frame dimensions are changed from time to time as new developments in motor technology make possible smaller units for a given horsepower rating.

4) Temperature—altitude. Insulating materials within a motor are classified by the

maximum temperatures they can withstand continuously: Class O—90 deg. C.; Class A—105 deg. C.; Class B—130 deg. C.; and Class H—180 deg. C. Motor nameplates are stamped with the maximum *ambient* (surrounding air) temperature at which they may be operated, which is 40 deg. C. (104 deg. F.); or with the allowable *temperature rise* during continuous operation. Typical values are 40 deg. C. and 55 deg. C. for motors under 200 HP, and 80 deg. C. and 90 deg. C. for larger motors. These ratings hold for elevations from sea level up to 3300 feet; above that a given motor will experience greater temperature rises than those given on the nameplate.

Motor Controls and Control Centers

Devices for starting motors must cope with a variety of economic, design, safety, and convenience problems. Manufacturers offer such equipment in these basic classifications:

1) *Across-the-Line* (full voltage) vs. *Part-Voltage* starters. When an across-the-line starter is connected, full line voltage is immediately applied to the motor; this type is used with motors ranging in size from less than one to fifteen hundred horsepower, but can only be used where the driven machine can withstand the high starting torque, and where a high initial surge of current will not damage the motor or upset the distribution system.

There are four types of part-voltage (also known as reduced voltage) starters used with polyphase induction motors: the *primary resistor* type, which offers very smooth acceleration on 65 percent—85 percent of the full voltage current; the *autotransformer,* which gives next-best acceleration characteristics and the highest torque output per unit of current drawn; the *part-winding* starter, which can only be used with motors which have double windings in each phase, is the cheapest of the reduced voltage methods, offers the least smooth acceleration, and operates by starting the motor on one winding and then connecting the second winding after it picks up the load; and the *wye-delta* starter which is arranged to start the motor in Y connection, but switches to delta after it is running. It offers good torque output per ampere of starting current, but is not as good as the autotransformer in smoothness of acceleration.

2) *Manual* vs. *Magnetic* starters. The manual starter makes and breaks contact by means .of a mechanical lever (similar to the familiar toggle switch) actuated by hand. It is limited to horsepower ratings not exceeding 7.5, and must be located near the motor.

In the magnetic starter a pushbutton actuates a magnetic coil which closes the contacts. The pushbutton can be located near the motor while the control mechanism can be remotely located in a more protected area. Motors above 7.5 HP are almost always equipped with magnetic starters.

3) *Reversing* vs. *Non-Reversing.* In many applications it is necessary or desirable to reverse the direction of rotation of the motor. This can be accomplished in the polyphase induction motor by switching any two of the phase connections, and the reversing starter provides a mechanism to do that at the touch of a button.

Motor starters are enclosed in steel boxes, usually with a hinged lid. A popular form is the *combination starter* which contains the motor starter, short circuit protection, overload devices, and a manual disconnect. Undervoltage protection may also be provided. Thermal overload devices called *heaters* provide protection against steady overload currents which are not high enough to trip the short circuit protection.

Motor control centers are steel structures built to house a number of starter units; they offer compactness, ease of wiring, and increased safety for those who must maintain them.

How to Cut Costs by Adjusting Power Factor

Unfortunately the equation, Power = Voltage x Current, is true only for DC circuits and

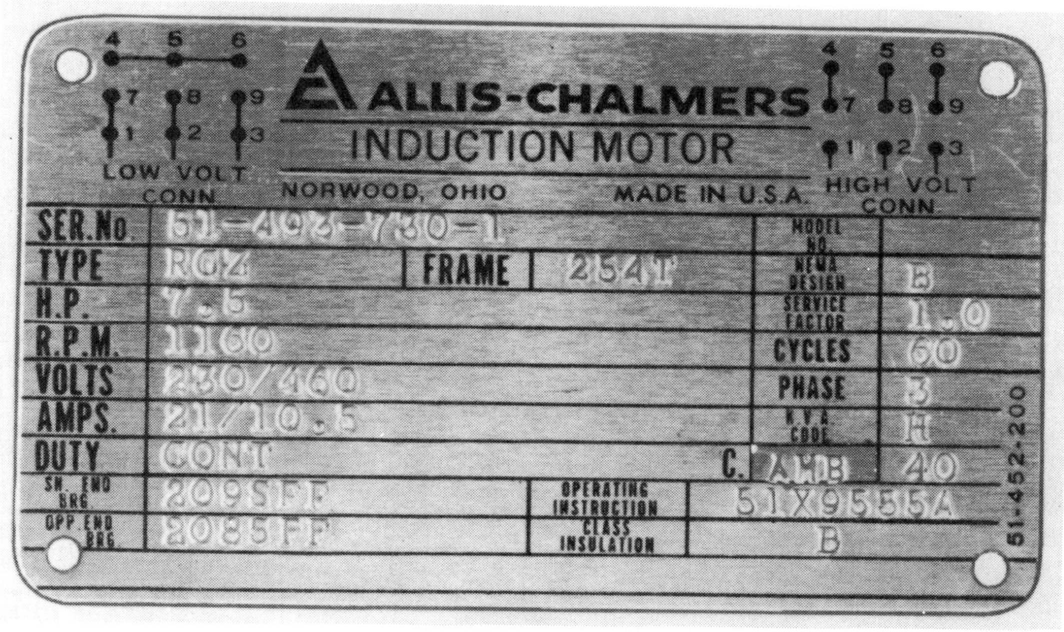

Exhibit 2. Typical industrial motor name plate. Manufacturer's name, identification as an induction motor, and diagrams of high and low voltage connections appear at top. Serial number, model number, and type classifications on the first two lines are manufacturer's designations. The frame size is 254; the letter T indicates that the motor can be used with a V-Belt drive (S would mean that it is built for direct connection only). NEMA design type is B (see page 215). This is a 7.5 horsepower (H.P.) motor, with a service factor of 1.0, which means that it is not designed to withstand any current overload. Shaft speed is 1160 revolutions per minute, and the motor operates on 60 cycle, 3-phase current. It can be connected to either 230 or 460 volt supply, and will draw rated current of 21 and 10.5 amperes respectively at those voltages. The letter "H" in the box marked "K.V.A. Code" refers to the locked-rotor KVA/HP classification, and means that the KVA/HP for this motor is 6.3 to 7.1; from this data the starting current can be calculated. The motor is designed for continuous (as opposed to intermittent) duty in ambient air not exceeding 40 deg. C., and is equipped with Class B insulation. "SH. END BRG." means shaft end bearing, and "OPP. END BRG." means opposite end bearing; the numbers refer to standard bearing sizes and are included to facilitate replacement. The number in "Operating Instruction" refers to a manufacturer's instruction manual.

some AC circuits under special conditions. In most AC circuits the power utilized is less than the product of the voltage and current supplied, and the ratio between them is called *power factor:*

$$\frac{\text{Power Utilized}}{\text{Voltage x Current Supplied}} = \text{Power Factor}$$

Power factor takes on values ranging up to a maximum of 1.0 and is usually expressed as a decimal (.80) or as a percentage (80%). (The electrical engineer further defines power factor as the cosine of the angle $\ominus$ by which the voltage leads the current, and expresses the power equation thus: Power = Voltage x Current x Cosine $\ominus$.)

Power factor values above .90 are usually considered acceptable, and no corrective action is taken. Below this level a number of cost and operating liabilities are encountered: power is being paid for which is not utilized; in some localities power companies bill penalty charges for low power factor; voltage regulation suffers; and higher rated distribution equipment (transformers and transmission lines) is required. Stated another way, more load can be added to an existing system is low power factor is corrected.

Inductive loads create low power factor in which the voltage leads the current, and appear most often in the form of the widely used squirrel cage induction motor. On the other hand capacitive loads (such as synchronous motors and static capacitors) cause the current to lead the voltage, and can be used of offset the inductive loads. Take these steps to uncover the cost saving opportunities in your electrical system:

1) Determine what the power factor is. Your maintenance department, engineering group, outside contractor, or possibly the power company can take voltage, ampere, and wattmeter readings to determine power factor.

2) Your electrical engineer and the power company can help you calculate the periodic cost savings as well as the additional load which can be added to the system after power factor is corrected.

3) Choose among these techniques to correct power factor:

   a. Install synchronous motors. If some of the motor applications are suited to the use of synchronous motors, they can be applied to offset the effect of the induction motors.

   b. Install static capacitors. Small units can be connected at each motor or inductive load, or larger units can be installed at substations to handle entire branch circuits. The first method is preferred when the primary object is to increase the load carrying capacity of the branch, the second when the objective is the cutting of power costs.

Are Standby Generators Needed?

The answer is not an automatic "yes." Evaluate these factors before making the decision:

1) What are the electrical usages? Make a list of all the facilities and equipment which would become inoperative in a power failure:

Process Machinery	Elevators	Heating & Ventilating Units
Electric Furnaces	Boilers	Instrumentation
Illumination	Lift Truck Chargers	Data Processing
Refrigeration	Cooling Towers	Air Conditioners

2) What is the risk of power failure? Plant records will give the number, duration, and incurred losses of power outages in the last five years. Contact the local power company to

supplement this information and to discuss the likelihood of future power failures. Combine all the available information into probabilities of occurrence and duration.

3) What are the consequences? Safety and cost are the principal concerns:

a. Safety. Is emergency lighting required for orderly shutdown of the process and safe evacuation of personnel? Will process materials be subject to overheating, fire, or explosion? Is standby power needed for ventilating equipment to remove dangerous fumes? Will important fire-fighting equipment (pumps, signal systems) be knocked out of service?

b. Cost. Will there be damage to any equipment if the outage exceeds a certain length of time? Will in-process materials suffer quality deterioration or possibly have to be scrapped? Will personnel have to be dismissed but paid anyway?

If the answer to any of the safety questions is "yes," standby equipment is clearly needed. The same answer for any of the cost questions requires a calculation of how much money is at stake in each situation.

4) What equipment is needed? Rarely will the combined factors of outage probability, safety hazard, and cost risk call for 100 percent standby generating capacity; instead a few critical usages will be selected, and their total consumption in kilowatts determined.

a. Batteries. Storage batteries are sometimes used as sources of emergency power for lighting, communications, and alarm systems. Because they are limited to direct current and relatively low power output they are not suitable for general supply of electricity.

b. Standby generators. They consist of a fuel-burning engine coupled to an electric generator. Fuel choices are gasoline, natural gas, and diesel fuel; the engines are internal combustion, diesel, reciprocating natural gas, and gas turbines. Output of standard models ranges from 1 to 1,000 kilowatts; single and three-phase current; and voltages from 110 to 4,160. All units require periodic startups and preventive maintenance to assure reliability in an emergency.

What Is "Explosion-Proof" Equipment and When Should It Be Used?

Electrical equipment is intrinsically spark-producing, and when used in atmospheres which may contain flammable vapors or combustible dusts creates a serious explosion hazard. Fortunately, manufacturers of this equipment are able to supply virtually all types in explosion-proof form: motors, switches, starters, lights, telephones, clocks, thermostats, forklift trucks, water coolers, refrigerators, and many kinds of instruments. Such items are built according to the standards of the National Electrical Code (available from the National Fire Protection Association, 60 Batterymarch Street, Boston, Mass. 02110), and are designed to contain any ignition which occurs so that it cannot spread to the surrounding atmosphere. Physical characteristics are use of rigid conduit, threaded joints, heavy enclosures, seals, and enclosure covers which have carefully machined mating surfaces and no gaskets. Use these criteria for the selection and use of explosion-proof equipment:

1) Decide which class, group, and division best describes the surroundings in which the equipment will be used. Turn to Exhibit 3, Chapter 10. Across the top of the page are headings for Class I, Class II, and Class III locations; under each heading is a description of the type of hazard encountered—e.g., Class II concerns locations where combustible dusts are present. Under Class I and Class II are a series of Groups (A, B, C, etc.), each of which deals with specific substances under its class. For instance, Group E concerns Class II locations where the hazard is metal dust. Beneath the groups in each class are shown two divisions; they describe the frequency of and the conditions under which the hazard may

arise. As an example of this, Division 2 under Class III covers locations in which ignitible fibers are handled and stored, but not manufactured.

A paint plant installed a process involving the use of lacquer solvent in drums. The contents of the drums were to be poured through open manholes into the mixing kettles; the final product was removed by gravity through the bottom and packed directly into five gallon pails.

Refer again to Exhibit 3, Chapter 10 (although this table was developed for use of industrial trucks, its upper section is a tabular summary of the hazardous location designations of the National Eelctrical Code). Because the new area would be exposed to flammable vapors in sufficient quantities to produce ignitible mixtures, it was designated as a Class I location. The specific flammable material—lacquer solvent—classified it in Group D. And the periodic presence of the vapors as part of normal operating conditions placed it in Division 1. Therefore when the electrical equipment was ordered for the new area, all components were specified for Class I, Group D, Division 1 service.

2) On the purchase order or in the equipment contract, require that the equipment supplied carry the Underwriters Laboratory label (usually a metal tag on industrial equipment) showing the class, group, and division for which the equipment is rated. Some suppliers may represent their equipment as being "explosion-proof" but not want to go through the procedure of obtaining the Underwriter's label. If you buy such equipment, you are entirely dependent on the supplier's word, and without the benefit of third party control and inspection of the way in which the equipment is constructed.

3) Once installed, explosion-proof equipment is effective only if it is properly maintained. Allow only qualified personnel who understand and will follow the manufacturer's instructions to disassemble the equipment. Do not attempt to install gaskets where none are provided originally. When reassembling draw up all screwed and bolted fittings tight. Make sure that all bolts are replaced.

WHAT THE PLANT MANAGER SHOULD KNOW ABOUT LIGHTING

Whether concerned with upgrading the illumination in older buildings or approving the lighting designs for new facilities, the plant manager's goal is to provide adequate light of good quality for the tasks to be performed at optimum cost. These are the factors involved in evaluating a lighting system:

1) The language of lighting. The *candle* is the basic unit of light intensity, and is roughly equivalent to the luminous intensity of a burning candle viewed horizontally (also *candlepower*). The *foot-candle* is the illumination on a surface one foot away from (and perpendicular to) a one candlepower source. *Lumen*: the quantity (as opposed to the intensity) of light emitted by a source in all directions. One lumen is the quantity of light falling on any area of one square foot on the inside of a sphere with a radius of one foot and a light source of one candlepower at its center. So far we have been dealing with point sources; the brightness of an object with a substantial surface area is measured in *footlamberts*. An object which gives off (by reflection or emission) one lumen per square foot of its area has a brightness of one footlambert.

2) How much light is needed? Illumination levels at working surfaces in various plant areas should have these minimum values, expressed in footcandles: Production areas and machine shops: 20, 50, and 100, depending on fineness of the work. Stairways: 10-20. Offices: 30, 50, or 150 depending on fineness of the work. Warehouses: 20-50. Laboratories and test areas: 50-500, depending on fineness of work. For more detailed listings of types of areas and the illumination required for them, consult the Illuminating Engineering Society Lighting Handbook and publications of manufacturers of lamps and fixtures.

3) Tie-in with other plant systems. It has already been pointed out that in a three-phase, four-wire distribution system single phase loads can be connected to one of the phases and to the neutral wire, drawing a voltage equal to the system voltage divided by 1.73. Thus, in a 208V three-phase system lamps connected across one of the phases would draw 208 + 1.73 = 120 volts. Lighting systems have been developed to operate at 277V, that being the single phase voltage from a 480V three-phase distribution system.

In buildings which have extensive lighting systems advantage can be taken of the heat given off by the lamps. Blowers are set up to move air across the banks of lights, and the air thus warmed is distributed for space heating. Economies are realized not only in the reduction of heat which must be supplied from other sources, but also in the prolonged life of the lamps resulting from their operation at lower temperatures.

4) Choose from available equipment types to optimize cost. *Incandescent* lamps yield about 15 lumens per watt, have the lowest initial equipment cost. But because they convert a relatively high proportion of the energy consumed to heat and are therefore costly to operate, they are used only in basements, unfrequented areas, and temporary installations. Fluorescent lamps produce about 60 lumens per watt, are the universal choice for offices, laboratories, and light manufacturing areas. In most situations they represent the best cost combination of initial and operating expenses. *Mercury vapor* lamps yield about 40 lumens per watt, are more costly to buy and operate, but are well adapted to heavy industrial operations where dust is a problem. *Luminaires* are the various reflectors, lenses, and "egg crate" devices used to enhance, diffuse, and remove objectionable glare from the lamp.

Compare lighting systems on the basis of *total annual cost,* that is, the cost of lamps, luminaires, electric power, lamp replacement, and cleaning, all reduced to a yearly base. For an excellent system of cost analysis see B.C. Cooper, "Choose Right to Save on Light," *Modern Manufacturing,* December 1970, pp. 55-57. For a detailed cost analysis form, see *Standard Handbook for Mechanical Engineers* (7th ed.) Ed.-in-Chief Theodore Baumeister, (New York, McGraw-Hill Book Company, 1967).

Group relamping is a maintenance system in which all lamps in a given area are replaced and fixtures cleaned and repaired at the same time. For a thorough account of the cost and performance benefits of this system, see John Molnar, "Cost Savings Through Group Relamping," in *Plant Operation Manual* (Englewood Cliffs, N.J.: Prentice-Hall, Inc., 1967), pp. 39-52.

CONCLUSION

Managers are understandably inclined to focus their search for cost reduction and performance improvement opportunities on the production processes peculiar to their plants. But the less visible network of wiring and electrical equipment must be carefully designed and operated if it is to make its full contribution to the reliability, cost, and safety of plant processes.

Distribution systems carry the highest practicable voltages to minimize capital expenses; they are arranged in radial or loop combinations as the need for reliability demands. Transformers step voltages up and down to serve the needs of the distribution system, and are connected in a variety of methods to improve cost and reliability. Circuit breakers protect the system against overloads; cost increases with complexity, and the more sophisticated types are chosen to meet compelling needs in continuity of service and isolation of defective branch circuits. Motors and starters are matched to the horsepower, torque, speed control, and environmental conditions of the loads to which they are connected. Hazardous locations may require "explosion-proof" motors and other electrical equipment as well.

Adjustment of power factor offers the single greatest opportunity for cost reduction in an existing plant; cost control, safety, and employee performance are all affected by the choices made in the design of lighting systems. And the ultimate reliability device—the standby generator—is employed if a thorough examination of the risk of power failure and its consequences justifies the cost of installation and maintenance.

Chapter 17

Understanding
the Selection and Operation
of Mechanical Equipment
for Maximum Reliability

Every plant has an assortment of "taken for granted" equipment—steam boilers, compressors, mechanical drives, bearings and couplings—whose continued functioning is essential to keeping the plant in operation. Because performance reliability is the key attribute, it is important that the plant manager understand the fundamentals of design, selection, and maintenance of these kinds of equipment, and this chapter will supply the information he needs.

STEAM BOILERS

These are the important definitions and classifications relating to boilers:

1) *Field erected* vs. *packaged* units. In package boilers all of the essential components— tube section, fuel burner, controls and safety devices, air fans—are assembled at the factory and mounted on a steel skid framework for support and easy handling. When delivered they need only be connected to the appropriate piping and electrical systems. If the package boiler is a *firetube* type (hot gases from the fuel combustion are passed through the tubes while the water to be heated is contained in the surrounding space) it can be obtained in capacity ratings up to 24,000 pounds per hour of steam; if it is a *watertube* type (water is inside the tubes while hot gases are passed through the surrounding space) capacity ratings up to 200,000 pounds per hour are available.

Field erected units are constructed on the plant site, are often custom designed to meet local conditions, and while some have been constructed with capacities as low as 30,000 lb/hr their most frequent application is in the capacities above the limits of packaged boilers, i.e., over 200,000 lb/hr.

2) Number of "passes." A *pass* is a one-way trip through the length of the boiler. In a four pass firetube boiler the gases travel from the burner through a set of tubes to the other end, where direction is reversed by a baffle, and return to the front end; the process is repeated to obtain a total of four trips.

**Exhibit 1. Packaged firetube boiler, showing essential external operating components.
(Courtesy of Cleaver-Brooks Division of Aqua-Chem, Inc.)**

3) Auxiliary equipment. A primary objective of boiler design is to extract the maximum heat value from the fuel consumed. In the *economizer* waste heat from the flue gases is used to raise the temperature of water fed to the boiler; in the *feedwater heater* the same result is obtained by using exhaust steam. The *air preheater* takes heat from the waste flue gases to raise the temperature of the air fed to the furnace, improving the efficiency of the combustion process.

To provide the required quantity of air for combustion, *forced-draft fans* supply fresh air under pressure to the furnace. In larger installations *induced-draft fans* are located just ahead of the exhaust stack to pull the flue gases through the system.

Steam is obtained from water at the boiling point temperature (212 deg. F. at 0 psi gauge; 338 deg. F. at 100 psi gauge), but in some processes it is advantageous to heat the steam to temperatures well above the boiling point. That is accomplished by means of a *superheater*, a bank of tubes containing steam which may be fired separately or, more often, is included in the boiler furnace.

4) Boiler ratings. Boilers are usually specified by number of pounds per hour of steam which they generate. Because the heat content of steam varies with the temperature and pressure, those two conditions must be specified. For example, a boiler might be rated for 10,000 pounds per hour from and at 212 deg. F. and atmospheric pressure (= 0 psi gauge). This means that the boiler has an energy output equivalent to the evaporation of 10,000 pounds of water per hour into steam at the stated temperature and pressure.

Another method of boiler rating is the *boiler horsepower*. It is equivalent to the evaporation of 34.5 lb/hr of water into steam from and at 212 deg. F. and atmospheric pressure. It is also equivalent to 33,475 BTU/hr. (It should be noted that boiler horsepower has nothing to do with the standard physical definition of one horsepower, which is equal to 2,545 BTU/hr.) A boiler rated at 200 HP will have a steam capacity of 6,900 lb/hr from and at 212 deg. F. and atmospheric pressure.

Choice of fuel is a matter of economics, and the costs of using various available fuels vary widely throughout the country. But consider these factors when making a choice: Very few new installations are designed to use coal, and those that are tend to be the larger units (3,000 HP and up). Not only does coal present problems of fuel storage space and materials handling, but increasingly stringent air pollution laws have resulted in a steady long-term trend toward oil and gas. Many of the newer installations are equipped to burn both oil and gas for greater reliability, and to take advantage of lower costs for interruptible and seasonal supplies. Chemical additives are now available to make combustion more efficient and reduce the output of pollutants. A number of companies improve cost efficiency and handle otherwise difficult pollution problems by burning waste products; pulp and paper companies burn tree bark and "black liquor," while chemical and petroleum plants burn residual oils and gases.

Effective operation and maintenance of boilers is a matter of direct and deep concern to the plant manager who must worry about cost efficiency, continuity of operations, and the physical safety of the plant. Make sure that your boiler operation includes these basic controls:*

1) Require operators to keep a written log of all pressure, temperature, liquid level, and flow gauge readings, as well as a notation of any unusual circumstances.

2) Maintain chemical treatment of boiler water at specified levels (see section below for a discussion of boiler water chemistry) with a program of daily testing by qualified personnel. Record results in a log book.

3) Get rid of sludge formation by periodic or continuous *blowdown*—i.e., draining a small proportion of the water out of the boiler.

4) Analyze flue gases to achieve maximum burner efficiency. Oxygen content should not exceed 1-2 percent; carbon monoxide level should be zero; and carbon dioxide content should be 8.5 to 10 percent when burning gas, 12.5 to 13.8 percent when burning #6 oil, and the higher the better in both cases.

5) Diagnose combustion problems by monitoring stack temperature. If the temperature of the existing flue gases rises and remains above normal levels, the tube surfaces may have become clogged with soot and need cleaning. If the stack temperature exceeds the steam temperature by more than 150° F. heat is being wasted, and burner adjustment may be required.

6) Avoid thermal shock by preventing sudden addition of steam load and rapid introduction of cold feedwater. Always bring a boiler up to temperature from a cold start very gradually.

7) Make weekly checks of protective devices—low level cutoffs, relief valves, fuel cutoffs—to insure that they will operate properly when needed.

Use these techniques for an effective maintenance program:

1. Take the boiler out of service and open it up for inspection and repair semiannually.

2. Replace all handhole and manhole gaskets and seals.

3. Inspect the waterside for scale deposits, corrosion, and mud accumulation. If

---

*The basic procedures for sound boiler operation and maintenance listed here are contained in *Boiler Care Handbook,* published by the Cleaver-Brooks Division of Aqua-Chem, Inc.

scale is heavy, a chemical acid cleaning may be necessary; if corrosion is evident, chemical treatment of the water is needed; if mud accumulation is heavy, blowdown procedures and chemical treatment need adjustment.

4. Inspect tubes and tube sheet. Replace broken tubes and those showing severe corrosion. Re-roll or reweld tube ends at tube sheet if they appear loose, corroded, or leaking.

5. Inspect fireside. Stack should be clean; if it is sooty, adjust air-fuel ratio. Fill in cracks and eroded spots in refractory lining. Clean burner tip and nozzle.

6. Make detailed check of protective devices. Replace any components which past history indicates will fail before next overhaul.

7. Arrange for inspection of the boiler while it is open by state, municipal, or insurance inspector.

The chemical state of water in the boiler must be carefully controlled to avoid damage to the equipment. *Dissolved oxygen* causes pitting corrosion; it can be removed physically by passing the feedwater through a *deaerator,* or scavenged chemically in the boiler by the addition of hydrazine or sodium sulfite. *Acid corrosion* is prevented by the addition of alkali chemicals to keep the pH on the alkaline side—usually around 11. *Sludge accumulation* is retarded by the addition of chemical dispersants to keep solid particles in suspension, so that they can leave with the blowdown. *Scale formation* is inhibited by pre-softening the raw feedwater, and by the addition of sodium phosphate or organic sequestering agents to the boiler. *Condensate line corrosion* can be controlled by the addition of volatile amines to the boiler water, but this method must be reviewed carefully if the steam comes in contact with any process materials.

Boiler water chemistry is a complicated subject, and this review is not intended to provide recipes for water treatment. If your company cannot provide the technical expertise required to set up a water treatment program, a number of consulting firms can provide technical advice, chemicals, and periodic reviews of the effectiveness of treatment. (The author has had direct experience with Betz Laboratories Inc. and Nalco Chemical Company; many others are listed in industrial directories under Water Treatment Chemicals.)

COMPRESSORS

Compressors are part of the general class of machines used to move gases from one location to another. They are differentiated from fans and blowers, which move large volumes of gas with little change in pressure, by this definition: A compressor is a device which increases the density of the gas passing between its inlet and outlet by at least 7 percent. Air and refrigerant compressors are the types most often encountered, but there are many plants which use compressors to move process gases. These guidelines for the selection, installation, and operation of compressors apply to all types:

1) Types and range of application.

a. *Reciprocating* machines have one or more cylinders in which a sliding piston compresses and moves the gas. They are most often used for flows up to 10,000 cubic feet per minute (CFM) of inlet gas, and pressures up to 10,000 pounds per square inch (psi); both limits can be exceeded by specially built machines.

b. *Rotary* compressors are positive displacement machines in which a rotating element traps a slug of gas at the inlet side, carries it around through the machine, and discharges it at the high pressure outlet side. (The rotating element is designed to seal off the two sides of the machine from each other, so that leakage cannot occur back to the low pressure side.) Major types are the *sliding vane,* the *single-* and *double-lobe,* the *helical screw,* and the *liquid piston.* Application is in the 10 CFM to 20,000 CFM range, and from negative pressures (vacuum) to 500 psi.

c. In the *centrifugal* compressor the gas is discharged tangentially from a high-speed rotating impeller; the action is similar to that of a centrifugal liquid pump. It is used for flows from 200 CFM to 200,000 CFM, with some machines ranging close to 1,000,000 CFM. Discharge pressures range from below atmospheric to around 5,000 psi.

d. The *axial* compressor is similar to the centrifugal compressor in that neither is a positive displacement machine, but differs in that the flow is parallel to the rotating shaft, and moves through a system of stationary and rotating blades. Application starts around 10,000 CFM and exceeds 1,000,000 CFM, with discharge pressures ranging from below atmospheric to 150 psi.

e. Comparative application: Reciprocating compressors are the most efficient in terms of energy consumption, and at low flows and high pressures have an advantage in purchase cost. However, they are costly to install, and are subject to more frequent maintenance shutdowns. Rotary compressors have a first-cost advantage at low flows and pressures, deliver air without pressure surges, and require no valve maintenance. Centrifugal compressors excel at handling large volumes at constant pressure, require less floor space, and are cheaper to install. Maintenance outages are less frequent, but are longer in duration. Axial compressors are well adapted to constant volume applications, have some efficiency advantages over centrifugal types, but should only be used where some gas leakage is acceptable.

2) How to set up a compressor installation. The enemies of reliable, low-maintenance compressor service are vibration, stress, and the presence of liquid in the system. Be sure that your design for a new compressor installation covers these key points:

a. Foundation. Massive enough to absorb vibration and stress. Meet or exceed compressor manufacturer's recommendations. Dissociate from building structure as much as possible.

b. Piping. Install traps and drains at low points for removal of liquid accumulations. Use flexible suction connections. All piping close to the compressor must be measured carefully and connected so as to avoid strain on the casing. Slope piping away from unit so that liquid cannot run back into it. Do not install shutoff valves on suction side—accidental closing can damage a compressor.

c. Surroundings. The mistake is often made of jamming compressor equipment into small rooms or areas crowded with other machinery. Provide horizontal room sufficient for removal of piping and dismantling of equipment, and vertical room for installation of hoisting apparatus and lubrication units.

3) Effective operation and maintenance. Follow these principles for trouble-free operation:

a. Establish an operating log. Record pressures, temperatures, gas flows, cooling water rates, and oil levels.

b. Use the proper lubricant (ordinary oils may break down under the unusual heat and friction in a compressor), use the log as a control method to make sure the lubrication program is actually carried out.

c. Check out the operation of auxiliary equipment—traps, drains, filters, and air dryers—on a daily basis. These devices must function properly to protect expensive machinery.

d. Be careful not to run the compressor outside its design limits of flow, pressure, and continuous hours of operation.

e. Repair leaks in the compressed gas system. When the compressed gas is air, leaks are easily ignored. But they incur needless power costs, and can overload your machinery.

f. Inspect for mechanical vibration daily. Use an industrial stethoscope, the more elaborate electronic vibration detection and measurement devices, or simply train your mechanic to touch the point of a screwdriver to the casing, and put his ear to the other end. He will soon learn to pick up unusual noises, and will know when to shut the equipment down for preventive repair.

g. Implement a preventive maintenance program. Open up the compressor to check wear, alignment, bearing condition, clearances, and corrosion effects on a quarterly to annual basis. Replace parts whose failure or excessive wear may damage other parts of the machine.

MECHANICAL POWER TRANSMISSION

The spinning shaft of an electric motor represents the usual form in which mechanical power first arrives for use in an industrial plant. But most mechanical devices cannot operate at the high speeds of the motor shafts, and in many cases cannot receive the power in alignment with the motor. Three basic types of mechanical transmission devices commonly used to overcome the twin problems of speed reduction and transfer of power between planes are the gear drive, the chain drive, and the belt drive. A fourth device, the variable speed drive, accomplishes the work of the other types and in addition allows the speed of the driven shaft to be changed without dismantling the machine. Use these guidelines for the application and operation of MPT equipment in your plant:

A) Gear Drives. Capable of transmitting more power and operating at higher speeds than the other types, the gear drive consists of a metal housing with an input shaft and one or more output shafts. Inside the casing are gear combinations of the following types:

1. Types and application: *Spur gears* are the strongest, cheapest, noisiest, and are relatively efficient. They are universally used for moderate loads and speeds. *Helical gears* are used for higher loads and speeds, are quieter and more efficient, but more costly. *Worm gears* permit operation on intersecting axes, are good for high speed work, carry larger gear ratios, and are relatively quiet, but efficiency is low. *Bevel gears* are normally used for intersecting shafts at 90 degrees, but other angles are possible. They are relatively expensive.

2. Selection criteria. Manufacturers of gear drives provide tables of service factors based on the type of application (cranes, machine tools, screw conveyors, etc.), the uniformity of loading, and the number of hours per day of operation. The service factor is multiplied by the horsepower required at the driven machine to determine the size of gear reducer required. Torque requirement and ambient temperature also affect the size requirement.

3. Speed ratio. The rpm of the input shaft divided by the rpm of the output shaft is the speed reduction ratio of the unit. The most commonly employed ratios are 15 to 1, 30 to 1, and 50 to 1, but many other ratios ranging from 3:1 to 500:1 are available.

Helical Gears

Worm Gears

Bevel Gears

Spur Gears

Exhibit 2. Four common types of gears.
(Courtesy Akron Gear and Engineering Inc.)

4. Operation and maintenance. Gears operate under a film of oil constantly replenished by a reservoir in the casing. Be sure that this oil is the type recommended by the manufacturer, and maintained at the specified level (over-oiling can cause as much damage as under-oiling). Poor alignment of the gear drive shafts with connected equipment can cause bearing strain and rapid failure; check alignment periodically during preventive maintenance inspections.

B) Chain Drives. Falling between gear drives and belt drives in load-carrying capacity, chain drives retain the fixed speed ratios of the gear drives, but escape the space limitations of the fixed housing.

1. Chain technology. *Pitch* is the distance from the centerline of one link to that of the next. Most roller chain is manufactured to specifications of the American Standard Association and is designated by ASA number; No. 40 single strand roller chain has a pitch of ½ in., while No. 200 chain has a pitch of 2½ in. Each pitch consists of a roller, a bushing, side plates, pin, and spring clip, cotter pin, or rivet. When loading or speed is too great for a single strand chain, *multiple strand* chain is used; it is available in double, triple, or quadruple parallel strands, with specially-made types up to twenty-four strands. *Double pitch* chain has twice the centerline distance of comparable regular chain, and the ASA number has a prefix of 20; thus ASA No. 2040 designates a chain with a pitch of 1 in., rather than the ½ in. of No. 40 chain. The double pitch costs about half as much as regular chain, can only be used at slow speeds, and is not made in multiple strands. *Self-lubricating* chain is available for sensitive operations (such as food processing) where standard lubricants are prohibited. *Sprockets* are the toothed wheels on which the chain rides; they are designed to ASA standards for tooth profile and critical dimensions. Most manufacturers stock sprockets cut to popular bore sizes, but will rebore for a fee. The speed reduction of a chain drive is the ratio of the number of teeth on each of the two sprockets.

2. Design and installation. Manufacturer's catalogs (a good example is the

Dodge Engineering Catalog published by the Dodge Manufacturing Division of Reliance Electric Co.) usually contain design tables for the selection of chains and sprockets based on the horsepower which must be transmitted, the type of service, type of primary drive, the speed ratio, and the distance between shafts.

Speed ratios are usually limited to 7:1 for a single drive; above that, two chain drives should be used. The optimum center distance between shafts is 30 to 50 chain pitches, but the range can be spread from 20 to 80 in special cases. The chain should be in contact with the sprocket over at least 120 degrees of arc. Idler sprockets are sometimes used to change chain direction or maintain tension; current practice is to avoid them because they require additional flexing of the chain and hasten its wear. On horizontal installations it is good practice to have the slack portion of the chain on the lower side; when the sprockets must be placed one above the other, they should be offset from the vertical by 20-30 degrees.

3. Operation and maintenance. There are four standard methods of chain drive lubrication, depending upon the speed and severity of service: manual, drip lubrication, oil bath, and oil stream (supplied by a circulating pump). Lubricating oil grades are SAE 20 to 50; higher viscosity lubricants may not penetrate to the rubbing surfaces.

Chain adjustment should not be too tight (excessive wear) or too loose (tends to ride up and off sprocket teeth). The chain drive should be taken out of service periodically for lubrication check, tightness adjustment, and alignment of sprockets, which should be done with a straight edge. A set of the special tools required for adjustment and repair should be available to maintenace personnel.

C) Belt Drives. Widely used because of ease of installation, low first cost, simple maintenance, and relative convenience in making speed changes, belt drives can carry loads up to 1500 horsepower and operate at speeds up to 12,000 feet per minute.

1. Types and application. *Flat belts* made of leather or rubber and operating on grooveless pulleys are seldom specified for power transmission applications because of their tendency to slip and a speed limitation around 3,000 feet per minute. *V-Belt* drives are much more widely used because of greater load-carrying capacity and speeds up to 12,000 feet per minute. The V-belt has a trapezoidal cross-section, the slanted edges gripping the sides of a V-shaped groove in the pulley. The top of the belt rides at the top of the groove but the bottom of the belt does not touch the bottom of the groove.

V-Belt types and ratings are specified by the Rubber Manufacturers Association. Types 2L, 3L, 4L, and 5L are light-duty or fractional horsepower (FHP) belts, are used singly, and have HP ratings from under 0.1 to 1.1 at speeds from 200 fpm to 6,000 fpm. For higher ratings and multiple-belt drives, Types A, B, C, D, and E are used; the ranges of these belts overlap, with A having HP ratings of 0.69 to 4.38 and E of 14.7 to 57.6 HP per belt at speeds between 1200 and 6000 fpm and various small sheave diameters. Recent advances in materials engineering have made possible a series of Narrow V-Belts designated 3V, 5V, and 8V. They cover approximately the same range as the A through E belts, but can carry the same loads with fewer belts and smaller sheaves, reducing cost and space requirements. In multiple belt drives with long center distances, or subject to shock loading, individual belts may ride off the pulleys or turn over in the sheave groove; for these difficult applications sets of two to five belts banded together at the top by a solid web are available. *V-Flat* belt drives consist of a set of V-belts, a grooved small-diameter sheave, and a flat or grooveless large pulley. This arrangement is cheaper than having both sheaves grooved, and works well when center distances are short and speed ratios are high.

Synchronous belt drives (timing belts) employ a flat belt from ¼ in. to 14 in. wide with transverse rubber teeth on the inside surface. These teeth engage grooves in the surface of the pulley which are parallel to its axis. Available in ratings over 600 HP and speeds to 16,000 fpm, synchronous belt drives have the advantage of precise speed control, small space and weight requirements, and quiet operation.

2. Selection and installation. To choose the proper belts for a power application requires a series of tables and graphs found in manufacturer's catalogs (such as the Dodge catalog mentioned previously in this section). First a design horsepower is calculated by multiplying the rated horsepower of the motor by a service factor, which is derived from a table based on the type of load, torque characteristics of the driver, and continuity of service. Then a graph of design horsepower vs. rpm of the faster shaft is consulted to determine the type of belt—A, B, C, 3V, 5V, etc. Next the horsepower per belt is obtained from a table based on driver and driven pulley speeds and center distance between them. Design horsepower divided by HP per belt gives the number of belts required.

Provide an adjustable motor mount so that the belts can be installed loose, without prying over the pulley edges. Then adjust to proper tension using an inexpensive tension tester. Check pulley alignment with a straight edge. Finally, take precautions to protect the belts from excessive heat, chemical fumes, dripping oil, or abrasive dust.

3. Operation and maintenance. Follow these rules for reliable service and extended belt life:

a. Continue tension adjustments—within two weeks of installation, and on a periodic preventive maintenance schedule thereafter. Loose belts result in poor load-pulling performance and early wear; overly tight belts may burn out from excessive heat buildup.

b. Replace belts as matched sets. Attempts to economize by replacing part of a set results in uneven tension, erratic performance, and early wear of the new belts.

COUPLINGS

These devices are used to connect two shafts rotating on the same axis line. In most industrial applications one shaft is connected to a driver (such as an electric motor or internal combustion engine) and the other to a driven, work-performing machine (such as an agitator, hoist, pump, etc.), giving rise to a wide range of application problems—load capacity, torque, vibration, and shaft misalignment. Use this classification to select the proper type for your application:

1) Rigid couplings. As the name implies, this type is built of solid metal halves, either joined in mating flange faces or in bolted longitudinal sleeves. Capable of carrying heavy loads at high speeds, they are the cheapest and least complicated mechanically, but can only be used where there is *no* misalignment of the connected shafts.

2) Flexible couplings. The most widely used type, they are designed to overcome the three most common types of misalignment: 1) offset, in which the axes of the rotating

shafts are parallel, but displaced laterally, 2) angular, in which the axes are not parallel, but meet at a slight angle, and 3) end-float, in which the shaft ends change position in the axial direction because of mechanical thrust or temperature change. Flexible couplings can also cushion shock loads and dampen torsional vibration.

Types of shaft misalignment

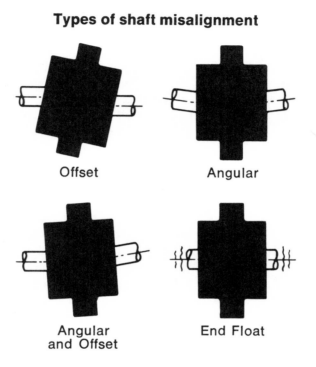

Offset   Angular

Angular   End Float
and Offset

Exhibit 3. Types of shaft misalignment at couplings.
(Courtesy of The Falk Corporation.)

Illustrative of the many varieties commercially available are the *gear* type, with the teeth of two face-mating gear wheels engaged by the internal teeth of a surrounding rim; the similar *chain coupling,* with two facing sprockets joined by a length of roller chain wrapped around their circumferences; the Falk Steelflex® coupling in which a sinuous circular spring-like grid is snapped into the grooves of two facing hubs; the elastomeric type, in which a synthetic rubber ring is used to connect the two metal rings joined to the connected shafts; and the *universal joint* which allows a high level (up to 30 degrees) of angular misalignment.

3) Fluid drives. The basic principle of the fluid drive—transmission of the input energy of the driver to a fluid which turns a rotor connected to the load—is used to build couplings which allow enough slip for the motor to come up to speed before it has to carry the full load. The result is smoother starts, and torque overload protection for the motor and the drive mechanism.

BEARINGS

Where the moving and stationary parts of a machine meet, a *bearing* is installed to reduce friction to a non-destructive level. The plant manager is seldom involved in the intricacies of bearing design, but he should understand these basic principles of application:

1) Type of load. A load whose direction is from the centerline of a rotating shaft toward the circumference is a *radial* load; a horizontal shaft supported by two bearings at either end always has a radial load resulting from the weight of the shaft and any wheels or devices attached to it. A load in the direction of the centerline is a *thrust* load; a vertically mounted shaft always has a thrust load at its lower end resulting from the weight of the shaft and attached devices, but many horizontal shafts carry thrust loads as well. Industrial bearings often must be designed to carry combined radial and thrust loads.

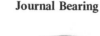
Journal Bearing

Sleeve Bearing

Exhibit 4. Sliding friction bearings.
(Courtesy of Dodge Manufacturing Division, Reliance Electric Company.)

2) Type of friction. *Journal* bearings and *sleeve* bearings are based on sliding friction. The bearing consists of a hollow cylinder of special antifriction alloy metal in which the shaft rotates; that part of the shaft inside the bearing is called the *journal.* The shaft may also oscillate back and forth, without rotation, as in a crankshaft or piston. *Ball* bearings and *roller* bearings take advantage of the lower frictional forces inherent in rolling friction, and consist of concentric rings with the rolling element lodged between them. Spherical balls of hardened steel are used in the raceways of ball bearings; cylindrical steel rollers are used in roller bearings, and when their length is more than four times the diameter, a *needle* bearing results.

3) Housing. The *pillow block* is a common form of bearing housing; circular and square *flanges* are also used. Because alignment is critical *take-up* housings and frames are available which permit fine adjustment of the bearing position. *Self-aligning* bearings are constructed internally to withstand some initial misalignment and that due to later settling of the bearing supports.

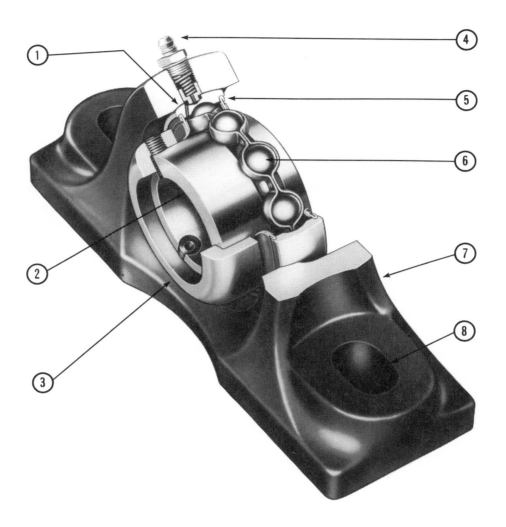

Exhibit 5. Cutaway view of ball bearing mounted in pillow block housing.
(Courtesy of Dodge Manufacturing Division, Reliance Electric Company.)

4) Life rating. Manufacturer's catalogs show the "Minimum Hours Life" (also called the "B-10 Life") for each bearing at various radial loads and shaft rpm. The minimum hours life ranges from 500 to 30,000 hours, and is the service time which may be expected from at least 90 percent of a group of the bearings operating under identical conditions. Average life is five times the minimum life.

LUBRICATION

No operation under the plant manager's jurisdiction has more impact on the performance reliability of process equipment than the lubrication program. Follow these action suggestions to build an effective lubrication program:

1) Use the right lubricant.

Flange Housing

Take-up Housing

Exhibit 6. Additional types of bearing housings.
(Courtesy of Dodge Manufacturing Division,
Reliance Electric Company.)

a. Comply with equipment manufacturer's instructions concerning type of lubricant and frequency of change, as shown in the operating manual or nameplate mounted on the equipment.

b. When it is important to reduce the number of kinds of lubricant used, or when the equipment is old and lubrication instructions are not available, try an oil company survey. Most major oil companies have lubrication experts who will review your needs and recommend specific oils and greases to meet them. A word of caution here—in one industrial checkup review it was found that on three critical operations oil company recommendations were in error twice. (O.S. Warner, "Why Hire a Lubrication Engineer?" *Plant Engineering,* October 15, 1970.) Be sure to supply the oil company representative with all the information you have on equipment manufacturer's recommendations.

c. Petroleum lubricants are the most widely used type in industry; they are often compounded with animal and vegetable oils and synthetic additives. Synthetic fluids such as silicones, polyalkylene glycols, and chlorinated hydrocarbons are used when high temperatures, equipment corrosion, and process contamination must be resisted.

Service classifications for gasoline engine lubricants are ML, MM, and MS for light, moderate, and severe operating conditions; DG, DM, and DS are the corresponding designations for diesel service (American Petroleum Institute). Greases are often classified by the soap base with which they are compounded— lime-base greases have good water resistance but are limited to 175° F., while soda-base greases are usable at 260° F., but have poor water resistance. EP (extreme pressure) lubricants are used on hypoid gears and in bearings subject to high internal contact forces.

d. Interchangeability. When it becomes necessary to change suppliers or efficiency demands that the plant consolidate a large inventory of grease and oil types, some method of correlating the various trade-name products is needed. One way is to compare them on the basis of the grade and class designations of such organizations as the Society of Automotive Engineers (S.A.E.) and the American Gear Manufacturers Association (AGMA).

2) Find the best method of getting it to the wear surface.

a. Manual. The simple oil can or the hand operated grease gun, used conscientiously, will suffice for most light-duty machine lubrication.

b. Immersion. Some mechanical devices are best lubricated when they are operated in or continuously passed through an oil bath. Frequently the oil is circulated by a pump and passed through a cooler and filter.

c. Gravity feed systems. They start with an oil reservoir, which for single-point application is a small cup made of glass or plastic and for multi-point application is an oil tank. Oil is conducted to the wear point by piping, where it is applied by means of a simple drip tube, wick, brush, or vibrating rod. On multi-point systems the use of sight feed valves is common; they permit adjustment and observation of the oil flow rate.

d. Pressure systems. Similar in design to the gravity systems, this type moves oil or other lubricants out of the reservoir by air pressure or by pump, achieving a force feed. A variation is the *spray* system, in which the oil is atomized by a pressurized air stream which delivers it to the wear point as a spray.

3) Establish a well-defined application and checkup system. It must have these three elements:

a. Trained and motivated lubrication personnel. Classify the lubricator's job at a high enough pay rate to attract capable people. Give them detailed training in technique and responsibility in classes conducted by your lubrication engineer, maintenance superintendent, or oil company representative. Repeat this training annually or more frequently as need arises.

b. Specific instructions. The lubricator must know exactly what machines he is to lubricate, when he is to do it, and the precise lubricant to be used. Some ways of communicating this information are punched cards or route sheets issued daily to the lubricators, and decals or plastic tags placed on each machine to be lubricated.

c. Checkoff reporting. Require the lubricator to sign or initial each task performed, using the punched card, the route sheet, or the plastic tag as a permanent record. Leave space for and invite his comments on the conditions he finds at the lubrication points.

CONCLUSION

A common set of principles evolves from the mechanical equipment guidelines developed in this chapter, whether for steam boilers, compressors, power transmission devices, bearings and couplings: thorough research before selection, sound operating procedures explicitly communicated, and effective preventive maintenance and lubrication practices. Accountability for applying them filters upward through the organization, arriving ultimately at the desk of the plant manager.

WEEK DUE 07-15-____
326-04-01

2200   WOOD HANDLING & PREPARATION ROOM
CONVEYOR UNDER NO. 1 CHIPPER
LINK BELT GEAR REDUCER
1 POINT
CHECK OIL LEVEL—ADD
EVERY MONTH MODE—
OIL BATH E.P. LUBRICANT
75

CHAIN DRIVE   2 POINTS
CHECK OIL LEVEL—ADD
EVERY WEEK MODE—DIP
LUBRICATION E.P. LUBRI-
CANT 75

DRIVE BELT GUIDE ROLL BEARINGS
2 POINTS
ADD GREASE EVERY
QUARTER MODE—PRES-
SURE GREASE FITTINGS
GREASE E.P. NO. 2

001-10-00   CHIP BIN
1600   HYDRAULIC TRUCK UNLOADER
HYDRAULIC SYSTEM
1 POINT
DRAIN, FLUSH & FILL
EVERY SIX MONTHS
MODE—RESERVOIR TUR-
BINE OIL 44

Exhibit 7. Lubricator's computerized instruction sheet.
(Courtesy of Gulf Oil Corporation)

Chapter 18

Utilizing Process Equipment
for Effective Conversion
and Movement of Material Streams

Plants of all descriptions increasingly find themselves taking advantage of the techniques used in the process industries to cut costs by handling and converting materials in continuous streams and in bulk. This chapter will examine a few of the more common kinds of equipment used for these unit operations, providing an overview of the types available and guidelines for selection and use.

VESSELS

Process vessels are roughly classified as *storage tanks* and *reaction kettles.* (See Chapter 10 for important considerations in the selection of tanks and the properties of process liquids.) Reaction kettles are vessels in which process fluids undergo a change in physical or chemical properties; they are typically equipped with an agitator for stirring the contents, exterior jackets or internal coils for heating and cooling, and instruments for measuring and recording temperature and pressure. Consider these points in the design and operation of both kinds of process vessels:

1) Design criteria.

   a. Density and weight. What is the density of the process fluid? Combined weight of contents and tank when full? Should it be mounted on load cell or lever scale? Will building structure support this weight without modification?

   b. Heat transfer. What will the temperatures of the contents be? What extremes will be reached? Will the fluid have to be heated or cooled? If so, how fast? Will the process or reaction generate heat which must be removed?

   c. Pressure. What is the maximum pressure which will be reached in the tank? In its jacket? Will either be subject to vacuum? Has the designer provided for these pressures at the maximum temperatures?

   d. Corrosion and finish. Will the process fluid corrode the vessel? Will the vessel material contaminate the fluid? Should the interior surface be given a special finish to minimize "skin" deposits on the walls or for sanitary cleaning?

   e. Volatility and flammability. What is the vapor pressure of the contained fluid? At temperature extremes? Is it flammable? If so, will inert gas blanketing of the vapor space be required?

f. Viscosity. How "thick" is the fluid? What are the maximum and minimum viscosities encountered during processing? Have agitation and outlet nozzles been designed for the worst conditions?

2) Auxiliary equipment.

a. Tanks. *Earth dikes* are built up around outdoor storage tanks so that surrounding areas will not be flooded if a leak occurs; if the process fluid is dangerous or expensive, *concrete pits* may be built so that it can be recovered. If more than one tank is built in a single pit, a good design rule is to size the pit to hold the contents of the largest tank plus 25 percent of the contents of the other tanks. *Dipstick nozzles* and *downpipes* permit direct measurement of the liquid level; a variety of *liquid level indicating instruments* provide indirect readings at ground level and remote stations. *Conservation vents* permit small build-ups of pressure and vacuum before venting the tank to the atmosphere; they reduce vapor loss of volatile materials. *Flame arrestors* (often used in combination with conservation vents) prevent flashback of ignited vapors to the interior of the tank.

b. Kettles. Pressure vessels may require *relief valves* or *rupture disks* for release of sudden pressure buildups. If visual inspection of the contents is required, *sight glasses* are mounted on manholes or nozzles in pairs—one for a light source, the other to look through. *Manholes* should be large enough to permit entry by personnel and removal of internal equipment; they may have to be fitted with *crossbars* to prevent personnel from falling in. Overhead *condensers* are used to liquefy vapors of volatile materials and return them to the vessel. *Jackets* can be of the *baffled, spiral,* or *dimpled* types, depending upon heat transfer and cost requirements. External *insulation* is used for heat conservation and personnel protection.

3) Operating precautions.

a. Inspect safety devices periodically. Flame arresters and conservation vents can become corroded and clogged with dust after long exposure to the atmosphere. The undersides of rupture disks become coated with process materials which can alter their pressure ratings.

b. Clean jackets annually. Even when "city water" is used as the coolant, scale deposits will build up on the heat transfer surface. Commercial services are available who will come into the plant and circulate cleaning chemicals through the jackets.

c. Clean interior kettle surfaces on a regularly scheduled basis; if deposits are allowed to accumulate uncontrolled the equipment will suffer emergency outages, and cleaning will be more costly. Tank entry by personnel may be required (make sure harsh tools do not damage finished or delicate surfaces), but often solvent or solutions which react with the buildup can be found to remove deposits without tank entry.

MIXERS

Process vessels usually require agitation to accomplish their objectives, which may be the blending of liquids, the dissolving or suspending of solids in liquids, the dispersion of gases in liquids, or heat transfer to and from liquids. Follow these steps from definition of the problem through to operation of the equipment:

1) How to define the mixing job. First, determine the *physical properties* of the materials being mixed: density, viscosity, and surface tension. Solubility relationships must be understood, and if solids are involved, the particle size must be known. If any of the materials are shear sensitive, the maximum allowable shear stress must be stated. When heat transfer is required, the thermal conductivity and specific heat of the mix components is essential data. Such information is available in handbooks of physical and chemical properties, in the research files of your company, from suppliers of the mixed materials, and from mixing equipment vendors.

Next, decide what *performance characteristics* must be achieved: How fast must the mixing job be accomplished? To what degree of physical or chemical conversion must it be carried? How big will the mixing vessel be? Are there any limitations on its dimensions? (Note: Give the mixing designer as much freedom as possible to determine the shape of the tank, i.e., the ratio of length to diameter.) If the vessel is part of a continuous flow-through system, how much residence time is available or required? Is foaming objectionable—or desired?

2) Choose from available equipment. Manufacturers of mixing equipment offer a large variety of standard components; expensive, custom-designed units are rarely required. These are the basic elements of a mixing system:

a. Impeller. Selection is based on the flow pattern desired, and the viscosity of the fluids. See Exhibit 1 for examples of these types: a) the *propeller,* which produces axial flow—fluid motion in the same direction as the centerline of the shaft. Used for thin fluids and relatively small vessels, propeller units provide the simplest and cheapest mixer installations; b) the *axial flow* (or *pitched paddle*) impeller is used for larger installations, but as its name implies, still gives an axial motion to the fluid; c) the *flat-blade turbine* handles larger volumes and viscosities up to 100,000 centipoises (curved blades are sometimes used in the higher viscosity ranges), imparting a radial motion to the fluid. It is the impeller of choice when gas-liquid contacting is required; d) the *helical* impeller is the most expensive of the group, and is used for viscosities above 100,000 centipoises.

b. Shaft. The shaft must be designed to withstand the bending and vibrational forces to which it will be subjected. Cost savings in its design can be realized if a steady bearing is installed in the bottom of the tank to support the lower end, but these savings will rapidly disappear if the process fluid is not a good enough lubricant to prevent frequent failure of the bearing. Another important design consideration arises at the point where the shaft passes through the top of the tank—if there are no pressure or vapor loss problems, a simple hole in the top of the tank and a conical sheet metal collar mounted on the shaft will provide sufficient protection. For pressures up to 150 psi. *packed seals* are used; the more expensive *mechanical seals* are used for higher pressures and applications where leakage of process materials cannot be tolerated.

c. Drive. Horsepower, torque, and speed reduction are the basic criteria for selection. But the buyer must also consider flexibility for future needs (can agitator speed be changed by a simple gear replacement?), service dependability and maintenance requirements, and whether variable speed control is required

a. Propeller

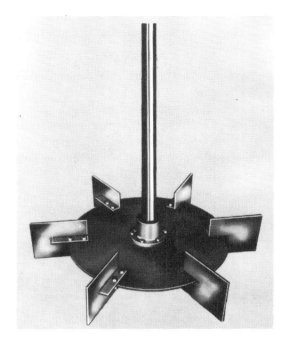

b. Axial flow impeller.

c. Flat-blade turbine.

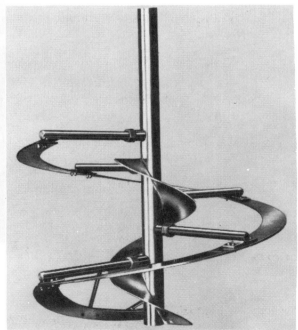

d. Helical impeller.

Exhibit 1. Types of mixing impellers.
(Courtesy of Mixing Equipment Company, Inc.)

(sometimes an expensive variable speed drive can be replaced by a simple two-or three-speed electric motor without real loss of process capability).

d. Baffles. An agitator mounted on the centerline of an unbaffled tank produces a swirling liquid motion, usually with a vortex forming around the shaft. This is the poorest of all mixing patterns and wasteful of power. To provide vertical as well as lateral motion, *baffles* are installed; typically they are flat metal plates mounted vertically in the tank (length about the same as the vertical wall of the tank), positioned on 90-degree radii (width about 1/12 of tank diameter), with several inches of clearance between the edge of the baffle and the tank wall.

3) Observe these operating precautions.

a. Don't run the agitator in an empty tank for more than a few seconds; damage to bearings and excessive shaft flexure could result.

b. Replace the packing in the stuffing box regularly; if it is allowed to "wear out" scoring of the shaft may result.

c. Keep the liquid level consistent from batch to batch. This is especially important when two (or more) impellers are mounted on the shaft, and the liquid level must be maintained at a minimum distance above the upper impeller to avoid excessive foaming or shear stress.

HEAT

The simplest method of transferring heat from one fluid to another is to mix them together, and this possibility ought to be seriously considered for each heat transfer situation. This section, however, is limited to a discussion of equipment for transferring heat between two fluids which must be handled in enclosed systems and kept separate from each other.

1) What to specify.

a. Operating conditions. For each fluid, the flow rate through the exchanger, the temperature in and desired temperature out, pressure, and allowable pressure drop through the equipment. In addition, the basic service of the unit: heater, cooler, evaporator, condenser, or reboiler.

b. Physical properties of the fluids. Density, viscosity, specific heat, thermal conductivity, and if one of the fluids is a vapor its latent heat and the quantity and nature of any non-condensable gases which might be present. The *fouling factor* must also be known or estimated; it is a numerical measure of the degree to which the fluid can be expected to deposit unwanted solid material on the heat transfer surfaces. Values for various fluids can be obtained from equipment manufacturers or from the published standards of the Tubular Equipment Manufacturer's Association (TEMA). They range from a low of .0005 for steam and clean organic vapors to a high of .01 for polluted river water or diesel exhaust fumes.

2) Equipment choices.

a. The basic categories are *tubular* and *plate* exchangers. Of the tubular types the simplest in construction is the *double-pipe* exchanger, which consists of a smaller pipe containing one fluid mounted concentrically inside a larger pipe, with the second fluid in the annual space. *Shell-and-tube* exchangers are the most common type, and are explained in a separate paragraph below. *Spiral-tube* exchanges are constructed by winding short lengths of tubing into flat coils, stacking them close together, and connecting the inlet and outlet ends to pipe manifolds. This assembly is inserted into a compact shell which has connections for entrance and exit of the shell-side fluid. The finished unit is a very compact device whose construction overcomes thermal expansion problems, and which is well-suited to the handling of viscous materials.

Plate exchangers include the basic *plate-frame* unit, which consists of a series of vertical plates mounted on horizontal guide rods. The plates are gasketed around the edges, and have holes at the corners for passage of the fluids. They are pressed tightly together by massive blocks tightened with a screw mechanism. If the spaces between the plates are imagined to be numbered consecutively, the plate holes are arranged so that one fluid passes through the odd numbered spaces, while the other flows through the even numbered spaces. This type of exchanger can readily be opened for cleaning, and is often used for fluids which deposit relatively large amounts of solids. The *spiral plate* exchanger has two parallel plates wound in a spiral and enclosed in a casing. It has many of the same advantages as the spiral tube. The *plate-and-fin* exchanger has corrugated metal sheets sandwiched between flat metal plates; the "sandwiches" are stacked together, with fluids in the alternate spaces. It is widely used in very low temperature applications.

b. Shell-and-tube exchangers. A number of long thin tubes are mounted inside a cylindrical shell; one fluid flows through the tubes, the other surrounds them as it passes through the shell. The ends of the tubes are fitted into circular discs called *tubesheets. Heads* are mounted on the tubesheets to serve as inlet and outlet reservoirs for the tubeside fluid; partitions can be installed in the heads to achieve as many passes through the tubes as desired (one to eight passes is considered "standard"). *Baffles* mounted inside the shell support the tubes and direct the flow of the shellside fluid so as to avoid dead spots. Exhibit 2 illustrates these features of a typical industrial heat exchanger.

The designer of this equipment must meet the obvious objectives of achieving the desired quantity of heat transfer at the lowest possible cost. He strives for the highest fluid velocities possible in order to maximize heat transfer and minimize fouling, but he must do this within the allowable pressure drops for each fluid stream. When temperature differences are large, or thermal cycling frequent, the design must accomodate expansion and contraction of the components. In many cases access must be provided to the exterior of the tubes so that they can be cleaned mechanically.

There are three basic designs to meet these requirements. One is the *fixed tubesheet*, in which a tubesheet at each end of the exchanger is welded to the shell; another is the "U-tube" type, with only one tubesheet and each tube bent into a long U-shape; and the "floating head" types, in which there is one fixed tubesheet and the other is free to move back and forth in thermal expansion and contraction. Sub-types of this last group are the *pull-through floating head exchanger,* the *floating head outside packed lantern-ring exchanger,* the *floating-head split backing ring* exchanger, and the *floating head outside packed stuffing box* exchanger. Features of the various designs are compared in Exhibit 3, which is taken from an excellent publication on this subject, *Heat Exchangers,* Manual 700-A, The Patterson-Kelley Co., Inc., East Stroudsburg, Pa.

3) Operating instructions.

a. Measure the performance (inlet and outlet temperatures and flow rates of both streams) while the exchanger is running well; the data will be needed for comparison when substandard performance is suspected.

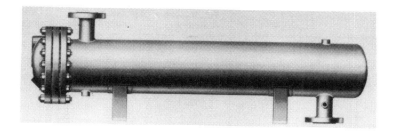

a).   Photograph of U—tube heat exchanger with threaded head connections.

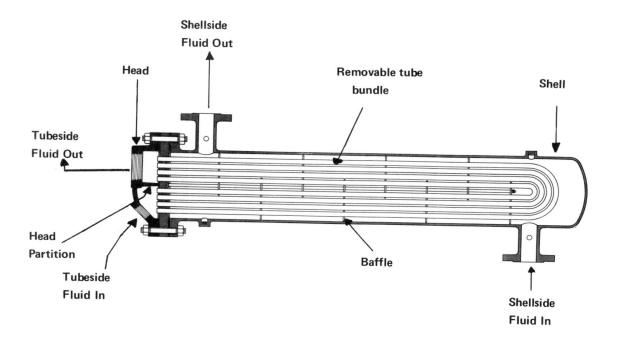

b).   Diagram of above exchanger, showing internal parts.

a). Photograph of U-tube heat exchanger with threaded head connections.
b). Diagram of above exchanger, showing internal parts.

Exhibit 2. Industrial heat exchanger.
(Courtesy of The Patterson-Kelley Co., Inc.)

Type of Design	"U"-Tube	Fixed Tubesheet	Floating Head Pull-Through Bundle	Floating Head Outside Packed Lantern-Ring	Floating Head Split Backing Ring	Floating Head Outside Packed Stuffing Box
Relative Cost Increases From (A) Least Expensive through (E) Most Expensive	A	B	C	C	D	E
Provision for Differential Expansion	individual tubes free to expand	expansion joint in shell	floating head	floating head	floating head	floating head
Removable Bundle	yes	no	yes	yes	yes	yes
Replacement Bundle Possible	yes	not practical	yes	yes	yes	yes
Individual Tubes Replaceable	only those in outside row	yes	yes	yes	yes	yes
Tube Interiors Cleanable	difficult to do mechanically can do chemically	yes, mechanically or chemically	yes, mechanically or chemically	yes, mechanically or chemically	yes, mechanically or chemically	yes, mechanically or chemically
Tube Exteriors With Triangular Pitch Cleanable	chemically only	chemically only	chemically only	chemically only	chemically only	chemically only
Tube Exteriors With Square Pitch Cleanable	yes, mechanically or chemically	chemically only	yes, mechanically or chemically	yes, mechanically or chemically	yes, mechanically or chemically	yes, mechanically or chemically
Double Tubesheet Feasible	yes	yes	no	no	no	yes
Number of Tube Passes	any practical even number possible	no practical limitations	no practical limitation (for single pass, floating head requires packed joint)	limited to single or 2 pass	no practical limitation (for single pass, floating head requires packed joint)	no practical limitation
Internal Gaskets Eliminated	yes	yes	no	yes	no	yes

Exhibit 3. Comparison of various heat exchanger design features.
(Courtesy of The Patterson-Kelley Co., Inc.)

b. Monitor both outlet streams for evidence of cross-contamination. If it occurs, the trouble may be a corroded tube, leaks at the tubesheet, or leaking head partition gaskets.

c. Leaking tubes can be taken out of service temporarily by tapping a soft metal plug into each end of the tube; the entire tube can be replaced at the next scheduled shutdown.

d. Arrange periodic shutdowns for cleaning of tubes and shell, replacement of head gaskets, replacement of defective tubes, and re-rolling of tube ends in the tube sheet. Chemical cleaning consists of circulating solutions through the tube and shell which can dissolve solid deposits; mechanical cleaning consists of scraping and rodding, or using motorized brushes and knives to clean out tube interiors.

DRYERS

Industrial materials which require drying cover a wide variety of forms—lumber, ceramic objects, plastic films, textiles, solutions, pastes, and slurries. The liquid to be removed is usually water, but can be any volatile liquid. And the final form can be the original solid object or sheet, a powder or granular solid. Use these guidelines to find your way through this extensive field:

1) Design and selection of dryers from the manager's point of view:

a. Make sure a broad economic review is made before selecting a particular drying technique. One process equipment catalog lists thirty-six categories of dryers. Comparisons should include not only the substantial first cost of such equipment, but energy consumption over its lifetime as well.

b. Can the dryer be included in the materials movement scheme? That is, can the material be dried while on a moving belt, in a bucket elevator, or on a screw conveyor? (See Chapter 10).

c. Mechanical separation of the liquid from the solid is much cheaper than evaporation in a dryer. Can a settling, screening, or centrifuging step be inserted ahead of the dryer to reduce the load on it?

d. Avoid overdesign. There is no point in being able to dry wood chips to a moisture content of 1 percent if later they will reach an equilibrium moisture content of 10 percent while in contact with the air in a warehouse.

2) Types of dryers available.

a. Continuous versus batch. The most common of the batch units is the *tray* dryer. An insulated cabinet (usually of walk-in height) is fitted with heating coils and fans. The material to be dried is placed on trays which are mounted on wheeled carts. The carts are moved into the cabinet, the doors closed, and the material subjected to hot air flow for as long as needed to reach desired dryness. Although first cost of this equipment is relatively low, labor cost is high, and it is limited to situations in which the material cannot tolerate agitation, in which relatively small amounts of a large number of different products are dried, or those in which long drying times are required.

The continuous dryers offer much more economical material handling. The tray dryer concept can readily be adapted to the continuous *tunnel* dryer, in which the carts are pulled through a long drying cabinet, with the residence time calculated to match the drying cycle. The most common of the continuous types is the *rotary* dryer, which consists of a horizontal cylinder mounted to rotate around its long axis. Fin-like sheet metal *flights* are attached to the interior surface. The wet feed enters at one end of the rotating cylinder, is picked up by the flights and cascaded through the air space. Hot air is passed through the cylinder, either *concurrently* or *countercurrently* to the direction of the feed flow. *Belt* dryers are really tunnel dryers which use a conveyor belt to transport the material; the belt can contain perforations or be a screen to allow air to pass up through the material as well as over it.

b. Direct versus indirect heating. All of the dryers described above are *direct heat* types, because the heat which evaporates the moisture is carried by the air (or gas) stream which comes in direct contact with the material being dried. Further illustrations of the direct heat type are the *spray* dryer, in which a solution is forced through a spray nozzle into a chamber through which hot gases flow, suspending the falling droplets until the water evaporates and a dry powder remains. Spray dryers are used for dilute solutions, heat-sensitive materials, and some types of slurries. The *fluid bed* dryer takes advantage of the fact that a mass with the properties of a fluid can be achieved by passing a gas flow through a bed of granular solids at velocities high enough to suspend or "fluidize" the particles. If the gas is heated, drying can be accomplished at the same time. Fluid bed dryers can be operated either as batch or continuous flow systems.

In *indirect heat* dryers the heat for drying is not carried by the gas flow, but comes through a metal wall with which the material to be dried is kept in contact. A prime example is the *drum* dryer, which is a slowly rotating cylinder, closed off at either end to form a hollow chamber. Steam or any desired heating medium is passed through the interior of the drum. The feed is applied to the hot exterior surface, dries as it rides around the periphery, and is scraped off as a flake or powder by a knife-edged bar. Drum dryers are often used when it is desired to recover the solids in flake form, are readily adapted to handling viscous feeds, and are suited to solvent-recovery applications. Another type is the double-cone shaped *tumble* dryer, which takes a batchwise charge and turns end over end during the drying cycle. Heat is supplied to an external jacket. The ordinary screw conveyor is converted to a *screw flight* dryer by adding a heating jacket to the trough.

c. Vacuum versus atmospheric pressure drying. Drying at less than atmospheric pressure lowers the operating temperature (a necessity for heat-sensitive materials), and facilitates the recovery of solvents. The tray, rotary, drum and tumble dryers already mentioned are adaptable to vacuum operation. Another type often equipped for vacuum operation is the *pan* dryer. It has a relatively shallow-dished circular container into which the feed flows. Heating is indirect, through a jacket, and an agitator sweeps the bottom of the pan effecting material discharge through a side port.

3) Operating hints.

a. Don't overdry. This point is similar to that raised previously in paragraph 1.d., and in Chapter 1, page 23. If the quality specification allows a moisture content of X, it is a waste of (sometimes considerable amounts of) money to dry it to one-tenth or even one-half X.

b. Schedule shutdowns. Of all the kinds of process equipment, dryers are among those which benefit most from pre-planned downtime for cleaning and maintenance. Heat transfer surfaces become fouled, plastic and rubber seals in rotating elements are subject to erosion by abrasive particles and plugging by solids buildups, air filters become plugged after so many hours of use. If these problems are not attended to *before* they cause trouble, emergency outages and accumulations of off-grade product will be the outcome *after* they become evident.

c. Monitor inlet (as well as outlet) streams. If the feed is wetter (or has other properties different) than design specifications, the dryer may be hopelessly overloaded. Operating managers then have to make the choice between shutting down and straightening out the problems in upstream equipment (decanters, centrifuges, settlers), or producing a "wet" product which will have to be re-dried.

FLUID SYSTEM PRINCIPLES

The ability to transport fluids—liquids, slurries, or gases—from one processing unit to another is a key element in the development of a continuous processing stream. The technology used in the design of fluid transportation systems is broad and complex, and its details cannot be compressed into a few pages. But the plant manager, who is interested in obtaining the most efficient fluid systems for his operations, will find useful the basic design principles and the economic balances which must be struck in using them, as they are outlined in the remainder of this chapter.

The designer of a piping system for liquid flow uses as a basic tool this form of the Bernoulli equation:

$$Z_1 + \frac{V_1^2}{2g} + \frac{p_1}{\rho_1} + W = Z_2 + \frac{V_2^2}{2g} + \frac{p_2}{\rho_2} + F$$

The subscripts 1 and 2 refer to values of the variables at two different points in the system, usually the starting and ending points. Z is the elevation in feet above a convenient datum line established by the designer, often through the lowest point in the system. V is the linear velocity of the fluid through the piping in feet per second; g is the acceleration of gravity, a constant with the value of 32.2 feet per second; p is the fluid pressure, expressed in squared pounds per *square foot* (multiply pressure in psi by 144 to obtain pressure in psf). ρ is the density of the fluid in pounds per cubic foot. It will be noticed that when the variables in the first three terms on each side of the equation are expressed in consistent units of pounds, feet, and seconds, the units in the numerators and denominators divide out in such a way that each expression evolves in units of feet. This measurement in terms of feet is called *head,* and the three terms of the equation are *elevation head, velocity head,* and *pressure head,* respectively.

W represents the head which must be supplied by the pump. When it is multiplied by the flow rate in pounds per second and the resulting product divided by 550, the theoretical horsepower is obtained. Dividing this figure by the pump efficiency gives the horsepower rating of the pump.

Before F is explained, a word is in order about the *Reynolds number.* It is the expression $\frac{DV\rho}{\mu}$, in which D is the pipe diameter in feet, V is the fluid velocity in feet per second, ρ is the fluid density in pounds per cubic foot, and μ is the viscosity in pounds per foot-second. When the Reynolds number takes on values below 2,000 the flow is classified as *laminar, viscous,* or *streamline.* When the Reynolds number exceeds 4,000 the flow is *turbulent.* The

a). Tray dryer (batch type). (Courtesy of Proctor & Schwartz, Inc.)

b). Rotary dryer (continuous type).
(Courtesy FMC Corp. Link-Belt Material Handling Systems Div.)

Exhibit 4. Examples of batch and continuous dryers.

classification of flow and the values of the Reynolds number are important in finding F and in many other hydraulic and heat transfer calculations.

F represents the combined frictional losses in the system. There is a frictional drag between the wall of a pipe and the fluid moving inside it which produces energy losses which must be made up by the pump. The rougher the interior surface of the pipe (commercial steel pipe is rougher than copper tubing), the greater the loss. Fittings in the pipe system (valves, elbows, tees, etc.), sudden enlargements and contractions (change from one pipe size to another), and pipe entrances and exits (e.g., to or from a large tank) contibute additional energy losses to F. To handle this complicated problem of finding F, the designer of the system:

1. Calculates the Reynolds number.

2. Finds the friction factor f, from one of several charts available in handbooks on hydraulic engineering,* which plot f against Reynolds number and pipe roughness.

3. Converts the total number of fittings, entrance and exit resistances, and enlargement and contraction resistances to equivalent lengths of straight pipe from tables in hydraulic handbooks. He adds this total to the actual length of straight pipe run to determine the total equivalent pipe length, L.

4. Finds F, the head loss of friction, from a formula supplied with the friction factor chart which relates F to f, L, and V, the fluid velocity.

The model given above is limited to noncompressible fluids (liquids) which do not undergo a temperature change. For compressible fluids (gases and vapors) more complicated equations, which take account of the change in fluid density with changes in pressure, must be used.

PIPING

Four major choices are involved in the design of a piping system: a) optimum size, b) appropriate material of construction, c) best method of joining, and d) selection of fittings.

1) Select optimum pipe size. Commercial pipe is made in nominal pipe sizes starting at 1/8 in. and increasing in 1/8 in. increments up to 1/2 in.; in 1/4 in. increments up to 1 1/2 in.; 1/2 in. increments up to 4 in.; 1 in. increments up to 6 in.; and 2 in. increments up to 42 in. It is also classified according to wall thickness under *Schedule Number*. Schedule 40 is the "normal" weight used in most plant applications. Wall thickness declines as schedule numbers go lower. From Schedule 40 the schedule numbers drop in increments of 10 to Schedule 10 (Schedule 10S and 5S are special designations for thin-walled pipe made of corrosion-resistant alloys, such as stainless steel), and rise in increments of 20 to 160 ("Double Extra Strong" pipe is designated as XX, and has a wall thickness greater than that of Schedule 160).

Choice of pipe size is based on flow velocity in feet per second (divide the flow rate in cubic feet per second by the crosssectional area of the pipe in square feet); typical values for liquids are 5 to 15 fps, and 70 to 1500 fps for steam. *Economic pipe diameter* is chosen on this basis: as pipe size goes up the cost of purchase and installation increases; on the other hand, the cost of energy to move fluid through it declines, because friction losses are lower. To find the economic diameter for any particular installation, a) plot a curve of pipe cost versus pipe size, b) on the same plot graph energy cost versus pipe size, c) plot a total cost line by adding the two costs for each pipe size. The economic pipe size is that corresponding to the lowest point on the total cost line.

---

*One publication offering this information as well as detailed analyses of practical flow problems, is *Flow of Fluids Through Valves, Fittings and Pipe* (Chicago: Crane Co., 1957).

2) Pick the right material. Apply these criteria: cost; projected life; resistance to corrosion, temperature and shock; non-contamination of process material; heat transfer; ease of cleaning (food and chemical plants); cost of maintenance. Select from this table of available materials:

METALS	NON-METALS	PIPE LININGS*
Carbon steel	Concrete	Asphalt
Wrought iron	Clay	Cement
Cast iron	Asbestos cement	Wood
Brass	Graphite	Glass
Aluminum	Porcelain	Rubber
Silicon-Iron	Glass	Plastic (many types,
Lead	Plastic	including fluoro-
Copper	(Many types, including	carbon polymers,
Stainless steel	polyethylene, polyvinyl	polyvinvylidene,
Nickel-copper	chloride, and glass fiber	chlorinated poly-
Nickel	reinforced polyester)	ether)
Nickel-chromium	Rubber	Metal (lead, stainless
Tin	Wood	steel, aluminum, nickel
Titanium		and its alloys, tantalum,
Tantalum		titanium)

3) Choose the best joining method. *Threaded* pipe is available in sizes up to 12 in.; although it dominates the field in sizes below 2 in., its use in larger sizes should be questioned in terms of economics, especially the labor cost of installation. Threaded joints are sealed by the application of pipe dope or wrapping with Teflon tape before final tightening. *Flanged* joints are available in sizes up to 24 in. They are normally employed in sizes above 2 in., but are useful in any size when higher temperatures, higher pressures, or a need for frequent disassembly are involved. Flanges may be formed as an integral part of the pipe when it is manufactured, or they can be shipped separately and welded or screwed to the pipe in the field. Flanged joints are sealed by inserting gaskets between the flange faces and compressing them by tightening the bolts which hold the flanges together. *Welded* joints are used in long runs in larger sizes, and when the nature of the fluid requires positive leak-proof joints.

4) Select appropriate fittings. They may be grouped according to the functions they perform:

    a. Connecting. Two pieces of pipe with external (male) threads can be connected with a *coupling,* a short pipe length with internal (female) threads. A short pipe length with male threads is called a *nipple.* If the joint must be disassembled without disturbing adjacent pipe arrangements, a *union* is used. It has two halves which are permanently threaded to the pipe ends, and are joined by a single threaded connection at the center which is easily undone with a pipe wrench.

    b. Change in pipe size. When (for example) a four-inch pipe must be connected to a two-inch pipe, a *reducer* is used. It is a short section of pipe with the large and small connections at opposite ends; it is a *concentric reducer* if the small connection is centered on the same axis line as the large connection, and an

---

*Note on linings. Plastic linings may either be fused to the base pipe, or inserted loose. Metal linings may either be electroplated, or inserted as "clad" plates and welded to the base pipe.

eccentric reducer if it is not. A *bushing* is a single ring with an external thread of one size, and an internal thread of a smaller size.

c. Change in flow direction. The common *elbow* effects a 90-degree change in direction. *Long radius elbows* have a longer arc of curvature, offer less resistance to flow. *Street elbows* have an external thread at one end, an internal thread at the other. 45-degree elbows effect change in direction at that angle. The *return bend* is U-shaped, effecting a 180-degree change in direction. The *tee* permits a 90-degree branch from the straight run. The *Y-branch* or *lateral* allows branching at other angles, usually 45 degrees. The *cross* provides double branching at 90 degrees. Most of the fittings mentioned are available with unequal size connections at the branches; such fittings are called *reducing tees, reducing elbows,* etc. Pipes ends can be blocked with *caps,* which have an internal thread, or *plugs,* which have an external thread.

d. Valves. *Gate* valves are good for positive cutoff of flow, but not for regulating or *throttling* flow; they should be left fully closed or fully open. *Plug cocks* offer positive flow cutoff with a quick-closing feature (usually one 90-degree turn of a handle). *Globe* valves have good throttling characteristics and positive cutoff; they are seldom used in sizes over 3 in. *Ball* valves have quick-closing, positive cutoff, and throttling features; they are often used for viscous fluids and slurries. *Butterfly* valves have good throttling characteristics and low pressure drop; tight shutoff is available in recent special models. *Diaphragm* valves separate the fluid from the moving metal parts by a rubber or plastic diaphragm; they are used for corrosive and abrasive fluids at pressures up to 150 psi. *Check* valves allow flow only in one direction, have a gate or ball mechanism which seals on backpressure; basic types are *lift, swing,* and *ball* checks.

PUMPS

These machines provide the driving force which moves fluids through the plant; they are briefly discussed in the context of materials movement in Chapter 10. *Centrifugal pumps,* which are the most commonly encountered type in plant work, are really part of a larger class of variable capacity devices which include the *axial flow* pump and the *regenerative* pump. The axial flow machine has a propeller mounted on a shaft within the pump casing, and imparts velocity to the fluid in the direction of the shaft. It is used when large volumes of fluid are moved against relatively low head, as in recirculation systems. The regenerative pump is also called a *turbine* pump; it moves fluid through a radial cavity at the periphery of the pump by means of vanes which are mounted on a radial disk and project into the radial cavity. Its application is the reverse of that of the axial flow types—it is used for low-volume high-head systems. The *centrifugal* pump uses a circular impeller with spiral vanes (mounted on a spinning shaft like a wheel on an axle) which rotates inside a casing. Liquid is drawn into the eye of the impeller, and discharged at the periphery. The casing is most often in the shape of a volute, which allows a smooth transformation of velocity head into pressure head.

In *positive displacement* pumps a slug of liquid is drawn into the pump, trapped in a chamber formed by the mechanism, and forced into the discharge section by some form of mechanical action. In *piston* and *plunger* pumps, liquid is drawn into a cylindrical chamber on the suction stroke and forced into the discharge line on the return power stroke. This action creates pressure pulsations in the discharge line; they can be smoothed out by mounting two or more pistons on the pump with staggered power strokes. The *triplex* pump (three pistons) is a common type.

Rotary pumps achieve a non-pulsating positive displacement by means of a continuously rotating mechanism. Typical is the *gear* pump, which has two gears mounted one above the other, so that they mesh in the center. Liquid is drawn into the pump by rotation of the gears, and trapped between the gear teeth and the pump casing which fits tightly around them. When the liquid reaches the discharge side it is prevented from flowing back to the suction side by the meshing of the gear teeth. Other variations of the rotary pump are the *vane* pump, *screw* pump, *rotating piston,* and *lobe* pumps.

How to Select a Pump

1) Choose a centrifugal pump whenever possible. This type is available in a wide variety of standard capacities, is usually lowest in first cost, has the simplest mechanism, and is easiest to install and operate. Specify a centrifugal pump *unless:*

a. The flow is outside the range of 5 gpm to 100,000 gpm.

b. Changes in flow rate caused by changes in system pressure are unacceptable.

c. Viscosity exceeds 1,000 centipoises.

d. The combination of flow rate and head requirements lies within the narrow ranges of the more specialized variable displacement pumps. Use the axial flow pump for flow rates from 1,000 to 1,000,000 gpm at heads less than 50 ft. At the other end of the scale, specify the regenerative pump for flows up to 200 gpm against heads up to 1200 ft.

Final selection of a particular centrifugal pump for a flow system is made from curves of flow rate vs. head published by manufacturers for each of their models. Examples of these curves, called *characteristics,* are given in Exhibit 5 for three pump models, A, B, and C. The characteristic shows the flow rates which will be delivered against various values of head; for example, when Pump C is operated against a 43 ft. head, it will deliver 200 gpm. Each pump will operate at only those points which lie on its characteristic; thus, if it is desired to operate Pump C at 100 gpm, the head would have to be increased to 49 ft.

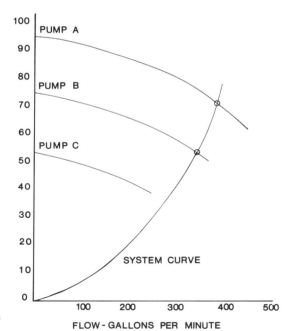

Exhibit 5. Pump Characteristic and System Curves

A further aid to selection is the plotting of a *system curve,* as shown in Exhibit 5. Using the equation and calculation method described on Pages 249-251, values of head required are determined for a number of flow rates in a given piping system and the results plotted on the pump curve graph. The intersection of a characteristic with the system curve represents one set of conditions at which the flow system can operate. Thus, in Exhibit 5, if the flow system can be operated at 340 gpm it will develop a head of 53 ft; if Pump B is operated against a head of 53 ft. it will produce a flow rate of 340 gpm. This combination of flow and head is the only one at which Pump B will operate in this system. If a higher flow rate is desired, the conditions at the intersection of the system curve and the Pump A characteristic can be used—385 gpm at 71 ft. of head. These intersections are the only two points on the graph at which the system can operate; if other flow rates are desired, other pumps whose characteristics intersect the system curve at those flow rates would have to be obtained.

2) Choose a positive displacement pump when:

a. Flow is less than 5 gpm.

b. Viscosity exceeds 1,000 centipoises.

c. Steady flow rate must be maintained against changes in head. Unlike the centrifugal pump, the positive displacement pump delivers at a virtually constant flow rate over a wide range of head.

d. The fluid might be injured by the high shear rate of a centrifugal pump (e.g., synthetic latex).

The centrifugal pump is usually connected directly to the motor shaft, and rotates at full motor speed. Positive displacement pumps are usually geared down to operate at lower speeds, and if a variable speed drive is used, can be adjusted to deliver accurate flows over a wide rate range. Because of their close-fitting internal parts, they should not be used with fluids containing suspended matter or those which have poor lubricating properties.

Cavitation and Net Positive Suction Head

If the pressure at the suction inlet of the pump is low enough to equal or almost equal the vapor pressure of the fluid, bubbles of vapor will form and then collapse as the fluid passes to the high pressure side of the pump. This action is known as *cavitation,* and can be identified by extreme vibration and noisiness. It causes erosion of the pump parts, and interferes with pump performance. To overcome this problem, two kinds of net positive suction head (NPSH) must be considered: 1) The NPSH required by the pump. It is determined by the manufacturer, and usually plotted as a curve of required NPSH vs. flow rate on the same graph as the characteristic curve of the pump. 2) The NPSH available at the suction inlet of the pump. Its value is the total of the elevation, pressure, and velocity heads minus the vapor pressure of the fluid. The available NPSH must equal or exceed the required NPSH if cavitation is to be avoided.

Checklist for Installing, Operating, and Maintaining Pumps

1) When Installing:

a. Mount pump level on firm foundation or base plate.

b. Connect piping so that there is no strain on pump casing. May require flexible connection.

c. Do not connect an elbow or other change of direction fitting directly to pump casing. Fluid should have a straight run into the pump suction.

d. Locate pump as close as possible to fluid supply. Keep suction line as short as possible.

e. Check coupling for misalignment. (See Chapter 17.)

f. An arrow showing the proper direction of rotation will be embossed on the casing or marked on the nameplate. Check for proper rotation before starting a new pump or one which has undergone electrical repairs; wires are commonly reversed, causing pump to run backwards.

2) Operating:

a. Startup. Flood casing by opening suction valve. If there is a vent cock on the casing, open it so that liquid can displace air or gas. Open discharge valve if pump is positive displacement type; if it is centrifugal type, close the discharge valve or open slightly. Check to see that all lubrication and cooling devices are in operation. Start motor, open discharge valve slowly.

b. Check for noise, vibration, overheating, and excessive motor current while pump is running. If any of these symptoms appear, take pump out of service until condition is corrected.

c. Never throttle suction valve on a pump. Never throttle discharge valve on a positive displacement pump.

d. Never run a pump dry—moving parts will wear and overheat.

3) Maintenance:

a. Put pump on routine lubrication schedule. Make sure that oil reservoirs and grease fittings are properly supplied at all times.

b. Repack stuffing box on regular schedule; don't wait until excessive leakage or scoring of shaft takes place.

c. Store spare parts as recommended by manufacturer. Moving parts—shaft, seals, bearings—are usually on the list. If pump has a mechanical seal, stock a complete spare seal assembly for quick return of the pump to service in the event of failure.

d. On preventive maintenance inspections, check coupling alignment, tightness of baseplate bolts and piping connections, functioning of lubrication systems, and condition of packing.

e. If there is a risk of damaging objects getting into the pump mechanism, install a large mesh screen or knockout pot in the suction line.

CONCLUSION

Even those plants which consider their operations to be totally machine-shop oriented are turning to the use of bulk and fluid processing systems to simplify operations and reduce costs. A wire-enamelling plant builds a central mixing and distribution system to control the properties of the enamel sent to each coating machine; a cigarette factory sets up bulk storage and distribution facilities for its adhesives, eliminating the handling of 55 gallon drums; a textile mill does the same thing with its bleaching chemicals. This chapter provides the plant manager with the fundamental ideas and necessary practical hints for making his contribution to the design, installation, and operation of storage tanks, reaction kettles, mixers, heat exchangers, dryers, and the pumps and piping systems which transport fluids between them.

Chapter 19

Building Coordinated Heating, Ventilating and Air Conditioning Systems for Employee Comfort and Safety

Some manufacturing operations demand close control of air quality—temperature, humidity, and dust content—in order to make an acceptable product. All manufacturing installations and their associated laboratories and offices must have adequate heat, ventilation, and possibly air conditioning for worker comfort, low labor turnover, and compliance with safety and health regulations.

While the three topics are treated separately for ease of understanding, they must be carefully coordinated in the design of any particular installation, and the material in this chapter is presented with the problems and opportunities of coordination in mind. Competent engineering work is essential in determining the needs to be met and the hardware to be used in building HVAC systems; if this important step is omitted, engineering, maintenance, and management people face long years of complaints and problems.

HEATING

Adquate building heat is the most elemental need for employee comfort, but it may also be required to prevent freezing damage to piping systems, raw materials, and products. The plant manager and his engineering staff should know how long it will take each building in the plant to cool down to unacceptable temperature levels in case of heating system failure in cold weather, and be prepared to supply emergency heat within that time period. Whether he is considering the heating system for a new building, replacement of heating equipment in an old facility, or expansion of an existing structure, the manager will need to deal with these aspects of design and equipment selection:

Choose Between Centralized and Decentralized Systems

The centralized heating system is typified by the familiar home furnace which burns fuel to produce steam, hot water, or warm air. The heated fluid is circulated through pipes or conduits to radiators, registers, or similar devices to diffuse the heat at the point of need. Return pipes and conduits bring the fluid back to the furnace for reheating. In decentralized systems, each local "heater" (space heater, rooftop unit, or infra-red device) is fired by its own supply of electricity or gas.

1) Centralized systems: *Advantages* are more efficient fuel consumption, low maintenance costs, monitoring and control from one point. *Disadvantages* are slower response to sudden demand, difficulty of expansion, complete loss of heat when the system is inoperative.

2) Decentralized systems: *Advantages* are low first cost, ease of expansion, partial supply of heat when one unit is inoperative. *Disadvantages* are difficulty of access for maintenance, hazards of gas piping or high-current electrical distribution networks.

Select a Fuel and the Medium

Central heating systems fire coal, oil, or gas, and the choice between these fuels is based on price but modified by considerations of convenience and pollution limits. (See Chapter 17.)

The medium for carrying the heat of the burning fuel to the spaces to be warmed can be steam, hot water, or warm air. Steam systems are the most common in industrial space heating; piping systems are relatively simple, the fluid is moved without the aid of a pump or fan, and the amount of heat transfer surface required at the point of use is minimized by the high temperatures available and by the change from gas to liquid (each pound of steam gives up approximately 900 BTU of heat as it condenses to water). Hot water systems have the advantage of fast response to demand, quieter operation, more flexibility in piping arrangements, and less corrosion in the piping system. *High temperature hot water* systems (over 250° F.) approach the economy of steam systems by requiring smaller piping and heat transfer surfaces than ordinary hot water systems while retaining their advantages. However, they do require very precise operating control to function effectively. Warm air systems are limited to smaller plants with relatively clean operations; they are inexpensive to build, have fast response to demand, and the air circulating systems can be used for ventilation in warm weather. Fuel efficiency is low, however, and if the recirculated air is contaminated by dust or odors, expensive removal devices must be installed.

Electric heat is less common in industrial plants, but the trend is up. Conditions which favor electric heating are: 1) cheap electricity and special rates for heating, 2) mild outdoor temperatures, 3) buildings which are heavily insulated for other reasons, and 4) a need to avoid air pollution which might result from the burning of fossil fuels at the plant site. Electric heaters can be installed as baseboard units, or placed in the air stream of central ventilating and recirculating systems, such as those required for air conditioning. Another way of applying electric heat is through infra-red units which radiate heat to localized areas which must be warmed, or are used for outdoor applications such as loading docks. In buildings and offices which require large banks of fluorescent lights, the heat from these lights can be used to supplement or completely replace conventional sources of heat. Air is passed over the banks of lamps to pick up heat and is distributed to areas which must be heated. This system has the double advantage of reducing operating temperature of the lamps, prolonging their life and improving efficiency. In warm weather the air from the light banks can be exhausted to the outside, reducing the load on the air conditioning system.

Pick the Best Heater

The apparatus which finally transfers the heat produced by the fuel to the air space where it is needed is called a "heat-emitting device," or simply a "heater." It is a key component of the heating system which affects overall performance and economy.

Two basic heat transfer devices used in many of the units described below are the *finned tube* and the *coil. Finned tubes* are made by mounting thin metal sheets (fins) with holes at their centers on tubing or pipe, and bonding them in such a way that heat conducts readily from the tube to the fin. The total heat transfer surface of the original tube is magnified as much as twentyfold. *Coils* consist of large fins with many holes; tubing is passed back and forth through the holes in a serpentine pattern, as in an automobile radiator, and attached to the fins with a heat-conducting bond. In both types heating or cooling fluids are passed through the tubes or pipes.

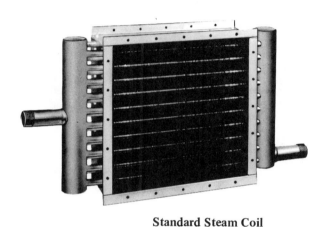

Standard Steam Coil

Finned Tube Electric "Coil"

Exhibit 1. Two types of heating coil.
(Courtesy of American Air Filter Company, Inc.)

Heaters for Centralized Systems

1) Baseboard units. Familiar in residential construction, these devices consist of a finned tube covered by a metal enclosure with a damper on the top side for temperature control. The tubes carry steam or hot water. In industrial applications two or more units may be run side by side, or mounted in stacks on a wall.

2) Unit heaters. These are compact units which can be hung from ceilings or mounted on wall brackets. The heating element is a coil supplied with steam or hot water, mounted in a finished metal cabinet. Louvers direct the air stream, which is supplied by a fan. Units mounted horizontally have the coil on the suction side of the fan; vertical units have the coil on the discharge side of the fan. An important characteristic of the unit heater is its "throw," the distance in feet from the unit at which the warm air stream is effective. Advantages are: 1) they take up no floor space, 2) high heat output from relatively small

units, 3) flexibility in location, so that they can be aimed at cold spots, and 4) powered air movement which helps circulation, and which can be used for ventilation in hot weather by simply shutting off the heat and running the fan.

Horizontal Delivery   **Vertical Delivery**

**Exhibit 2. Two types of unit heaters for use with steam or hot water.
(Courtesy of Modine Manufacturing Company.)**

3) Cabinet convectors. The old-fashioned cast-iron "radiator" is no longer specified for industrial heating applications, but in offices and relatively small rooms where forced air movement is not required to distribute heat, *cabinet convectors* can be used. They are usually wall-mounted, and consist of stacks of finned tubes or coils ranging from 1½ to 3½ feet high, surrounded by close-fitting sheet metal panels. They are effective in rooms with high heat requirements, and in locations where long runs of baseboard units are impractical.

4) Coils in central systems. Central air conditioning systems require a network of air ducts equipped with blowers to recirculate conditioned air to and from the occupied spaces. Heated coils can be installed in these ducts and the systems used during cold weather to supply heat.

5) Panel heaters. Formerly referred to as *radiant heating,* this system employs coils of hot water piping embedded in floors, wall panels, and even ceilings. Advantages are: 1) no loss of floor space, 2) transmission of heat at relatively low temperatures, 3) a feeling of comfort by the occupants at lower room temperatures. Disadvantages are: 1) temperature control is more difficult, especially in changeable situations, 2) heat losses to the ground or outside air are greater, and 3) access to the distribution piping is more difficult.

Heaters for Decentralized Systems

1) Rooftop Units. These are compact structures, enclosed in metal cabinets, and designed for mounting on the roof of the building section served. They are usually equipped for both cooling and heating, and contain an air conditioning unit for the cooling function. Heating is accomplished by the insertion of coils which may be steam or hot-water heated, or the use of electric or gas-fired coils. Supply and return air ducts are passed through the roof membrane. They have all the advantages previously mentioned in the section on centralized vs. decentralized systems. Problems can arise, however, in continuous exposure to the weather and in damage to the roof caused by installation and maintenance activities. Commercially available sizes are rated for 70,000 to 2,500,000 Btu per hour (Btuh) of heating, 5 to 40 tons of refrigeration for cooling, and have dimensions ranging from 4 x 3½ x 2½ feet to 35 x 8 x 6 feet.

2) Unit heaters. Basic characteristics are discussed above under centralized systems. They can readily be adapted to decentralized systems by the use of electric coils or gas-fired indirect heat exchangers. Smaller electric coils consist of bare-wire resistance elements; larger units have the resistance wire imbedded in refractory powder inside a finned tube. The gas-fired units require a vent to the outside for removal of combustion products; heat is transferred to the air stream from these gases by a venturi-tube heat exchanger.

3) Infra-red heaters. Because they transmit heat by radiation, and therefore are not dependent upon air movement to achieve proper heat distribution, infra-red units can be used for difficult heating jobs such as high factory bays, loading docks, and outside areas where work must be performed. Electric units use the familiar infra-red lamp or quartz lamps; gas units have a ceramic grid upon which the gas flame impinges, the grid giving off its radiation when it reaches 1650° F.

4) Fresh air heaters. A relatively new development in space heating, these devices are the simplest of all—they simply burn gas in an open flame inserted in the incoming air stream. Because the combustion products end up in the ventilating air, the units must be designed and operated carefully to be sure that sufficient dilution is achieved. Advantages are the highest possible fuel efficiency, simplest possible machinery, and often no need to install distribution ductwork.

Include All Gains and Losses in the Design

Heat is lost from a building at a rate which is determined by the temperature difference between the inside and the outside, wind velocity and other conditions of climate, the surface area of the building exposed to the elements, and the thermal properties of the walls and other building structures. The heating system must perform two functions: 1) replace the heat lost when the building is at its normal inside temperature, and 2) bring the building up to normal temperature within a specified time if it has cooled down for any reason.

But not all of the heat balance is described by losses. Activities inside a building can supply heat, and the designer must include these significant gains as well as losses in his calculations:

Heat Gains	*Heat Losses*
Manufacturing Operations	Transmission through walls and roof
Electric Motors	to outside atmosphere
Office Copiers	Conduction through floor to ground
Electric Lights	Ventilation air exhausted to outside

Exposure to sunlight   Infiltration of cold air through
Human beings (varies with   doors, windows, and cracks
   activity level)

VENTILATING

Ventilation involves movement of air for human comfort or the removal of contaminants. We have seen in the foregoing section that heating entails air movement, and it would seem obvious that the need for coordinating the two is compelling. Yet in many industrial buildings the two systems have "grown" without that coordination, resulting in poor efficiency, employee discomfort and complaints, and the high cost of constant additions and corrections to the system.

Reasons for Ventilation

1) Human comfort. Operating at a constant temperature of 98.6° F., the human body is a heat generator whose output (which grows with increased activity) must be transmitted to its surroundings. This transmission of heat is accomplished by *radiation* and *convection*. Radiation depends upon the temperature difference between the body and cooler objects around it, and would take place even if air were not present (conversely, objects hotter than the body will radiate heat to it). In convection, heat is transferred from the body to a stream of cooler air moving past it; the body improves on this process by *perspiration*, with evaporation of moisture from the skin achieving additional cooling effect.

2) Removal of toxic materials. Gases, vapors, dusts, aerosols must be removed from the plant air if they are concentrated enough to cause injury to human beings by intense exposure for a short time or lesser exposure for extended periods.

3) Removal of flammable vapors. Volatile flammable liquids evaporate to form flammable (or "explosive") mixtures with air, and each material has an upper explosive limit and a lower explosive limit expressed as percentage by volume. Gasoline, for instance, has a UEL of 7.6 percent and an LEL of 1.4 percent. When materials of this type are used in industrial processes, ventilation may be required to prevent accumulations of vapor in the flammable range.

4) Control of odors. Many plant operations involve the use of materials which are neither toxic nor flammable, but which generate odors seriously disturbing or downright intolerable to most people. Ventilation is a key means of reducing odors to acceptable levels.

5) Dusts. Mineral, organic, and metal dusts may be toxic, explosive, or damaging to equipment and process materials. Ventilation of work areas is used to remove dusts from the building or to concentrate them for collection and re-use.

Types of Ventilation

Industrial buildings and offices can be ventilated by a number of methods. Choose one or a combination of these ways of accomplishing the objectives listed in the previous section:

1) Exhaust. Removal of contaminated air from the interior of a building to the outside atmosphere is used for general ventilation as well as for localized ventilation of areas where production processes contaminate or overheat the air.

2) Dilution. Hot or contaminated air can often be brought to acceptable quality levels by mixing cool, fresh air with it.

3) Recirculation. Because convection cooling of the body depends on air movement, it is possible to maintain a sense of comfort by moving the same air around the ventilated space in a recycling pattern. The ability to do this becomes an important cost-saving factor when

the air must be heated in cold weather, or mechanically cooled in hot weather. A further advantage is that recirculated air can be passed through a cleaning system for removal of contaminants before it is returned to the occupied spaces.

4) Cleaning. Pollution laws may require the removal of odors, toxic material, or particulate matter before air can be exhausted to the atmosphere. The same will be true of air which is recirculated within a building, with the addition of flammable vapors to the list. The most common devices for cleaning are filters, washers, electrostatic precipitators, absorption beds, and cyclones.

Techniques of Ventilation

Listed below are the design criteria and operating systems used to accomplish ventilating goals. Apply these methods singly or in combination to overcome your ventilating problems:

1) Air changes. Technical literature and manufacturer's catalog references vary widely on their recommendations for the number of air changes per hour in different types of work areas. This table gives the average of a number of sources:

Type of Space	Air Changes per Hour
Manufacturing Buildings	15
Boiler Rooms	29
Laboratories	23
Offices	11
Toilets	18
Warehouses	4

2) Negative pressure. When air is exhausted from a room or building at a rate faster than make-up air is supplied, the pressure drops below that of the outside atmosphere or surrounding rooms. Air will then come in through wall cracks, openings around windows and doors, or any other apertures it can find. The results are uncontrolled drafts and wide temperature differences, especially in the winter; employee complaints are not far behind. Ventilation design should always include enough make-up air to keep the pressure positive, or, as in the case of heat-producing operations, provide for controlled flow of cold air into the work space.

3) Natural Ventilation. Two factors promote natural ventilation: one is height, and the other is the temperature difference between the inside air and the fresh air coming from the outside. For these reasons, natural ventilation tends to be limited to buildings with very high ceilings housing processes which give off a great deal of heat—in other words, heavy industry. Equipment consists of roof vents mounted at the highest point of the building and inlet louvers located near ground level. Designers usually specify the inlet louver area at one to one and one-half times that of the exhaust vent.

4) Forced Ventilation: Local exhaust systems. Wall and ceiling fans can be installed in those plant areas where fumes, odors, dusts, and excessive heat are generated. If the conditions are not severe, they can often handle the job at low cost. In more demanding situations, the ventilation designer will specify a *hood,* a sheet metal or plastic enclosure which is placed above the work station or surrounds it on one to three sides. The hood is attached to a ductwork through which the contaminated air is exhausted to the outside or sent to a cleaning station. Air movement is induced by a fan or blower, which may have to be explosion-proof or made of corrosion-resistant materials to meet special conditions. A key design parameter is the *capture velocity*, the linear velocity of the air at the opening of the hood, expressed in feet per minute, which is required to prevent the contaminant from

escaping into the surrounding air. It varies form 100 fpm for drying ovens to 2,000 fpm for grinding operations.

5) Forced Ventilation: Central distribution systems. Wall fans and roof ventilators are limited in their range of effectiveness, and when air must be distributed evenly over a large area, or returned to a central station for cooling or cleaning, a central air handling system must be used. These are the components and the main design considerations for its construction:

a. Ductwork. Available in rectangular or circular cross-sections, it is constructed of light gauge aluminum, copper, galvanized steel, or plastic. When carrying heated or cooled air, it may be insulated to prevent unwanted heat transfer and condensation. Design is based on air velocity. If the air stream is carrying industrial dusts the minimum *transport velocity* must be maintained—3,000 to 7,000 feet per minute. When noise is a problem, much lower velocities are employed—about 1,000 fpm for offices, and 2,000 fpm for light industry plants.

b. Fans and blowers. Fans are selected from manufacturers' tables which correlate speed, horsepower, flow rate, and discharge pressure for each model. Fans have characteristic curves similar to those shown in Exhibit 5, Chapter 18, and the air duct has its own system curve similar to that described for liquid flow. The fan will only operate at the intersection of its characteristic with the system curve. If noise is a problem, it is important to choose a fan which is operating close to its maximum efficiency.

The term "blower" is not precisely defined; flow-pressure ratings overlap fans on the one side and compressors on the other. In general, blowers are designed to deliver air at higher discharge pressures than fans, and are used to supply furnaces, air conveying systems, and heavy duty exhaust units.

c. Grilles and diffusers. These devices are mounted in the ductwork at the points where it is desired to introduce air into the ventilated room. The grille is a flat frame which can be installed horizontally or vertically, and usually has adjustable vanes to direct the air stream. It may be equipped with a damper to vary the air flow. The diffuser consists of a set of concentric cones, and like the grille, may be equipped with a variable-flow damper. It is mostly used in ceiling ducts. Whichever type is chosen, it should be selected to achieve rapid and thorough mixing of the air while avoiding uncomfortable drafts (air velocities over 50 feet per minute) and disturbing temperature differentials.

d. Balancing the system. Central air handling systems have many branches which vary in length, elevation, size of ducts, number of types of fittings, and volume of air to be moved. If the resistance to flow in any one branch is too high, it will not carry the desired air flow; if it is too low, it will rob other branches of their design flow rates. For systems in which it would be unwise to install adjustable dampers (such as exhaust ducts carrying heavy dusts), balancing is achieved by designing each branch so that its static pressure matches that of the main duct at the point where they meet. In systems which can use adjustable dampers, each branch is sized on desired air capacity and velocity, and the whole is balanced out by adjusting the dampers after construction.

6) Cleaning the air. Air brought in from the outside as well as that recirculated in a ventilating or air conditioning system can be contaminated with smoke, dust, lint, fumes, and odors. Use these devices singly or in combination to achieve accceptable air quality:

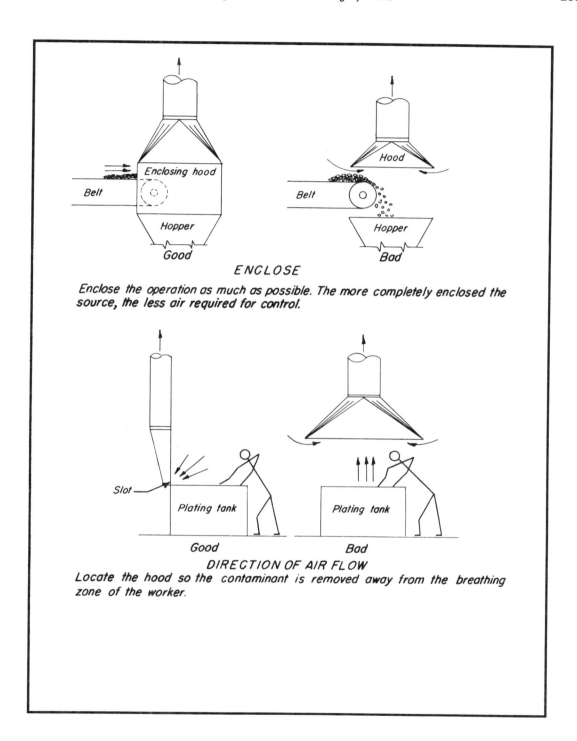

Exhibit 3. Principles of Exhaust Hood Design.
From *Industrial Ventilation, A Manual of Recommended Practice,* **(8th Edition, 1964)**
American Conference of Governmental Industrial Hygienists. (Used by permission.)

a. Odors. *Activated carbon* beds adsorb odors and some gases with excellent results. *Potassium permanganate* is effective in oxidizing many odor molecules to innocuous forms. *Air washers* have limited application in removing high concentrations of water-soluble gases, but are not widely used because of the humidity they inject into the treated air.

b. Particles. *Electrostatic air cleaners* are very effective for particles below two microns in diameter. *Viscous filters* consist of cloth or wire screen coated with oil or other viscous fluid; they are used for particle sizes over five microns. *Dry filters* may be woven or non-woven fibers of cotton, plastic, glass, asbestos, or metal. They are available as stationary panels, which can be discarded or washed for re-use after they become clogged; or in automatic roll-up units which move fresh sections into place from a continuous roll. They are available in almost any desired degree of removal efficiency and particle size. HEPA (high efficiency particulate air) filters stand at the top of the list with a removal effectiveness of up to 99.999 percent for particles down to 0.3 micron.

AIR CONDITIONING

Air conditioning is defined as the modification of temperature, humidity, and quantity of contaminants to predetermined values and delivery to the conditioned space. Since air cleaning and distribution were discussed in the previous section, this analysis will deal primarily with temperature and humidity control. *Comfort conditioning* is aimed at producing optimum conditions for human activity; *process air conditioning* controls air quality to meet the needs of special industrial operations (machining to close tolerances, formation of certain plastic films, handling of hygroscopic materials, micro-assembly).

Why Air Conditioning?

The manager and businessman, caught between the demands of his employees for greater comfort and the necessity of justifying to his superiors the cost of installing and operating air conditioning, often finds it difficult to separate facts from emotion in arriving at a decision. Weigh these factors when making decisions and developing rationales:

1) Employee efficiency. Various studies have shown that employee effectiveness can be expected to drop anywhere from 7.5 percent to 28 percent at various combinations of temperature above 90° F., excessive humidity, and still air. The cost of this loss of effort should be calculated for the number of days per year on which adverse weather conditions can be expected.

2) Employee turnover. Your personnel department can work up a correlation between the rate of employee turnover and occurrence of hot humid weather. The cost of training each new employee can be calculated in terms of the hours of non-productive time for which he must be paid, and the amount of defective output which is tolerated because he is new at the job. Combine these two to arrive at a total cost of employee turnover attributable to sultry plant conditions.

3) Process needs. For purposes of economic justification, process needs divide into two categories:

a. Air conditioning essential. When materials must be handled or manufacturing operations carried out within close tolerances of temperature, humidity, and cleanliness, an air conditioning system may be essential. If so, its cost should be included in the total project expenditure required to set up the operation, and justified on an overall return on investment calculation.

b. Air conditioning helpful. Controlled indoor climate can contribute to greater

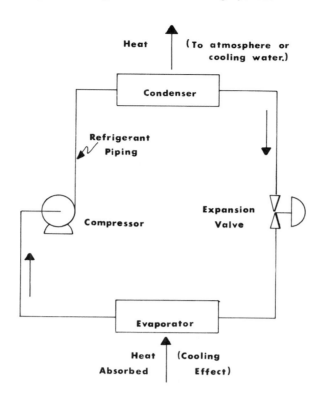

Exhibit 4. Vapor-compression refrigeration cycle.

accuracy and faster processing cycles in many types of industries without being essential. Justification in such cases is based on reduced scrap rate and improved output; it should stand on its own, and be kept separate from the calculations made to determine the profitability of the process. Reliable data for these calculations is hard to come by; if a process variable (such as drying time) is involved, tests can be made in an air conditioned laboratory. Scrap rate comparisons can be made using summertime quality records and those obtained under more ideal conditions in the spring or fall.

How Air Conditioning Works

Although the technical definition only mentions modifying air temperature, "air conditioning" always implies the ability to cool air. Cooling is accomplished by one of the three refrigeration methods described in this section, all of which come under the general heading of mechanical refrigeration. Cooling capacity of air conditioners is stated in Btuh (Btu per hour), or MBh (thousands of Btu per hour), and in *tons of refrigeration,* one ton being equivalent to heat removal of 12,000 Btuh, or 12 Mbh.

Refrigerating machines are based on a simple physical phenomenon: when a liquid evaporates it creates a cooling effect by absorbing the heat required for evaporation from its surroundings. (Water has a latent heat of evaporation of about 1,000 Btu/lb; most commonly used refrigerants have latent heats between 50 and 100 Btu/lb.) When the gas is condensed back to a liquid it gives up that same latent heat, allowing the development of a *refrigeration cycle* in which heat is absorbed from the space to be cooled and rejected to outside air (or cooling water).

1) Vapor-compression cycle. These principles are applied in the vapor-compression

refrigeration cycle illustrated in Exhibit 4. Starting with the arrow at the right side of the diagram, liquid refrigerant passes through the expansion valve, and changes to gas in the evaporator. This creates the cooling effect of the refrigerating machine. The gas then passes through the compressor, which raises the pressure sufficiently to change the gas back to a liquid in the condenser. The latent heat is released and transferred by the condenser surfaces to the outside atomsphere or to cooling water. The liquid refrigerant then goes to the expansion valve to start the cycle again.

In air conditioning machines both the condenser and the evaporator will have finned-tube coils for maximum heat transfer. One arrangement is to locate the evaporator coils directly in the space or air stream to be cooled; when this is done the cooling coils are called "DX" coils (direct expansion). Another method is to place the evaporator in a brine or other liquid coolant and circulate that to the coils in the air stream (indirect cooling).

Vapor-compression systems are by far the most commonly encountered in air conditioning practice, and are used in sizes ranging from small window units up to the largest central station installations.

2) Absorption cycle. No machinery with moving parts is required in this system, although some larger units may use auxiliary pumps. It is based on the principle that a concentrated solution of a chemical salt in water can absorb water vapor from the space above the liquid surface. If the vapor space of a tank containing concentrated lithium bromide solution is connected to the vapor space of a tank containing water, water vapor will be absorbed by the solution (in effect condensing out of the vapor space). Water will then evaporate from the liquid surface in the water tank (to replace the vapor removed by absorption), creating a cooling effect.

As absorption continues the concentrated salt solution becomes dilute, and must be regenerated. It is sent to a third compartment called the *generator*, where water is removed by heating the dilute solution with a steam coil, gas flame, or any other convenient method. Water vapor is driven off, liquefied in a condenser, and returned to the pure water compartment. The cooling water for the condenser is first passed through the absorber for removal of the rejected heat.

The absorption and evaporation compartments are operated under a vacuum of 29.7 inches of mercury so that the water evaporation will take place at a low enough temperature (38-40° F.) to produce a useful chilling effect.

Absorption units can be built in a wide range of sizes (3 to 1500 tons), but most applications are in sizes above 25 tons. They are especially economical when exhaust steam is available, extra boiler capacity is available during the summer months, or natural gas is plentiful and cheap. Some systems are built with ammonia, rather than pure water, as the refrigerant.

3) Evaporative cooling. The simplest application of the principle that evaporation causes cooling is to spray water into a moving air stream, let it evaporate, and in so doing cool the air. The difficulty with this method is that it raises the humidity of the circulated air, and thus limits its application in many parts of the United States. In most units water is collected in a sump after it falls through the air, and is recycled to the sprays by pump. In some applications it is chilled by external refrigeration before recirculation.

Despite their humidity limitations, evaporative coolers are the most economical to install and operate, and find application in industrial situations where large volumes of air must be cooled. These conditions tend to favor evaporative cooling: a) air to be cooled is hot, but has low humidity; b) large quantities of air are needed to cool industrial areas where processes generate much heat; c) raw materials or the process itself requires high humidity;

and d) the space to be cooled would develop high humidity anyway—e.g., a room with open tanks containing hot water.

Choose the Right Equipment

The widespread popularity of air conditioning in the United States has resulted in the availability of many types of reliable equipment. But selection must be discriminating to get the best cost advantage, maximum reliability, and satisfaction of the personnel being served. Select from these major types:

1) Room air conditioners. Installed in a window or through a wall, the room conditioner has its evaporator coil in the room to be cooled, and rejects heat to the outside air through the condenser. It has fans to move air past the coils on both sides of the wall, and a dry filter to remove dust from the recirculated room air.

Sizes range from 5,000 to 34,000 Btuh. Smaller units operate on 115-volt current; above 10,000 Btuh 208V or 230V currrent is required.

Advantages of the room air conditioner are that it is readily available, easy to install, adaptable to individual preferences, and can be easily replaced when its useful life is over. Disadvantages are that it uses the highest amount of electric power per ton of refrigeration, can be costly to install if a large number of units requiring new electric outlets are involved, and can be expensive to service if a large number of units must be maintained.

2) Unitary air conditioners. This classification includes room air conditioners mentioned in the previous section, and rooftop units covered in the following section. The unitary air conditioner is one which has all its essential components (compressor, coils, fans, controls, filter, and condenser) factory assembled. It can be free-standing, wall or ceiling mounted, inside or outside the space to be served, connected to ductwork or discharging freely into the room. Capacities range from 2 to 60 tons.

Manufacturers have steadily increased the reliability, efficiency, and appearance of these units, and they have the advantages of being mountable in many kinds of available space and not requiring cutting through the roof.

3) Rooftop units. Some thirty suppliers turn out 185 models ranging from 5 to 45 ton capacity, attesting to the increasing demand for this type of unit. The factory-assembled unit contains refrigeration equipment for air cooling, a fan for air distribution, and maybe a heating system for winter use, all combined in a single cabinet designed for roof mounting. Air is transported to the conditioned space through relatively short ducts.

Rooftop units have all the advantages of decentralized systems: a) they are readily adjustable to area needs (without having to balance a central system to varying loads), b) they can be easily added as the building expands—a sometimes difficult problem with a central system. They also have the disadvantages: a) decentralized units cannot match the power efficiency of a central station, b) a large number of scattered units means a spread-out maintenance responsibility which can be costly as the units get older.

When planning a rooftop unit installation, be sure that funds are provided for a good roof cutting and patching job. Examine the building steel to see if it is heavy enough to carry the weight and vibration of the proposed unit. Review the manufacturer's design to be sure that parts exposed to the weather will resist corrosion and leakage.

4) Central systems. When the refrigeration load for an air conditioning system exceeds 45 tons, the built-up central station is resorted to. It is usually connected to a complex ductwork system serving areas which require different temperatures and air flow rates. Central stations may be constructed entirely from component parts, or partly constructed from packaged equipment combinations.

Exhibit 5 shows the components which may go to make up a centralized unit. Fresh air is introduced from the left side through an automatic damper, and mixed with the return air from the conditioned space. It then passes through the *filter,* which not only removes particles to improve the quality of the air for ultimate consumption, but to reduce fouling of the heat transfer coils in the central station. The *preheat coil* is used in connection with downstream water sprays, adding enough heat to be sure that the spray equipment does not freeze. It can also help carry the heating load when the central station is used as a winter air heater. The *cooling coil* is required when vapor-compression or absorption refrigeration is used, but is absent when the system employs evaporative cooling. As indicated by the diagram and described on Page 268, the coil can either be of the direct expansion or indirect cooling type. The water spray can serve a number of purposes: 1) to spray upon the cooling coils, improving heat transfer between them and the air; 2) to wash out particles not screened by the filter, especially bacteria; 3) to humidify the air for some process and comfort needs; and 4) to supply the main cooling effect when the system is based on evaporative cooling. Not shown on the diagram are drift eliminators, which would be installed downstream from the sprays to catch any droplets carried by the air stream; a basin beneath the sprays to catch the water and fitted with a pump to recirculate it; and a separate chilling system to cool the recirculated water. The *reheat coil* is used to restore heat to air which has been cooled below design temperature in order to dehumidify it; like the preheat coil it can be used to help carry the heating season load. Both preheat and reheat coils can use steam or hot water. *Non-freezing* steam coils are available for systems which must handle air below 32° F. The last component to handle the air is the *fan,* which must have sufficient capacity to move the air through the ductwork at acceptable noise levels.

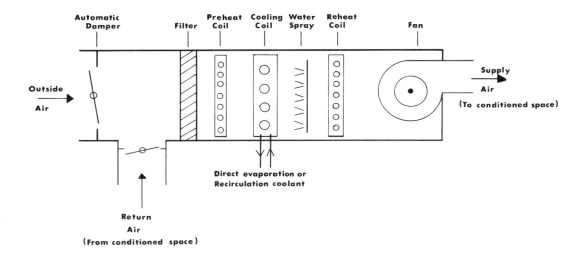

Exhibit 5. Components of Central Air Conditioning Station

Tables—Appendix

TABLES—APPENDIX

64ths		64ths		32nds		16ths		8ths		4ths		Fractions with De-
1	.01562	33	.5156	1	.03125	1	.0625	1	.1250	1	.2500	nominators 11-19
3	.04688	35	.5469	3	.09375	3	.1875	3	.3750	2	.5000	1/11 .09091
5	.07812	37	.5781	5	.1562	5	.3125	5	.6250	3	.7500	1/12 .08333
7	.1094	39	.6094	7	.2188	7	.4375	7	.8750			1/13 .07692
9	.1406	41	.6406	9	.2812	9	.5625			9ths		1/14 .07143
11	.1719	43	.6719	11	.3438	11	.6875	7ths		1	.1111	1/15 .06667
13	.2031	45	.7031	13	.4062	13	.8125	1	.1428	2	.2222	1/16 .06250
15	.2344	47	.7344	15	.4688	15	.9375	2	.2857	3	.3333	1/17 .05882
17	.2656	49	.7656	17	.5312			3	.4286	4	.4444	1/18 .05556
19	.2969	51	.7969	19	.5938	6ths		4	.5714	5	.5555	1/19 .05263
21	.3281	53	.8281	21	.6562	1	.1667	5	.7143	6	.6667	
23	.3594	55	.8594	23	.7188	2	.3333	6	.8571	7	.7778	
25	.3906	57	.8906	25	.7812	3	.5000			8	.8889	
27	.4219	59	.9219	27	.8438	4	.7500					
29	.4531	61	.9531	29	.9062	5	.8333					
31	.4844	63	.9844	31	.9688							

Table 1. Decimal Equivalents of Fractions

English-Metric		Metric-English	
Length			
1 inch	2.540 centimeters	1 centimeter	.3937 inch
1 foot	.3048 meters	1 meter	39.37 inches
1 yard	.9144 meters	1 meter	3.281 feet
1 mile	1.609 kilometers	1 kilometer	.6214 mile
Area			
1 square inch	6.452 square cm.	1 square cm.	.1550 sq. inch
1 square foot	.09290 square m.	1 square m.	10.76 sq. feet
1 square yard	.8361 square m.	1 square m.	1.196 sq. yards
1 acre	4,047 square m.	1 hectare	2.471 acres
1 square mile	259.0 hectares	1 sq. kilometer	.3861 sq. mile
(1 hectare equals 10,000 sq. meters and 0.1 sq. kilometers.)			
Volume: Liquid			
1 ounce	29.57 cubic cm.	1 cubic cm.	.03381 ounce
1 quart	.9464 liters	1 liter	1.057 quarts
1 gallon	3.785 liters	1 liter	.2642 gallon
(Ounces, quarts, and gallons are U.S. measure; 1 liter equals 1,000 cu. cm.)			
Volume: Dry			
1 cubic inch	16.39 cubic cm.	1 cubic cm.	.06102 cu. in.
1 cubic foot	.02832 cubic m.	1 cubic m.	35.31 cu. ft.
1 cubic yard	.7646 cubic m.	1 cubic m.	1.308 cu. yd.
1 dry quart	1.101 liters	1 hectoliter	2.838 bushels
1 bushel	35.24 liters	(1 hectoliter equals 100 liters)	

		Weight	
1 ounce (avoir.)	28.35 grams	1 gram	.03527 oz. (avoir.)
1 pound	453.6 grams	1 kilogram	2.205 lbs.
1 short ton (2,000 lbs)	907.2 kilograms	1 metric ton (1,000 kg)	1.102 short tons
1 long ton (2,240 lbs)	1,106 kilograms	1 metric ton	.9842 long tons

		Work-Heat	
1 foot-pound	.1383 kg-meter	1 kilogram-meter	7.233 foot-pound
1 kilowatt-hour	3.671×10^5 kg-m	1 kg-m	$.2724 \times 10^{-5}$ kw-hr
1 Btu	107.6 kg-m	1 kg-m	.009296 Btu
1 Btu	.2520 kg-calorie	1 kg-cal	3.968 Btu

		Power	
1 ft-lb/second	.1383 kg-m/sec	1 kg-m/sec	7.233 ft-lb/sec
1 U.S. horse-power	76.04 kg-m/sec	1 metric hp	542.5 ft-lb/sec
1 kilowatt	102.0 kg-m/sec	1 kg-m/sec	.009807 kw

(1 U.S. hp equals 550 ft-lb/sec; 1 metric hp equals 75 kg-m/sec.)

		Pressure	
1 psi (lb/sq in)	.07031 kg/sq cm	1 kg/sq cm	14.22 psi
1 atmosphere	1.033 kg/sq cm	1 kg/sq cm	.9678 atm
1 atmosphere	760 mm mercury	1 kg/sq cm	28.96 in mercury
1 atmosphere	10.34 meters of water	1 kg/sq cm	32.84 ft water

(Mercury at 0 deg C and water at 15 deg C.)

Table 2. Metric Conversion

Table 3. Temperature Conversion

1. To use the following table, find the temperature you desire to convert in the boldface column in the center; its Centigrade equivalent will be in the left-hand column, and the Fahrenheit equivalent in the right-hand column.

2. The formulas for temperature conversion are:
deg F = 1.8 deg C + 32   deg C = (deg F - 32)/1.8

3. Temperature span: One degree Centigrade is equivalent to 1.8 degrees Fahrenheit; one degree Fahrenheit is equivalent to .5556 degrees Centigrade.

4. Absolute temperature scales. For certain heat transfer and thermodynamic calculations, the *absolute temperature* scales are used. Absolute zero on the Centigrade scale is -273.2 degrees; to convert to degrees Kelvin add 273.2 to the Centigrade value. Absolute zero on the Fahrenheit scale is -459.7 degrees; to convert to degrees Rankine add 459.7 to the Centigrade value.

Deg C		Deg F	Deg C		Deg F	Deg C		Deg F	Deg C		Deg F
-273.2	-459.7		-73.3	-100	-148	-21.1	-6	21.2	-16.1	3	37.4
-268	-450		-45.6	-50	-58.0	-20.6	-5	23.0	-15.6	4	39.2
-240	-400		-40.0	-40	-40.0	-20.0	-4	24.8	-15.0	5	41.0
-212	-350		-34.4	-30	-22.0	-19.4	-3	26.6	-14.4	6	42.8
-184	-300		-28.9	-20	-4.0	-18.9	-2	28.4	-13.9	7	44.6
-170	-273.2	-459.7	-23.3	-10	+14.0	-18.3	-1	30.2	-13.3	8	46.4
-157	-250	-418	-22.8	-9	15.8	-17.8	0	32.0	-12.8	9	48.2
-129	-200	-328	-22.2	-8	17.6	-17.2	1	33.8	-12.2	10	50.0
-101	-150	-238	-21.7	-7	19.4	-16.7	2	35.6	-11.7	11	51.8

Deg C		Deg F	Deg C		Deg F	Deg C		Deg F	Deg C		Deg F
-11.1	12	53.6	1.7	35	95.0	13.9	57	134.6	26.7	80	176.0
-10.6	13	55.4	2.2	36	96.8	14.4	58	136.4	27.2	81	177.8
-10.0	14	57.2	2.8	37	98.6	15.0	59	138.2	27.8	82	179.6
-9.4	15	59.0	3.3	38	100.4	15.6	60	140.0	28.3	83	181.4
-8.9	16	60.8	3.9	39	102.2	16.1	61	141.8	28.9	84	183.2
-8.3	17	62.6	4.4	40	104.0	16.7	62	143.6	29.4	85	185.0
-7.8	18	64.4	5.0	41	105.8	17.2	63	145.4	30.0	86	186.8
-7.2	19	66.2	5.6	42	107.6	17.8	64	147.2	30.6	87	188.6
-6.7	20	68.0	6.1	43	109.4	18.3	65	149.0	31.1	88	190.4
-6.1	21	69.8	6.7	44	111.2	18.9	66	150.8	31.7	89	192.2
-5.6	22	71.6	7.2	45	113.0	19.4	67	152.6	32.2	90	194.0
-5.0	23	73.4	7.8	46	114.8	20.0	68	154.4	32.8	91	195.8
-4.4	24	75.2	8.3	47	116.6	20.6	69	156.2	33.3	92	197.6
-3.9	25	77.0	8.9	48	118.4	21.1	70	158.0	33.9	93	199.4
-3.3	26	78.8	9.4	49	120.2	21.7	71	159.8	34.4	94	201.2
-2.8	27	80.6	10.0	50	122.0	22.2	72	161.6	35.0	95	203.0
-2.2	28	82.4	10.6	51	123.8	22.8	73	163.4	35.6	96	204.8
-1.7	29	84.2	11.1	52	125.6	23.3	74	165.2	36.1	97	206.6
-1.1	30	86.0	12.2	53	127.4	23.9	75	167.0	36.7	98	208.4
-0.6	31	87.8	12.2	54	129.2	24.4	76	168.8	37.2	99	210.2
0.0	32	89.6	12.8	55	131.0	25.0	77	170.6	37.8	100	212.0
+0.6	33	91.4	13.3	56	132.8	25.6	78	172.4	43.3	110	230
1.1	34	93.2				26.1	79	174.2			

Deg C		Deg F	Deg C		Deg F	Deg C		Deg F	Deg C		Deg F
48.9	120	248	171	340	644	426	800	1472	1593	2900	5252
54.4	130	266	177	350	662	454	850	1562	1649	3000	5432
60.0	140	284	182	360	680	482	900	1652			
65.6	150	302	188	370	698	510	950	1742			
71.1	160	320	193	380	716	538	1000	1832			
76.7	170	338	199	390	734	593	1100	2012			
82.2	180	356	204	400	752	648	1200	2192			
87.8	190	374	210	410	770	704	1300	2372			
93.3	200	392	215	420	788	760	1400	2552			
98.9	210	410	221	430	806	815	1500	2732			

100.0	**212**	413	226	**440**	824	871	**1600**	2912
104	**220**	428	232	**450**	842	927	**1700**	3092
110	**230**	446				982	**1800**	3272
116	**240**	464	238	**460**	860	1038	**1900**	3452
121	**250**	482	243	**470**	878	1093	**2000**	3632
			249	**480**	896			
127	**260**	500	254	**490**	914	1149	**2100**	3812
132	**270**	518	260	**500**	932	1204	**2200**	3992
138	**280**	536				1260	**2300**	4172
143	**290**	554	288	**550**	1022	1316	**2400**	4352
149	**300**	572	315	**600**	1112	1371	**2500**	4532
			343	**650**	1202			
154	**310**	590	371	**700**	1292	1427	**2600**	4712
160	**320**	608	399	**750**	1382	1482	**2700**	4892
165	**330**	626				1538	**2800**	5072

A	Atmosphere (Standard)	=	33.93	feet of water @ 60°F.
	Atmosphere (Standard)	=	29.92	inches of mercury @ 32°F.
	Atmosphere (Standard)	=	760.0	millimeters of mercury @ 0°C.
	Atmosphere (Standard)	=	14.696	pounds per square inch
B	Barrel	=	5.6146	cubic feet
	Barrel	=	42.0	gallons
	Barrel of water @ 60°F.	=	0.1588	metric ton
	Barrel (36° A.P.I.)	=	0.1342	metric ton
	Barrel per hour	=	0.0936	cubic feet per minute
	Barrel per hour	=	0.700	gallon per minute
	Barrel per hour	=	2.695	cubic inches per second
	Barrel per day	=	0.02917	gallon per minute
	British Thermal Unit	=	252.	calories
	British Thermal Unit	=	0.2931	Int. Watt Hours
	British Thermal Unit	=	0.2932	watt hour (abs.)
	B.T.U. per minute	=	0.02359	horse-power
	British Thermal Unit	=	778.57	foot pounds
C	Calorie	=	.003968	British Thermal Units
	Centimeter	=	0.3937	inch
	Centimeter of mercury	=	0.1934	pounds per square inch
	Cubic centimeter	=	0.06102	cubic inch
	Cubic foot	=	0.1781	barrel
	Cubic foot	=	7.4805	gallons
	Cubic foot	=	0.02832	cubic meter
	Cubic foot per minute	=	10.686	barrels per hour
	Cubic foot per minute	=	28.800	cubic inches per second
	Cubic foot per minute	=	7.481	gallons per minute
	Cubic inch	=	16.387	cubic centimeters
	Cubic meter	=	6.2898	barrels
	Cubic meter	=	35.314	cubic feet
	Cubic meter	=	1.308	cubic yards
	Cubic yard	=	4.8089	barrels
	Cubic yard	=	46,656.	cubic inches
	Cubic yard	=	0.7646	cubic meter
F	Foot	=	30.48	centimeters
	Foot	=	0.3048	meter
	Foot	=	0.3600	vara (Texas)
	Foot of water @ 60°F.	=	0.4331	pound per square inch
	Foot per second	=	0.68182	mile per hour
	Foot pound	=	0.001284	British Thermal Unit
	Foot pound per second	=	0.001818	horse-power
G	Gallon (U.S.)	=	0.02381	barrel
	Gallon (U.S.)	=	0.1337	cubic foot
	Gallon (U.S.)	=	231.000	cubic inches
	Gallon (U.S.)	=	3.785	liters
	Gallon (U.S.)	=	0.8327	gallon (Imperial)
	Gallon (Imperial)	=	1.2009	gallons (U.S.)
	Gallon (Imperial)	=	277.274	cubic inches
	Gallon per minute	=	1.429	barrels per hour
	Gallon per minute	=	0.1337	cubic foot per minute
	Gallon per minute	=	34.296	barrels per day
	Grain (Avoirdupois)	=	0.06480	gram
	Grain per gallon	=	17.118	parts per million
	Grain per gallon	=	142.86	pounds per million gals.
	Grain per gallon	=	0.017118	gram per liter
	Gram	=	15.432	grains
	Gram	=	0.03527	ounce
	Gram per liter	=	58.415	grains per gallon
H	Horse-power	=	42.39	B.T.U.'s per minute
	Horse-power	=	33,000.	foot-pounds per minute
	Horse-power	=	550.	foot-pounds per second
	Horse-power	=	1.014	horse-power (metric)
	Horse-power	=	0.7457	kilowatt (abs.)
I	Horse-power	=	.7455	kilowatt (int.)
	Horse-power hour	=	2,543.	British Thermal Units
	Inch	=	2.540	centimeters
	Inch of mercury @ 32°F.	=	1.133	feet of water @ 39.1°F.
	Inch of mercury @ 32°F.	=	0.4912	pound per square inch
	Inch of water @ 60°F.	=	0.0361	pound per square inch
K	Kilogram	=	2.2046	pounds
	Kilogram per square cm.	=	14.223	pounds per square inch
	Kilogram per square mm.	=	1,422.32	pounds per square inch
	Kilometer	=	3,281.	feet
	Kilometer	=	0.6214	mile
	Kilowatt	=	1.3415	horse-power
L	Link (Surveyor's)	=	7.92	inches
	Liter	=	0.2642	gallon
	Liter	=	1.0567	quarts
M	Meter	=	3.281	feet
	Meter	=	39.37	inches
	Mile	=	5,280.	feet
	Mile	=	1.609	kilometers
	Mile per hour	=	1.4667	feet per second
O	Ounce	=	437.5	grains
	Ounce	=	28.3495	grams
P	Part per million	=	0.058415	grain per gallon
	Part per million	=	8.345	pounds per million gals.
	Pound	=	7,000.	grains
	Pound	=	0.4536	kilogram
	Pound per cubic inch	=	27.680	gm. per cu. cm.
	Pound per square inch	=	2.309	feet of water @ 60°F.
	Pound per square inch	=	2.0360	inches of mercury @ 32°F.
	Pound per square inch	=	51.713	millimeters of mercury @ 32°F.
	Pound per square inch	=	0.0703	kilogram per sq. cent.
	Pound per million gals.	=	0.00700	grain per gallon
	Pound per million gals.	=	0.11983	part per million
Q	Quart (Liquid)	=	0.946	liter
S	Square centimeter	=	0.1550	square inch
	Square foot	=	0.0929	square meter
	Square foot	=	0.1296	square vara (Texas)
	Square inch	=	6.452	square centimeter
	Square kilometer	=	0.3861	square mile
	Square meter	=	10.76	square feet
	Square mile	=	2.590	square kilometers
T	Temp. Centigrade	=	5/9 (Temp. Fahr. −32)	
	Temp. Fahrenheit	=	9/5 Temp. Cent. +32	
	Temp. Absolute C.	=	Temp. °C. +273	
	Temp. Absolute F.	=	Temp. °F. +460	
	Therm	=	100,000 B.T.U.	
	Ton (Long)	=	2,240.	pounds
	Ton (Metric)	=	2,205.	pounds
	Ton (Short or Net)	=	2,000.	pounds
	Ton (Metric)	=	1.102	ton (short or net)
	Ton (Metric)	=	1,000.	kilograms
	Ton (Metric)	=	6.303	barrels of water @ 60°F.
	Ton (Metric)	=	7.454	barrels (36° A.P.I.)
	Ton (Short or Net)	=	0.907	ton (metric)
W	Watt-hour (Int.)	=	3.4115	British Thermal Units
	Watt-hour (abs.)	=	3.4103	British Thermal Units
Y	Yard	=	0.9144	meter

Barrel, above, always means oil barrel = 42 gallons.
Gallon, unless otherwise noted, means U.S. gallon.

British Thermal Unit = 1054.1 absolute joules.
British Thermal Unit per pound = 5/9 (cal./gram.)
British Thermal Unit per pound per °F. = calorie per gram per °C.

Table 4. General Conversion Factors
Courtesy of the Patterson-Kelley Co., Inc.

Circumferences and Areas of Circles

Diam.	Circum.	Area	Diam.	Circum.	Area	Diam.	Circum.	Area	Diam.	Circum.	Area	Diam.	Circum.	Area
1/64	0.0491	0.0002	3	9.4248	7.0686	8	25.1327	50.265	16	50.2655	201.06			
1/32	0.0982	0.0008	1/16	9.6211	7.3662	1/8	25.5254	51.849	1/8	50.6582	204.22			
1/16	0.1964	0.0031	1/8	9.8175	7.6699	1/4	25.9181	53.456	1/4	51.0509	207.39			
3/32	0.2945	0.0059	3/16	10.0138	7.9798	3/8	26.3108	55.088	3/8	51.4436	210.60			
1/8	0.3927	0.0123	1/4	10.2102	8.2958	1/2	26.7035	56.745	1/2	51.8363	213.82			
5/32	0.4909	0.0192	5/16	10.4065	8.6179	5/8	27.0962	58.426	5/8	52.2290	217.08			
3/16	0.5890	0.0276	3/8	10.6029	8.9462	3/4	27.4889	60.132	3/4	52.6217	220.35			
7/32	0.6872	0.0376	7/16	10.7992	9.2806	7/8	27.8816	61.862	7/8	53.0144	223.65			
1/4	0.7854	0.0491	1/2	10.9956	9.6211	9	28.2743	63.617	17	53.4071	226.98			
9/32	0.8836	0.0621	9/16	11.1919	9.9678	1/8	28.6670	65.397	1/8	53.7998	230.33			
5/16	0.9817	0.0767	5/8	11.3883	10.321	1/4	29.0597	67.201	1/4	54.1925	233.71			
11/32	1.0799	0.0928	11/16	11.5846	10.680	3/8	29.4524	69.029	3/8	54.5852	237.10			
3/8	1.1781	0.1105	3/4	11.7810	11.045	1/2	29.8451	70.882	1/2	54.9779	240.53			
13/32	1.2763	0.1296	13/16	11.9773	11.416	5/8	30.2378	72.760	5/8	55.3706	243.98			
7/16	1.3745	0.1503	7/8	12.1737	11.793	3/4	30.6305	74.662	3/4	55.7633	247.45			
15/32	1.4726	0.1726	15/16	12.3700	12.177	7/8	31.0232	76.589	7/8	56.1560	250.95			
1/2	1.5708	0.1964	4	12.5664	12.566	10	31.4159	78.540	18	56.5487	254.47			
17/32	1.6690	0.2217	1/16	12.7627	12.962	1/8	31.8086	80.516	1/8	56.9414	258.02			
9/16	1.7672	0.2485	1/8	12.9591	13.364	1/4	32.2013	82.516	1/4	57.3341	261.59			
19/32	1.8653	0.2769	3/16	13.1554	13.772	3/8	32.5940	84.541	3/8	57.7268	265.18			
5/8	1.9635	0.3068	1/4	13.3518	14.185	1/2	32.9867	86.590	1/2	58.1195	268.80			
21/32	2.0617	0.3382	5/16	13.5481	14.607	5/8	33.3794	88.664	5/8	58.5122	272.45			
11/16	2.1598	0.3712	3/8	13.7445	15.033	3/4	33.7721	90.763	3/4	58.9049	276.12			
23/32	2.2580	0.4057	7/16	13.9408	15.466	7/8	34.1648	92.886	7/8	59.2976	279.81			
3/4	2.3562	0.4418	1/2	14.1372	15.904	11	34.5575	95.033	19	59.6903	283.53			
25/32	2.4544	0.4794	9/16	14.3335	16.349	1/8	34.9502	97.205	1/8	60.0830	287.27			
13/16	2.5525	0.5185	5/8	14.5299	16.800	1/4	35.3429	99.402	1/4	60.4757	291.04			
27/32	2.6507	0.5591	11/16	14.7262	17.257	3/8	35.7356	101.62	3/8	60.8684	294.83			
7/8	2.7489	0.6013	3/4	14.9226	17.721	1/2	36.1283	103.87	1/2	61.2611	298.65			
29/32	2.8471	0.6450	13/16	15.1189	18.190	5/8	36.5210	106.14	5/8	61.6538	302.49			
15/16	2.9452	0.6903	7/8	15.3153	18.665	3/4	36.9137	108.43	3/4	62.0465	306.35			
31/32	3.0434	0.7371	15/16	15.5116	19.147	7/8	37.3064	110.75	7/8	62.4392	310.24			
1	3.1416	0.7854	5	15.7080	19.635	12	37.6991	113.10	20	62.8319	314.16			
1/16	3.3379	0.8866	1/16	15.9043	20.129	1/8	38.0918	115.47	1/8	63.2246	318.10			
1/8	3.5343	0.9940	1/8	16.1007	20.629	1/4	38.4845	117.86	1/4	63.6173	322.06			
3/16	3.7306	1.1075	3/16	16.2970	21.135	3/8	38.8772	120.28	3/8	64.0100	326.05			
1/4	3.9270	1.2272	1/4	16.4934	21.648	1/2	39.2699	122.72	1/2	64.4026	330.06			
5/16	4.1233	1.3530	5/16	16.6897	22.166	5/8	39.6626	125.19	5/8	64.7953	334.10			
3/8	4.3197	1.4849	3/8	16.8861	22.691	3/4	40.0553	127.68	3/4	65.1880	338.16			
7/16	4.5160	1.6230	7/16	17.0824	23.221	7/8	40.4480	130.19	7/8	65.5807	342.25			
1/2	4.7124	1.7671	1/2	17.2788	23.758	13	40.8407	132.73	21	65.9734	346.36			
9/16	4.9087	1.9175	9/16	17.4751	24.301	1/8	41.2334	135.30	1/8	66.3661	350.50			
5/8	5.1051	2.0739	5/8	17.6715	24.850	1/4	41.6261	137.89	1/4	66.7588	354.66			
11/16	5.3014	2.2365	11/16	17.8678	25.406	3/8	42.0188	140.50	3/8	67.1515	358.84			
3/4	5.4978	2.4053	3/4	18.0642	25.967	1/2	42.4115	143.14	1/2	67.5442	363.05			
13/16	5.6941	2.5802	13/16	18.2605	26.535	5/8	42.8042	145.80	5/8	67.9369	367.28			
7/8	5.8905	2.7612	7/8	18.4569	27.100	3/4	43.1969	148.49	3/4	68.3296	371.54			
15/16	6.0868	2.9483	15/16	18.6532	27.688	7/8	43.5896	151.20	7/8	68.7223	375.83			
2	6.2832	3.1416	6	18.8496	28.274	14	43.9823	153.94	22	69.1150	380.13			
1/16	6.4795	3.3410	1/8	19.2423	29.465	1/8	44.3750	156.70	1/8	69.5077	384.46			
1/8	6.6759	3.5466	1/4	19.6350	30.680	1/4	44.7677	159.48	1/4	69.9004	388.82			
3/16	6.8722	3.7583	3/8	20.0277	31.919	3/8	45.1604	162.30	3/8	70.2931	393.20			
1/4	7.0686	3.9761	1/2	20.4204	33.183	1/2	45.5531	165.13	1/2	70.6858	397.61			
5/16	7.2649	4.2000	5/8	20.8131	34.472	5/8	45.9458	167.99	5/8	71.0785	402.04			
3/8	7.4613	4.4301	3/4	21.2058	35.785	3/4	46.3385	170.87	3/4	71.4712	406.49			
7/16	7.6576	4.6664	7/8	21.5984	37.122	7/8	46.7312	173.78	7/8	71.8639	410.97			
1/2	7.8540	4.9087	7	21.9911	38.485	15	47.1239	176.71	23	72.2566	415.48			
9/16	8.0503	5.1572	1/8	22.3838	39.871	1/8	47.5166	179.67	1/8	72.6493	420.00			
5/8	8.2467	5.4119	1/4	22.7765	41.282	1/4	47.9093	182.65	1/4	73.0420	424.56			
11/16	8.4430	5.6727	3/8	23.1692	42.718	3/8	48.3020	185.66	3/8	73.4347	429.13			
3/4	8.6394	5.9396	1/2	23.5619	44.179	1/2	48.6947	188.69	1/2	73.8274	433.74			
13/16	8.8357	6.2126	5/8	23.9546	45.664	5/8	49.0874	191.75	5/8	74.2201	438.36			
7/8	9.0321	6.4918	3/4	24.3473	47.173	3/4	49.4801	194.83	3/4	74.6128	443.01			
15/16	9.2284	6.7771	7/8	24.7400	48.707	7/8	49.8728	197.93	7/8	75.0055	447.69			

Table 5. Circumferences and Areas of Circles
(Reprinted from Dodge General Engineering Catalog by special permission of Dodge Manufacturing Division, Reliance Electric Co.)

Circumferences and Areas of Circles (Continued)

Diam.	Circum.	Area	Diam.	Circum.	Area	Diam.	Circum.	Area	Diam.	Circum.	Area
24	75.3982	452.39	32	100.531	804.25	40	125.664	1256.6	48	150.796	1809.6
1/8	75.7909	457.11	1/8	100.924	810.54	1/8	126.056	1264.5	1/8	151.189	1819.0
1/4	76.1836	461.86	1/4	101.316	816.86	1/4	126.449	1272.4	1/4	151.582	1828.5
3/8	76.5763	466.64	3/8	101.709	823.21	3/8	126.842	1280.3	3/8	151.975	1837.9
1/2	76.9690	471.44	1/2	102.102	829.58	1/2	127.235	1288.2	1/2	152.367	1847.5
5/8	77.3617	476.26	5/8	102.494	835.97	5/8	127.627	1296.2	5/8	152.760	1857.0
3/4	77.7544	481.11	3/4	102.887	842.39	3/4	128.020	1304.2	3/4	153.153	1866.5
7/8	78.1471	485.98	7/8	103.280	848.83	7/8	128.413	1312.2	7/8	153.545	1876.1
25	78.5398	490.87	33	103.673	855.30	41	128.805	1320.3	49	153.938	1885.7
1/8	78.9325	495.79	1/8	104.065	861.79	1/8	129.198	1328.3	1/8	154.331	1895.4
1/4	79.3252	500.74	1/4	104.458	868.31	1/4	129.591	1336.4	1/4	154.723	1905.0
3/8	79.7179	505.71	3/8	104.851	874.85	3/8	129.983	1344.5	3/8	155.116	1914.7
1/2	80.1106	510.71	1/2	105.243	881.41	1/2	130.376	1352.7	1/2	155.509	1924.4
5/8	80.5033	515.72	5/8	105.636	888.00	5/8	130.769	1360.8	5/8	155.902	1934.2
3/4	80.8960	520.77	3/4	106.029	894.62	3/4	131.161	1369.0	3/4	156.294	1943.9
7/8	81.2887	525.84	7/8	106.421	901.26	7/8	131.554	1377.2	7/8	156.687	1953.7
26	81.6814	530.93	34	106.814	907.92	42	131.947	1385.4	50	157.080	1963.5
1/8	82.0741	536.05	1/8	107.207	914.61	1/8	132.340	1393.7	1/8	157.472	1973.3
1/4	82.4668	541.19	1/4	107.600	921.32	1/4	132.732	1402.0	1/4	157.865	1983.2
3/8	82.8595	546.35	3/8	107.992	928.06	3/8	133.125	1410.3	3/8	158.258	1993.1
1/2	83.2522	551.55	1/2	108.385	934.82	1/2	133.518	1418.6	1/2	158.650	2003.0
5/8	83.6449	556.76	5/8	108.778	941.61	5/8	133.910	1427.0	5/8	159.043	2012.9
3/4	84.0376	562.00	3/4	109.170	948.42	3/4	134.303	1435.4	3/4	159.436	2022.8
7/8	84.4303	567.27	7/8	109.563	955.25	7/8	134.696	1443.8	7/8	159.829	2032.8
27	84.8230	572.56	35	109.956	962.11	43	135.088	1452.2	51	160.221	2042.8
1/8	85.2157	577.87	1/8	110.348	969.00	1/8	135.481	1460.7	1/8	160.614	2052.8
1/4	85.6084	583.21	1/4	110.741	975.91	1/4	135.874	1469.1	1/4	161.007	2062.9
3/8	86.0011	588.57	3/8	111.134	982.84	3/8	136.267	1477.6	3/8	161.399	2073.0
1/2	86.3938	593.96	1/2	111.527	989.80	1/2	136.659	1486.2	1/2	161.792	2083.1
5/8	86.7865	599.37	5/8	111.919	996.87	5/8	137.052	1494.7	5/8	162.185	2093.2
3/4	87.1792	604.81	3/4	112.312	1003.8	3/4	137.445	1503.3	3/4	162.577	2103.3
7/8	87.5719	610.27	7/8	112.705	1010.8	7/8	137.837	1511.9	7/8	162.970	2113.5
28	87.965	615.75	36	113.097	1017.9	44	138.230	1520.5	52	163.363	2123.7
1/8	88.357	621.26	1/8	113.490	1025.0	1/8	138.623	1529.2	1/8	163.756	2133.9
1/4	88.750	626.80	1/4	113.883	1032.1	1/4	139.015	1537.9	1/4	164.148	2144.2
3/8	89.143	632.36	3/8	114.275	1039.2	3/8	139.408	1546.6	3/8	164.541	2154.5
1/2	89.535	637.94	1/2	114.668	1046.3	1/2	139.801	1555.3	1/2	164.934	2164.8
5/8	89.928	643.55	5/8	115.061	1053.5	5/8	140.194	1564.0	5/8	165.326	2175.1
3/4	90.321	649.18	3/4	115.454	1060.7	3/4	140.586	1572.8	3/4	165.719	2185.4
7/8	90.713	654.84	7/8	115.846	1068.0	7/8	140.979	1581.6	7/8	166.112	2195.8
29	91.106	660.52	37	116.239	1075.2	45	141.372	1590.4	53	166.504	2206.2
1/8	91.499	666.23	1/8	116.632	1082.5	1/8	141.764	1599.3	1/8	166.897	2216.6
1/4	91.892	671.96	1/4	117.024	1089.8	1/4	142.157	1608.2	1/4	167.290	2227.0
3/8	92.284	677.71	3/8	117.417	1097.1	3/8	142.550	1617.0	3/8	167.683	2237.5
1/2	92.677	683.49	1/2	117.810	1104.5	1/2	142.942	1626.0	1/2	168.075	2248.0
5/8	93.070	689.30	5/8	118.202	1111.8	5/8	143.335	1634.9	5/8	168.468	2258.5
3/4	93.462	695.13	3/4	118.596	1119.2	3/4	143.728	1643.9	3/4	168.861	2269.1
7/8	93.855	700.98	7/8	118.988	1126.7	7/8	144.121	1652.9	7/8	169.253	2279.6
30	94.248	706.86	38	119.381	1134.1	46	144.513	1661.9	54	169.646	2290.2
1/8	94.640	712.70	1/8	119.773	1141.0	1/8	144.906	1670.9	1/8	170.039	2300.8
1/4	95.033	718.69	1/4	120.166	1149.1	1/4	145.299	1680.0	1/4	170.431	2311.5
3/8	95.426	724.64	3/8	120.559	1156.6	3/8	145.691	1689.1	3/8	170.824	2322.1
1/2	95.819	730.62	1/2	120.951	1164.2	1/2	146.084	1698.2	1/2	171.217	2332.8
5/8	96.211	736.62	5/8	121.344	1171.7	5/8	146.477	1707.4	5/8	171.609	2343.5
3/4	96.604	742.64	3/4	121.737	1179.3	3/4	146.869	1716.5	3/4	172.002	2354.3
7/8	96.997	748.69	7/8	122.129	1186.9	7/8	147.262	1725.7	7/8	172.395	2365.0
31	97.389	754.77	39	122.522	1194.6	47	147.655	1734.9	55	172.788	2375.8
1/8	97.782	760.87	1/8	122.915	1202.3	1/8	148.048	1744.2	1/8	173.180	2386.6
1/4	98.175	766.99	1/4	123.308	1210.0	1/4	148.440	1753.5	1/4	173.573	2397.5
3/8	98.567	773.14	3/8	123.700	1217.7	3/8	148.833	1762.7	3/8	173.966	2408.3
1/2	98.960	779.31	1/2	124.093	1225.4	1/2	149.226	1772.1	1/2	174.358	2419.2
5/8	99.353	785.51	5/8	124.486	1233.2	5/8	149.618	1781.4	5/8	174.751	2430.1
3/4	99.746	791.73	3/4	124.878	1241.0	3/4	150.011	1790.8	3/4	175.144	2441.1
7/8	100.138	797.98	7/8	125.271	1248.8	7/8	150.404	1800.1	7/8	175.536	2452.0

Circumferences and Areas of Circles (Concluded)

The four side-by-side column groups form one continuous sequence and are combined below into a single table.

Diam.	Circum.	Area
88	276.460	6082.1
1/8	276.853	6099.4
1/4	277.246	6116.7
3/8	277.638	6134.1
1/2	278.031	6151.4
5/8	278.424	6168.8
3/4	278.816	6186.2
7/8	279.209	6203.7
89	279.602	6221.1
1/8	279.994	6238.6
1/4	280.387	6256.1
3/8	280.780	6273.7
1/2	281.173	6291.2
5/8	281.565	6308.8
3/4	281.958	6326.4
7/8	282.351	6344.1
90	282.743	6361.7
1/8	283.136	6379.4
1/4	283.529	6397.1
3/8	283.921	6414.9
1/2	284.314	6432.6
5/8	284.707	6450.4
3/4	285.100	6468.2
7/8	285.492	6486.0
91	285.885	6503.9
1/8	286.278	6521.8
1/4	286.670	6539.7
3/8	287.063	6557.6
1/2	287.456	6575.5
5/8	287.848	6593.5
3/4	288.241	6611.5
7/8	288.634	6629.6
92	289.027	6647.6
1/8	289.419	6665.7
1/4	289.812	6683.8
3/8	290.205	6701.9
1/2	290.597	6720.1
5/8	290.990	6738.2
3/4	291.383	6756.4
7/8	291.775	6774.7
93	292.168	6792.9
1/8	292.561	6811.2
1/4	292.954	6829.5
3/8	293.346	6847.8
1/2	293.739	6866.1
5/8	294.132	6884.5
3/4	294.524	6902.9
7/8	294.917	6921.3
94	295.310	6939.8
1/8	295.702	6958.2
1/4	296.095	6976.7
3/8	296.488	6995.3
1/2	296.881	7013.8
5/8	297.273	7032.4
3/4	297.666	7051.0
7/8	298.059	7069.6
95	298.451	7088.2
1/8	298.844	7106.9
1/4	299.237	7125.6
3/8	299.629	7144.3
1/2	300.022	7163.0
5/8	300.415	7181.8
3/4	300.807	7200.6
7/8	301.200	7219.4
96	301.593	7238.2
1/8	301.986	7257.1
1/4	302.378	7276.0
3/8	302.771	7294.9
1/2	303.164	7313.8
5/8	303.556	7332.8
3/4	303.949	7351.8
7/8	304.342	7370.8
97	304.734	7389.8
1/8	305.127	7408.9
1/4	305.520	7428.0
3/8	305.913	7447.1
1/2	306.305	7466.2
5/8	306.698	7485.3
3/4	307.091	7504.5
7/8	307.483	7523.7
98	307.876	7543.0
1/8	308.269	7562.2
1/4	308.661	7581.5
3/8	309.054	7600.8
1/2	309.447	7620.1
5/8	309.840	7639.5
3/4	310.232	7658.9
7/8	310.625	7678.3
99	311.018	7697.7
1/8	311.410	7717.1
1/4	311.803	7736.6
3/8	312.196	7756.1
1/2	312.588	7775.6
5/8	312.981	7795.2
3/4	313.374	7814.8
7/8	313.767	7834.4
100	314.159	7854.0
1/4	314.945	7893.3
1/2	315.730	7932.7
3/4	316.515	7972.2
101	317.301	8011.8
1/4	318.086	8051.6
1/2	318.872	8091.4
3/4	319.657	8131.3
102	320.442	8171.3
1/4	321.228	8211.4
1/2	322.013	8251.6
3/4	322.799	8291.9
103	323.584	8332.3
1/4	324.369	8372.8
1/2	325.155	8413.4
3/4	325.940	8454.1
104	326.726	8494.9
1/4	327.511	8535.8
1/2	328.296	8576.6
3/4	329.082	8617.8
105	329.867	8659.0
1/4	330.653	8700.3
1/2	331.438	8741.7
3/4	332.223	8783.2
106	333.009	8824.7
1/4	333.794	8866.4
1/2	334.580	8908.2
3/4	335.365	8950.1
107	336.150	8992.0
1/4	336.936	9034.1
1/2	337.721	9076.3
3/4	338.507	9118.5
108	339.292	9160.9
1/4	340.077	9203.3
1/2	340.863	9245.9
3/4	341.648	9288.6
109	342.433	9331.3
1/4	343.219	9374.2
1/2	344.004	9417.1
3/4	344.790	9460.2
110	345.575	9503.3
1/4	346.360	9546.6
1/2	347.146	9589.9
3/4	347.931	9633.3
111	348.717	9676.9
1/4	349.502	9720.5
1/2	350.287	9764.3
3/4	351.073	9808.1
112	351.858	9852.0
1/4	352.644	9896.1
1/2	353.429	9940.2
3/4	354.214	9984.4
113	355.000	10,028.7
1/4	355.785	10,073.2
1/2	356.570	10,117.7
3/4	357.356	10,162.3
114	358.141	10,207.0
1/4	358.927	10,251.9
1/2	359.712	10,296.8
3/4	360.497	10,341.8
115	361.283	10,386.9
1/4	362.069	10,432.1
1/2	362.854	10,477.4
3/4	363.639	10,522.8
116	364.425	10,568.3
1/4	365.210	10,613.9
1/2	365.995	10,659.6
3/4	366.781	10,705.4
117	367.566	10,751.3
1/4	368.352	10,797.3
1/2	369.137	10,843.4
3/4	369.922	10,889.6
118	370.708	10,935.9
1/4	371.493	10,982.3
1/2	372.279	11,028.8
3/4	373.064	11,075.3
119	373.849	11,122.0
1/4	374.635	11,168.8
1/2	375.420	11,215.7
3/4	376.206	11,262.7
120	376.991	11,309.7
1/4	377.776	11,356.9
1/2	378.562	11,404.2
3/4	379.347	11,451.5
121	380.133	11,499.0
1/4	380.918	11,546.6
1/2	381.703	11,594.2
3/4	382.489	11,642.0
122	383.274	11,689.9
1/4	384.060	11,737.8
1/2	384.845	11,785.9
3/4	385.630	11,834.0
123	386.416	11,882.3
1/4	387.201	11,930.6
1/2	387.987	11,979.1
3/4	388.772	12,027.6
124	389.557	12,076.3
1/4	390.343	12,125.0
1/2	391.128	12,173.9
3/4	391.914	12,222.8
125	392.699	12,271.8
1/4	393.484	12,321.0
1/2	394.270	12,370.2
3/4	395.055	12,419.5
126	395.841	12,469.0
1/4	396.626	12,518.5
1/2	397.411	12,568.1
3/4	398.197	12,617.9
127	398.982	12,667.7
1/4	399.768	12,717.6
1/2	400.553	12,767.6
3/4	401.338	12,817.7
128	402.124	12,868.0
1/4	402.909	12,918.3
1/2	403.695	12,968.9
3/4	404.480	13,019.2
129	405.265	13,069.8
1/4	406.051	13,120.5
1/2	406.836	13,171.3
3/4	407.621	13,222.2
130	408.407	13,273.2
1/4	409.192	13,324.3
1/2	409.978	13,375.5
3/4	410.763	13,426.8
131	411.549	13,478.2
1/4	412.334	13,529.7
1/2	413.119	13,581.3
3/4	413.905	13,633.0
132	414.690	13,684.8
1/4	415.476	13,736.7
1/2	416.261	13,788.6
3/4	417.046	13,840.7
133	417.832	13,892.9
1/4	418.617	13,945.2
1/2	419.402	13,997.6
3/4	420.188	14,050.0
134	420.973	14,102.6
1/4	421.759	14,155.3
1/2	422.544	14,208.0
3/4	423.329	14,260.9
135	424.115	14,313.9
1/4	424.900	14,366.9
1/2	425.686	14,420.1
3/4	426.471	14,473.4
136	427.257	14,526.7
1/4	428.042	14,580.2
1/2	428.827	14,633.7
3/4	429.613	14,687.4
137	430.398	14,741.1
1/4	431.184	14,795.0
1/2	431.969	14,848.9
3/4	432.754	14,903.0
138	433.540	14,957.1
1/4	434.325	15,011.4
1/2	435.110	15,065.7
3/4	435.896	15,120.1
139	436.681	15,174.7
1/4	437.467	15,229.3
1/2	438.252	15,284.0
3/4	439.037	15,338.9
140	439.823	15,393.8
1/4	440.608	15,448.8
1/2	441.394	15,504.0
3/4	442.180	15,559.2

MANUFACTURERS' STANDARD GAGE FOR SHEET STEEL

Thickness equivalents are based on 0.0014945 in. per oz. per sq. ft.; 0.023912 in. per lb. per sq. ft. (reciprocal of 41.820 lb. per sq. ft. per in. thick) ; 3.443329 in. per lb. per sq. in.

Manufacturers' Standard Gage No.	Ounces per Square Foot	Pounds per Square Inch	Pounds per Square Foot	Inch Equivalent for Sheet Steel Thickness	Manufacturers' Standard Gage No.
3	160	0.069444	10.0000	0.2391	3
4	150	.065104	9.3750	.2242	4
5	140	.060764	8.7500	.2092	5
6	130	.056424	8.1250	.1943	6
7	120	.052083	7.5000	.1793	7
8	110	.047743	6.8750	.1644	8
9	100	.043403	6.2500	.1495	9
10	90	.039062	5.6250	.1345	10
11	80	.034722	5.0000	.1196	11
12	70	.030382	4.3750	.1046	12
13	60	.026042	3.7500	.0897	13
14	50	.021701	3.1250	.0747	14
15	45	.019531	2.8125	.0673	15
16	40	.017361	2.5000	.0598	16
17	36	.015625	2.2500	.0538	17
18	32	.013889	2.0000	.0478	18
19	28	.012153	1.7500	.0418	19
20	24	.010417	1.5000	.0359	20
21	22	.0095486	1.3750	.0329	21
22	20	.0086806	1.2500	.0299	22
23	18	.0078125	1.1250	.0269	23
24	16	.0069444	1.0000	.0239	24
25	14	.0060764	0.87500	.0209	25
26	12	.0052083	.75000	.0179	26
27	11	.0047743	.68750	.0164	27
28	10	.0043403	.62500	.0149	28
29	9	.0039062	.56250	.0135	29
30	8	.0034722	.50000	.0120	30
31	7	.0030382	.43750	.0105	31
32	6.5	.0028212	.40625	.0097	32
33	6	.0026042	.37500	.0090	33
34	5.5	.0023872	.34375	.0082	34
35	5	.0021701	.31250	.0075	35
36	4.5	.0019531	.28125	.0067	36
37	4.25	.0018446	.26562	.0064	37
38	4	.0017361	.25000	.0060	38

Table 6. Sheet Metal Gages
(Courtesy of American Iron and Steel Institute.)
a. Manufacturer's Standard Gage

GALVANIZED SHEET GAGE NUMBERS, UNIT WEIGHTS AND THICKNESSES

Galvanized Sheet Gage No.	Ounces Per Square Foot	Pounds Per Square Foot	Pounds Per Square Inch	Thickness Equivalent for Galvanized Sheet Gage No.	Galvanized Sheet Gage No.
8	112.5	7.03125	0.048828	0.1681	8
9	102.5	6.40625	.044488	.1532	9
10	92.5	5.78125	.040148	.1382	10
11	82.5	5.15625	.035807	.1233	11
12	72.5	4.53125	.031467	.1084	12
13	62.5	3.90625	.027127	.0934	13
14	52.5	3.28125	.022786	.0785	14
15	47.5	2.96875	.020616	.0710	15
16	42.5	2.65625	.018446	.0635	16
17	38.5	2.40625	.016710	.0575	17
18	34.5	2.15625	.014974	.0516	18
19	30.5	1.90625	.013238	.0456	19
20	26.5	1.65625	.011502	.0396	20
21	24.5	1.53125	.010634	.0366	21
22	22.5	1.40625	.0097656	.0336	22
23	20.5	1.28125	.0088976	.0306	23
24	18.5	1.15625	.0080295	.0276	24
25	16.5	1.03125	.0071615	.0247	25
26	14.5	.90625	.0062934	.0217	26
27	13.5	.84375	.0058594	.0202	27
28	12.5	.78125	.0054253	.0187	28
29	11.5	.71875	.0049913	.0172	29
30	10.5	.65625	.0045573	.0157	30
31	9.5	.59375	.0041233	.0142	31
32	9.0	.56250	.0039062	.0134	32

b. Galvanized Sheet

SIZES OF WIRE RODS

Inch	Steel Wire Gage No.	Decimal Equivalent	Inch	Steel Wire Gage No.	Decimal Equivalent
47/64		0.734	27/64		0.422
23/32		0.719	13/32		0.406
45/64		0.703		4/0	0.394
11/16		0.688	25/64		0.391
43/64		0.672	3/8		0.375
21/32		0.656		3/0	0.363
41/64		0.641	23/64		0.359
5/8		0.625	11/32		0.344
39/64		0.609		2/0	0.331
19/32		0.594	21/64		0.328
37/64		0.578	5/16		0.313
9/16		0.563		1/0	0.307
35/64		0.547	19/64		0.297
17/32		0.531		1	0.283
33/64		0.516	9/32		0.281
1/2		0.500	17/64		0.266
	7/0	0.490		2	0.263
31/64		0.484	1/4		0.250
15/32		0.469		3	0.244
	6/0	0.462	15/64		0.234
29/64		0.453		4	0.225
7/16		0.438	7/32		0.218
	5/0	0.431			

Table 7. Wire and Wire Rod Gages
(Courtesy of American Iron and Steel Institute.)
a. Wire Rod

STEEL WIRE GAGE
SPLIT GAGE NUMBERS AND DECIMAL EQUIVALENTS

Gage	Decimal	Gage	Decimal	Gage	Decimal	Gage	Decimal
7/0	.490	6	.192	18	.0475	30	.014
7/0 ¼	.483	6 ¼	.188	18 ¼	.0459	30 ¼	.0138
7/0 ½	.476	6 ½	.185	18 ½	.0443	30 ½	.0136
7/0 ¾	.469	6 ¾	.181	18 ¾	.0426	30 ¾	.0134
6/0	.4615	7	.177	19	.0410	31	.0132
6/0 ¼	.454	7 ¼	.173	19 ¼	.0394	31 ¼	.0131
6/0 ½	.446	7 ½	.170	19 ½	.0379	31 ½	.0130
6/0 ¾	.438	7 ¾	.166	19 ¾	.0363	31 ¾	.0129
5/0	.4305	8	.162	20	.0348	32	.0128
5/0 ¼	.421	8 ¼	.159	20 ¼	.0340	32 ¼	.0126
5/0 ½	.412	8 ½	.155	20 ½	.0332	32 ½	.0123
5/0 ¾	.403	8 ¾	.152	20 ¾	.0325	32 ¾	.0121
4/0	.3938	9	.1483	21	.0317	33	.0118
4/0 ¼	.386	9 ¼	.145	21 ¼	.0309	33 ¼	.0115
4/0 ½	.378	9 ½	.142	21 ½	.0301	33 ½	.0111
4/0 ¾	.370	9 ¾	.138	21 ¾	.0294	33 ¾	.0108
3/0	.3625	10	.135	22	.0286	34	.0104
3/0 ¼	.355	10 ¼	.131	22 ¼	.0279	34 ¼	.0102
3/0 ½	.347	10 ½	.128	22 ½	.0272	34 ½	.0100
3/0 ¾	.339	10 ¾	.124	22 ¾	.0265	34 ¾	.0097
2/0	.331	11	.1205	23	.0258	35	.0095
2/0 ¼	.325	11 ¼	.117	23 ¼	.0251	35 ¼	.0094
2/0 ½	.319	11 ½	.113	23 ½	.0244	35 ½	.0093
2/0 ¾	.313	11 ¾	.109	23 ¾	.0237	35 ¾	.0091
1/0	.3065	12	.1055	24	.0230	36	.0090
1/0 ¼	.301	12 ¼	.102	24 ¼	.0224	36 ¼	.0089
1/0 ½	.295	12 ½	.099	24 ½	.0217	36 ½	.0087
1/0 ¾	.289	12 ¾	.095	24 ¾	.0211	36 ¾	.0086
1	.283	13	.0915	25	.0204	37	.0085
1 ¼	.278	13 ¼	.089	25 ¼	.0198	37 ¼	.0084
1 ½	.273	13 ½	.086	25 ½	.0193	37 ½	.0083
1 ¾	.268	13 ¾	.083	25 ¾	.0187	37 ¾	.0081
2	.2625	14	.080	26	.0181	38	.0080
2 ¼	.258	14 ¼	.078	26 ¼	.0179	38 ¼	.0079
2 ½	.253	14 ½	.076	26 ½	.0177	38 ½	.0078
2 ¾	.248	14 ¾	.074	26 ¾	.0175	38 ¾	.0076
3	.2437	15	.072	27	.0173	39	.0075
3 ¼	.239	15 ¼	.070	27 ¼	.0170	39 ¼	.00737
3 ½	.235	15 ½	.067	27 ½	.0168	39 ½	.00725
3 ¾	.230	15 ¾	.065	27 ¾	.0165	39 ¾	.00712
4	.2253	16	.0625	28	.0162	40	.007
4 ¼	.221	16 ¼	.060	28 ¼	.0159	40 ¼	.0069
4 ½	.216	16 ½	.058	28 ½	.0156	40 ½	.0068
4 ¾	.212	16 ¾	.056	28 ¾	.0153	40 ¾	.0067
5	.207	17	.054	29	.0150	41	.0066
5 ¼	.203	17 ¼	.052	29 ¼	.0148	41 ¼	.0065
5 ½	.200	17 ½	.051	29 ½	.0145	41 ½	.0064
5 ¾	.196	17 ¾	.0491	29 ¾	.0143	41 ¾	.0063

b. Steel Wire Gages

GAGE NUMBERS				DIAMETER			GAGE NUMBERS				DIAMETER		
Steel Wire Gage	American Wire Gage (B. & S.)	Birmingham or Stubs	British Imperial Standard	Inches — Reduction by 64ths	Inches — Decimally	Milli-meters (Decimally)	Steel Wire Gage	American Wire Gage (B. & S.)	Birmingham or Stubs	British Imperial Standard	Inches — Reduction by 64ths	Inches — Decimally	Milli-meters (Decimally)
				1	1.0000	25.40				4/0		.4000	10.16
				63/64	.984375	25.00	4/0					.3938	10.00
				31/32	.96875	24.61					25/64	.390625	9.922
				61/64	.953125	24.21			2/0			.3800	9.652
				15/16	.9375	23.81					3/8	.3750	9.525
				59/64	.921875	23.42				3/0		.3720	9.449
				29/32	.90625	23.02		2/0				.3648	9.266
				57/64	.890625	22.62	3/0					.3625	9.208
				7/8	.8750	22.23					23/64	.359375	9.128
				55/64	.859375	21.83				2/0		.3480	8.839
				27/32	.84375	21.43					11/32	.34375	8.731
				53/64	.828125	21.03			1/0			.3400	8.636
				13/16	.8125	20.64	2/0					.3310	8.407
				51/64	.796875	20.24					21/64	.328125	8.334
				25/32	.78125	19.84		1/0				.3249	8.252
				49/64	.765625	19.45				1/0		.3240	8.230
				3/4	.7500	19.05					5/16	.3125	7.938
				47/64	.734375	18.65	1/0					.3065	7.785
				23/32	.71875	18.26			1	1		.3000	7.620
				45/64	.703125	17.86					19/64	.296875	7.541
				11/16	.6875	17.46		1				.2893	7.348
				43/64	.671875	17.07			2			.2840	7.214
				21/32	.65625	16.67	1					.2830	7.188
				41/64	.640625	16.27					9/32	.28125	7.144
				5/8	.6250	15.88				2		.2760	7.010
				39/64	.609375	15.48					17/64	.265625	6.747
				19/32	.59375	15.08	2					.2625	6.668
	6/0				.5800	14.73			3			.2590	6.579
				37/64	.578125	14.68		2				.2576	6.543
				9/16	.5625	14.29				3		.2520	6.401
				35/64	.546875	13.89					1/4	.2500	6.350
				17/32	.53125	13.49	3					.2437	6.190
	5/0				.5165	13.12			4			.2380	6.045
				33/64	.515625	13.10					15/64	.234375	5.953
		5/0	7/0	1/2	.5000	12.70				4		.2320	5.893
7/0					.4900	12.45		3				.2294	5.827
				31/64	.484375	12.30	4					.2253	5.723
				15/32	.46875	11.91			5			.2200	5.588
			6/0		.4640	11.79					7/32	.21875	5.556
6/0					.4615	11.72				5		.2120	5.385
	4/0				.4600	11.68	5					.2070	5.258
		4/0			.4540	11.53		4				.2043	5.189
				29/64	.453125	11.51					13/64	.203125	5.159
				7/16	.4375	11.11			6			.2030	5.156
			5/0		.4320	10.97	6			6		.1920	4.877
5/0					.4305	10.93					3/16	.1875	4.763
		3/0			.4250	10.80		5				.1819	4.620
				27/64	.421875	10.72			7			.1800	4.572
	3/0				.4096	10.40	7					.1770	4.496
				13/32	.40625	10.32				7		.1760	4.470

c. Comparison of Wire Gage Systems

GAGE NUMBERS — Steel Wire Gage	American Wire Gage (B. & S.)	Birmingham or Stubs	British Imperial Standard	DIAMETER (Inches) — Reduction by 64ths	Decimally	Millimeters (Decimally)
				11/64	.171875	4.366
		8			.1650	4.191
8	6				.1620	4.115
			8		.1600	4.064
				5/32	.15625	3.969
9					.1483	3.767
		9			.1480	3.759
	7				.1443	3.665
			9		.1440	3.658
				9/64	.140625	3.572
10					.1350	3.429
		10			.1340	3.404
	8				.1285	3.264
			10		.1280	3.251
				1/8	.1250	3.175
11					.1205	3.061
		11			.1200	3.048
			11		.1160	2.946
	9				.1144	2.906
				7/64	.109375	2.778
		12			.1090	2.769
12					.1055	2.680
			12		.1040	2.642
	10				.1019	2.588
		13			.0950	2.413
				3/32	.09375	2.381
			13		.0920	2.337
13					.0915	2.324
	11				.0907	2.304
		14			.0830	2.108
	12				.0808	2.052
14			14		.0800	2.032
				5/64	.078125	1.984
15	13	15	15		.0720	1.829
		16			.0650	1.651
	14				.0641	1.628
			16		.0640	1.626
16				1/16	.0625	1.588
		17			.0580	1.473
	15				.0571	1.450
			17		.0560	1.422
17					.0540	1.372
	16				.0508	1.290
		18			.0490	1.245
			18		.0480	1.219
18					.0475	1.207
				3/64	.046875	1.191
	17				.0453	1.151
		19			.0420	1.067
19					.0410	1.041
	18					.0403	1.024
			19		.0400	1.016
			20		.0360	.9144
	19				.0359	.9119
		20			.0350	.8890
20					.0348	.8839
	20	21	21		.0320	.8128
21					.0317	.8052
				1/32	.03125	.7938
22					.0286	.7264
	21				.0285	.7239
		22	22		.0280	.7112
23					.0258	.6553
	22				.0253	.6426
		23			.0250	.6350
			23		.0240	.6096
24					.0230	.5842
	23				.0226	.5740
		24	24		.0220	.5588
25					.0204	.5182
	24				.0201	.5105
		25	25		.0200	.5080
26					.0181	.4597
		26			.0180	.4572
	25				.0179	.4547
27					.0173	.4394
			27		.0164	.4166
28					.0162	.4115
		27			.0160	.4064
	26				.0159	.4039
29				1/64	.015625	.3969
					.0150	.3810
			28		.0148	.3759
	27				.0142	.3607
30		28			.0140	.3556
			29		.0136	.3454
31					.0132	.3353
		29			.0130	.3302
32					.0128	.3251
	28				.0126	.3200
			30		.0124	.3150
		30			.0120	.3048
33					.0118	.2997
			31		.0116	.2946
	29				.0113	.2870
			32		.0108	.2743
34					.0104	.2642
	30	31	33		.0100	.2540
35					.0095	.2413
			34		.0092	.2337

Steel Wire Gage	American Wire Gage (B. & S.)	Birmingham or Stubs	British Imperial Standard	Reduction by 64ths	Decimally	Milli-meters (Decimally)
36		32			.0090	.2286
	31				.00893	.2268
37					.0085	.2159
			35		.0084	.2134
38		33			.0080	.2032
	32				.00795	.2019
			36		.0076	.1930
39					.0075	.1905
	33				.00708	.1798
40		34			.0070	.1778
			37		.0068	.1727
41					.0066	.1676
	34				.0063	.1600
42					.0062	.1575
43			38		.0060	.1524
44					.0058	.1473
	35				.00561	.1425
45					.0055	.1397
46			39		.0052	.1321
47	36	35			.0050	.1270
48			40		.0048	.1219
49					.0046	.1168
	37				.00445	.1130
50			41		.0044	.1118
		36	42		.0040	.1016
	38				.00396	.1006
			43		.0036	.09144
	39				.00353	.08966
			44		.0032	.08128
	40				.00314	.07976
	41		45		.00280	.07112
	42				.00249	.06325
			46		.00240	.06096
	43				.00222	.05639
			47		.00200	.05080
	44				.00198	.05029
	45				.00176	.04470
			48		.00160	.04064
	46				.00157	.03988
	47				.00140	.03556
	48				.00124	.03150
			49		.00120	.03048
	49				.00111	.02812
			50		.00100	.02540
	50				.000986	.02504
	51				.000878	.02230

NEMA Electric Motor Dimensions

for Squirrel Cage, Drip Proof★
General Purpose Motors

The motor ratings and dimensions listed on these pages are in accord with the National Electrical Manufacturers Association Standards. NEMA has conducted several re-rating programs which have led to reductions in frame size requirements. "Old" (pre-1953) NEMA frames were replaced by "U" frames in the 1953 standard and in 1963 "T" frames were established.

NEMA Design B Motors account for 90% of the 3-phase motors sold and are the most widely stocked. They have low starting current-normal torque and normal slip and are suitable for most fan, blower, pump and machine tool applications of 15 HP and below.

NEMA Design C Motors are next in popularity having low starting current, high breakaway torque, and normal slip. They are available from limited stocks in 7½ @ 1800 RPM and larger. They usually need not be specified below 15 HP. Desirable for "hard-to-start" applications such as plunger pumps, conveyors, and compressors.

NEMA Design D Motors are available on special order. They have high breakaway torque combined with high slip and are recommended for punch presses, shears and other high inertia machinery or multi-motor conveyor drives where motors operate in mechanical parallel.

The most popular motor-mounting style for industry is the rigid or foot mounting as shown in drawing on next page.

Motors with **NEMA C Face Mounting** (essentially a flat machined face with male pilot) use the suffix letter C; for example, 143 TC. They are popular for use with NEMA C-Face Speed Reducers. The mounting is available with or without the standard rigid base in all frames.

Table 2 shows dimensions for the T and U frames and for reference Table 1 includes some of the "old" frames. Dimensions are provided for reference only. Certified dimension drawings should be requested from the motor supplier.

Table 1—Old NEMA Frame Assignments

Old Frames, Design A, B & C, 1.15 Service Factor▲ 60 Cycles, Class B Insulation			
HP ♦	Speed, RPM		
	3450⧫	1750	1160
⅛—⅓	...	48	...
⅛—½	48	...	56
⅙	...	...	48
⅓—1	...	56	...
¾—1	56	...	...

Table 2—T and U NEMA Frame Assignments

T Frames, Design B, 1.15 Service Factor▲, 60 Cycles, Class B Insulation				
HP	Speed, RPM			
	3450	1750	1160	870
½	....	....	....	143T
¾	....	....	143T	145T
1	....	143T	145T	182T
1½	143T	145T	182T	184T
2	145T	145T	184T	213T
3	145T	182T	213T	215T
5	182T	184T	215T	254T
7½	184T	213T	254T	256T
10	213T	215T	256T	284T
15	215T	254T	284T	286T
20	254T	256T	286T	324T
25	256T	284T	324T	326T
30	284TS	286T	326T	364T
40	286TS	324T	364T	365T
50	324TS	326T	365T	404T
60	326TS	364TS*	404T	405T
75	364TS	365TS*	405T	444T
100	365TS	404TS*	444T	445T
125	404TS	405TS*	445T	....
150	405TS	444TS*	....	....
200	444TS	445TS*	....	....
250	445TS	....	....	....

U Frames, Design B & C, 1.5 Service Factor▲, 60 Cycles, Class A Insulation				
HP	Speed, RPM			
	3450	1750	1160	870
½	....	....	....	182*
¾	....	....	182*	184*
1	....	182*	184*	213*
1½	182*	184*	184*	213*
2	184*	184*	213*	215*
3	184*	213*	215†	254U†
5	213*	215†	254U†	256U†
7½	215*	254U†	256U†	284U†
10	254U*	256U†	284U†	286U†
15	256U*	284U†	324U†	326U†
20	284U*	286U†	326U†	364U†
25	286U*	324U†	364U†	365U†
30	324S*	326U†	365U†	404U†
40	326S*	364U†	404U†	405U†
50	364US*	365U†, 365US♠	405U†	444U†
60	365US*	404U†, 404US♠	444U†	445U†
75	404US*	405U†, 405US♠	445U†	....
100	405US*	....	....	....
125	444US*	....	....	....
150	445US*	....	....	....
...	....	....	....	....
...	....	....	....	....

★ Most manufacturers' standard motors are drip-proof although they are commonly referred to as "open."

▲ Multiplying the rated HP by the service factor yields the maximum permissible HP loading, if the motor is applied under the service conditions specified by NEMA and if voltage and frequency values, as specified on nameplates, are maintained.

⧫ Applies to design A and B motors only.

* Applies to design B motors only.

† Applies to design B and C motors only.

♦ Normal HP range, Consult Manufacturer.

♠ When motors are to be used with V-Belt or chain drives, the correct frame size is the one shown with the suffix "S" omitted.

Table 8. NEMA Electric Motor Dimensions

(Reprinted from Dodge General Engineering Catalog by special permission of Dodge Manufacturing Division, Reliance Electric Co.)

NEMA Electric Motor Dimensions
(Continued)

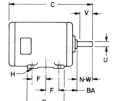

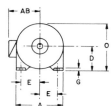

Table 3—Standard Dimensions of Electric Motors

Frame Desig-nation	Frame No.	A Max.	B Max. Δ	C §	D ⧗	E	F	G §	H	N-W	O §	U	V Min.	AB §	BA	Shaft Keyseat		Key Lgth.
																Width	Depth	
"Old" Frames	48	5 5/8§	3 1/2§	10 3/8	3	2 1/8	1 3/8	3/32	11/32 Slot	1 1/2	5 13/16	1/2	1 1/2§	. . .	2 1/2	Flat	3/64	. . .
	56	6 1/2§	4 1/4§	11 3/8	3 1/2	2 7/16	1 1/2	1/8	11/32 Slot	1 7/8	6 11/16	5/8	1 7/8§	. . .	2 3/4	3/16	3/32	1 3/8
"U" Frames	182	9	6 1/2	12 1/4	4 1/2	3 3/4	2 1/4	9/16	13/32	2 1/4	9	7/8	2	7 3/8	2 3/4	3/16	3/32	1 3/8
	184	9	7 1/2	13 1/4	4 1/2	3 3/4	2 3/4	9/16	13/32	2 1/4	9	7/8	2	7 3/8	2 3/4	3/16	3/32	1 3/8
	213	10 1/2	7 1/2	15 5/16	5 1/4	4 1/4	2 3/4	5/8	13/32	3	10 1/2	1 1/8	2 3/4	8 1/8	3 1/2	1/4	1/8	2
	215	10 1/2	9	16 7/8	5 1/4	4 1/4	3 1/2	5/8	13/32	3	10 1/2	1 1/8	2 3/4	8 1/8	3 1/2	1/4	1/8	2
	254U	12 1/2	10 3/4	20 1/4	6 1/4	5	4 1/8	3/4	17/32	3 3/4	12 1/2	1 3/8	3 1/2	10 1/8	4 1/4	5/16	5/32	2 3/4
	256U	12 1/2	12 1/2	22 1/16	6 1/4	5	5	3/4	17/32	3 3/4	12 1/2	1 3/8	3 1/2	10 1/8	4 1/4	5/16	5/32	2 3/4
	284U	14	12 1/2	23 5/8	7	5 1/2	4 3/4	7/8	17/32	4 7/8	14	1 5/8	4 5/8	10 13/16	4 3/4	3/8	3/16	3 3/4
	286U	14	14	25 3/16	7	5 1/2	5 1/2	7/8	17/32	4 7/8	14	1 5/8	4 5/8	10 13/16	4 3/4	3/8	3/16	3 3/4
	324U	16	14	26 3/8	8	6 1/4	5 1/4	1	21/32	5 5/8	16	1 7/8	5 3/8	12 3/8	5 1/4	1/2	1/4	4 1/4
	324S	16	14	24 1/16	8	6 1/4	5 1/4	1	21/32	3 1/4	16	1 5/8	3	12 3/8	5 1/4	3/8	3/16	1 7/8
	326U	16	15 1/2	27 7/8	8	6 1/4	6	1	21/32	5 5/8	16	1 7/8	5 3/8	12 3/8	5 1/4	1/2	1/4	4 1/4
	326S	16	15 1/2	25 1/2	8	6 1/4	6	1	21/32	3 1/4	16	1 5/8	3	12 3/8	5 1/4	3/8	3/16	1 7/8
	364U	18	15 1/4	29 1/8	9	7	5 5/8	1 1/8	21/32	6 3/8	18	2 1/8	6 1/8	16	5 7/8	1/2	1/4	5
	364US	18	15 1/4	26 7/8	9	7	5 5/8	1 1/8	21/32	3 3/4	18	1 7/8	3 1/2	16	5 7/8	1/2	1/4	2
	365U	18	16 1/4	30 1/8	9	7	6 1/8	1 1/8	21/32	6 3/8	18	2 1/8	6 1/8	16	5 7/8	1/2	1/4	5
	365US	18	16 1/4	27 1/2	9	7	6 1/8	1 1/8	21/32	3 3/4	18	1 7/8	3 1/2	16	5 7/8	1/2	1/4	2
	404U	20	16 1/4	32 3/8	10	8	6 1/8	1 1/4	13/16	7 1/8	20	2 3/8	6 7/8	17	6 5/8	5/8	5/16	5 1/2
	404US	20	16 1/4	29 1/2	10	8	6 1/8	1 1/4	13/16	4 1/4	20	2 1/8	4	17	6 5/8	1/2	1/4	2 3/4
	405U	20	17 3/4	33 7/8	10	8	6 7/8	1 1/4	13/16	7 1/8	20	2 3/8	6 7/8	17	6 5/8	5/8	5/16	5 1/2
	405US	20	17 3/4	31	10	8	6 7/8	1 1/4	13/16	4 1/4	20	2 1/8	4	17	6 5/8	1/2	1/4	2 3/4
	444U	22	18 1/2	37 3/4	11	9	7 1/4	1 1/4	13/16	8 5/8	22	2 7/8	8 3/8	19 1/8	7 1/2	3/4	3/8	7
	444US	22	18 1/2	33 7/16	11	9	7 1/4	1 1/4	13/16	4 1/4	22	2 1/8	4	19 1/8	7 1/2	1/2	1/4	2 3/4
	445U	22	20 1/2	39 3/4	11	9	8 1/4	1 1/4	13/16	8 5/8	22	2 7/8	8 3/8	19 1/8	7 1/2	3/4	3/8	7
	445US	22	20 1/2	35 3/8	11	9	8 1/4	1 1/4	13/16	4 1/4	22	2 1/8	4	19 1/8	7 1/2	1/2	1/4	2 3/4
"T" Frames	143T	7	6	12 5/8	3 1/2	2 3/4	2	3/8	11/32	2 1/4	7	7/8	2	5 5/8	2 1/4	3/16	3/32	1 3/8
	145T	7	6	12 5/8	3 1/2	2 3/4	2 1/2	3/8	11/32	2 1/4	7	7/8	2	5 5/8	2 1/4	3/16	3/32	1 3/8
	182T	9	6 1/2	12 3/4	4 1/2	3 3/4	2 1/4	9/16	13/32	2 3/4	9	1 1/8	2 1/2	7 3/8	2 3/4	1/4	1/8	1 3/4
	184T	9	7 1/2	13 3/4	4 1/2	3 3/4	2 3/4	9/16	13/32	2 3/4	9	1 1/8	2 1/2	7 3/8	2 3/4	1/4	1/8	1 3/4
	213T	10 1/2	7 1/2	15 13/16	5 1/4	4 1/4	2 3/4	5/8	13/32	3 3/8	10 1/2	1 3/8	3 1/8	8 1/8	3 1/2	5/16	5/32	2 3/8
	215T	10 1/2	9	17 5/16	5 1/4	4 1/4	3 1/2	5/8	13/32	3 3/8	10 1/2	1 3/8	3 1/8	8 1/8	3 1/2	5/16	5/32	2 3/8
	254T	12 1/2	10 3/4	20 1/2	6 1/4	5	4 1/8	3/4	17/32	4	12 1/2	1 5/8	3 3/4	10 1/8	4 1/4	3/8	3/16	2 7/8
	256T	12 1/2	12 1/2	22 1/4	6 1/4	5	5	3/4	17/32	4	12 1/2	1 5/8	3 3/4	10 1/8	4 1/4	3/8	3/16	2 7/8
	284T	14	12 1/2	23 5/16	7	5 1/2	4 3/4	7/8	17/32	4 5/8	14	1 7/8	4 3/8	10 13/16	4 3/4	1/2	1/4	3 1/4
	284TS	14	12 1/2	22	7	5 1/2	4 3/4	7/8	17/32	3 1/4	14	1 5/8	3	10 13/16	4 3/4	3/8	3/16	1 7/8
	286T	14	14	24 7/8	7	5 1/2	5 1/2	7/8	17/32	4 5/8	14	1 7/8	4 3/8	10 13/16	4 3/4	1/2	1/4	3 1/4
	286TS	14	14	23 1/2	7	5 1/2	5 1/2	7/8	17/32	3 1/4	14	1 5/8	3	10 13/16	4 3/4	3/8	3/16	1 7/8
	324T	16	14	26 1/2	8	6 1/4	5 1/4	1	21/32	5 1/4	16	2 1/8	5	12 3/8	5 1/4	1/2	1/4	3 7/8
	324TS	16	14	24 5/8	8	6 1/4	5 1/4	1	21/32	3 3/4	16	1 7/8	3 1/2	12 3/8	5 1/4	1/2	1/4	2
	326T	16	15 1/2	27 3/4	8	6 1/4	6	1	21/32	5 1/4	16	2 1/8	5	12 3/8	5 1/4	1/2	1/4	3 7/8
	326TS	16	15 1/2	26 1/8	8	6 1/4	6	1	21/32	3 3/4	16	1 7/8	3 1/2	12 3/8	5 1/4	1/2	1/4	2
	364T	18	15 1/4	28 3/4	9	7	5 5/8	1 1/8	21/32	5 7/8	18	2 3/8	5 5/8	16	5 7/8	5/8	5/16	4 1/4
	364TS	18	15 1/4	26 9/16	9	7	5 5/8	1 1/8	21/32	3 3/4	18	1 7/8	3 1/2	16	5 7/8	1/2	1/4	2
	365T	18	16 1/4	29 3/4	9	7	6 1/8	1 1/8	21/32	5 7/8	18	2 3/8	5 5/8	16	5 7/8	5/8	5/16	4 1/4
	365TS	18	16 1/4	27 9/16	9	7	6 1/8	1 1/8	21/32	3 3/4	18	1 7/8	3 1/2	16	5 7/8	1/2	1/4	2
	404T	20	16 1/4	32 5/8	10	8	6 1/8	1 1/4	13/16	7 1/4	20	2 7/8	7	17	6 5/8	3/4	3/8	5 5/8
	404TS	20	16 1/4	29 5/8	10	8	6 1/8	1 1/4	13/16	4 1/4	20	2 1/8	4	17	6 5/8	1/2	1/4	2 3/4
	405T	20	17 3/4	34 1/8	10	8	6 7/8	1 1/4	13/16	7 1/4	20	2 7/8	7	17	6 5/8	3/4	3/8	5 5/8
	405TS	20	17 3/4	31 1/8	10	8	6 7/8	1 1/4	13/16	4 1/4	20	2 1/8	4	17	6 5/8	1/2	1/4	2 3/4
	444T	22	18 1/2	37 7/8	11	9	7 1/4	1 1/4	13/16	8 1/2	22	3 3/8	8 1/4	19 1/8	7 1/2	7/8	7/16	6 7/8
	444TS	22	18 1/2	34 1/8	11	9	7 1/4	1 1/4	13/16	4 3/4	22	2 3/8	4 1/2	19 1/8	7 1/2	5/8	5/16	3
	445T	22	20 1/2	39 7/8	11	9	8 1/4	1 1/4	13/16	8 1/2	22	3 3/8	8 1/4	19 1/8	7 1/2	7/8	7/16	6 7/8
	445TS	22	20 1/2	36 1/8	11	9	8 1/4	1 1/4	13/16	4 3/4	22	2 3/8	4 1/2	19 1/8	7 1/2	5/8	5/16	3

Note: Suffix "S" indicates short shaft for direct coupled service only.

§ These dimensions are not NEMA standard—they are average dimensions that are common to a number of manufacturers. Certified drawings should be requested from Motor Manufacturer for accurate dimensions.

Δ Not necessarily on same centerline as F dimension.

⧗ Dimension will never be larger, but may be less, requiring shims for coupled service.

Table 9. Steel Pipe Dimensions[1]

Nominal Pipe Size, in.	Outside Diameter, in.	Wall Thickness, in.	Inside Diameter, in.	Inside Cross-sectional Area, sq. in.
		Standard Wall[2]		
1/8	0.405	0.068	0.269	0.0568
1/4	0.540	0.088	0.364	0.104
3/8	0.675	0.091	0.493	0.191
1/2	0.840	0.109	0.622	0.304
3/4	1.050	0.113	0.824	0.533
1	1.315	0.133	1.049	0.864
1¼	1.660	0.140	1.380	1.496
1½	1.900	0.145	1.610	2.036
2	2.375	0.154	2.067	3.356
2½	2.875	0.203	2.469	4.788
3	3.500	0.216	3.068	7.392
3½	4.000	0.226	3.548	9.887
4	4.500	0.237	4.026	12.730
5	5.563	0.258	5.047	20.006
6	6.625	0.280	6.065	28.890
8	8.625	0.322	7.981	50.026
10	10.750	0.365	10.020	78.853
12	12.750	0.375	12.000	113.096
14	14.000	0.375	13.250	137.885
16	16.000	0.375	15.250	182.652
18	18.000	0.375	17.250	233.703
20	20.000	0.375	19.250	291.036
22	22.000	0.375	21.250	354.653
24	24.000	0.375	23.250	424.552
26	26.000	0.375	25.250	500.735
28	28.000	0.375	27.250	583.201
30	30.000	0.375	29.250	671.950
32	32.000	0.375	31.250	766.982
34	34.000	0.375	33.250	868.298
36	36.000	0.375	35.250	975.896
		Extra Strong Wall[3]		
1/8	0.405	0.095	0.215	0.0363
1/4	0.540	0.119	0.302	0.0716
3/8	0.675	0.126	0.423	0.140
1/2	0.840	0.147	0.546	0.234
3/4	1.050	0.154	0.742	0.432
1	1.315	0.179	0.957	0.719
1¼	1.660	0.191	1.278	1.283

[1]First three columns extracted from American National Standard Wrought Steel and Wrought Iron Pipe, ANSI B 36.10-1970, with the permission of the publisher, The American Society of Mechanical Engineers, 345 East 47th Street, New York, N.Y. 10017.

[2]Same as Schedule 40 for pipe sizes up to and including 10-in.

[3]Same as Schedule 80 for pipe sizes up to and including 8-in.

Nominal Pipe Size, in.	Outside Diameter, in.	Wall Thickness, in.	Inside Diameter, in.	Inside Cross-sectional Area, sq. in.
1½	1.900	0.200	1.500	1.767
2	2.375	0.218	1.939	2.953
2½	2.875	0.276	2.323	4.238
3	3.500	0.300	2.900	6.605
3½	4.000	0.318	3.364	8.888
4	4.500	0.337	3.826	11.497
5	5.563	0.375	4.813	18.194
6	6.625	0.432	5.761	26.066
8	8.625	0.500	7.625	45.663
10	10.750	0.500	9.750	74.661
12	12.750	0.500	11.750	108.433
14	14.000	0.500	13.000	132.731
16	16.000	0.500	15.000	176.713
18	18.000	0.500	17.000	226.978
20	20.000	0.500	19.000	283.526
22	22.000	0.500	21.000	346.357
24	24.000	0.500	23.000	415.471
26	26.000	0.500	25.000	490.869
28	28.000	0.500	27.000	572.549
30	30.000	0.500	29.000	660.513
32	32.000	0.500	31.000	754.760
34	34.000	0.500	33.000	855.290
36	36.000	0.500	35.000	962.103

Weights of Materials

Material	Average Wt. per Cu. Ft., Pounds	Angle of Repose	Material	Average Wt. per Cu. Ft., Pounds	Angle of Repose
Acid Phosphate, fertilizer	60		Cocoa Nibs	35-40	30-45°
Air, 60° F—14.7 PSIA	0.0765		Cocoanut, meal	32	
Alfalfa, ground	16	45° & Up	Cocoanut, shredded	20-25	45° & Up
Alum, lumpy	50-60	30-45°	Coffee, fresh beans	30-40	30-45°
Alum, pulverized	45-50	30-45°	Coffee, roasted beans	22-30	Up to 30°
Alumina	60	30-45°	Coke, loose	23-32	30-45°
Aluminum, solid mass	165		Coke, pulverized	25-35	45° & Up
Aluminum Oxide	70-120	Up to 30°	Coke, petroleum calcined	35-45	30-45°
Ammonium Sulfate	45-60		Concrete, cinder with Portland cement	112	
Apples	40		Concrete, gravel & sand with Portland cement	150	
Asbestos, shredded	20-25	45° & Up	Copper Ore	120-150	30-45°
Asbestos, solid	153		Copper, cast	542	
Asbestos Brake Lining, molded	178		Copper, rolled	556	
Asbestos Brake Lining, woven	110		Cork, solid	15	
Ash, American White, dry (wood)	38		Cork, ground	5-15	45° & Up
Ashes, dry	35-40	45° & Up	Corn, on cob	45	
Ashes, wet	45-50	45° & Up	Corn, shelled	45	Up to 30°
Ashes, gas producer, saturated	78		Corn, grits	40-45	30-45°
Ashes, soft coal	35-45	40°	Cottonseed, dry, de-linted	35	30-45°
Asphalt, crushed	45	30-45°	Cottonseed, dry, not de-linted	18-25	45° & Up
Asphaltum	87.3		Cottonseed cake, lumpy	40-45	30-45°
Bagasse	7.5	45° & Up	Cottonseed, hulls	12	45° & Up
Bakelite, powder	30-40	45° & Up	Cottonseed, meal	35-40	30-45°
Bakelite, molded	82-88		Cottonseed, meats	40	30-45°
Baking Powder	40-50	30-45°	Cryolite	90-110	30-45°
Bark, wood, refuse	10-20	45° & Up	Cullet	80-120	30-45°
Barley	38	Up to 30°	Culm	45-50	
Baryte, crushed	180		Cypress	29	
Basalt	184		Dolomite, solid	181	
Batch, glass	90-100	30-45°	Dolomite, pulverized	46	
Bauxite, crushed	75-85	30-45°	Dolomite, lumpy	90-100	30-45°
Beans, castor, whole	36	Up to 30°	Earth, common dry	70-80	30-45°
Beans, cocoa	37		Earth, moist	75-85	30-45°
Beans, navy	48-54	Up to 30°	Earth, fullers dry	30-35	23°
Beans, soy	45	Up to 30°	Elm, dry	35	
Beets	45		Feldspar, solid	160	
Bentonite, crude	34-40	45° & Up	Feldspar, lumps	85-95	
Bones, pulverized	50-60		Feldspar, dust	75-80	45°
Borax, fine	50-55	30-45°	Fibre, hard	87	
Bran	16	30-45°	Fir	24-33	
Brass, cast	519		Fish, scrap	40-50	
Brass, rolled	534		Fish, meal	35-40	45° & Up
Brewers Grain	25-30	45° & Up	Flaxseed, whole	45	Up to 30°
Brick, best pressed	150		Flour, wheat	35-40	45° & Up
Brick, common hard	125		Fluorspar, solid	200	
Brick, fire	137		Fluorspar, lumps	80-110	45° & Up
Brick, soft inferior	100		Fluorspar, dust	80-95	45° & Up
Brickwork, fine	140		Foundry, refuse	60-80	
Bronze, copper 8, tin 1	546		Foundry, sand, loose	80-90	
Buckwheat	40-42	Up to 30°	Foundry, sand, rammed	100-110	
Calcium Carbide	70-80	30-45°	Garbage, average	30	
Carbon, black pellets	25	Up to 30°	Glass, window or plate	161	
Carbon, powder	4-6		Glass, batch	90-100	30-45°
Carbon, solid	134		Glass, broken	80-100	
Cedar, red	35		Glue, animal, flaked	35	
Cement, bulk	75-85		Glue, vegetable, powdered	40	
Cement, clinker	75-95		Gluten, meal	39	30-45°
Cement, Portland (376 lbs. net per bar.)	90-100	30-45°	Granite, solid	150-170	
Cement, slurry	90		Granite, lumps	96	30-45°
Cement mortar, Portland 1:2½	135		Graphite, flake	40	30-45°
Chalk, lumpy	82-95	45° & Up	Gravel, dry, round or sharp	90-100	30-40°
Chalk, fine	65-75	45° & Up	Gravel, wet	100-120	
Chalk, solid	156		Greenstone, crushed, loose	107	
Charcoal, wood	15-30		Gypsum, solid	142	
Cherry wood, dry	42		Gypsum, lumps	90-100	30-45°
Chestnut wood, dry	41.2		Gypsum, ground	75-80	
Chocolate, powder	40		Gypsum, pulverized	60-80	45° & Up
Chromium ore	125-140	30-45°	Hay, loose	5	
Cinders, (coal, ashes and clinkers)	40	25-40°	Hay, pressed	24	
Clay, potter's dry	100-120		Hemlock, dry	25	
Clay, dry in lumps	65	25-45°	Hickory, dry	53	
Coal, Anthracite, solid	94		Hops, moist	35	45° & Up
Coal, Anthracite, loose	52-57	30-45°	Ice, solid	57.4	
Coal, Bituminous, solid	84		Ice, crushed	35-40	Up to 30°
Coal, Bituminous, loose or slack	43-50	30-45°	Ilmenite	144	30-45°

Table 10. Weights of Materials and Angle of Repose
(Reprinted from Dodge General Engineering Catalog by special permission of Dodge Manufacturing Division, Reliance Electric Co.)

Weights of Materials

Material	Average Wt. per Cu. Ft., Pounds	Angle of Repose	Material	Average Wt. per Cu. Ft., Pounds	Angle of Repose
Iron Ore	120-180	....	Rosin	67	....
Iron, cast gray	450	....	Rubber, caoutchouc	59	....
Iron, cast ductile	444	....	Rubber, manufactured	95	....
Iron, wrought	480	....	Rubber, scrap (ground)	25-35	45° & Up
Iron, borings	130-200	....	Rye	42-45	Up to 30°
Lead, commercial	710	....	Salt cake	80-95	30-45°
Lead, red	230	....	Salt, coarse	45-55	30-45°
Lead Ore, crushed	180-270	....	Salt, fine	70-80	30-45°
Lead, white pigment	250-260	....	Saltpeter	70-80	30-45°
Lignite, air dried	45-55	30-45°	Sand, wet	110-130	45° & Up
Lignum Vitae, dry	41-83	....	Sand, dry	90-110	34°
Lime, briquettes	60	....	Sand, loose, foundry	80-100	30-45°
Lime, burned pebble	53-56	45° & Up	Sand, rammed	100-110	....
Lime, quick, crushed	64	....	Sand, voids full of water	110-130	15-30°
Lime, hydrated	20-40	30-45°	Sandstone, quarried and piled	82-86	....
Limestone, solid	165	....	Sawdust	10-25	....
Limestone, loose	100	....	Scale, rolling mill	125-160	....
Limestone, pulverized	85-90	45° & Up	Sewage, sludge	40-50	....
Linseed, whole	45-50	Up to 30°	Shales, solid	162	....
Linseed, meal	28-40	30-45°	Shales, broken	85-100	30-45°
Locust, dry	44	....	Silica, flour	80	....
Magnesite, solid	188	....	Slag, solid	160-180	....
Magnesium, solid	109	....	Slag, furnace, granulated	60-65	30-45°
Magnesium Sulfate, crystal	70	....	Slag, Birmingham	80-95	....
Mahogany, Spanish, dry	53	....	Slate, solid	165-175	....
Mahogany, Honduras, dry	35	....	Slate, fine ground	80-90	30-45°
Malt	20-22	30-45°	Slate, flakes	70-85	....
Manganese, solid	475	....	Snow, fresh fallen	5-12	....
Manganese Ore	125-140	....	Snow, compacted by rain	15-50	....
Manganese Oxide	120	....	Soap, solid	50	....
Manure	25	....	Soap, chips	5-15	30-45°
Maple, dry	49	....	Soap, flakes	5-15	30-45°
Marble, crushed	90-95	30-45°	Soap, powder	20-25	30-45°
Marl	79	30-45°	Soda Ash, heavy	55-65	30-45°
Masonry, granite or limestone	165	....	Soda Ash, light	20-35	30-45°
Mercury, 32° F.	849	....	Sodium Aluminate, ground	72	....
Mica, solid	181	....	Sodium Nitrate, ground	70-80	....
Mica, ground	75-80	30-45°	Soybeans, whole	45-50	Up to 30°
Milk, malted	25-35	45° & Up	Spruce, California, dry	28	....
Milk, powdered	28	45° & Up	Starch, powdered	25-45	....
Molybdenum Ore, powdered	107	....	Steel, solid	489.6	....
Mortar, wet	150	....	Steel, chips	100-150	30-45°
Oak, live, dry	59	....	Steel, turnings	60-120	45° & Up
Oak, red	32-45	....	Sugar, brown	45	....
Oats	26-28	32°	Sugar, powdered	45-55	....
Oats, rolled	19	30-45°	Sugar, granulated	50-55	30-45°
Oil Cake	48-50	....	Sugar, raw cane	55-65	45° & Up
Oil, linseed	58.8	....	Sugarbeet Pulp, dry	12-15	....
Oil, petroleum	55	....	Sugarbeet Pulp, wet	24-45	....
Oyster Shells, ground	53	30-45°	Sugarcane, knifed	15-18	45° & Up
Paper, writing and wrapping	65-90	....	Sulphur, solid	125	....
Paraffine	45	....	Sulphur, lumps	80-85	30-45°
Peanuts, shelled	35-45	30-45°	Sulphur, dust	50-70	30-45°
Peanuts, not shelled	15-20	30-45°	Sycamore, dry	37	....
Pebbles	90-100	....	Talc, solid	165-170	....
Petroleum, coke	35-45	....	Talc, granulated	50-65	....
Phosphate, rock	200	30-45°	Tanbark, ground	55	....
Phosphate, sand	90-100	30-45°	Tankage	50-70	....
Pine, White, dry	26	....	Tar	69-75	....
Pine, Yellow Northern, dry	34	....	Tin, cast	459	....
Pine, Yellow Southern, dry	45	....	Tobacco, scraps	15-25	45° & Up
Pitch	72	....	Tobacco, stems	16-25	45° & Up
Potash	80	....	Traprock, compact	187	....
Potassium Chloride	120-130	30-45°	Traprock, crushed	95-110	30-45°
Potatoes, white	48	....	Turf	20-30	....
Pumice, ground	40-45	45° & Up	Walnut, black, dry	38-42	....
Pyrites, pellets	120-130	30-45°	Water, pure	62.4	....
Quartz, solid	165	....	Water, sea	64.08	....
Quartz, lumps	95-100	....	Wheat	48	28°
Quartz, sand	70-80	....	Wheat, cracked	40-45	30-45°
Redwood, California, dry	26-30	....	Wood Chips	10-30	45° & Up
Resin, synthetic, crushed	30-40	....	Wood Flour	16-35	....
Rice, hulled and polished	45-48	Up to 30°	Zinc, calcines	75-80	30-45°
Rice, rough	36	30-45°	Zinc, cast	443	....
Rice Grits	42-45	30-45°	Zinc Ore, granular	160	....
Rip-rap	80-105	....	Zinc Oxide	10-35	45° & Up

LEGEND

A = EXCELLENT
B = GOOD
C = FAIR
D = NOT SUITABLE
E = EXPLOSIVE
I = IGNITES
• = INFORMATION NOT AVAILABLE

No.	Chemicals	Concentration %	Temperature °F	Carbon Steel	Copper	Red Brass	Muntz	Admiralty	Copper Silicon	90-10 Cupro-Nickel	70-30 Cupro-Nickel	Aluminum	304 Stainless Steel	316 Stainless Steel	Nickel	Monel	Inconel	Hastelloy	Titanium	Zirconium	Tantalum
1.	Acetaldehyde	100	70	A	E	E	E	E	E	D	B	B	A	A	A	A	A	A	B	A	A
2.	Acetic Acid (Aerated)	100	70	A	D	E	E	E	D	C	B	B	B	A	A	A	B	A	A	A	A
3.	Acetic Anhydride	100	70	D	B	C	D	C	B	D	A	A	B	B	B	B	B	B	A	A	B
4.	Acetone	100	70	A	A	A	A	C	B	D	A	A	A	A	A	A	A	A	A	A	A
5.	Acetylene	100	70	A	E	E	E	E	E	E	E	E	A	A	A	A	A	A	A	•	A
6.	Aluminum Chloride	10	70	D	A	A	A	A	A	B	B	B	D	C	B	B	D	A	A	A	A
7.	Aluminum Hydroxide	10	70	B	A	A	A	A	A	A	B	B	B	B	B	B	B	B	•	•	B
8.	Ammonia (Anhydrous)	100	70	A	B	B	B	B	B	A	A	C	B	B	D	D	B	B	A	A	A
9.	Ammonium Chloride	10	70	A	A	A	A	A	A	D	C	C	C	B	B	B	B	B	A	A	A
10.	Ammonium Sulfate	10	70	C	C	C	C	C	C	D	D	D	C	C	B	B	B	B	A	A	A
11.	Ammonium Sulfite	10	70	D	C	C	C	C	C	B	B	B	C	C	B	B	B	•	A	•	A
12.	Amyl Acetate	100	70	B	B	A	A	B	B	B	B	B	A	A	B	B	B	B	A	A	A
13.	Aniline	100	70	B	A	A	A	C	B	B	B	B	A	A	B	D	B	B	A	•	A
14.	Aroclor	100	70	B	A	A	A	A	A	A	A	A	A	B	B	B	B	B	A	•	A
15.	Barium Chloride	30	70	B	B	B	B	D	B	B	B	C	B	B	B	B	B	B	A	A	A
16.	Benzaldehyde	100	70	B	B	B	A	A	A	B	B	B	B	B	B	B	B	B	A	•	A
17.	Benzene	100	70	A	A	A	A	A	A	B	B	B	A	A	B	B	B	B	A	•	A
18.	Benzoic Acid	10	70	A	A	A	A	A	A	B	B	C	B	B	B	B	B	B	A	•	A
19.	Boric Acid	10	70	D	B	B	B	B	B	B	B	B	B	B	B	B	B	B	A	•	A
20.	Butadiene	100	70	A	A	A	A	A	A	A	A	A	A	A	B	B	B	B	A	A	A
21.	Butane	100	70	A	A	A	A	A	A	A	A	A	A	A	B	B	B	B	A	•	A
22.	Butanol	100	70	A	A	A	A	A	A	B	B	B	A	A	B	B	B	B	A	A	A
23.	Butyl Acetate	100	70	A	B	B	B	B	B	B	B	B	A	A	B	B	B	B	A	•	A
24.	Butyl Chloride	100	70	A	A	A	A	A	A	B	B	B	B	B	B	B	B	B	A	•	A
25.	Calcium Chloride	20	70	B	B	B	B	D	B	C	B	B	C	B	B	B	B	A	A	A	A
26.	Calcium Hydroxide	10	70	B	B	B	B	D	B	C	B	B	B	B	B	B	B	B	A	•	A
27.	Carbon Dioxide (Wet)	100	70	B	C	C	C	C	C	C	C	B	B	B	B	B	B	B	A	•	A
28.	Carbon Tetrachloride (Dry)	100	70	B	C	C	C	C	C	B	B	C	B	B	B	B	B	B	A	A	A
29.	Carbonic Acid	100	70	C	C	C	C	C	C	C	C	B	B	B	B	C	B	A	A	•	A
30.	Chlorine Gas (Dry)	100	70	B	B	B	B	B	B	B	B	B	B	D	B	B	B	B	I	A	A
31.	Chloroform (Dry)	100	70	B	B	B	B	B	B	B	B	A	A	A	B	B	B	B	A	•	A
32.	Chromic Acid	20	70	D	D	D	D	D	D	D	D	C	B	A	D	D	B	B	A	•	A
33.	Citric Acid	20	70	D	C	C	C	C	C	C	C	B	A	A	B	B	B	C	A	•	A
34.	Creosote	100	70	B	B	B	B	B	B	B	B	A	B	B	B	B	B	B	A	•	A
35.	Dibutylphthalate	100	70	A	A	A	A	A	A	B	B	B	A	A	A	B	B	B	A	•	A
36.	Dichlorobenzene	100	70	B	B	B	B	B	B	B	B	B	B	B	B	B	B	B	B	•	B
37.	Dichlodifluoromethane (F-12)	100	70	B	B	B	B	B	B	B	B	B	B	B	B	B	A	A	B	•	A
38.	Diethanolamine	100	85	A	A	A	A	A	A	A	A	B	A	A	B	B	A	A	A	•	A
39.	Diethyl Ether	100	70	A	B	B	B	B	B	B	B	A	B	B	B	B	B	B	A	•	A
40.	Diethylene Glycol	100	70	A	A	B	B	B	B	B	B	A	B	B	B	B	B	B	B	•	A
41.	Diphenyl	100	160	B	B	B	B	B	B	B	B	B	B	B	B	B	B	B	A	A	A
42.	Diphenyl Oxide	100	85	B	B	B	B	B	B	B	B	A	A	A	B	B	B	B	A	•	A

LEGEND

A = EXCELLENT
B = GOOD
C = FAIR
D = NOT SUITABLE
E = EXPLOSIVE
I = IGNITES
• = INFORMATION NOT AVAILABLE

No.	Chemicals	Concentration %	Temperature °F	Carbon Steel	Copper	Red Brass	Muntz	Admiralty	Copper Silicon	90-10 Cupro-Nickel	70-30 Cupro-Nickel	Aluminum	304 Stainless Steel	316 Stainless Steel	Nickel	Monel	Inconel	Hastelloy	Titanium	Zirconium	Tantalum
78.	Naphtha	100	70	A	B	B	B	B	B	B	B	A	A	A	B	B	B	B	B	•	A
79.	Naphthalene	100	70	A	B	B	B	B	B	B	B	B	A	A	A	A	B	B	B	•	A
80.	Nickel Chloride	20	70	D	B	B	D	C	B	B	B	B	D	B	B	A	D	B	B	A	B
81.	Nickel Sulfate	10	200	B	B	B	B	B	B	B	B	B	B	B	B	B	B	B	A	A	A
82.	Nitric Acid	50	200	D	D	D	D	D	D	D	D	A	B	B	D	D	B	D	A	B	A
83.	Nitrous Acid	10	70	D	D	D	D	D	D	D	D	D	B	B	D	D	C	•	•	•	A
84.	Oleic Acid	100	70	B	B	B	C	C	B	B	B	B	B	A	A	A	B	B	B	B	B
85.	Oxalic Acid	10	70	D	B	B	C	B	B	C	C	C	B	B	B	B	B	D	A	B	A
86.	Perchloric Acid (Dry)	100	70	D	D	D	D	D	D	D	D	D	B	B	D	D	B	•	A	•	A
87.	Perchloroethylene	100	70	A	A	B	B	B	B	B	B	A	B	B	B	B	B	•	A	•	A
88.	Phenol	10	120	B	B	B	C	B	B	B	B	B	B	B	B	B	B	•	A	•	A
89.	Phosphoric Acid (Aerated)	50	200	D	D	D	D	D	D	D	D	A	B	B	D	B	B	C	A	D	B
90.	Phthalic Anhydride	100	300	D	B	B	B	B	B	B	B	B	B	B	B	B	B	B	A	•	A
91.	Potassium Bicarbonate	30	200	B	B	B	C	B	B	B	B	B	B	B	B	B	B	B	B	•	A
92.	Potassium Carbonate	40	200	B	B	B	B	B	B	B	B	A	B	B	B	B	B	B	A	•	A
93.	Propylene Glycol	100	70	B	B	B	B	B	B	B	B	A	B	B	B	B	B	B	A	•	A
94.	Pyridine	100	70	A	B	B	B	B	B	B	B	A	B	B	B	B	B	B	B	•	A
95.	Silver Chloride	10	70	D	D	D	D	D	D	D	D	B	D	D	D	D	B	B	B	•	A
96.	Silver Nitrate	10	70	D	D	D	D	D	D	D	D	A	B	B	D	D	B	B	A	A	A
97.	Sodium Acetate	10	70	D	B	B	B	B	B	B	B	B	A	A	B	B	B	B	A	B	A
98.	Sodium Hydroxide	50	300	B	B	C	C	C	C	B	C	D	A	A	A	A	B	B	B	B	D
99.	Sodium Nitrate	40	70	B	B	B	B	B	B	B	B	A	A	A	B	B	B	B	B	C	A
100.	Sodium Sulfate	10	200	B	B	B	C	B	B	B	B	A	A	A	B	B	B	B	A	•	A
101.	Sulfur Dioxide (Dry)	100	300	B	D	D	D	D	D	D	D	B	D	D	C	D	C	B	B	•	A
102.	Sulfuric Acid (Aerated)	60	200	D	D	D	D	D	D	D	D	B	D	D	D	D	B	B	D	A	A
103.	Toluene	100	200	A	A	A	A	A	A	A	A	A	A	A	A	A	A	A	A	A	A
104.	Trichloroethylene (Dry)	100	150	B	B	B	B	B	B	B	B	B	B	B	B	B	A	B	A	•	A
105.	Turpentine	100	70	B	B	B	B	B	B	B	B	B	B	B	B	B	B	B	B	•	B
106.	Vinyl Chloride (Dry)	100	70	A	B	B	B	D	C	B	B	A	B	A	A	A	A	A	A	•	A
107.	Water (Fresh)	100	70	C	B	B	C	A	A	A	A	B	A	A	A	B	B	A	A	A	A
108.	Water (Sea)	100	70	C	B	B	C	A	A	A	A	A	B	A	A	B	B	B	A	A	A
109.	Xylene	100	200	B	A	A	A	A	A	A	A	A	A	A	A	A	A	A	A	A	A
110.	Zinc Chloride	10	70	D	D	D	D	D	D	D	D	C	B	B	B	D	A	D	B	A	A
111.	Zinc Sulfate	20	70	D	B	B	D	B	B	B	B	D	A	B	A	B	A	B	A	•	A

Table 11. Corrosion Resistance of Metals
(Courtesy of the Patterson-Kelley,, Inc.)

Table 12. Tank Volumes
a. Capacities of Vertical Cylinders

Diameter Ft	In	Gallons per Ft of Height	Diameter Ft	In	Gallons per Ft of Height	Diameter Ft	In	Gallons per Ft of Height
1	—	5.9	5	6	177.7	10	—	587.5
1	6	13.2	5	8	188.6	10	6	647.7
2	—	23.5	5	10	199.9	11	—	710.9
2	6	36.7	6	—	211.5	11	6	777.0
3	—	52.9	6	2	223.4	12		846.0
3	2	58.9	6	4	235.7	13		992.9
3	4	65.3	6	6	248.2	14		1152
3	6	72.0	6	8	261.1	15		1322
3	8	79.0	6	10	274.3	16		1504
3	10	86.3	7	—	287.9	17		1698
4	—	94.0	7	2	301.8	18		1904
4	2	102.0	7	4	316.0	19		2121
4	4	110.3	7	6	330.5	20		2350
4	6	119.0	7	8	345.3	21		2591
4	8	128.0	7	10	360.5	22		2844
4	10	137.2	8	—	376.0	23		3108
5	—	146.9	8	6	424.5	24		3384
5	2	156.8	9	—	475.9	25		3672
5	4	167.1	9	6	530.2			

b. Contents of Horizontal Tanks (Flat Ends)

Gallons per Foot of Length

Diam Ft	— Depth of Liquid, Inches									
	6	12	18	24	30	36	42	48	54	60
3	5.8	15.4	26.4	37.4	47.1	52.9	—	—	—	—
4	6.8	18.4	32.2	47.0	61.8	75.6	87.2	94.0	—	—
5	7.6	20.8	37.0	54.9	73.4	92.0	109.8	126.0	139.2	146.9
6	8.4	23.2	41.3	61.6	83.4	105.8	128.1	149.9	170.2	188.3
7	9.1	25.2	45.2	67.9	92.3	117.9	143.9	170.0	195.6	220.0
8	9.8	27.2	48.7	73.5	100.4	128.8	158.2	188.0	217.8	247.2
9	10.4	28.9	52.1	78.7	107.9	138.7	171.2	204.3	238.0	271.6
10	11.0	30.6	55.2	83.6	114.9	148.2	183.3	219.5	256.4	293.8

Diam Ft	Depth of Liquid, Inches									
	66	72	78	84	90	96	102	108	114	120
6	203.1	211.5	—	—	—	—	—	—	—	—
7	242.6	262.7	278.8	287.9	—	—	—	—	—	—
8	275.6	302.5	327.2	348.9	366.2	376.0	—	—	—	—
9	304.7	337.2	368.0	397.2	423.8	447.0	465.5	475.9	—	—
10	331.1	368.1	404.3	439.3	472.7	503.9	532.3	557.0	576.6	587.5

Table 13. Properties of Saturated Steam*

Absolute Pressure Psi**	Temperature Deg F	Specific Volume of Vapor cu ft/lb	Enthalpy, Btu/lb		
			Saturated Liquid	Evaporation	Saturated Vapor
1	101.7	333.6	69.70	1036.3	1106.0
5	162.2	73.52	130.13	1001.0	1131.1
10	193.2	38.42	161.17	982.1	1143.3
14.696	212.0	26.80	180.07	970.3	1150.4
15	213.0	26.29	181.11	969.7	1150.8
20	228.0	20.09	196.16	960.1	1156.3
25	240.1	16.30	208.42	952.1	1160.6
30	250.3	13.75	218.82	945.3	1164.1
35	259.3	11.90	227.91	939.2	1167.1
40	267.2	10.50	236.03	933.7	1169.7
45	274.4	9.401	243.36	928.6	1172.0
50	281.0	8.515	250.09	924.0	1174.1
55	287.1	7.787	256.30	919.6	1175.9
60	292.7	7.175	262.09	915.5	1177.6
65	298.0	6.655	267.5	911.6	1179.1
70	302.9	6.206	272.61	907.9	1180.6
75	307.6	5.816	277.43	904.5	1181.9
80	312.0	5.472	282.02	901.1	1183.1
85	316.2	5.168	286.39	897.8	1184.2
90	320.3	4.896	290.56	894.7	1185.3
95	324.1	4.652	294.56	891.7	1186.2
100	327.8	4.432	298.40	888.8	1187.2
110	334.8	4.049	305.66	883.2	1188.9
120	341.2	3.728	312.44	877.9	1190.4
130	347.3	3.455	318.81	872.9	1191.7
140	353.0	3.220	324.82	868.2	1193.0
150	358.4	3.015	330.51	863.6	1194.1
160	363.5	2.834	335.93	859.2	1195.1
170	368.4	2.675	341.09	854.9	1196.0
180	373.1	2.532	346.03	850.8	1196.9
190	377.5	2.404	350.79	846.8	1197.6
200	381.8	2.288	355.36	843.0	1198.4
225	391.8	2.042	366.09	833.8	1199.9
250	401.0	1.844	376.00	825.1	1201.1
275	409.4	1.680	385.21	816.9	1202.1
300	417.3	1.543	393.84	809.0	1202.8
350	431.7	1.326	409.69	794.2	1203.9
400	444.6	1.161	424.0	780.5	1204.5
450	456.3	1.032	437.2	767.4	1204.6
500	467.0	0.9278	449.4	755.0	1204.4
600	486.2	0.7698	471.6	731.6	1203.2
700	503.1	0.6554	491.5	709.7	1201.2

*Excerpted from *Thermodynamic Properties of Steam,* J.H. Keenan and F.G. Keyes (New York: John Wiley & Sons, Inc., 1936) by permission of the publishers.
**Subtract 14.696 psi to obtain gage pressure.

800	518.2	0.5687	509.7	688.9	1198.6
900	532.0	0.5006	526.6	668.8	1195.4
1000	544.6	0.4456	542.4	649.4	1191.8
1500	596.2	0.2765	611.6	556.3	1167.9
2000	635.8	0.1878	671.7	463.4	1135.1
2500	668.1	0.1307	730.6	360.5	1091.1
3000	695.4	0.0858	802.5	217.8	1020.3
3206.2	705.4	0.0503	902.7	0	902.7

INDEX